AF777367

IM Instant Messaging Security

Computer Security and Computer Forensic Related Book Titles:

Rittinghouse & Hancock, *Cybersecurity Operations Handbook*, ISBN 1-55558-306-7, 1336pp, 2003.

Rittinghouse & Ransome, *Instant Messaging Security*, ISBN 1-55558-338-5, 432pp, 2005.

Rittinghouse, *Wireless Operational Security*, ISBN 1-55558-317-2, 496pp, 2004.

Ransome & Rittinghouse, *VoIP Security*, ISBN 1-55558-332-6, 450pp, 2005.

De Clercq, *Windows Server 2003 Security Infrastructures: Core Security Features*, ISBN 1-55558-283-4, 752pp, 2004.

Erbschloe, *Implementing Homeland Security for Enterprise IT*, ISBN 1-55558-312-1, 320pp, 2003.

Erbschloe, *Physical Security for IT*, ISBN 1-55558-327-X, 320pp, 2005.

Speed & Ellis, *Internet Security*, ISBN 1-55558-298-2, 398pp, 2003.

XYPRO, *HP NonStop Server Security*, ISBN 1-55558-314-8, 618pp, 2003.

Casey, *Handbook of Computer Crime Investigation*, ISBN 0-12-163103-6, 448pp, 2002.

Kovacich, *The Information Systems Security Officer's Guide*, ISBN 0-7506-7656-6, 361pp, 2003.

Boyce & Jennings, *Information Assurance*, ISBN 0-7506-7327-3, 261pp, 2002.

Stefanek, *Information Security Best Practices: 205 Basic Rules*, ISBN 0-878707-96-5, 194pp, 2002.

For more information or to order these and other Digital Press titles, please visit our website at www.books.elsevier.com/digitalpress!
At www.books.elsevier.com/digitalpress you can:
•Join the Digital Press Email Service and have news about our books delivered right to your desktop
•Read the latest news on titles
•Sample chapters on featured titles for free
•Question our expert authors and editors
•Download free software to accompany select texts

IM Instant Messaging Security

John W. Rittinghouse, Ph.D., CISM
James F. Ransome, CISM, CISSP

ELSEVIER
DIGITAL
PRESS

AMSTERDAM • BOSTON • HEIDELBERG • LONDON
NEW YORK • OXFORD • PARIS • SAN DIEGO
SAN FRANCISCO • SINGAPORE • SYDNEY • TOKYO

Elsevier Digital Press
30 Corporate Drive, Suite 400, Burlington, MA 01803, USA
Linacre House, Jordan Hill, Oxford OX2 8DP, UK

Copyright © 2005, John W. Rittinghouse and James F. Ransome. All rights reserved.

No part of this publication may be reproduced, stored in a retrieval system, or transmitted in any form or by any means, electronic, mechanical, photocopying, recording, or otherwise, without the prior written permission of the publisher.

Permissions may be sought directly from Elsevier's Science & Technology Rights Department in Oxford, UK: phone: (+44) 1865 843830, fax: (+44) 1865 853333, e-mail: permissions@elsevier.com.uk. You may also complete your request on-line via the Elsevier homepage (http://elsevier.com), by selecting "Customer Support" and then "Obtaining Permissions."

∞ Recognizing the importance of preserving what has been written, Elsevier prints its books on acid-free paper whenever possible.

Library of Congress Cataloging-in-Publication Data
Application Submitted.

ISBN: 1-55558-338-5

British Library Cataloguing-in-Publication Data
A catalogue record for this book is available from the British Library.

For information on all Elsevier Digital Press publications
visit our Web site at www.books.elsevier.com

05 06 07 08 09 10 9 8 7 6 5 4 3 2 1

Printed in the United States of America

Contents

List of Figures and Tables

Acknowledgments

Lots of people besides the author contribute to the great effort that is required to take an idea from scratch and see it become a finished product. In reality, the author usually depends on quite a few others to help in keeping things in order. This is something that is very true in the case of getting this book out the door and into your hands. Many people deserve our gratitude and thanks. My wife, Naree Rittinghouse, is certainly among those I would like to thank for her love and understanding, her encouragement, and, most of all, her faith in my work. I would like to thank Dr. Tony Dubendorf for his contributions and for providing such timely and excellent feedback. Murray Fish deserves special thanks for always being there to bounce ideas around and provide sanity on days when none could be found. Bill Hancock is another individual who helped contribute to the success of this book. His expertise in the security realm knows no bounds—he worked many late nights reviewing, editing, and validating the work herein to ensure its accuracy and relevancy to our cyberenvironment of today. Finally, I would like to thank all of the folks at Elsevier/Digital Press, especially Theron Shreve, Alan Rose, and Tim Donar for their continued support of my work.

—John W. Rittinghouse

I would like to take this opportunity to give thanks to my wife Gail for her continual patience with me as I completed my third security book in a rather short period of time. I would like to thank both Dr. Tony Dubendorf and Terry Dalby for their contributions to the book, and Theron Shreve of Elsevier/Digital Press for his continued support of my work. A special thanks to Howard Schmidt for writing the foreword to this book on a subject and message that we both share a passion for and want to get out to the practitioners and decision makers as quickly as possible. And, finally, to those of you who worked for and with me in the earlier part of my corporate career, I leave you with the following quote by Walter Bagehot: *"The greatest pleasure in life is doing that which people say we cannot do."*

—James F. Ransome

Foreword

Securing Instant Messaging (IM) is one of the top three priorities for IT managers to consider in the next 12 months. If IM security problems have been keeping you up at night . . . they should! According to research firm IDC, corporate IM users will jump from nearly 50 million in 2003 to over 181 million by 2005.[1] If your company is like many others, contributing to that exponential growth in IM usage, it likely means that the potential for major security breaches in your organization is very high. By their very nature, popular IM services can introduce major security vulnerabilities to the organization. Once used simply to send short notes out among computer experts at MIT and other institutions of higher learning, IM is now a widespread, efficient medium for everyday business users to collaborate, organize strategy meetings, and share internal files and information. According to the analyst firm Yankee Group, IM will continue to grow at an explosive rate of 150 percent per year between 2003 and 2005.

IM is moving toward ubiquity through increased use of IM within enterprises and IM integration within mission-critical business applications. With this ubiquity, there are at least five major security risks identified for use of IM in an enterprise:

1. First of all, because many of the most popular IM solutions weren't originally designed with enterprise users in mind, they can benefit from third-party security and management solutions. For a corporation, the correct answer to this problem is not to ban IM from being used internally but to embrace IM to capitalize on the business benefit it provides while mitigating its risks.

1. IM Logic. (2004). "Top Instant Messaging Security Risks for 2004." Retrieved February 5, 2005 from http://www.unipalm.ie/library/t25121_3.pdf.

2. IM systems are rapidly working their way into corporations because of their efficiency and convenience. Unfortunately, few companies have standardized on any particular IM solution, leaving users to choose for themselves and potentially compromise security within the organization. Many of today's IM systems were built for consumer chatting rather than secure corporate communications; consequently, they create new and often hidden vulnerabilities within the corporation.
3. IM has entered the enterprise and network environment by the back door, creating special challenges for security managers. While IM is now standard in many industries and trusted, enterprise-quality solutions are readily available, IM still brings its own set of challenges. To date, providers of IM security and privacy solutions have relied upon regulated industries such as financial services and energy for the bulk of their business.
4. Most IM systems presently in use were designed with scalability rather than security in mind. Virtually all freeware IM programs lack encryption capabilities, and most have features that bypass traditional corporate firewalls, making it difficult for administrators to control IM usage inside an organization. Many of these systems have insecure password management and are vulnerable to account spoofing and denial-of-service (DoS) attacks.
5. IM systems meet all the criteria required to make them an ideal platform for rapidly spreading computer worms and blended threats: They are ubiquitous; they provide a communications infrastructure; they have integrated directories (buddy lists) that can be used to locate new targets; and they can, in many cases, be controlled by easily written scripts. Even worse, no firewall on the market today can scan IM transmissions for viruses.

IM is gaining popularity with workers trying to get around the restrictions placed on what they can do with e-mail. Currently, few firms subject IM programs to the same scrutiny that e-mail receives to stop spam, viruses, or abuse by employees. The risks and dangers that emerged with early use of e-mail are happening all over again as use of IM grows. Security strategies to stop viruses, worms, and SPAM can be thwarted by unauthorized use of IM. As more companies crack down on misuse of e-mail, we have seen people moving more and more toward freer communications such as IM. The security threats from IM are straightforward. Since deployment isn't controlled, the enterprise can't keep a rein on how the systems are used. With the public IM networks, the individual employee registers for service. If the employee leaves the company, the firm has no (technology-based) way to prevent him or her from continuing to use the account or from even continuing to represent him- or herself as still working for the company. Without additional tools, the company has no way of archiving IM messages for legal or regulatory purposes or of monitoring and controlling the content of messages to filter for inappropriate communications.

There are the obvious holes that are opened up on the corporate network. Each of the IM networks uses a well-known port that must either be left open on the corporate firewall to allow traffic in, or closed, which, at least in theory, bans that service to end users. Given IM's pervasiveness, enterprises can't think about security in a vacuum; it has to be part of a larger management structure. The tough thing about IM security and management isn't that it's technically hard to do, it's that adoption is happening so quickly that network managers are playing catch-up. Due to the efficiency and convenience of their communications, IM systems are rapidly becoming very important tools within corporations. Unfortunately, many of the current IM systems are inadequately secured and in turn are exposing some enterprises to serious security and economic breaches.

Ideally, corporations looking to leverage IM should deploy a secure, corporate-focused IM solution within the company network, and then layer suitable security systems on top of this solution (firewalls, vulnerability management, antivirus, etc.). However, many companies continue to permit employees to use popular free IM services. These organizations need to understand the associated security risks and plan accordingly. Clearly, the growth of IM systems will bring greater efficiencies to the global workplace. Only by appropriately securing these systems will businesses be able to reap their full economic benefits.

Drs. Rittinghouse and Ransome have done an excellent job at addressing the technology and the risks of using IM at work or home. This book will give you the tools and methods to embrace the technology securely. I highly recommend this book for anybody interested in securing IM.

Howard A. Schmidt joined eBay as Vice President and Chief Information Security Officer in May 2003. He now serves as chairman of the U.S. Computer Emergency Readiness Team, a public/private security monitoring organization based at Carnegie Mellon University in Pittsburgh. He retired from the White House after 31 years of public service. He was appointed by President Bush as the Vice Chair of the President's Critical Infrastructure Protection Board and as the Special Adviser for Cyberspace Security for the White House in December 2001. He assumed the role as the Chair in January 2003 until his retirement in May 2003. Prior to the White House, Howard was Chief Security Officer for Microsoft Corp., where his duties included CISO, CSO, and forming, and directing the Trustworthy Computing Security Strategies Group. Before Microsoft, Howard was a supervisory special agent and director of the Air Force Office of Special Investigations (AFOSI) Computer Forensic Lab and Computer Crime and Information Warfare Division. While there, he established the first dedicated computer forensic lab in the government. Before AFOSI, Howard was with the FBI at the National Drug Intelligence Center, where he headed the Computer Exploitation Team. He is recognized as one of the pioneers in the field of computer forensics and computer evidence collection. Before working at the FBI, he was an officer with the Chandler, Arizona Police Department. Howard has had leadership positions with the Information Systems Security Association (ISSA), the Information Technology Information Sharing and Analysis Center (IT-ISAC), the International Organization of Computer Evidence, and the Federal Computer Investigations Committee. He is a member of the American Academy of Forensic Scientists. He is on the advisory board for the Technical Research Institute of the National White Collar Crime Center, and was a distinguished special lecturer at the University of New Haven, Connecticut, teaching a graduate certificate course in forensic computing. He served as an augmented member to the President's Committee of Advisors on Science and Technology in the formation of an Institute for Information Infrastructure Protection. He has testified before congressional committees on computer security and cybercrime, and has been instrumental in the creation of public and private partnerships and information-sharing initiatives. Howard has been appointed to the Information Security Privacy Advisory Board (ISPAB) to advise the National Institute of Standards and Technology (NIST), the Secretary of Commerce, and the Director of the Office of Management and Budget on information security and privacy issues pertaining to federal government information systems, including a thorough review of proposed standards and guidelines developed by NIST. Howard holds a bachelor's degree in business administration and a master's degree in organizational management from the University of Phoenix. He also holds an Honorary Doctorate in Humane Letters.

—Howard A. Schmidt, CISM, CISSP

1

Introduction

1.1 Purpose and Audience

IM is expected to influence the drop of e-mail usage by 40 percent in 2006 [1] and is resulting in new legal, regulatory, and privacy issues that are challenging security professionals and users to reevaluate the security, technology, and employee productivity issues with regard to IM. We believe there is also a gap in the current commercial literature with regard to IM security. According to research firm Gartner, over 70 percent of corporate employees depend on Instant Messaging for business communications, despite the fact that, according to Nemertes Research, 70 percent of IT executives claim to have banned the use of commercial IM services [2]. The reality for IT organizations is that—authorized or not—IM is being used on most networks, and—authorized or not—it poses a serious security threat if left unchecked. Not surprisingly, Gartner recently labeled IM security one of "five technologies you need to know," and research firm Yankee Group called securing IM one of the top three priorities for IT managers in 2004. Senior IT executives overwhelmingly concur, as 62 percent told Nemertes Research that they worry about IM security. IM is quickly becoming prevalent as a business-critical communications tool, and with its use come new security challenges for businesses around the world [3]. The security concerns with the use of IM are myriad and range from technical vulnerabilities, such as client buffer overflow attacks, to inappropriate usage risks, such as the leakage of intellectual property. This book is designed to help you fully understand, prepare for, and mediate current IM security risks in today's ever-changing network environment. We will address the potentially costly security challenges that IM brings to the workplace and home. As with our recent books on Wireless and VoIP security, this book will provide a holistic approach to IM Security in that it covers both the fundamentals and advanced topics of IM technology, with a specific focus on IM security, architecture, and management. As such, this book is appropriate reading for both the IT professionals and laypersons who have an interest in secure IM communications use in the workplace or at home.

1.2 What to Expect from This Book

IM Security will teach you how to mitigate security risks inherent to IM and its costly challenges while maximizing its business potential. This book is an essential and timely source of information to help both you and your organization secure this rapidly growing and ubiquitous technology.

1.3 What Is IM?

IM is an Internet protocol (IP)–based application that provides convenient communication between people using a variety of different device types. The most familiar form today is computer-to-computer instant text messaging, but IM also can work with mobile devices, such as digital cellular phones, and can incorporate voice or video [4].

Figure 1.1
ICQ Lite Edition with Xtraz.

1.3.1 IM and Its History

In our fast-paced world there are times when even the rapid response of e-mail is not fast enough. There is no way for you to know if the person you are sending e-mail to is online at that moment. This is one of the reasons why IM has gained popularity, acceptance, and become a desired tool in the workplace. IM provides us with the ability to maintain a list of people, often called a buddy list or contact list, whom we want or need to interact with. IM monitors our list of people and their status of being online or offline. If they are online, we can send messages back and forth. Businesses today are increasingly viewing IM as an excellent productivity and communication tool that complements voice mail and e-mail. In order for there to be complete acceptance, there needs to be specific security, accountability, and uniformity among IM solution providers. There needs to be policies that protect critical organizational interests and comply with federal mandates and regulations. Corporations want IM solutions that provide seamless security, full audit trails, identity controls, and administrative controls. Most corporations agree that message encryption is essential.

There are three basic types of IM, as follows:

1. Public messaging
2. Enterprise messaging
3. Wireless messaging

In 1987, a computer scientist at MIT developed an instant-messaging program called Zephyr in order to provide a system that was faster than e-mail, which had begun to be bogged down, so that urgent messages regarding the school's network and server could be received instantly in case, for example, the school's network server was going down. Soon, students adopted Zephyr as a form of easy communication that could be used while they worked at their computers. This technology was quickly adopted by other universities, and the simple early warning system that Zephyr was originally designed to be was repurposed, becoming a popular tool of conversation and information exchange called IM. IM as we know it today was created in July 1996 by four young Israeli entrepreneurs. Yair Goldfinger, Arik Vardi, Sefi Vigiser, and Amnon Amir, started a company called Mirabilis in order to introduce a new way of communication over the Internet. They created a technology that would enable Internet users to locate each other online on the Internet and create peer-to-peer communication channels easily. They called their technology ICQ (I seek you) and released it in November 1996. Within six months, 850,000 users had been registered by Mirabilis. By June 1997, Mirabilis was able to handle 100,000 concurrent users and had become the world's largest Internet communications network. Mirabilis and ICQ were acquired by America Online, Inc., in June 1998 for $287 million. AOL had also created its own Instant Messenger system. By that time, Microsoft had created its own IM client and service, MSN Messenger, and another Internet heavyweight, Yahoo!, created one as well. Because IM services evolved from proprietary systems created by companies to make a profit, their systems remain unable to interoperate because of the desire to control the IM market. AOL and ICQ, even though owned by the same company, are not interoperable. ICQ currently has two clients: ICQ4 Lite Edition with Xtraz (Figure 1.1) and ICQPro™ (Figure 1.2) [5,6].

The AOL and ICQ clients cannot communicate with one another, and AOL maintains both systems and market dominance in the IM field. All this may change soon. Conditions of the AOL–Time Warner merger required AOL to open up its IM systems [7]. In its analysis of IM, the FCC concluded that the merger would combine an essential input of AOL's dominant IM service and future IM-based services—chiefly, the Names and Presence Directory (NPD)—with assets of Time Warner, including its cable

Figure 1.2
ICQ™Pro.

facilities and Road Runner ISP. An IM provider's NPD consists of a database of its users' unique IM names, their Internet addresses, and a "presence detection" function, which indicates to the provider that a certain user is online and allows the provider to alert others to this information. The FCC noted that these features created a market with strong network effects. AOL, with by far the largest NPD, resisted making its IM services interoperable with other providers' services. The merger brought Time Warner's cable Internet platform and content library under AOL's control and gave AOL Time Warner a significant and anticompetitive first-mover advantage in the market for advanced, IM-based high-speed services (AIHS). Potential AIHS applications include those using streaming video (lengthy, high-quality, one- or two-way video). The merger would frustrate the objectives of the Communications Act by preventing the emergence of a competitive and innovative market for advanced, IM-based services. This would violate key Communications Act principles, including the further development of healthy competition in the Internet and interactive services arena. The FCC did not establish an interoperability protocol. Rather, the FCC's remedy requires AOL Time Warner to follow a protocol developed by the industry or to create a protocol with other IM providers pursuant to contracts. Thus, the FCC did not create and will not review an Internet protocol.

The FCC imposed an "IM condition" on the merger to avert market harm now so that it would not be required to regulate IM in the future. Given AOL Time Warner's likely domination of the potentially competitive business of new, IM-based services, especially advanced, IM-based high-speed services applications, the FCC ruled that AOL Time Warner may not offer any AIHS steaming video applications that use a Names and Presence Directory (NPD) over the Internet via AOL Time Warner broadband facilities until the company demonstrates that it has satisfied one of three pro-competitive options filed by the FCC. AOL Time Warner must file a progress report with the FCC, 180 days from the release date of the order and every 180 days thereafter, describing in technical depth the actions it has taken to achieve interoperability of its IM offerings and other offerings. These reports will be placed on public notice for comment. The IM condition was set to sunset five years after the release of the order.

AOL Time Warner was directed to show that it had implemented an industry-wide standard for server-to-server interoperability. AOL Time Warner had to show that it had entered into a contract for server-to-server interoperability with at least one significant, unaffiliated provider of NPD-based services within 180 days of executing the first contract. AOL Time Warner also had to show that it entered into two additional contracts with significant, unaffiliated, actual or potential competing providers. AOL Time Warner was given the opportunity to seek relief by showing by clear and convincing evidence that this condition no longer serves the public interest, convenience, or necessity because there has been a material change in circumstances.

Since the FCC ruling, several competing companies have joined together to advocate an IM protocol similar to those that allow the interoperability of e-mail systems. Other companies have taken a different approach rather than wait for an agreed-upon standard. Jabber is one company that has created a client program capable of communicating with various IM systems. In less than two decades, the concept of IM has become an international tool of communication.

1.3.2 IM as an Integrated Communications Platform

The IM platform can be the basis for true integrated communications by incorporating additional technology (such as extending it into the wireless realm with mobile phones and personal digital assistants [PDAs]) or by adding other means of communication (such as voice chat or video chat). With the addition of IP telephony (VoIP) capability, the messaging service can even extend to telephony, making it possible to communicate with anyone at any time. It can be used as a personal communications portal to create a single point of contact for all methods of communication, allowing a user to initiate any kind of communication from one place, using a single contact list. Using IM as an integrated communications platform allows for one-click communication. Instead of having to run through a list of home, office, mobile, pager numbers, and e-mail addresses, someone trying to reach another person can simply click on that person's name. It also enables users to control how others communicate with them. If they prefer that calls go to their mobile phones when they are away from the office, they can set their profile so that the system directs calls that way. The system would route communications according to that person's preferences. When additional features such as integrated communications, reachability, and communications profiles are part of IM, the market for IM will increase from personal to professional use, creating better business markets for messaging services and making these services more of a revenue-generating opportunity for service providers [8].

1.3.3 Common IM Application Approaches

An IM service can be either network-based or device-based. We will discuss each in the following paragraphs.

Network-based Approaches

In a network-based approach, user information is stored on a network-based server, so users have access to the same customized services and information, regardless of how they access the system. Client software will have to be loaded on devices used to access the service, but the same contact list, addresses, and other personal information will be available whenever users log in to the system. If a change is made to information, that change will then affect all the devices that user uses. Users have the same information and the same services whether logging on from their home computers, office computers, or mobile phones. Because this information is located centrally, users also have the option of updating their own information for all other users. For example, if Lois changes her e-mail address, she can make that change in the system. Then everyone who has Lois on their contact list will automatically have their contact lists updated the next time they log in to the system. Lois won't have to send an e-mail to all her contacts asking them to change her address on their contact lists [9].

Device-based Approaches

In the device-based approach, user information is located on the device used to access the system and the user downloads a client application to the device, most likely a computer. The user's list of contacts and other preferences specific to the user are saved on that computer. When a user accesses the system from multiple devices such as a home computer and an office computer, the same user information will have to be created on each device; this will also require a manual change on both computers in the case where information such as an address on the contact is changed. The user won't have access to personal contact lists or other personal information if the user accesses the system as a guest from a device that normally is not used [10].

1.3.4 Who Uses IM?

Recent Survey Trends

IM consumers generally use one of four publicly available IM networks: America Online's AIM, ICQ, MSN Messenger, and Yahoo! Messenger (Figure 1.3). A recent survey by AOL has shown that 90 percent of surveyed teens and young adults, 48 percent of those aged 55 or over, seven out of

Figure 1.3 *IM consumers use one of the four IM networks: AOL's AIM, ICQ, MSN Messenger, and Yahoo! Messenger.*

ten 22- to 34-year-olds, and 55 percent of adults aged 35–54 use IM at home, at work, or on any number of mobile devices. According to the survey, the top ten markets for IM are New York, New York; Miami, Florida; Chicago, Illinois; Philadelphia, Pennsylvania; Orlando, Florida; Dallas Fort Worth, Texas; Atlanta, Georgia; Washington, DC; Los Angeles, California; and Houston, Texas [11]. It is clear from these survey results that IM has become a mainstream application and is part of the fabric of our daily lives, enabling communications for both personal and professional use.

Corporate Usage

Twenty-seven percent of all IM users say they use IM in the workplace, a 71 percent increase over last year, and 43 percent of employed IM users say they use desktop IM to communicate quickly in the workplace. Nineteen percent of IM users now send IMs or SMS text messages from mobile phones and PDAs, as compared with 10 percent who did so last year. Thirty-two percent of these mobile messengers say they stay in touch with coworkers via mobile IM or SMS text messages while on business travel. Seventy percent of business users send instant messages while at work to communicate with colleagues, 63 percent say they send IMs to get answers and make business decisions, 34 percent say they use IM to interact with clients or customers, and 11 percent say they have used IM at work to avoid a potentially difficult in-person conversation [12] (Figure 1.4).

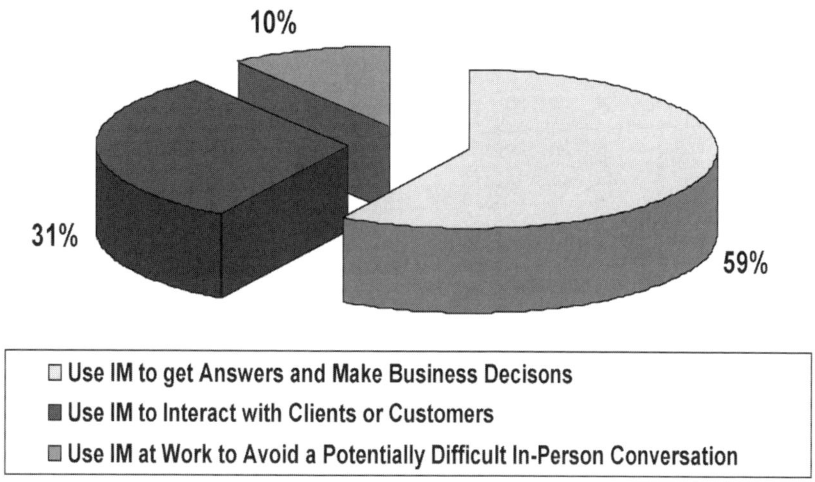

Figure 1.4 *Business usage of IM.*

Home Usage

In the at-home market, AOL's Instant Messenger (AIM) is the most popular, MSN Messenger is second, Yahoo! Messenger is third, and with ICQ is fourth. Last year's AOL survey indicated that 90 percent of those surveyed send IMs to keep in touch with family or friends, 28 percent use IM to share photos, 22 percent to set up weekend or evening activities, 14 percent to play games, and 11 percent to get to know dates better [13].

Criminal Usage

E-mail and IM have provided a faster, more efficient, and often more convenient form of peer-to-peer communication. However, along with new methods of communication, there has emerged a new medium for criminals. Criminals have found it easier and often safer to communicate via e-mail and IM as opposed to the telephone, because this avoids the possibility of wiretaps. The anonymous, ubiquitous, and document/photograph attachment capabilities of IM make it an attractive medium for criminal use such as:

- Computer intrusion (i.e., hacking)
- Password trafficking
- Copyright (software, movie, sound recording) piracy
- Theft of trade secrets
- Trademark counterfeiting

- Counterfeiting of currency
- Child exploitation
- Internet fraud
- Internet SPAM
- Internet harassment
- Internet bomb threats
- Trafficking in explosive or incendiary devices or firearms over the Internet

All suspicions or knowledge of these types of criminal activities can be reported to the Department of Justice at http://www.usdoj.gov/criminal/cybercrime/reporting.htm.

IM can also be used as a communications vehicle for criminals and as a means by which the transfer of documents for use by terrorists, drug traffickers, and industrial or state espionage can take place. Perhaps the most troublesome and highly reported use of IM for criminal activity has been its use for child exploitation. Today, companies are compelled by law to act on IM logs as evidence, just as with e-mails. In the state of Vermont, for example, the Vermont Supreme Court affirmed a conviction based on IM evidence [14]. The appellate court affirmed the trial court's finding that IM text was sufficient evidence to support the defendant's conviction of incitement and attempt to use a child in a sexual performance. The state introduced evidence recovered from a computer forensic examination of the computer system and floppy disks taken from the child's home. The computer forensic expert recovered text from IM conversations in which the defendant discussed with the child's mother a plan to have a lewd photo shoot. At trial, the expert noted that IM is not usually saved on a computer and that saving it to floppy disks required "concentrated effort." Based on the IM evidence, the jury found the defendant guilty. The defendant argued that the IM text was "meager evidence" of guilt, since the text had allegedly been altered and edited. The court rejected this claim, finding that the retrieved electronic conversations, together with witness testimony, offered ample evidence to support the jury's findings.

Law enforcement officers worldwide are dealing with the growing problem of major criminal activity that is taking place in chat rooms, IM applications, and e-mail. These modes of communication have given predators and pedophiles access to online playgrounds where they find children to exploit or molest. The Internet has provided these criminals with a means of communicating with millions of children. The fact that they have anonymity means that they are free to pose as anyone they want to impersonate [15,16].

1.3.5 What Are the Advantages of Using IM?

Presence awareness is one of the key attributes of IM software that enables it as a real-time communication tool for individuals so they can quickly see who of their contacts are online and available and can then establish immediate real-time communications with them. Depending on the particular IM tool they are using, after the connection has been made, they can invite others into the conversation to have a group conversation; have a voice conversation; use video (in one-on-one conversations); transfer files; share applications running on their desktop; share a whiteboard; save the transcript (by copying and pasting) for later review; or set their status to busy, away, or offline if they don't want to be disturbed . . . all in real time.

Instant (Message) Communications

IM users can query available colleagues instantly while on a conference call or making a sales call, which increases employee productivity. Through the use of presence, the user can tell which colleagues are available to help solve a problem or provide information immediately, which means IM helps reduce response times.

Remote teams can have interactive communication more cost efficiently across disparate locations communicating in real time through IM. It reduces the use of other, more costly means of communications, such as the excessive use of long-distance phone calls and voice mail caused by phone tag. Presence management tools can automatically indicate who is online even across organizational boundaries and geographic regions. Automatic activity detection can update a user's presence information without user input. Users can add customized text messages to presence status to more accurately describe their availability or location. In addition, they can choose to be "invisible," which enables them to see the presence of others but not appear online.

Enhanced Customer Service

IM and presence awareness add great value to call center and customer service operations. When customers call in for assistance, they no longer have to wait for a customer service representative while being put on hold and listening to elevator music. Instead, they can work on other things and will be alerted when a customer service representative becomes available.

When customers or prospects can't find information on a Web site, their first impulse is to call the toll-free number, which is costly for the recipient. In contrast, an automated answer delivered by an IM query costs just a fraction of an answer delivered by a human speaking on a toll-free line. For online shoppers, they can get quick answers without resorting to the phone or to e-mail. IM can provide an alternative for business help lines, and customers can use it while remaining online. The use of IM is also advantageous for those customers with a single phone line, who cannot shop online and call customer service simultaneously. This use of IM can help in preventing a business from losing customers because their attention is interrupted outside the store's online environment simply to make a phone call. IM can also automatically create a written transcript of the dialog between a customer and a customer service agent. Written transcripts are easier to archive and search than voice recordings, so businesses can use them to monitor customer interactions for quality control. It is also easier for a service agent to cut and paste scripted answers to frequently asked questions through the use of IM, while also giving a better impression of a personal response than through e-mail or from a Web site.

Improved Employee Productivity

IM has evolved from a novelty to an effective way to communicate with colleagues in diverse geographies. As a real-time IM solution, IM enables companies to communicate and make better decisions faster by integrating presence and communication capabilities into their business applications and processes. Users can also see when a colleague is at his or her desk and can send an instant message to that person, rather than pick up the phone or walk to the colleague. This option is especially helpful for international communication because employees can contact others, even in other countries, without incurring hefty long-distance telephone charges. IM also allows a meeting participant to get additional information from a coworker without interrupting the meeting. IM provides employees the ability to communicate and make more informed decisions more quickly by integrating presence and communication capabilities into the company's applications and processes.

IM allows desktop support or technically savvy users to help others on the network through the use of its remote assistance functionality. This ability to share knowledge helps people get back to business quickly and keeps small issues from halting productivity in the workplace. This also provides increased customer satisfaction from users, because they know that the other person is there and working with them simultaneously. Additional features, such as the whiteboard utility, enables users to share their ideas dynamically and graphically. Users can work together to sketch and outline their ideas across the continents in real time, leading to improved productivity and faster decision making.

Ease of Multitasking

IM takes multitasking to a new level. IM provides a vehicle of communication unique from a voice conversation that might be had in person, over the phone, or via teleconference. IM is also distinctly different from e-mail, written mail, or other non-real-time modes of interaction and can provide the best of both for information exchange. IM provides this revolutionary new way of multitasking to the users by allowing two or more participants to simultaneously contribute their thoughts, reading responses and calculating replies. Employees can be on conference calls and simultaneously ask for additional information or for project status without leaving the conversation, while also managing several IM windows for online Web research.

Greater Accountability for Off-site Employees

We have stated that presence is a key feature of IM. It provides the ability to see when someone is online and available to communicate with applications. Through presence, a manager can use the IM system to see if off-site workers are online and available for a conversation.

Comprehensive Features

IM can provide a rich feature set of real-time communication capabilities to include text chat, VoIP conferencing, application sharing, and remote control—all within a secure, centrally managed framework. Comprehensive IM features also enable the timely delivery of business communications, and IM improves productivity by reducing the delays traditionally associated with e-mail, phone, fax, and voice mail, with add-ons such as VoIP conferencing to enhance interactions between employees, customers, and vendors—both person-to-person and group-to-group.

The comprehensive feature set of an enterprise-level product will extend beyond traditional IM and usually includes text-based chat conferencing, presence management, application sharing, advanced encryption for security, VoIP conferencing, and Citrix and Terminal Server support. In addition, strong administration capabilities must be included for corporate users, such as a comprehensive set of tools to manage the IM function as part of the network and enable the IT manager to remotely control the entire IM infrastructure. Advanced IM system administration features, such as remote control, enable help desks to interact with the end-user's computer from a remote location, allowing quicker resolution of support issues. Some applications allow administrators to manage their entire IM infrastructure from anywhere in the world.

Cost Savings on Long Distance and Travel

IM provides the ability for multiple people to join in real-time conversation without incurring the expense of air travel and group conference calls, which can cost hundreds or thousands of dollars or more. Team members can converse with one another by IM all day and, when necessary, all night about work in progress. IM allows employers to give employees the option to work and live wherever they want as road warriors, local field staff, or telecommuters by staying "on IM." Companies that have overseas employees, partners, or customers may also find IM particularly cost effective.

Access to Content

The ability to access and interact with content is an essential component of IM. This has become both a major attraction and a security risk for IM. Rich media features are currently supported on nearly every IM platform used today. Exchange of pictures, slides, video clips, and other types of media are commonplace and can enrich the IM user experience—often at the cost of security breaches that spread virus-laden content across the IM user community. Caution must be taken to prevent such catastrophes from occurring within a corporate environment.

Elimination of Phone Tag

It is estimated that between 40 percent and 60 percent of business phone calls are unsuccessful, because callers fail to reach the called parties when they are busy or away from their desk [17]. Presence management features of IM significantly mitigate the risk of phone tag and provide for more productive communications to take place. The integration of IM and presence management has enabled a caller to know when a person is present even if he or she is using a handheld or other portable device. Individuals can both communicate with others and be connected with clients and coworkers when they are in airplanes, airports, hotels, rental cars, conferences, and so on.

More Responsive Conversations and Collaboration

There is an increasing need for people to work together on the different aspects of data and documents. Such collaboration often starts with several people authoring, editing, and reviewing a document at the same time. The technology of IM real-time communications has made it possible to have a framework in which multiple people, sitting in different locations, can communicate and collaborate together in a (nearly) seamless way.

1.3.6 What Are the Risks of Using IM?

Although IM has significant advantages, including ease of use and instantaneous communication, it also provides a significant security risk. Unfortunately, proper security reviews are usually the last thing to be incorporated into the development and deployment of new technology this is certainly the case with IM. Public IM providers originally developed instant-messaging software to expand their consumer services. Consumers liked the convenience it offered and the fact that is was free, so they quickly adopted it. Business employees wanted to use IM's advantages, so they began downloading and using the software (often without permission).

IM poses significant risk to business users. IT departments typically do not have control over each employee's desktop and often dramatically underestimate the number of workers who are using IM and the ease with which employees can deploy it. As the unmanaged use of consumer IM clients proliferates, the potential for harmful consequences increases. IM-delivered viruses, IM spam (a.k.a., SPIM), lack of communication audit trails (required of financial services firms), and the unchecked dissemination of proprietary company information are some of the dangers associated with uncontrolled IM use.

Content Concerns

Public IM products generally contain no provisions for message logging, confidentiality, or security. IM protocols are generally very difficult to control with existing network security products, because they were designed to allow communication between consumers across the public Internet under any possible configuration. Attempts by administrators or security personnel to block IM traffic by closing firewall ports will fail, because most of these applications are "port agile," often rolling over to other ports that must remain open for users to access the Internet.

Regulatory Issues

Just as with e-mail, IM is also regulated by government and industry regulatory requirements governing content, privacy, and retention. Logging IM content has emerged as either a business need or a regulatory requirement across several industries. For instance, the Securities and Exchange Commission (SEC), NASD, and NYSE require U.S. brokerages to retain and archive all digital communications with customers for periods up to six years. The SEC also mandates that all communications with external investment banking clients be logged and analyzed for potential securities trading violations. Similar regulatory issues apply to the pharmaceutical and petrochemical industries. Logging is a critical business need for call center operations, as well as an operational requirement for government and defense systems. Without the ability to properly control and log IM sessions, financial organizations find themselves unable to meet regulatory compliance. As a form of e-mail, IM creates a written business record that can be subpoenaed and used as evidence in litigation or regulatory investigations. The *Zubulake v. UBS Warburg* case [18] was a landmark series of rulings that focused on cost-shifting and its effect on the management of e-mail and IM. On May 13 and July 24, 2003, U.S. District Court Judge Shira A. Scheindlin (S.D.N.Y.) issued orders [19] that could significantly impact the developing issue of which party must bear the costs of restoring and producing "inaccessible" electronic data, such as e-mails, that have been deleted from an active system.

The *Zubulake* case was a gender discrimination case, where the court confronted the question of whether UBS Warburg should be required to spend approximately $450,000 to restore and produce e-mails that existed only on its backup tapes. In the first instance, UBS Warburg argued that the plaintiff should bear the cost if UBS Warburg were required to do so. In its May 13, 2003 order, the court found that "inaccessible" e-mails are generally discoverable so long as they are relevant to the plaintiff's case. A new three-step analysis was adopted by the court to determine whether it would be appropriate to shift the costs of the production to the plaintiff:

1. The data at issue must be categorized as either (a) "accessible," such as information that is active online or near online and immediately retrievable, or (b) "inaccessible," such as data that is stored on backup tapes like deleted e-mails. Cost-shifting is only typically appropriate for "inaccessible" data.

2. Before considering cost-shifting, the court should conduct a factual analysis to determine which information may be found on the inaccessible media. One way to accomplish this is to require the responding party to restore and produce responsive documents from a small sample of the backup tapes. In the *Zubulake* case, the court required restoration and production of five backup tapes of the plaintiff's choosing.
3. The court should apply the following seven factors (in order of importance) as a guide to help determine whether the requesting party's discovery needs are outweighed by the burdens of the production:
   a. The extent to which the request is specifically tailored to discover relevant information
   b. The availability of such information from other sources
   c. The total cost of production, compared with the amount in controversy
   d. The total cost of production, compared with the resources available to each party
   e. The relative ability of each party to control costs and its incentive to do so
   f. The importance of the issues at stake in the litigation
   g. The relative benefits to the parties of obtaining the information

After reviewing the sampling of the backup tapes and applying its new seven-factor analysis, on July 24, 2003, the court shifted 25 percent of the cost of restoring e-mails from backup tapes to the plaintiff, but the court found that none of the production costs, such as attorney time for reviewing the data, could qualify for shifting.

In the *Zubulake* case, the cost of restoring the backup tapes was approximately \$175,000, while the estimated cost of producing them was \$273,649. Since the production costs of large volumes of documents will often dwarf restoration costs, the judge's decision to shift *only* the cost of restoring backup tapes, and not the costs of production, to include the attorney reviewing time, was significant. Even where it is appropriate to shift the entire cost of restoring backup tapes to the requesting party, the judge ruled that the producing party must bear the costs of reviewing the documents before the production [20].

What does this judgment mean to a corporation and its management of e-mail and IM? If this case becomes a precedence in future rulings, the consequences could be as follows:

- Despite the enormous attorney review time that is often associated with searching active e-mail servers for responsive documents, the cost of searching and producing accessible data must be borne by the producing party.
- *Zubulake* showed us that even if a corporate defendant can succeed in convincing the court that some cost-shifting is appropriate, the defendant still must bear the entire cost of review and production, as UBS Warburg was required to.
- The burden will be great where regulations require a corporation or its employees, such as in the securities industry, to retain e-mails for relatively long periods of time.
- The *Zubulake* decisions will also increase the burden on corporate parties with respect to searching backup media, such as e-mail backup tapes.
- Careful consideration must be given to any corporate electronic document retention program, especially with respect to the protocol for scope and duration of backup of e-mails and e-mail, like systems, including IM and PDA-type communications. All of these backup tapes are fair game for discovery, and it appears that the attendant costs of that discovery will fall primarily on the producing party.

The *Zubulake v. UBS Warburg LLC* case showed that rulings on lost or destroyed electronic data could mean significant sanctions. In a continuation of this case, in a later ruling on October 22, 2003, U.S. District Court Judge Shira A. Scheindlin (S.D.N.Y.) issued a fourth ruling [21] that is relevant to corporate electronic data preservation practices. In the previous ruling on July 24, 2003, the court ordered the parties to share costs of recovering relevant e-mails contained on UBS Warburg's backup tapes. During the process of restoring the e-mails, the parties discovered that certain of the tapes were missing and that certain isolated e-mails had been deleted from the system after being saved, while others had not been saved at all. In response to this discovery, Zubulake moved for sanctions against

UBS Warburg to include the full costs of restoration, an adverse inference instruction with respect to the backup tapes that were missing, and the costs of redeposing some individuals concerning the issues raised in the e-mails. In this latest ruling, the court declined all but one of Zubulake's sanction requests, ordering UBS Warburg to pay only for the costs of redeposing certain witnesses. The court ruled that UBS Warburg had a duty to preserve the e-mails in question and had breached this duty by failing to do so and, as a consequence, the judge formed a standard to determine *when* the duty to retain documents arises and *which* documents must be retained. The court recognized that even when faced with litigation, a company does not need to preserve *every* electronic document and summarized a company's preservation obligations as follows:

- Once a company *reasonably anticipates* litigation, it is its duty to preserve documents, and at that point, it must suspend its regular policies and put in place a "litigation hold" to ensure the preservation of *relevant* documents.
- "Litigation hold" does not apply to backup tapes that are inaccessible, such as those maintained solely for the purpose of disaster recovery; however, if the backup tapes are actively used for information retrieval, they would likely be subject to the "litigation hold."
- In the case where a company can identify where particular employee documents are stored on backup tapes, then the company should preserve tapes that contain the documents of "key players" in the existing or threatened litigation, unless the information is available elsewhere.

In *Zubulake IV*, the court found that all but one of the elements for an adverse inference instruction existed. Those elements included:

1. The party with control over the evidence had a duty to preserve it.
2. The evidence was destroyed with a "*culpable state of mind.*"
3. The evidence was relevant to the party's claim or defense.

The court found that UBS Warburg breached its duty to preserve the e-mails and that the bank's negligence in destroying the data was sufficiently culpable conduct. The only element missing was evidence that the destroyed e-mails had specific relevance to Zubulake's claims. The court ordered the bank to pay for the costs of redeposing certain witnesses, because UBS Warburg had breached its duty to preserve the e-mails in question. UBS Warburg narrowly missed a much more serious penalty—an adverse inference instruction to the jury—authorizing the jury to infer that the destroyed evidence would have been favorable to Zubulake and harmful to UBS Warburg; however, the court had no reason to believe that the evidence would have been harmful to UBS Warburg in this case. Although UBS Warburg avoided the extreme sanction of an adverse inference instruction, corporate defendants should take no comfort in this result; however, if evidence of relevance had existed, the inadvertent destruction of e-mails may have effectively guaranteed a jury verdict in favor of Zubulake.

Continuing a line of groundbreaking and influential decisions relevant to corporate electronic data preservation and discovery, on July 24, 2004, U.S. District Court Judge Shira A. Scheindlin issued a fifth ruling [22]. Although companies and their consul should be familiar with all the rulings of *Zubulake v. UBS Warburg*, this ruling is perhaps the most important because it may significantly affect the way parties to litigation and their in-house and outside counsel approach electronic document retention.

In this latest ruling by the court, in *Zubulake V*, the court found that UBS had not produced e-mails relevant to the plaintiff's gender discrimination claims against the company. Previously, in *Zubulake IV*, the court allowed the plaintiff to redepose several key UBS employees after UBS produced additional e-mails it had recovered and disclosed that certain e-mails had been inadvertently deleted or written over. But, lacking evidence that the lost and deleted e-mails were particularly relevant to the plaintiff's claim, the court declined to grant an adverse inference jury instruction, which would authorize the jury that eventually hears the case to infer that the destroyed evidence would have been favorable to Zubulake and harmful to UBS. During the redepositions ordered by the court in *Zubulake IV*, the plaintiff uncovered evidence that a few UBS employees had inadvertently deleted e-mails that were relevant to her claim. The plaintiff also discovered that responsive documents that existed at the time of her document requests were produced late because counsel had never specifically asked for their production.

As a result, Zubulake once again moved for sanctions against UBS, renewing her request that an adverse inference instruction be given to the jury. This time the court granted the request. At trial, the jury was instructed, in part, as follows:

> *If you find that UBS could have produced this evidence, and that the evidence was within its control, and that the evidence would have been material in deciding facts in dispute in this case, you are permitted, but not required, to infer that the evidence would have been unfavorable to UBS.*

The court also required the company to restore additional backup tapes, awarded the plaintiff any costs associated with redeposing witnesses, and awarded the plaintiff the costs associated with the motion for sanctions. While the court found UBS's counsel shared some blame for the company's failure to preserve and produce e-mails, the court did not sanction counsel [23]. The court found that UBS and its counsel could have done more to preserve and produce the relevant documents but also acknowledged that UBS's in-house and outside counsel had properly instituted a "litigation hold," which suspended the company's document retention policy. Indeed, counsel had issued "litigation hold" instructions before and after Zubulake filed her complaint and had repeated the instruction several times. Moreover, outside counsel had made clear that the hold applied to backup tapes as soon as the tapes became an issue in the litigation. Outside counsel also communicated directly with many of the key players in the litigation. Finally, outside counsel directly instructed most (but not all) UBS employees to produce copies of their active computer files.

Despite these efforts, however, Judge Scheindlin found that UBS did not fully satisfy its duty to locate relevant information in its possession and failed to take necessary steps to ensure that relevant data was retained. Even though both in-house and outside counsel had sent numerous "litigation hold" memoranda, certain UBS employees had failed to retain relevant e-mails. The court found that counsel should have communicated better with a key employee about how she "archived" her e-mails in a separate active file on her computer so that the employee could have been asked to produce those files. In addition, the court ruled that counsel should have directly communicated the "litigation hold" instructions to several key employees, should have directly asked certain additional employees to produce files, and should have put better protections in place for backup tapes so that they would not be inadvertently recycled. The clear lesson of *Zubulake V* is as follows:

> *In short, it is not sufficient to notify all employees of a litigation hold and expect that the party will retain and produce all relevant information. Counsel must take affirmative steps to monitor compliance so that all sources of discoverable information are identified and searched.*

This instruction will likely change the standard practice of many lawyers and clients who have, until now, assumed that issuing a "litigation hold" memo at the outset of a case satisfies their obligation in this area. What are the "affirmative steps" contemplated by Judge Scheindlin? According to her, the best way for counsel and parties to avoid spoliation claims is to do the following [24]:

1. **Issue and reissue a "litigation hold."** As explained by the court in both *Zubulake IV* and *Zubulake V*, a party that "reasonably anticipates" litigation must suspend its regular policies and put in place a "litigation hold" for relevant documents. This "litigation hold" would generally apply to "accessible" backup tapes (i.e., those actively used for information retrieval) but not to "inaccessible" backup tapes (e.g., those typically maintained solely for the purpose of disaster recovery at a remote location). Counsel must reissue the hold so that new employees are aware of it and so that it is fresh in the minds of all employees.
2. **Locate all sources of relevant information.** Once the "litigation hold" is in place, a party and counsel must endeavor to identify all sources of potentially relevant information. To do so, counsel should become familiar with the party's document retention policies and computer system. This will require affirmative communication and coordination with IT personnel, as well as key players, in order to understand how documents are stored at both the institutional and individual levels. While much of the preservation can be done at the system level by the IT personnel at a firm, counsel must directly interface with the key players to ensure that their individual electronic records are preserved. For example, an employee's individual archive system may contain documents long ago deleted from the company's general system (e.g., e-mails saved to a local archive that no longer are retained because of recycling of backup tapes). Therefore, one cannot rely on backup tapes and fail to pursue individually retained electronic materials.
3. **Ensure continual preservation and production.** Once the sources of potentially relevant information are located, counsel must take several additional steps to monitor the preservation of that information. Counsel must clearly and directly communicate the preservation duty to IT personnel and key players and must remind them of it periodically in a manner that will ensure preservation of relevant material. In addition, counsel must directly

> instruct employees to produce copies of their relevant active files. Counsel cannot simply assume that employees will do so.

In the growing literature on electronic document production, the *Zubulake* opinions are undoubtedly among the leading authorities, at least at the district court level. We note, however, that Judge Scheindlin has set a demanding standard for parties and counsel. Other courts may not agree fully that the duties addressed by Judge Scheindlin extend quite as far, and definitive guidance will have to await further development in the courts (particularly appellate courts). If courts uniformly adopt an exacting standard similar to Judge Scheindlin's, the burdens of electronic discovery will fall especially hard on the securities industry, where regulations mandate the retention of business-related e-mails and IM longer than is customary for most companies. In any case, corporate defendants and their counsel should consider themselves on notice: Failure to comply with the obligation to preserve and produce electronic data may result in harsh monetary sanctions and damaging adverse inference instructions.

Security Breaches

According to research firm Gartner, over 70 percent of corporate employees depend on IM for business communications despite the fact that, according to Nemertes Research, 70 percent of IT executives claim to have banned the use of commercial IM services in their organizations. Authorized or not, IM is being used on most networks, and it poses a serious security threat if left unchecked. Gartner also recently labeled IM security as one of "five technologies you need to know," and research firm Yankee Group called securing IM one of the top three priorities for IT managers in 2004. Senior IT executives overwhelmingly concur, as 62 percent told Nemertes Research that they worry about IM security [25].

Incompatibility of Communication Software

There is currently a high degree of incompatibility between the different downloadable IM clients and ISP systems. Unlike the phone and e-mail systems, IM technology is far from universal. The various competing networks have become a complex web of incompatibility in which users of one system can't communicate with those on another. There are now seven major IM networks in the United States and as many as 40 minor ones. Some allow users to freely send and receive messages from competing networks, while others protect their users behind closed walls. For example, the most widely used public IM network is AOL, with four of every five

IM users on its two huge networks, AOL Instant Messenger (AIM) and ICQ. AIM is used by 23 million AOL members, as well as by 61 million others who have downloaded the free software, which lets them chat with AOL users.

Monitoring, Retention, and Archiving Challenges

Logging IM content has emerged as either a business need or a regulatory requirement across several industries. For instance, the SEC, NASD, and NYSE require U.S. brokerages to retain and archive all digital communications with customers for periods up to six years. Similar regulatory issues apply to the pharmaceutical and petrochemical industries. Logging is a critical business need for call center operations, as well as an operational requirement for government/defense systems. Pressured by fines and threats of imprisonment for noncompliance with federal and state regulations, IT executives are cautiously deploying systems that archive their e-mail and instant-messaging communications. Specific language in the Sarbanes-Oxley Act of 2002 says, in part:

> *Whoever knowingly alters, destroys, mutilates, conceals, covers up, falsifies, or makes a false entry in any record, document—with intent to impede—shall be fined under this title, imprisoned not more than 20 years, or both.*

A variety of regulations are causing organizations to look at e-mail archiving. Among the regulations that affect public companies are Sarbanes-Oxley, the Heath Information Portability and Accountability Act of 1996 (HIPAA), and the Uniform Electronic Transactions Act, which says e-mail can be used to form contracts. In addition, the threat of a lawsuit for offensive comments or behavior or for corporate wrongdoing is a concern.

It is a difficult task to decide which e-mail needs to be archived, involving the assessment of different business units in a company and deciding not only which department but also which employee e-mails need to be retained. Although some companies fearing litigation elect to archive all e-mails, others will either delete everything on a regular basis and eliminate incriminating evidence that might arise during a legal action; keep everything long term, including all the nonessential information; or keep only the most important types of information. Other issues can arise even after a decision has been made as to what is to be retained, such as users reaching their mailbox size quota and erratically deleting messages or saving them to personal file folders.

False Sense of Security Regarding Retention

Logging of IM has become a reality, and, as previously discussed, it is being driven by various regulatory and industry requirements. IM users can gain a false sense of personal security with regard to the content of their IM messages, because the message vanishes after it is read and the window closes; but, in fact, IM conversations can be logged and archived by a corporation or by the recipient without the knowledge or consent of the originating party.

Decrease in productivity as chat increases

In terms of productivity, IM is a double-edged sword. Although some companies have found IM to be an indispensable communication tool, other organizations have identified it as just another distraction for employees by creating a "virtual water cooler," which cannot be controlled or monitored. Many companies want to control the use of IM to ensure that their staffs are not spending excessive time with personal communications. IM file-sharing applications can also bog down the corporate network at the expense of normal business traffic, impacting the response time for employees and customers and leading to lower productivity.

Rogue Use

The security risks associated with rogue protocols include exposing outsiders to confidential content and/or infecting systems with viruses and opening the corporation to external attacks. Rogue protocol-based applications, such as peer-to-peer file sharing and IM, allow outsiders to view unauthorized information or files. Confidential information can be willfully disclosed by employees or captured surreptitiously. For example, with peer-to-peer file sharing, an employee could unintentionally share access to confidential information on the corporate network or on his or her system. With IM, the traffic from two communicating employees sitting across from each other actually travels outside the organization, through a public messaging server and back to the other employee. Eavesdroppers can intercept instant messages en route to the recipient. Furthermore, conversations can be logged indefinitely on a public messaging server, and confidential conversations can easily be recorded by unauthorized third parties.

With both IM and peer-to-peer file-sharing applications, content can pass through firewall and virus protection systems, introducing damaging viruses, worms, and Trojan horses into the network. These infections can result in serious damage to important network assets and may even provide access to or control of employee computers. Some Web browsers have integrated IM, resulting in the potential for attack without even activating the IM part of the browser. Peer-to-peer file sharing and IM applications that share files often allow third parties to view the user's IP addresses, increasing the risk of an attack.

Applications that use rogue protocols often go unrecognized by IT departments, making it difficult to enforce corporate and government policies. In the financial industry, regulators mandate that financial services companies log all electronic communication with customers, including instant messages. Because IM traffic is not logged by existing network security systems, corporations cannot fully comply with regulations. Enforcing corporate policy is challenging if the activities in question are undetected. Corporations may not want employees using the network to transfer music or other files to outside entities. Simply blocking ports will not solve the usage problem, because IM and peer-to-peer file-sharing applications scan for open ports and may also tunnel through port 80 (the port used for Web traffic).

Messages Not Read or Acted upon

IM only has the potential for real-time communication if the recipient is actually at his or her desk or not otherwise engaged in a phone call or in a meeting. It is also possible that the recipient has been buried with other messages that have masked your message or put it at the top of the stack, where it is possible to go unnoticed (in which case there is a high probability that your message will not be read or acted upon).

Misuse of User IDs or Corporate Domain Names

Unlike e-mail, with IM, users can establish their personalities and can use any name they wish. This is problematic, because it can lead to the misuse of user IDs and the misappropriation of corporate domain names in a corporate setting. An adversary, such as a competitor, could represent itself as an employee of a target company and communicate with the company's clients under false pretenses, adopt an inappropriate name associated with a company, or generally spoof any identity within or external to a company. This is a particularly challenging authentication issue.

1.4 Summary

IM is here to stay, with its combination of speed, privacy, and convenience; it can enable new business practices that early adopting end-users love and that neither e-mail nor the telephone can support. IM is already changing the way we communicate. IM is changing corporate communications, combining the real-time advantages of a phone call with the convenience of e-mail. IM is so compelling, it often gets implemented through the back door, with distributed workgroups downloading public IM clients and using them without getting approval from corporate IT departments. IM is a compelling business tool, but if not properly controlled, IM can lead not only to a decrease in productivity, but also to the inadvertent exposure of sensitive business information, resulting in serious security risks and further resulting in regulatory and legal risks. IM programs enable downloading and exchange of offensive imagery or text with clients or other employees, exposing your organization to potential harassment lawsuits. Downloading copyrighted music files or unlicensed software could also expose your organization to legal action or significant fines. Newly established statutes in the finance and healthcare industries require that organizations take the appropriate steps to ensure that nonpublic customer information is kept confidential. In addition, recent court cases have set a new precedence for the handling and storage of both e-mail and IM logs. Failure to comply with these laws can result in steep fines, or even jail time, in addition to the damaging effects it may have on your reputation. With the escalating use of IM in the enterprise sector, and the growing number of vendors and solutions, it has become a major challenge for companies to evaluate IM advantages and balance the cost security with the business needs and advantages.

1.5 Endnotes

1. B. Deagon. (July 2, 2003). "Top Brass Slow to Embrace Instant Messaging Technology—Explaining IM Benefits." *Investors Business Daily.*

2. M. Turek. "Opinion: The Messaging Years—2004 and 2005," online article. Retrieved from URL http://www.messagingpipeline.com/56900302, January 30, 2005.

3. Akonix. (2004). "Security." Retrieved December 14, 2004 from http://www.akonix.com/solutions/security.asp.

4. International Engineering Consortium. (2004). "Instant Messaging: Definition and Overview." Retrieved December 14, 2004 from http://www.iec.org/online/tutorials/instant_msg/.

5. ICQ. (2004). "What is ICQ?" Retrieved January 4, 2005 from http://www.icq.com/products/whatisicq.html.

6. ICQ. (2004). "ICQ Tour?" Retrieved January 4, 2005 from http://www.icq.com/icqtour/

7. FCC Ruling—CS Docket No. 00-30, MEMORANDUM OPINION AND ORDER, adopted: January 11, 2001, by the Commission; Chairman Kennard, Commissioners Ness and Tristani issuing separate statements; Commissioners Furchtgott-Roth and Powell concurring in part, dissenting in part, and issuing separate statements.

8. International Engineering Consortium. (2004). "Instant Messaging—IM as an Integrated Communications Platform." Retrieved December 14, 2004 from http://www.iec.org/online/tutorials/instant_msg/topic02.html.

9. International Engineering Consortium. (2004). "Instant Messaging—Network-Based versus Device-Based Approaches." Retrieved December 14, 2004 from http://www.iec.org/online/tutorials/instant_msg/topic03.html.

10. Ibid.

11. R. Demarco. (August 24, 2004). "America Online Inc.'s Second Annual Instant Messaging Trends Survey Shows Instant Messaging Has Gone Mainstream." Retrieved December 14, 2004 from http://imframe.blogspot.com/2004/08/america-online-incs-second-annual.html.

12. Ibid.

13. Ibid.

14. *State of Vermont v. Voorheis*, 2004 WL 258178, VT, February 13, 2004.

15. The U.S. Department of Justice. (2004). "Computer Crime and Intellectual Property Section (CCIPS)— How to Report Internet-Related Crime." Retrieved December 14, 2004 from http://www.usdoj.gov/criminal/cybercrime/reporting.htm.

16. IEE. (2002). "Internet Education for Educators: Helping Educators Protect Children." Retrieved December 14, 2004 from http://www.nerac.com/family/NeracReports/Cybercrimes.htm.
17. Tech Warehouse. (2004). "Instant Messaging." Retrieved December 16, 2004 from http://www.techiwarehouse.com/Articles/2003-05-12.html.
18. *Zubulake v. UBS Warburg LLC*, et al., No. 02 Civ. 1243 (S.D.N.Y.), May 13, 2003.
19. *Zubulake v. UBS Warburg LLC*, et al., No. 02 Civ. 1243 (S.D.N.Y.), July 24, 2003.
20. *Zubulake v. UBS Warburg LLC*, et al., No. 02 Civ. 1243 (S.D.N.Y.), July 24, 2003.
21. *Zubulake v. UBS Warburg LLC*, et al., No. 02 Civ. 1243 (S.D.N.Y.) 22 October, 2003.
22. *Zubulake v. UBS Warburg LLC*, et al., No. 02 Civ. 1243 (S.D.N.Y.) ("Zubulake V") 24 July, 2004.
23. Ibid.
24. Ibid.
25. Akonix. (2004). "Security." Retrieved December 16, 2004 from http://www.akonix.com/solutions/security.asp.

2

How Does IM Work?

In this chapter, we take a long, hard look at IM from a user perspective. We will also try to relate the user perspective to the technical details that take place behind the scenes to help you gain a fuller understanding of what IM is, how it works, and how it is used in both business and personal settings. This chapter will provide you with a solid understanding of the capabilities and features of IM software today. It should help you to decide whether or not IM is right for you, whether or not it is suitable for use in your home or business, and the benefits (and risks) that using IM brings with it.

2.1 High-Level View of IM

IM is one of the most widely used software applications in the world. In a recent (August 2004) study [1], the researchers' findings provided some surprising information:

- Over 53 million American adults now use IM—it is used mostly among young adults and techno-savvy users.
- Most IM users still use email more frequently than IM; however, many are turning to IM more often than they do email.
- IM is moving into the American workplace. At-work, IM users report feeling positively about how IM improves workflow and the quality of the workday. However, some think that the use of IM encourages gossip, distracts them from work, or even adds stress to the workplace.
- IM use differs markedly among age groups. Most notably, younger Internet users employ IM in greater numbers and more ardently than older generations.

- IM users often utilize special features of IM programs to enhance their ability to communicate and stay connected with other IM users. Yet, they do not spend a great deal of time using exclusionary features, such as blocking and removing buddies.

So, what exactly is this phenomenon called IM? A presence and IM system allows users to subscribe to each other and be notified of changes in state, as well as permitting users to send each other short (almost instant) text messages. The IM and presence model we describe herein consists of the various entities involved, descriptions of the basic functions they provide, and, most importantly, precise definition of a vocabulary that can be used to facilitate discussion. Throughout this chapter, the precise terminology that is used within the IM model is presented in all uppercase letters to help you distinguish between the common vernacular and IM-specific usage of a given term. The model itself defines two types of services: a PRESENCE SERVICE and an INSTANT MESSAGE SERVICE.

2.1.1 The Presence Service

The PRESENCE SERVICE serves to accept information, store it, and distribute it. The information stored is known as PRESENCE INFORMATION. Examples of this type of information would be client status (online, away, busy, etc.), user name, public profile information, and so on. Basically, this is what users are allowed to see or know about other users. Let's walk through an example of how the process works from a user's perspective. In this case, Lois wants to become a SUBSCRIBER to the PRESENCE SERVICE (Figure 2.1).

In order to accomplish this, she must use an Internet Service Provider (ISP) to gain Internet access and find the PRESENCE SERVICE online. She may have to download software and install that software on her computer before being able to use the IM service. Figure 2.2 illustrates an example of Lois going to the MSN Messenger download Web site and initiating the download process. Once Lois has successfully downloaded and installed the client software, she can go through the online sign-up process that MSN Messenger requires to allow her to subscribe to its PRESENCE SERVICE.

The PRESENCE SERVICE (MSN Messenger in this case) accepts, stores, and distributes PRESENCE INFORMATION from Lois, who is now referred to as a PRESENTITY (i.e., a PRESence ENTITY). The service may require authentication of PRESENTITIES and/or WATCHERS, and it may have different authentication requirements for different

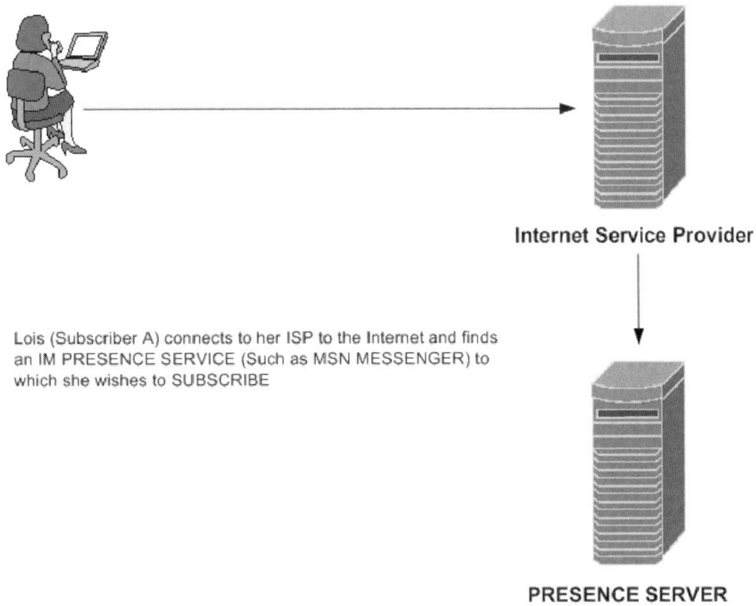

Figure 2.1 *Example of subscribing to a Presence Service.*

PRESENTITIES. For example, MSN Messenger currently uses the Microsoft Passport technology to maintain authentication data for its service subscribers. The service may have different authentication requirements for different WATCHERS, and it could also have different authentication requirements for different PRESENTITIES that are being watched by any given WATCHER.

It is important to note that a PRESENCE SERVICE does not need to operate on a single, distinct SERVER. The service may be implemented on multiple servers or it could be operating with direct communication among a PRESENTITY and one or more WATCHERS. The service may have an internal structure involving other PRESENCE SERVICES, which may be independently accessible in their own right as well as being reachable through the initial PRESENCE SERVICE. The PRESENCE SERVICE itself may have an internal structure involving multiple SERVERS and/or PROXIES, as shown in Figure 2.3. There may be complex patterns of redirection and/or proxying while retaining logical connectivity to a single PRESENCE SERVICE.

The process of using an IM service generally takes a standard sequence of events. Let's take a look at a typical example of a person wanting to become a subscriber to an IM service. In our next example, John has also decided to use IM. He chose to join an existing public IM service such as Yahoo! Instant

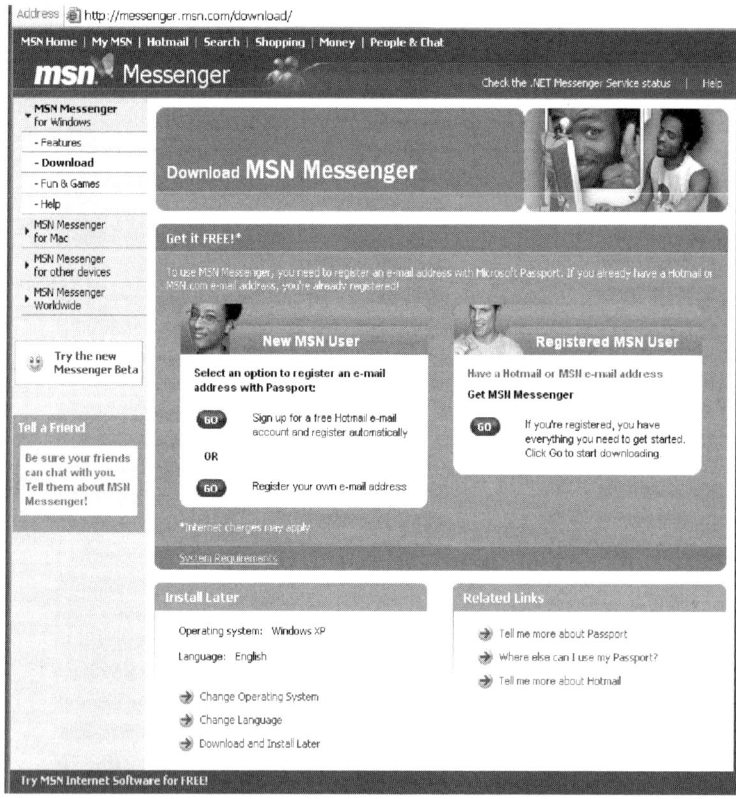

Figure 2.2 *Downloading MSN Messenger™ on the Internet.*

Messenger, ICQ, or MSN Messenger. He used his ISP to get on the Internet and find the IM Service he wanted to use at http://messenger.msn.com, where he created an IM subscriber account and downloaded the IM client software MSN Messenger) to install on his machine. Once John completed the install of the software and started the IM client, he was required to sign on to the MSN Messenger Service, as shown in Figure 2.4.

The process of signing on to the service sets his subscriber status to OPEN, and the PRESENCE SERVICE updates his PRESENCE INFO using a PRESENCE TUPLE sent via the PRESENCE PROTOCOL. The protocol is simply a predefined set of rules each party in the communications process has agreed to use in order to communicate successfully. The PRESENCE TUPLE used in this protocol is a set of data in three parts. It consists of a STATUS section, an optional COMMUNICATION ADDRESS, and optional OTHER PRESENCE MARKUP data. The optional presence markup data allows for different service providers to carry varying data about the subscriber, along with the presence data transmitted from the PRESENCE SERVICE, to a user. The PRESENCE SERVICE

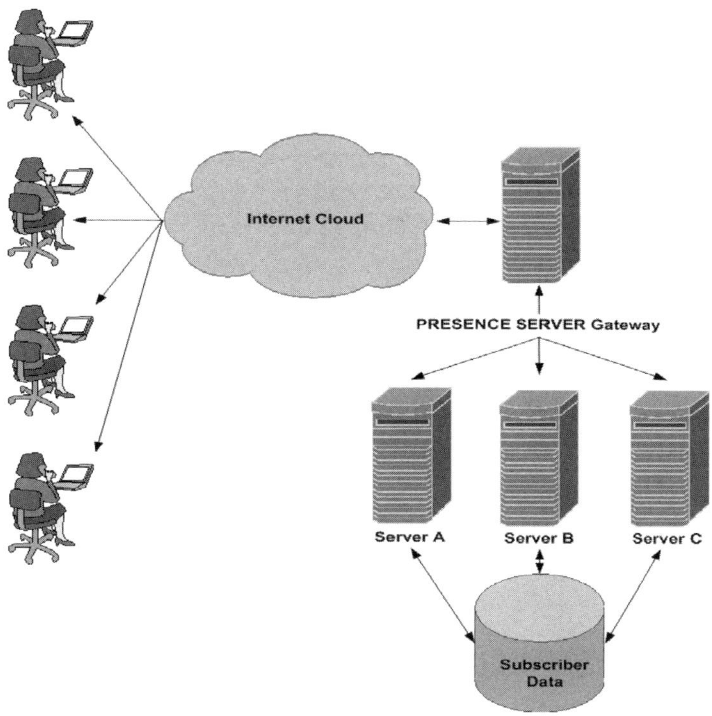

Figure 2.3 *Internet subscribers using a Presence Service with multiple servers.*

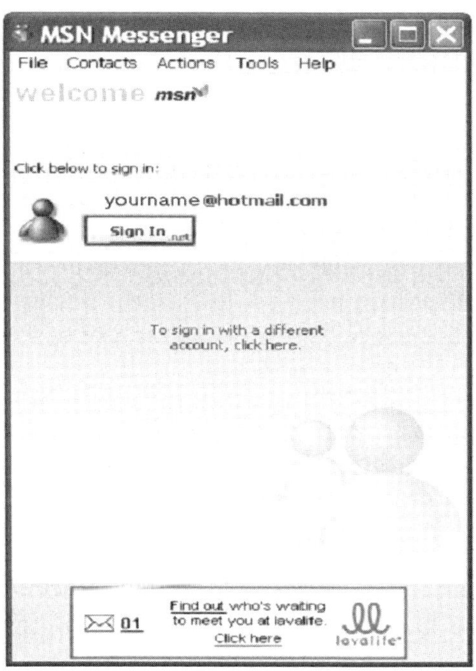

Figure 2.4 *MSN sign-on process.*

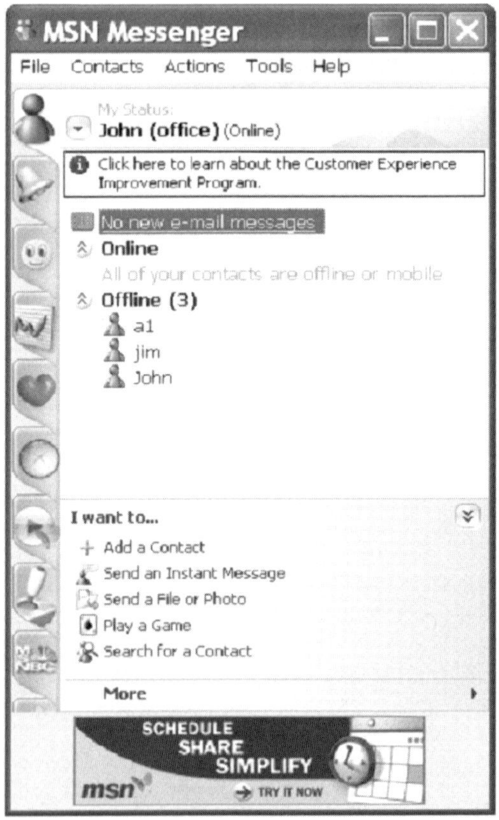

Figure 2.5 *Client software after sign-on.*

maintains all the subscription data relevant to each subscriber of the IM service, and it sends notifications of status change to subscribers as those changes occur.

Once John has authenticated successfully and signed on to the service, he will immediately begin to receive notifications from the PRESENCE SERVICE. What happens behind the scenes is that the client software has initiated a FETCHER (which is one form of a WATCHER) process to request current status for each contact John has stored in his subscriber data file. The FETCHER requests PRESENCE INFO regarding the contacts from the PRESENCE SERVICE, which in turn checks its PRESENCE INFO using the PRESENCE PROTOCOL for each contact in John's list of contacts.

Here is what the client software looks like (Figure 2.5) after successfully signing on to the service. In this case, none of John's contacts are online. Note that the presence info for his contacts is displayed as *online* or *offline* and that there are many options for John to use in order to make the best possible use of IM.

In order for John to receive such change notifications, the software must initiate a POLLER (which is yet another form of the WATCHER). The POLLER is used to make periodic update requests to the PRESENCE SERVICE for PRESENCE INFO relevant to John's contacts. The client software supports many features that allow subscribers to perform online chat, share files, video, and audio clips, collaborate on a document, and so on. Enhancements to the basic performance features allow users to display images of themselves or to use icons to represent themselves. The list of features is almost endless, with the number of software products competing for subscribers, so the consumer/subscriber is definitely the winner in this case. More features translate to more capability for the user, and those capabilities are often put to use in creative ways. Online education, training, or distance learning, as it has been called, is just one of many uses IM supports today.

An example of the many choices available to a subscriber is shown in Figure 2.6. Under the **Actions** menu, a subscriber can choose to send IMs, files, and photos, begin talking in an audio conversation, send video from a webcam, or even conduct a video conference. Other features allow interactive game playing with other subscribers, the ability to send email, text, or images to a mobile device, such as a cell phone or pager, and even to receive breaking news over IM. There are even more features that allow users to permit other subscribers to remotely assist in managing their machine, to share an application between themselves, have a common whiteboard for presentations, and so on. Sharing a machine is useful in situations such as with a help desk in a corporate environment, where a user can contact the help desk via IM and request assistance in using an application, setting proper user configurations, and so on. The ability for users to share an application or to share a whiteboard is quite handy when providing presentations over the Internet. Rather than have each person look at an emailed copy of a presentation, the whiteboard allows all users to see the same presentation at the same time. The advantage here is that the author/presenter can be assured that all users are seeing the latest version of the same presentation at the same time. To this point, we have covered the essentials of the PRESENCE SERVICE. Now, let's look at the INSTANT MESSAGING SERVICE.

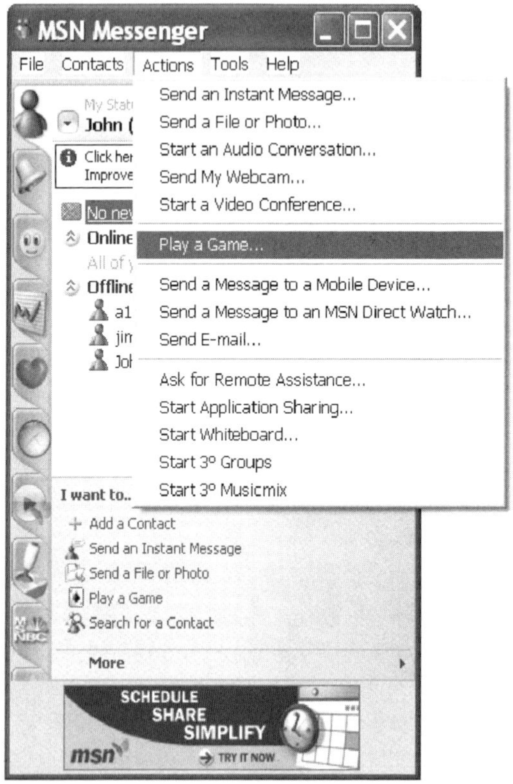

Figure 2.6
An example of the wide variety of features available in IM software today.

2.1.2 The Instant Messaging Service

The INSTANT MESSAGE SERVICE serves to accept and deliver INSTANT MESSAGES to INSTANT INBOXES. Each client SUBSCRIBER (also known as a PRINCIPAL) is set up with an INSTANT INBOX for instant messages. When an IM is received, it goes into the inbox and a notification is displayed immediately. The notification itself may display the message or allow the user to click to see the message. The notification can usually be set to provide the subscriber with audio or visual notices (or both). Responses are processed and sent out to the remote party in the same manner. As an example, let's assume John has previously downloaded and installed the client software mentioned in the previous section. When he gets on the Internet and logs into the PRESENCE SERVICE, several things occur. First of all, the act of logging into the PRESENCE SERVICE establishes John's status as OPEN and notifies the service that John is ONLINE and ready to accept notifications. John may choose to change his visible status to any one of several options available with his client software (BUSY, OFFLINE, etc.), but the PRESENCE SERVICE maintains his status as OPEN until he logs off, and then it becomes CLOSED. The PRESENCE SERVICE uses ACCESS RULES to determine how other subscribers will see John's presence from their client software. John can choose to be "invisible" to all but a few of his contacts, or he can allow everyone to see he is online and ready to accept notifications. Once John has successfully logged in, his client software initiates a WATCHER in the form of a FETCHER to request presence information about people in his contact list. A POLLER (which is another form of a WATCHER) periodically checks on presence information for each contact in John's list to maintain updated, current status for each of those contacts. As a contact's status changes, his or her PRESENCE INFORMATION is updated at the PRESENCE SERVICE, and that status change is updated when the next POLLER requests status.

If any of the contacts on John's list are logged in to the PRESENCE SERVICE and their status is set to OPEN and their access rules allow John to see that they are ONLINE, John will receive a NOTIFICATION MESSAGE for each such contact. If any of the contacts on John's list chooses to set his or her status to BUSY, for example, John would receive a notice that the person is BUSY, and the PRESENCE SERVICE would apply that contact's ACCESS RULES to prevent other SUBSCRIBERS from sending notifications to him or her.

The PRESENCE SERVICE manages the POLLER, WATCHER, and FETCHER requests from all subscribers. Each subscriber uses his or her client software, written to use IM and presence protocols, to communicate with the PRESENCE SERVICE, to update PRESENCE INFORMATION (using PRESENCE TUPLES), and exchange instant messages. INSTANT MESSAGES are delivered to and from subscribers' INSTANT INBOXES as they are sent from one subscriber to another. However, each message really goes through the PRESENCE SERVICE, has PRESENCE INFO and ACCESS RULES validated against the recipient subscriber's settings, and is then delivered based on the recipient subscriber's INSTANT INBOX settings. The INSTANT INBOX uses an INBOX USER AGENT to apply the DELIVERY RULES. What appears to be instantaneous, collaborative communication between two subscribers is, in fact, handled through the PRESENCE SERVICE and has rules applied to both ends as the messages and notifications are delivered. The transmission of such small amounts of text, and constant updates of each subscriber's presence information, provides an illusion of a directly connected communications session. Much the same way that a telephone connects two talkers in a phone call, the IM users really don't care what goes on behind the scenes or how many switches, routers, hubs, etc., the messages will traverse to get from John to Lois. So, to make all this work seamlessly, the PRESENCE SERVICE and the INSTANT MESSAGING SERVICE operate under known protocols (RFC 2778[2] and RFC 2779[3]) that allow each service to coexist and leverage features offered by the other service through a client software package that a SUBSCRIBER installs and uses. Let's now take a look at some of the most common IM features available today.

2.2 Basic IM Features

The presence and IM model was intended to provide a means for understanding, comparing, and describing systems that support the services typically referred to as IM. The model consists of a number of *named entities* (features) that appear, in some form or other, in existing systems. No actual implementation is likely to have every entity of the model as a distinct component. Instead, there will almost always be parts of the implementation that embody two or more entities of the model. However, different implementations may combine entities in different ways. What follows is a brief overview of some of the more common features provided in IM software today. Table 2.1 summarizes each of these features by product, comparing four of the most popular IM software products currently in operation.

The IM features listed in Table 2.1 are described as follows:

Table 2.1 *Common Public IM Features by Provider*

IM Feature	AIM	MSN	YAHOO!	ICQ
Instant Messaging	√	√	√	√
Voice Chat	√	√	√	√
Video Chat	×	√	√	√
Application Sharing	×	√	×	×
File Transfer	√	√	√	√
File Sharing	√	×	√	√
Game Requests	√	×	×	×
Remote Assistance	×	√	×	×
Whiteboard	×	√	×	×
IM Images	√	×	×	×

Instant Messaging—(*also known as IM*) The transmission of HTML-encoded text from one user to another via an IM service. These messages generally have no security and are always routed over the Internet.

Voice/Video Chat—A direct connection must be established between two users to enable voice/video chat. The data is typically transferred via UDP connections. AIM does not support video chat, but it does support voice chat (which is handled similarly to its IM images capability).

Application Sharing (NET Messenger)—Application sharing allows a remote user access to programs installed on another computer. Optionally, a user may give control of a program to a remote user. If a user accepts the invitation to share an application, the initiating user may select which programs he or she wishes to share with the other user. To achieve application sharing, a direct TCP connection is established between the clients.

File Transfers—File transfers require a direct connection to be established between users. However, once a file transfer is completed, the direct connection is closed.

File Sharing (AIM, Yahoo! and ICQ)—File sharing allows a user to browse a selected directory structure and download files. File sharing is an optional capability that must be enabled in AIM and ICQ before any sharing can take place. However, file sharing is enabled by default in Yahoo! The connection method for file sharing is the same as for a regular file transfer.

Game Requests (AIM only)—Game requests are simply requests for remote users to execute certain external programs, usually games. During game requests, no direct connection is made with users via AIM. If the external application or game requires a direct connection, one may be set up. This feature is not supported in AIM.

Remote Assistance (.NET Messenger)—Windows XP Professional and Home Edition contain the Remote Assistance utility, which allows a remote user to control another computer. The Remote Assistance feature in .NET Messenger launches this utility.

Whiteboard (.NET Messenger)—Whiteboard sharing is a way to share a Microsoft Paint document over a direct connection. It is identical to Application Sharing. Starting a whiteboard session with another user is a shortcut of invoking Application Sharer, then selecting Microsoft Paint as the application to share.

IM Images (AIM only)—IM images are sent via a direct connection with another user. The request is sent to the AIM™ server and is relayed to the target user. The request packet used for direct connection contains the TCP/IP address and port information of the requester. These direct connections reveal the IP address of each participant.

The process of selecting an IM client becomes a bit more complicated when dealing with hundreds or even thousands of users in an enterprise. The next section will discuss some of the factors that should be considered when selecting an IM solution for your company.

2.3 Enterprise Instant Messaging Considerations

Enterprise Instant Messaging (EIM) is quickly replacing consumer-based IM tools in the workplace. A host of new solutions on the market are designed specifically with the enterprise in mind, offering internal installation and control, regulatory compliance, security features, and more. The process of selecting an EIM solution is now as important as any other purchasing decision [4], according to Maxime Seguineau of Antepo, Inc. In the following excerpt, he suggests that before you select an EIM vendor, make sure to ask the following questions:

Does the EIM system require a specific operating system to run?

Does the EIM system require a specific database product to run?

Does the EIM system require a specific directory product to run?

Does your system federate natively with other EIM systems?

Is directory schema extension a prerequisite for the EIM system to operate?

Does your EIM system allow third-party IM clients to connect to your server?

Does the EIM solution offer built-in compliance and policy management?

Which options are available for remote access and mobile users?

What's my true final cost?

2.3.1 Operating System

If the EIM system is tied to a single operating system, it may be limited in its ability to grow and change with your organization. Support for multiple operating systems is very important. If you ever outgrow your installation and need to change or scale with a different hardware and operating system platform, this becomes a crucial gating factor.

2.3.2 Database

Databases are used to store transient presence and IM-related data such as buddy lists, subscription states, and privacy guards. It's especially important if you want to leverage multiple databases simultaneously for different purposes (e.g., archiving, offline messages, presence) that you have flexibility in selecting storage. Database licenses are expensive and need to be planned carefully. Last, but not least, your licensing agreement for database licenses might be managed by a different department, and therefore your EIM system should seamlessly operate with any database choices today and tomorrow.

2.3.3 Directory Services

Supporting multiple directories is also a critical requirement. Most enterprises today rely on a variety of LDAP-based applications to support their internal authentication and overall policy management rules. The EIM system you select should leverage your current directory infrastructure but also allow for flexibility in future decisions. Should you ever decide to migrate your directory operations to another vendor, your EIM system should seamlessly adapt.

2.3.4 Interoperability

An EIM system that only interoperates with itself jeopardizes your ability to aggregate and federate presence data from third-party products and limits your ability to remain agnostic with regard to your business partners, suppliers, and affiliates. Make sure your EIM vendor offers native and comprehensive federation features—not only with its own products but with other vendors using XMPP and/or all variations of SIP/SIMPLE.

2.3.5 Schema Change Requirements

Schema extension and any alteration of the corporate directory structure should be performed with great caution, especially during the trial phase of the product—in other words, it should be optional, not mandatory. While it allows more flexibility in the provisioning and management of IM users, it should be planned as an operational deployment item and reviewed carefully.

2.3.6 Standards Based for Third-Party Support

Organizations today have a variety of Windows, Mac, and even Linux desktops. As your deployment universe and the number of devices connected to your enterprise grows, you will be asked to extend presence and IM capabilities beyond the Windows desktop. Your chosen EIM system should allow third-party developers to develop client applications through standards-based protocol connectivity. Proprietary client/server protocol implementations or unique SDKs prevent innovation around the system you purchase.

2.3.7 Compliance Management

Many companies require the existence of "walls" between users to meet regulatory requirements. Make sure this can be achieved via simple configuration and not with additional programming. Being able to rethread archived conversations without additional SQL programming is vital. Ideally, SMTP logging should also be an option for integration with standard email/IM archive systems, archiving all conversations, whether one-to-one or many-to-many. You will also be well served if policy management is natively built in, as opposed to being dependent on third-party add-ons. Your EIM system should offer message and presence boundaries based on directory groups, prepopulated contact lists, and filters.

2.3.8 Remote Access

Mobile and handheld users epitomize the value of IM. Be sure to include these users in your EIM system by providing not only remote desktop access but also BlackBerry, Palm, Treo, and Pocket PC support. All of the capabilities of your in-house EIM system should be easily extended to your mobile workforce.

2.3.9 Cost Considerations

An EIM system should be easy to deploy and grow in your organization. Adding servers shouldn't increase your software costs beyond the addition of extra users. Also, make sure your EIM system can talk to other systems using different operating systems and/or protocols.

2.4 An Enterprise EIM Nightmare Scenario

The following situation, reported by Security firm F-Secure [5], discusses a recent worm transmitted through IM use, named Bropia.A. The worm spreads through MSN Messenger. Its immediate side effects include disabling the right mouse button of the victim computer and disabling access to the sound mixer. According to the report, it also deposits a variant of Rbot, which can gather keystrokes, collect system information, and make a computer an unwitting spam relay. When run, the worm checks for the existence of the following files:

- adaware.exe
- VB6.EXE
- iexplore.exe
- Win32.exe

If these files are not found, it drops a file named ***oms.exe*** onto the victim's system and executes it. This file is a variant of Rbot. When this file is run, it copies itself as "iexplore.exe" and adds the following registry keys to the system registry:

```
[HKLM\Software\Microsoft\Windows\CurrentVersion\Run]
"iexplore" = "iexplore"

[HKLM\Software\Microsoft\Windows\CurrentVersion\RunServices]
"iexplore" = "iexplore"
```

This registry edit ensures that the dropped file will be executed the next time the system is restarted. The bot can also be used as a backdoor, collecting system information, logging keystrokes, relaying spam, and for various other purposes. Bropia.A can spread when the worm copies itself into the local C directory using one of the following filenames:

- Drunk_lol.pif
- Webcam_004.pif
- sexy_bedroom.pif

- naked_party.pif
- love_me.pif

Once copied, it attempts to send the copied file over MSN Messenger to all active MSN contacts. The MSN Messenger window has to be open on the infected computer's desktop for this attack to be successful.

From an enterprise perspective, it is not hard to imagine the complications that would arise from a situation where your entire customer support section became infected and subsequently began spreading this worm to clients connected to your support agent's infected client, where the worm would spread out and grow by orders of magnitude in a very, very short time. Worse even, the implications of lawsuits for having spread such an infection from your company out to your clients, and quite possibly to their companies' desktops, conjures up a nightmare situation that no CIO or CISO (Chief Information Security Officer) would want to face.

2.5 An Overview of Mobile and Wireless Instant Messaging

So far, we have discussed IM in the fixed environment, which has a large base of IM users that typically use IM on a client such as a laptop computer. Such clients often include a rich user interface and support high bandwidth. The success of Short Message Service (SMS) and the increasing popularity of IM has made the concept of mobile IM a reality.

2.5.1 What Is Mobile Instant Messaging?

Mobile Instant Messaging (MIM) is the ability to engage in an IM session from a mobile handset via various standards or protocols, such as SMS, WAP, or GPRS. The growth of SMS on mobile phones is another factor in the increasingly widespread use of IM. Now, the same sort of short, chatty messages that have been sent using IM on personal computers (PCs) can be sent to mobile phones. Some Internet messaging services allow messages to be delivered to mobile phones, but most providers truly have not integrated the wireless and wireline messaging systems. MIM is typically used to describe IM through the use of handheld devices such as mobile phones.

2.5.2 What Is Wireless Instant Messaging?

The term Wireless IM (WIM) is used in a more general sense, denoted by the use of IM on mobile devices. Before we discuss WIM, we will describe the SMS, WAP, and GPRS protocols specific to MIM to give you a better understanding between the challenges of IM over mobile phones versus that of IM over laptops or more sophisticated PDAs with laptop-type operating systems and protocols.

2.5.3 Short Message Service

Short Message Service (SMS) is a message service offered by the GSM digital cellular telephone system. It is characterized by the transmission of short text messages to and from a mobile phone, fax machine, or mobile IP address. Messages must be no longer than 160 alphanumeric characters and contain no images or graphics. Once a message is sent, it is received by a Short Message Service Center (SMSC), which must then get it to the appropriate mobile device. Using SMS, a short alphanumeric message can be sent to a mobile phone to be displayed to the recipient of the message. It works much like an alphanumeric pager system. The message is buffered by the GSM network until the phone becomes active. Global System for Mobile Communications (GSM) is a standard for digital cellular communications and is currently used in the 900-MHz and 1800-MHz bands. SMS without WIM enabled does not allow the sender to have a high degree of confidence that the recipient will receive the message in real time, because, by itself, SMS is transaction based rather than session based. SMS does not include alias capabilities nor does it allow for confirmation that the intended recipient is available. Adding the capabilities of WIM to SMS allows the community of users to register as being a presentity and to set their status as online or offline. This approach allows for more real-time text messaging and communications than would be possible with traditional mobile messaging.

2.5.4 Wireless Application Protocol

The Wireless Application Protocol (WAP) is an open international standard and secure specification for applications that use wireless communication. The standard allows users to access information instantly via handheld wireless devices such as mobile phones, pagers, two-way radios, smartphones, and communicators with wireless Internet access. WAP supports most wireless networks and is supported by all operating systems. WAP uses displays and can access the Internet by using software utilities called micro-browsers. Micro-browsers are browsers with small file sizes that can accommodate low-memory constraints typical of handheld devices. They can also support low-bandwidth constraints of a wireless handheld network. Although WAP supports HTML and XML scripting, WAP also supports WMLScript. It is similar to JavaScript but makes minimal demands on memory and CPU power, because it does not contain many of the unnecessary functions commonly found in other scripting languages. WML is capable of supporting displays ranging from two-line text displays to graphic screens similar to those found on items such as smart phones and communicators. The WML language, which is an XML application, is specifically devised for small screens and one-handed navigation without requiring the use of a keyboard.

2.5.5 General Packet Radio Service

General Packet Radio Service (GPRS) is a standard for wireless communications that runs at speeds up to 115 kilobits per second, compared with current GSM systems that run at 9.6 kilobits per second. It is a data transmission technique that does not set up a continuous channel from a portable terminal for the transmission and reception of data. It transmits and receives data in packets. It makes very efficient use of the available radio spectrum and is particularly suited for sending and receiving small bursts of data, such as email and Web browsing. Users typically pay a provider only for the volume of data they have sent and received.

In a mobile environment, the user is constrained by bandwidth and the user interface. Such constraints are a tradeoff that is made to provide the advantage of mobility. WIM users message with other WIM users as well as fixed IM users on networks such as AOL, MSN, and Yahoo!. WIM allows users to address messages to other users through the use of one of the protocols described previously. By using an alias or user name and an address book, WIM allows the sender to know when his or her "buddies" are available.

2.5.6 The Future of WIM

A fusion of services designed to form WIM has made mobile IM move from a mere possibility to reality. By using WIM while being connected to the Internet using GPRS, it provides a chance for mobile users to check instant availability of individuals, communicate instantly on a nonvoice basis, and use a chat-like environment for exchanging ideas and information. With the lines blurring between wireless and wireline Internet access, and with the growth of multiservice providers, there are new opportunities for service providers to use messaging to attract and retain customers and to add new features and benefits that are not possible on today's stripped-down "fun" messaging services.

2.5.7 The Future of MIM

Future MIM systems will likely include rich and robust presence- and location-based service capabilities, which will enable users to detect the presence, availability, and/or the location of fellow MIM/WIM users. This will make the WIM systems more robust and pervasive, providing more valuable functionality. Interoperability between MIM/WIM systems should be possible by leveraging network mediation processes to enable messaging. By providing such fixed IM system features, it is expected that it will lead to a much wider scale of adoption and usage in the future.

2.6 Selecting and Securing a WIM Solution

Most of our book describes how to secure stationary IM and wireless systems as they relate to mobile laptops. Securing mobile systems such as phones and PDAs will have you feeling more at the mercy of the vendor than with the fixed and wireless LAN systems. For that reason, we have chosen to give an overview of what you should expect (and require) a vendor to provide, rather than what you should do yourself. As a selection guideline, the following requirements should be considered when selecting a WIM enterprise solution:

- *It must support multiple clients.* Most businesses have not standardized on mobile devices and have allowed departments or users to make the decision. Rapid innovation of device selection and falling hardware and connectivity costs have contributed to the diversity of devices within the enterprise. Therefore, enterprises that deploy wireless IM systems must select a solution that supports a multitude of clients. For example, you must consider the support for RIM, Palm OS, J2ME/BREW, Pocket PC, and two-way SMS when selecting a solution.
- *The solution should be able to act as a gateway/proxy between user devices and each of the back-end corporate and/or public IM services.* This will require features such as multiple "connectors," which can speak to the

native protocol of the back-end service. In this regard, the server should be able to connect to all of the back-end services, consolidate profiles and features from all services, and make them available via a single client interface. This type of extensible architecture will allow additional IM services to be supported in the future without the need to upgrade client software.

- *Any solution should allow users to connect to any combination of enterprise IM services and public IM services simultaneously.* Your solution should be able to support public IM systems such as AOL Instant Messenger, MSN Messenger, Yahoo! Instant Messenger, ICQ, and Jabber.
- *The proposed solution should not restrict wireless device selection.* It should be able to support devices such as RIM, Palm OS, any two-way SMS capable device, BREW, J2ME, and Pocket PC.
- *Any chosen solution should preserve the familiar desktop IM experience.* Wireless IM must be easy to learn and use, replicating the PC-based experience, in order to be effective.
- *It should integrate with existing network management tools.* Enterprises should not make the mistake of integrating point solutions, and they should not accept solutions requiring multiple systems management tools. Vendors with wireless IM solutions that integrate with popular network management tools such as Microsoft's Active Directory for unified communications infrastructure management should be given preference.
- *It should feature strong authentication, such as 3DES encryption, with two-factor authentication implemented in order to verify user identity.* It should encrypt all data sent over-the-air to wireless devices. It should be able to prevent corporate information from being sent outside the firewall unencrypted. It should also authenticate users by integrating directly with corporate directory services through Active Directory or LDAP.
- *Any solution should integrate with corporate email.* The solution should allow users to send email to offline IM contacts and it should connect to enterprise email systems such as Microsoft Exchange, Lotus Domino, POP3, and IMAP mail servers.
- *It should provide carrier-grade reliability and scalability.* Since Enterprise Wireless IM serves as a cornerstone of corporate communications infrastructure, the solution must be scalable and reliable. Preferred solutions should be hardware independent, fully cluster-

aware, and developed using open standards. The solution should also be capable of accommodating large amounts of traffic without compromising performance. For example, if the solution is hardware independent, it should allow an organization to choose the hardware size best suited to its specific, unique performance needs. A flexible solution architecture will allow it to be fully clusterable for even greater scalability and fault tolerance. Enterprises should only select wireless IM solutions that can scale linearly with hardware, ranging from hundreds to tens of thousands of users.

- *Any proposed solution should include flexible enterprise reporting tools.* Corporations require reporting to analyze usage patterns in order to accurately forecast billing, enforce compliance to propriety standards, and manage data for legal purposes. Businesses must select IM software that offers reporting at both the aggregate and user level, and, at the very least, such solution reporting should include the number of messages sent and received (by user) and preserve and maintain message content logs. These reports can be used to show usage at the aggregate and individual user levels. Web-based reports should be able to be run at any time and exported in various output formats, such as HTML, XML, .pdf, .doc, and so on.

2.7 Summary

In this chapter, we have discussed the ever-growing prevalence of IM usage, both at home and in the workplace. The widespread usage of IM continues to move it from a public forum to a commonplace tool in enterprise workplaces. We distinguished between the presence service and the IM service, introducing specific terminology that is used in the IM world. A high-level overview of how IM worked, from download and installation of a client to subscription and activation, was presented. We compared the basic IM features across four of the major public IM solution providers, and, finally, we took a look at some of the additional considerations the enterprise IM (EIM) implementers must consider before deciding whether or not to introduce IM into their environment.

Clearly, IM usage is gaining momentum. It is still a decision that a manager should not make lightly, because it introduces other factors into the business, such as policy changes, disposition of records, management of evidentiary materials, training, susceptibility to malware attacks, and so on. A company could be held responsible if its negligent use of IM did harm in some manner to another company or to an individual during the course of business. This is still a new, evolving area of interest in the legal offices of corporations around the world. Much more needs to be done to standardize practices in this area. In the next chapter, we take a look at the development of protocols and standards that have evolved to support IM as we know it today.

2.8 Endnotes

1. E. Shiu and A. Lenhart. "How Americans Use Internet Messaging." Washington, DC: Pew Internet & American Life Project, August 31, 2004.
2. FC 2778, "A Model for Presence and Instant Messaging," February 2000, ed. M. Day et al., IETF NWG, http://www.ietf.org.
3. FC 2779, "Instant Messaging/Presence Protocol Requirements," February 2000, ed. M. Day, et al., IETF NWG, http://www.ietf.org.
4. M. Sequineau. "Choosing the Right EIM Solution," JupiterMedia/CIO update online article, January 3, 2005. Retrieved from http://www.cioupdate.com/trends/article.php/3453731.
5. http://www.f-secure.com/v-descs/bropia_a.shtml#details

3

IM Standards and Protocols

As we mentioned earlier, there are a lot of players in the public IM space today. Many of these IM players (and many other players less known than MSN, AOL, ICQ, and Yahoo!) are vying to establish the dominant IM standard in this new arena. All of the players are continually introducing new applications and features to take advantage of all IM has to offer and to stand out from their competitors. It seems fairly obvious that having all these incompatible players is problematic at best. It appears that things will likely converge on some combination of SIP (Session Initiation Protocol) and SIMPLE (SIP for IM and Presence Leveraging Extensions) versus XMPP (Extensible Messaging and Presence Protocol). There is a question as to whether there will be just one standard or if some blend of one or more standards will prevail. Of course, this is assuming the standard comes from the IETF and is not driven by another organization, such as the mobile carrier forum called Wireless Village, which is not only pushing an architecture that's very similar to the other two architectures but is also developing and publishing a completely separate set of protocols. If it (or others) adds yet another protocol, the mix of interoperability will become even more interesting and challenging.

3.1 Extensible Messaging and Presence Protocol—RFC 2778

The Extensible Messaging and Presence Protocol (XMPP) is the IETF's formalization of the core protocols created by the Jabber community in 1999 [1]. A brief chronology of activity related to Jabber and XMPP in the IETF standards process is warranted. In August 1999, Jeremie Miller of the Jabber open-source project submitted a statement pledging the Jabber community's support for the IETF standards process. This statement was consistent with the founding impetus of the Jabber project: to foster and support open standards and interoperability in the area of IM and presence. In June 2000, Jeremie and other members of the Jabber project submitted an Internet Draft to the IM and Presence Protocol Working Group (IMPP) documenting the Jabber protocol. Unfortunately, the Jabber community was not well organized in those days, nor was it strongly focused on protocol development. Thus, the initial Internet Draft expired without the Jabber community following up or working closely with the IMPP or any other IETF efforts.

However, in 2001, the Jabber Software Foundation (JSF) was formed to provide some organization among the growing number of open-source projects and commercial entities building or using Jabber technologies. One of the core mandates of the JSF has been to document the XML protocol used by the Jabber community, and to manage the growth of that protocol. This organizational effort has led to the more recent involvement of the Jabber community in the IETF standards process.

In late 2001 and early 2002, prominent members of the Jabber community decided to once again submit the Jabber protocol to the IETF. The first submission was made in February 2002 as an informational Internet Draft. Following on the success of this submission, it was decided to explore the possibility of forming an IETF Working Group devoted to discussion of the Jabber protocol, under the neutral name of XMPP. As a result, three interrelated Internet Drafts were submitted on June 21, 2002.

On July 15, 2002, an XMPP "Birds of a Feather" session was held at the 54th IETF meeting in Yokohama, Japan. Given the overall favorable reaction to XMPP at that meeting, it was decided to proceed further by submitting a proposed working group charter to the Internet Engineering Steering Group (IESG). The IESG is responsible for technical management of IETF activities and the Internet standards process. As part of the Internet Society (ISOC), it administers the process according to the rules and procedures that have been ratified by the ISOC trustees. The IESG is directly responsible for the actions associated with entry into and movement along the Internet "standards track," including final approval of specifications as Internet standards. On October 31, 2002, the XMPP Working Group was approved. On November 3, 2002, updated Internet Drafts were submitted for **xmpp-core** and **xmpp-im**. The first meeting of the XMPP Working Group was held at the 55th IETF meeting in Atlanta, Georgia, on November 19, 2002, including presentations by Jeremie Miller, Joe Hildebrand, and Peter Saint-Andre.

In early 2003, the two base XMPP drafts went through several revision cycles and were published defining stringprep profiles for node identifiers and resource identifiers, as well as an updated protocol for end-to-end object encryption. A meeting of the XMPP Working Group was held on March 17, 2003, where a draft for using Session Description Protocol (SDP) over XMPP was also published. The SDP provides a mechanism for describing multimedia sessions, which are advertised and negotiated over the Internet. This document described how to use SDP to build a framework for media stream/session initiation and negotiation between Jabber entities. In particular, SDP [2] over XMPP [3] is used to provide a semantic framwork for signaling call setup (similar to the semantics provided by the Session Initiation Protocol [SIP] as defined in RFC 3261 [4]). The resulting mechanism was called the "*Transport for Initiating and Negotiating Sessions,*" or TINS.

In 2004, the IESG approved XMPP core and XMPP IM specifications as proposed standards on January 29 and February 5, respectively. The XMPP-CPIM Mapping specification was approved on May 19, 2004, and it was approved on July 26, 2004. In October 2004, these documents were published as the following RFCs:

- RFC 3920: Extensible Messaging and Presence Protocol (XMPP): Core
- RFC 3921: Extensible Messaging and Presence Protocol (XMPP): Instant Messaging and Presence
- RFC 3922: Mapping the Extensible Messaging and Presence Protocol (XMPP) to Common Presence and Instant Messaging (CPIM)
- RFC 3923: End-to-End Signing and Object Encryption for the Extensible Messaging and Presence Protocol (XMPP)

Upon publication of the XMPP RFCs, the IETF announced the conclusion of the XMPP Working Group. However, the XMPP WG mailing list remains active, and development of further XMPP extensions is being pursued through the Jabber Enhancement Proposals (a.k.a., JEP Series) produced by the Jabber Software Foundation.

RFC 3920

RFC 3920 [5] defines the core features of XMPP, a protocol for streaming Extensible Markup Language (XML) elements in order to exchange structured information in close to real time between any two network endpoints. While XMPP provides a generalized, extensible framework for exchanging

XML data, it is used mainly to build IM and presence applications that meet the requirements of RFC 2779. XMPP is an open XML protocol for near-real-time messaging, presence, and request-response services. The basic syntax and semantics were developed originally within the Jabber open-source community, mainly in 1999. In 2002, the XMPP WG was chartered with developing an adaptation of the Jabber protocol that would be suitable as an IETF IM and presence technology. As a result of work by the XMPP WG, the current memo defines the core features of XMPP 1.0; the extensions required to provide the IM and presence functionality as defined in RFC 2779 are specified in the XMPP: IM and presence document.

RFC 3921

RFC 3921 [6] describes extensions to and applications of the core features of the XMPP that provide the basic IM and presence functionality as defined in RFC 2779. XMPP is a protocol for streaming XML elements in order to exchange messages and presence information in close to real time. The core features of XMPP are defined in XMPP: Core. These features—mainly XML streams, use of TLS and SASL, and the <message/>, <presence/>, and <iq/> children of the stream root—provide the building blocks for many types of near-real-time applications, which may be layered on top of the core by sending application-specific data qualified by particular XML namespaces. This memo describes extensions to and applications of the core features of XMPP that provide the basic functionality expected of an IM and presence application as defined in RFC 2779.

RFC 3922

RFC 3922 [7] describes a mapping between the XMPP and the Common Presence and Instant Messaging (CPIM) specifications. The IM and Presence Protocol (IMPP) Working Group has defined an abstract framework for interoperability among IM and presence systems that are compliant with various other XMPP protocols. This framework is commonly called Common Presence and IM, or CPIM. The CPIM family of specifications includes a Common Profile for IM (also called *CPIM*), a Common Profile for Presence (CPP), a CPIM Message Format, and a Common Presence Information Data Format [8].

RFC 3922 describes how the XMPP-CORE and XMPP-IM map to the abstract model contained in the CPIM specifications. This is used mainly for establishing gateways between XMPP services and non-XMPP services that conform to IMP-REQS. Such a gateway, referred to herein as an "XMPP-CPIM gateway," may be established to interpret the protocols of

Figure 3.1 *XMPP-CPIM service.*

one service and translate them into the protocols of the other service. We can visualize this relationship as illustrated in Figure 3.1.

RFC 3922 defines a mapping for use by a gateway that translates between XMPP and a non-XMPP protocol via the CPIM specifications. Such a gateway is not an intermediate hop on a network of non-XMPP servers (whose native formats may or may not be defined by the CPIM specifications), but a dedicated translator between XMPP and a non-XMPP protocol, where the CPIM specifications define the common formats into which the protocols are translated for purposes of interworking. The mapping defined in RFC 3922 applies to instant messages and presence information that are not encrypted or signed for end-to-end security. For information about secure communications to or from an XMPP service through an XMPP-CPIM gateway, refer to the XMPP-E2E proposal. This document defines a method for end-to-end object signing and encryption in the XMPP.

RFC 3923

RFC 3923 [9] defines methods of end-to-end signing and object encryption for the XMPP. The method specified herein enables a sender to sign and/or encrypt an instant message sent to a specific recipient, sign and/or encrypt presence information that is directed to a specific user, and sign and/or encrypt any arbitrary XMPP stanza directed to a specific user. This memo thereby helps the XMPP specifications meet the requirements specified in the IMP-REQS.

3.1.1 Jabber and the IM Community

The noun *Jabber* is attached to many things in the IM world. Not only does it represent *This is Jabber, Inc.,* the commercial software company based in Denver, Colorado, but it also represents other areas related to both IM and Jabber Inc. Jabber, Inc. delivers a presence, messaging, and XML routing infrastructure for powering real-time applications, systems, and services. This infrastructure includes enterprise IM (EIM), conversational trading systems, and presence-enabled customer service applications. As a sponsor

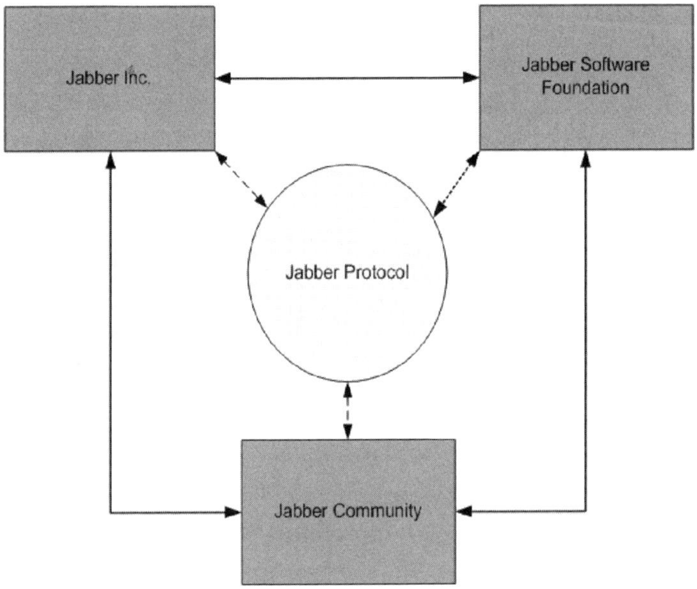

Figure 3.2 *Illustration of the Jabber world.*

of the Jabber Software Foundation, Jabber, Inc. also embraces the spirit of freedom that drives the worldwide open-source community.

Jabber is based upon XMPP, an open, XML-based protocol for IM and other presence-powered applications. XMPP is the only Internet Engineering Task Force (IETF)–approved protocol for real-time messaging and presence. The Jabber community is a growing, global body of developers that create Jabber-based solutions. Finally, there is the Jabber Software Foundation (JSF), which is a not-for-profit membership organization that manages the Jabber protocol and is also known as jabber.org [10]. Figure 3.2 illustrates this relationship among entities working with the Jabber protocol.

3.2 Jabber Protocol and XMPP

The term *Jabber* is widely used to refer to a set of open protocols for streaming XML elements between any two points on a network and to the technologies built using those protocols [11]. The architecture of Jabber IM systems is similar to that of the most time-tested messaging system on the planet: e-mail. While there are some key differences, if you think of Jabber as "instant e-mail," you would not be making a bad assumption.

So how does it really work? To understand how, let's first look at a quick example of how John and Lois might use Jabber in the workplace. Lois doesn't send a message directly (peer to peer) to John, at least not in the Jabber world. Lois has an account on a Jabber server, and her Jabber Identifier (or JID) looks a lot like an e-mail address. Since Lois is an ABC employee, she registers the user name Lois with the Jabber server running at ABC.com, so her JID is Lois@ABC.com. Similarly, John has an account on his company (XYZ) IM server and his JID is John@XYZ.net.

Once Lois has logged in to the ABC.com server, she can send messages to her business associate John. Here is what happens when Lois starts the client on her laptop:

- Lois sends a message addressed to John@XYZ.net.
- The message is handled by the Jabber server at ABC.com.
- The ABC.com server opens a connection to XYZ.net if one is not already open.
- Assuming that the IM administrators have not disabled server-to-server communications between ABC.com and XYZ.net, Lois's message is routed to the Jabber server at XYZ.net.
- The server at XYZ.net sees that the message is addressed to a user named "John" and delivers it to the Jabber client running on John's PDA, where the message appears on screen for John.

There are a lot of pieces here: clients running on different operating systems, multiple servers, a communication channel between the servers, and two business associates. Jabber handles everything but the last part. The process is illustrated in Figure 3.3.

3.2.1 Architectural Design

Figure 3.3 probably looks familiar, because it resembles the architecture of e-mail. Communications in Jabber are accomplished using a distributed network of servers, where each use a common protocol. Jabber clients connect to servers to receive messages from other Jabber users. They send messages to other users regardless of whether they reside on the same server or on any other server connected to the network. Jabber servers deliver messages in near real time. Real-time delivery is possible, because a Jabber server manages your presence status and knows when you are offline or online. Jabber contacts can also see when you are online (*if you grant them permission*).

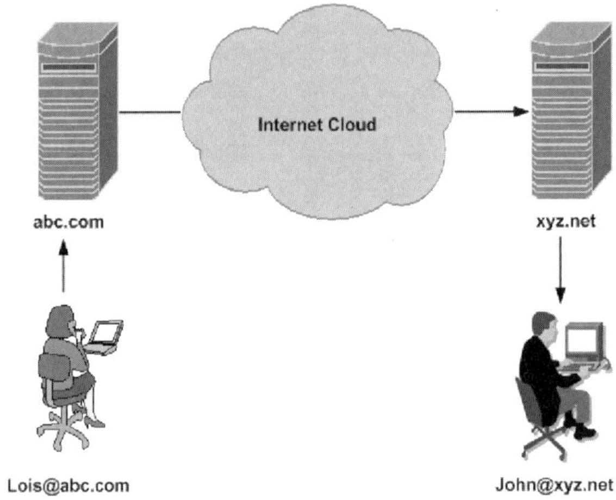

Figure 3.3 *A Jabber IM session.*

Presence knowledge is the key factor that enables IM to be instant. Jabber combines standard IM characteristics with some additional features to make Jabber unique. These features include:

1. Jabber uses a set of open, well-documented, easy-to-understand protocols.
2. Jabber protocols are 100 percent XML, which enables structured, intelligent messaging between human users and also between software applications.
3. Jabber uses addresses based on DNS and recognized URL schemes, resulting in addresses of the same form as those used in e-mail (user@host).
4. Jabber technologies use a client/server architecture, not a direct peer-to-peer architecture as some other messaging systems do.
5. Jabber supports a distributed network architecture.
6. Jabber has a modular server and simple client architecture.

Each of these key features is described in more detail in the following text.

Open Protocols

Jabber technologies started in the open-source community with the **jabberd** server and clients for Microsoft Windows, MacOS, and Linux. As part of its work, the original Jabber team defined an open protocol for streaming

XML over the Internet. This protocol continues to grow in depth and breadth. The depth comes mainly from work completed by the XMPP Working Group, the group that formalized the core XML streaming protocols under the name *Extensible Messaging and Presence Protocol.* The breadth comes mainly from work by the Jabber Software Foundation in defining extensions to the core protocols for a wide variety of features, including group chat, file transfer, service discovery, avatars, and much more. Because Jabber technologies all use an open protocol, anyone can implement the protocols, and they can use any manner of code license for their product. This has produced an explosion of Jabber software, including completely open-source servers and clients as well as proprietary commercial software.

XML Data Format

XML is an integral part of Jabber technologies. Why? Because it makes them fundamentally extensible and able to express almost any structured data. When a client connects to a server, it opens a one-way XML stream from the client to the server, and the server responds with a one-way XML stream from the server to the client. Thus, each session involves two XML streams. All communication between the client and the server happens over these streams, in the form of small data snippets or "stanzas" of XML, such as the following message from Lois to John:

```
<message from='Lois@ABC.com' to='John@XYZ.net'>
 <body>Where are you, John?</body>
</message>
```

While many Jabber stanzas are that simple, Jabber's XML format can also be extended through official XML namespaces (managed by the Jabber Software Foundation) and through custom namespaces needed for specialized applications. This makes Jabber a powerful platform for transferring any structured data, including things like XML-RPC and SOAP procedure calls, RSS syndication feeds, and SVG graphics.

Standards-Based Addressing

Within the Jabber network, many different entities need to communicate with each other. These entities can represent servers, gateways, group chat rooms, a single Jabber user, and so on. Jabber IDs are used both externally and internally to express ownership or routing information. Key characteristics of Jabber IDs include the fact that they uniquely identify individual objects or entities for communicating instant messages and presence information.

They are easy for users to remember and are flexible enough to enable inclusion of other IM and presence schemes. Also, each Jabber Identifier (JID) contains a set of ordered elements. JIDs are formed of a node, domain, and resource in the following format:

```
[node]@domain[/resource]
```

The domain is the primary identifier. It represents the Jabber server to which the entity connects. Every usable Jabber domain should resolve to a fully qualified domain name. The Node Identifier is the secondary identifier. It represents the user. All nodes live within a specific domain. However, the Node Identifier is optional, and a specified domain (e.g., special.jabber.org) is considered to be a valid JID. The Resource Identifier is an optional third identifier. All resources belong to a node. In Jabber protocols, the Resource Identifier is used to identify specific parameters associated with the user, such as peripheral devices or locations. Resources enable a single user to maintain several simultaneous connections to the same Jabber server. Jabber users always connect to a server through a specific resource and have an address of **node@domain/resource** (e.g., Lois@ABC.com/stargate) while they are connected to the Jabber server. Because the resource is session specific, the user's address can be communicated as node@domain (e.g., Lois@ABC.com), which is more familiar to people because it is of the same form as an e-mail addresses.

Client/Server Architecture

Jabber technologies use a client/server architecture. Some messaging systems use a direct peer-to-peer architecture. Client/server architecture requires that all Jabber data sent from one client to another must traverse at least one Jabber server. A Jabber client connects to a Jabber server on a TCP socket over port 5222. Servers connect to each other on a TCP socket over port 5269. This connection is persistent for the life of the client session with the server. This means the client does not have to poll for messages as an e-mail client would do. Any message intended for delivery to the Jabber client is immediately pushed out to the client if he or she is connected. The server keeps track of presence information and, when it detects that a client has gone to offline status, it stores any messages sent to that client for delivery when he or she next connects with the Jabber server.

Figure 3.4
Client/Server IM.

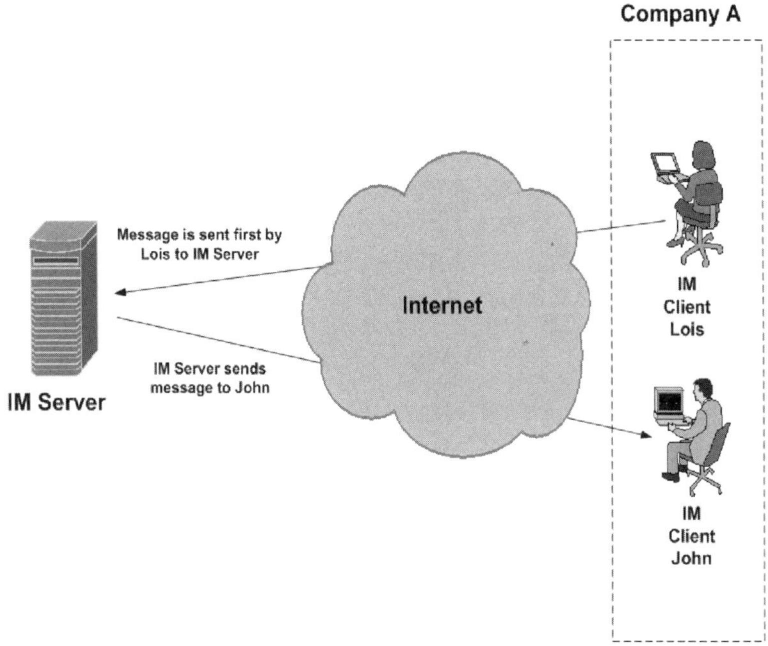

The client/server architecture is used in virtually all IM systems. IM clients are installed on client machines, which then communicate with an IM server in the messaging provider's infrastructure to locate other users and exchange messages. IM messages are sent first to an IM server and then from the IM server to the intended recipient, rather than directly from the initiating user's computer to the recipient's computer. The data is typically sent unencrypted (Figure 3.4).

Although most IM systems use client/server architectures to transmit their messages, some systems do use peer-to-peer messaging (P2P messaging). The chief advantage of P2P is that it can provide better security than a client/server architecture because both users are on the same local area network and because messages do not travel over the Internet. Peer-to-peer clients contact the IM server to locate other clients. Once the client chat program has located its peer, it contacts the peer directly (Figure 3.5). Of course, if one user is located outside the corporate network, the peer-to-peer model will be just as insecure as the client/server model, because messages sent between machines are exposed to potential eavesdroppers once the transmission hits the open Internet.

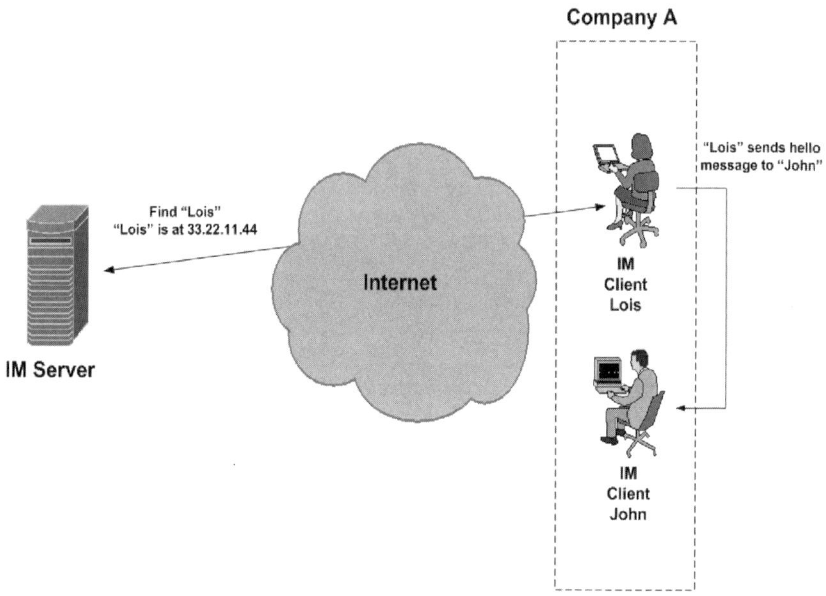

Figure 3.5
Peer-to-peer IM.

Distributed Network

Jabber's architecture is modeled after that of e-mail. Users connect to a home server, which will receive information on their behalf and transfer data to other servers on behalf of their home users. Thus, any domain can run a Jabber server. Each server functions independently and maintains its own user list. Any Jabber server can talk to any other Jabber server that is accessible via the Internet (if server-to-server communications are enabled). A particular user is associated with a specific server either through registration with a service provider or administrative setup within an enterprise. Jabber addresses are of the same form as e-mail addresses. The result is a flexible, controllable network of servers, which can scale much higher than the monolithic, centralized services run by legacy IM vendors such as AOL, Microsoft, and Yahoo!

Modular Servers and Simple Clients

A Jabber server performs three primary tasks: handling client connections and communicating directly with Jabber clients; communicating with other Jabber servers; and coordinating the various components associated with the server itself. Jabber servers are designed to be modular. They are constructed of specific code packages, which each handle a specific functionality, such as registration, authentication, presence, contact lists, offline message storage, and so on. Jabber servers can be extended with external component features that enable server administrators to supplement the core services with additional services, such as gateways to other messaging systems. Such components can introduce greater complexity into a Jabber deployment without sacrificing the simplicity of the core server. Furthermore, Jabber does not require such external components to be added or implemented by the core server team.

Flexibility is always a key consideration in the Jabber community. One of the design criteria for Jabber IM systems was that it must be easy to write a client, and the Jabber architecture imposes very few restrictions on clients. The only things a Jabber client *must* do are communicate with the Jabber server over TCP sockets, parse and interpret well-formed XML stanzas over an XML stream, and understand the core Jabber data types. The preference in Jabber is to move complexity from clients to the server. This makes it relatively easy to write clients and update them without forcing users to download new clients. Many low-level functions of the client are handled by Jabber client libraries. These libraries allow developers to focus on the user interface and let the libraries or server core handle the details that go on behind the screen. Jabber protocols and technologies provide an open alternative to proprietary services offered by legacy IM vendors. Jabber enables developers to create robust, near-real-time messaging and presence solutions for IM.

3.3 Instant Messaging/Presence Protocol—RFC 2779

Presence and IM have recently emerged as a new medium of communications over the Internet. In Chapter 2, we explained that presence is a means for finding, retrieving, and subscribing to changes in the presence information (e.g., online or offline) of other users. We also described IM as a means for sending small, simple messages that are delivered immediately to online users. Applications of presence and IM currently use independent, nonstandard, and noninteroperable proprietary protocols developed by the multitude of IM vendors. The goal of the IETF's IM and Presence Protocol Working Group (IMPPWG) is to define a standard protocol so that independently developed IM and/or presence applications can interoperate across the Internet [12]. This working group will eventually define the protocols and data formats necessary to build a cohesive Internet-scale messaging system capable of end-user presence awareness/notification, IM, user authentication, message integrity, encryption, and access control. RFC 2779[13] defines a minimal set of requirements that IMPP must meet.

The IMPPWG is the standards committee driving the IM world. IMPPWG chief contributors include the likes of AOL, Microsoft, and so on. Much confusion surrounds the efforts to standardize on an IM protocol. Different IM communities have appeared and, other than some work to make AOL and Microsoft interoperate with ICQ, little progress had been made until recently. IMPPWG has now established requirements for a standard protocol and defined a Common Profile for IM (CPIM) that sets out an architecture (Figure 3.1) and discusses server-to-server interoperability in a multiprotocol environment. SIP is one of three proposed protocols in the IETF's IMPPWG—the others are PRIM and APEX (formerly IMXP). SIP is explained in the next section. PRIM and APEX are both designed specifically for the needs of IM, whereas SIP would require some extensions to fulfill the requirements of the IMPPWG. PRIM takes the stance that a standard protocol should be based on existing proprietary architectures for IM. APEX does IM and presence on top of a Blocks Extensible Exchange Protocol (BEEP), which is an XML protocol.

Due to the obvious need for presence to be used in voice communications, SIP is a strong contender as the mechanism by which users and applications communicate their presence data to and from the network. The PRIM group has acknowledged this and allows the possibility of interfacing with SIP for voice applications. The strongest argument for SIP is probably that of convergence, while other initiatives would require an IM-specific infrastructure. SIP, of course, can also be used for many other purposes. Significant in this respect is the decision by Microsoft to adopt SIP for real-time communications on the .NET framework. The CPIM document shows there is some consensus being reached on this matter. A likely outcome, however, is that each of the groups will pursue their own protocol but will support some sort of base-level interoperability.

3.4 Session Initiation Protocol

The Session Initiation Protocol [14] (SIP) is a fundamental building block that service providers can use to harness the power of the Internet Protocol and transform their traditional revenue streams. The world of networking is undergoing a sea of change: Fixed and mobile networks are converging; computing and communications are becoming inseparable. The ubiquity of IP is transforming the data infrastructure into an all-encompassing communications capability that overshadows the telephone network. At the center of this evolution is SIP: It is the mechanism that unites services across platforms, thus creating a multiplicity of new possibilities.

SIP carries the banner of Internet-style innovation into the traditional world of Telco voice services. With SIP, services can be created that combine elements from telephony and other Web applications, such as e-mail, messaging, the Internet, and video streaming. The use of open Application Programming Interfaces (APIs) means that ISPs, ASPs, and even end users can program their own services. SIP achieves all of this by establishing, modifying, and terminating sessions over IP networks. These sessions could be as basic as a telephone call or as complex as a multiparty mixed-media session. SIP doesn't care: It specifies only what is needed.

SIP was originally intended to create a mechanism for inviting people to large-scale multipoint conferences on the Internet Multicast Backbone (Mbone). At this stage, IP telephony didn't really exist. It was soon realized that SIP could be used to set up point-to-point conferences—phone calls. The SIP approach exemplifies classic Internet-style innovation: Build only what you need to address only what is lacking in existing mechanisms. Because the SIP approach is modular and free from underlying protocol or architectural constraints, and because the protocols themselves are simple, SIP has caught on as an alternative to H.323 and to vendor-proprietary mechanisms for transporting the telecommunications community Signaling System 7 (SS7) protocols over IP.

SIP is a signaling protocol used for establishing sessions in an IP network [15]. A session could be a simple two-way telephone call or it could be a collaborative multimedia conference session. The ability to establish these sessions means that a host of innovative services become possible, such as voice-enriched e-commerce, Web page click-to-dial, IM with buddy lists, and IP Centrex services.

Over the last couple of years, the Voice over IP community has adopted SIP as its protocol of choice for signaling. SIP is an RFC standard (RFC 3261) from the Internet Engineering Task Force (IETF), the body responsible for administering and developing the mechanisms that comprise the Internet. SIP is still evolving and being extended as technology matures and SIP products are socialized in the marketplace.

The IETF's philosophy is one of simplicity: Specify only what you need to specify. SIP follows this philosophy, but having been developed purely as a mechanism to establish sessions, it does not know about the details of a session—it just initiates, terminates, and modifies sessions. This simplicity means that SIP scales, it is extensible, and it sits comfortably in different architectures and deployment scenarios.

3.4.1 SIP Security

SIP is considerably less complex to implement than H.323 when simple calls are to be performed. SIP is text based and because of that it avoids certain ASN.1-associated parsing issues the H.323 protocol suite must contend with if S/MIME is not used. Also, SIP is an application-level protocol. It exists independently from the protocol layer it is transported across. It can be based in TCP, UDP, or with a number of different IP protocols. UDP may be used to decrease overhead and increase speed and efficiency or TCP may be used if SSL/TLS is incorporated for security services. Unlike H.323, only one port is used in SIP (note that H.323 may also be used in a way that uses only one port—direct routed calls). The default value for this port is 5060.

The architecture of a SIP network is different from the H.323 structure. A SIP network is made up of endpoints, a redirect server, a proxy server, a location server, and a registrar. In the SIP model, a user is not bound to a specific host. Users initially report their location to a registrar, which may be integrated into either a proxy or a redirect server. This information is in turn stored in the external location server. Messages from endpoints must be routed through a proxy or redirect server. The proxy server intercepts messages from endpoints or other services, inspects their "To:" field, contacts the location server to resolve the user name into an address, and forwards the message to the appropriate endpoint. Redirect servers perform the same resolution function, but the onus is placed on the endpoints to perform the actual transmission. That is, redirect servers obtain the actual address of the destination from the location server and return this information to the original sender, which then must send its message directly to the resolved address.

The SIP protocol itself is modeled on the three-way handshake method implemented in TCP. The call setup process is similar with a redirect server, but with the extra step of returning the resolved address to the source endpoint. During the setup process, communication details are negotiated between the endpoints using Session Description Protocol (SDP), which contains fields for the codec used, the caller's name, and so on. Here is an example:

- If Bob wishes to place a call to Alice, he sends an INVITE request to the proxy server containing SDP info for the session.

- The proxy server then takes the INVITE request and forwards it to Alice's client via Bob's proxy, which could even be her proxy server.
- Eventually, assuming Alice wants to talk to Bob, she will send an "OK" message back containing her call preferences in SDP format.
- Bob will respond with an "ACK." SIP provides for the ACK to contain SDP instead of the INVITE, so that an INVITE may be seen without protocol-specific information.
- After the "ACK" is received, the conversation may commence along the RTP/RTCP ports previously agreed upon.

Notice that all the traffic was transported through one port in a simple (text) format, without any of the complicated channel/port switching associated with H.323. Still, SIP presents several challenges for firewalls and NAT.

3.4.2 Existing Security Features in the SIP Protocol

RFC 3261 [16] describes several security features for SIP and deprecates several security features that were advocated in the original RFC 2543 [17], such as the usage of PGP and HTTP Basic Authentication. Because of its weak security, and to avoid attacks by downgrading the required security level of the authentication, the HTTP Basic Authentication was deprecated in the current document RFC 3261.

3.4.3 Signaling Authentication Using HTTP Digest Authentication

The Digest authentication scheme is based on a simple challenge-response paradigm. The digest authentication scheme challenges the remote end using a nonce value. SIP digest authentication is based on the digest authentication defined in RFC 2617 [18]. Here, a valid response contains a checksum (by default, the MD5 checksum) of the user name, the password, the given-once value, the HTTP method, and the requested URL. In this way, the password is never sent in the clear.

3.4.4 S/MIME Usage within SIP

SIP messages carry MIME bodies. MIME itself defines mechanisms for the integrity protection and the encryption of the MIME contents. SIP may utilize S/MIME to enable mechanisms such as public-key distribution, authentication and integrity protection, or confidentiality of SIP signaling data. S/MIME may be considered as a replacement for PGP used in RFC 2543 to provide means for integrity protection and encryption of SIP messages. To be able to protect SIP header fields as well, tunneling of SIP messages in MIME bodies is specified. Generally, the proposed SIP tunneling for SIP header protection will create additional overhead. S/MIME requires certificates and private keys to be used, whereas the certificates may be issued by a trusted third party or may be self-generated. The latter case may not provide real user authentication but may be used to provide a limited form of message integrity protection. The following sections explain the usage of S/MIME more deeply.

The current document RFC 3261 recommends that S/MIME be used for UAs. Moreover, if S/MIME is used to tunnel messages, it is recommended to use a TCP connection because of the larger messages. This is to avoid problems that may arise by the fragmentation of UDP packets. Services such as authentication, integrity protection, and confidentiality of signaling data are possible.

3.4.5 Confidentiality of Media Data in SIP

SIP itself does not consider the encryption of media data. Using the RTP encryption as defined in RFC 1889[19] may provide confidentiality for media data. Another option for media stream security is the use of SRTP (DSRTP). For key management, SDP (RFC 2327 [20]) may be used. SDP can convey session keys for media streams. Note that using SDP for the key exchange provides no method to send an encrypted media stream key (Appendix A). Therefore, the signaling request should be encrypted, preferably by using end-to-end encryption.

3.4.6 TLS Usage within SIP

RFC 3261 mandates the use of TLS for proxies, redirect servers, and registrars to protect SIP signaling. Using TLS for UAs is recommended. TLS is able to protect SIP signaling messages against loss of integrity, confidentiality, and replay. It provides integrated key management with mutual authentication and secure key distribution. TLS is applicable hop-by-hop between UAs/proxies or between proxies. The drawback of TLS in SIP scenarios is the requirement of a reliable transport stack (TCP-based SIP signaling). TLS cannot be applied to UDP-based SIP signaling.

3.4.7 IPsec Usage within SIP

IPsec may also be used to provide security for SIP signaling at the network layer. This type of security is most suited to securing SIP hosts in a SIP VPN scenario (SIP user agents/proxies) or between administrative SIP domains. IPsec works for all UDP, TCP, and Control Transmission Protocol (SCTP) SIP signaling. IPsec may be used to provide authentication, integrity, and confidentiality for the transmitted data and supports end-to-end as well as hop-by-hop scenarios. At this time there is no default cipher suite for IPsec defined in SIP. Note: RFC 3261 does not describe a framework for the use of IPsec. Especially, no information is given as to how the key management is to be realized or which IPsec header and mode are to be used.

3.4.8 Security Enhancements for SIP

Currently, within the IETF several drafts concerning security are being discussed, with a view toward providing a general security solution to SIP scenarios. Several drafts have been produced concerning authentication, integrity, and confidentiality for SIP. The following sections provide a short overview of Internet drafts, which may be of interest for a discussion of security enhancements for common SIP scenarios. The list of Internet drafts considered here is not complete and should rather reflect that this is an important topic, where work remains to be done.

3.4.9 SIP Authenticated Identity Body

SIP Authenticated Identity Body (AIB) defines a generic SIP authentication token. The token is provided by adding an S/MIME body to a SIP request or response in order to provide reference integrity over its headers. The document defines a format for this message body named as authenticated identity body (AIB). This is a digitally signed SIP message (SIP/message) or message fragment (SIP/FRAG).

3.4.10 SIP Authenticated Identity Management

The existing mechanisms for expressing identity in SIP often do not permit an administrative domain to verify securely the identity of the originator of a request. This document recommends practices and conventions for authenticating end users and proposes a way to distribute cryptographically secure authenticated identities within SIP messages by including an authentication token (as a MIME body). This token is added to the message. There are basically three ways to add a MIME body to a request. They are:

- Redirection
- Authentication service acts as B2BUA
- Content indirection

3.4.11 SIP Security Agreement

SIP has a number of security mechanisms. Some of them have been built in to the SIP protocol directly, such as HTTP authentication. These mechanisms have even alternative algorithms and parameters. The idea originates from the Third Generation Partnership Project (3GPP), a collaboration of telecommunications companies, and provides a mechanism for selecting which security mechanisms to use between two entities. RFC 3261 itself does not provide any mechanism agreement options. Moreover, even if some mechanisms, such as OPTIONS, were used to perform a mechanism agreement, the agreement would be vulnerable to bidding-down attacks. Three header fields are defined for negotiating the security mechanisms within SIP between a SIP entity and its next SIP hop. Five mechanisms are currently supported:

- TLS
- HTTP Digest
- IPsec with IKE
- Manually keyed IPsec without IKE
- S/MIME

Connection Reuse

Connection reuse defines a method to reuse TCP connections that have already been established between a user agent and a proxy for the backward direction from the proxy to the client. The TLS security approach can also leverage from this, since clients often do not possess a certificate and corresponding private key. Thus, it would not be possible to open a TLS connection to these clients (except via TLS anonymous mode).

3.4.12 SIP End-to-Middle, Middle-to-Middle, Middle-to-End Security

Currently, there are two drafts being discussed within the IETF dealing with end-to-middle, middle-to-middle, and middle-to-end security. The first of these drafts, *"End-to-Middle Security in the Session Initiation Protocol (SIP),"* [21] was created to address the need to enable intermediaries to utilize some of the SIP message header and body when end-to-end security is applied. Examples include logging services for enterprise use, firewall traversal, transcoding, and early media extortion. Intermediaries may not be able to trace the SIP message body for certain information (e.g., port numbers to be opened) if the body is encrypted. There is still a discussion about this draft within the working group.

The second draft, *"A Mechanism to Secure SIP Information Inserted by Intermediaries"* [22] aims at a mechanism to secure information inserted by intermediaries. This document has a strong relation to the history-inserted draft. Proxies sometimes need to delete a message body in a request in order to delete user authentication data (e.g., proxy authorization) that is protected with S/MIME, but the SIP standard (RFC 3261) does not allow this. RFC 3261 is designed so that a proxy does not break integrity of the body.

The security requirements between both approaches are slightly different, since here information is added by intermediaries and used by intermediaries. Nevertheless, these approaches share the same fundamental problems to be solved in SIP. It is anticipated that there will be further discussion on this item, since certain scenarios exist where this functionality is needed.

3.4.13 SIP Security Issues

The text encoding of SIP makes it easier to analyze using standard parsing tools such as Perl or lex and yacc. Still, some new requirements are placed on the firewall in a SIP-based VoIP network. First, firewalls must be stateful and monitor SIP traffic to determine which RTP ports are to be opened and made available to which addresses. This responsibility is similar to the task firewalls on an H.323-based network perform, except the call setup and header parsing are much simpler. The other issues SIP-based VoIP encounters with firewalls are associated with RTP traffic and incoming calls. As with H.323, the big problem for SIP is NAT.

NAT inhibits SIP's registration and communication mechanisms and requires innovative solutions to resolve. The problems exist because in a SIP-based network, the SIP proxy is normally outside the NAT device. There are three main scenarios for using a SIP proxy:

- The proxy is within the corporate LAN and the teleworker connects from outside.
- The proxy is at the telecom side, and clients from, for instance, smaller companies connect to this proxy for VoIP service.
- Two administrative domains are connected; both have their own proxy.

So the problem is bartering communication between a proxy server that deals with global IP addresses and a machine that has been assigned a private network address. Schulzrinne et al. [23] classify three different sets of problems SIP traffic has in such an architecture: originating requests, receiving requests, and handling RTP. We have already dealt with the incompatibilities of RTP with NAT, and now we will see the issues NAT presents to the call setup process itself.

To initialize a session from behind the NAT, a caller can simply send an INVITE message as always. The outgoing port number (5060) will be preserved by the NAT, but response communication could be disturbed. If SIP is implemented over UDP (recall SIP is protocol independent), the proxy server must send the UDP response to the address and port the request arrived on. A simpler solution is to use the standard practice of routing SIP communication over TCP. With TCP, the response from the callee will come over the same channel as the original INVITE, and so NAT will not present a problem.

We have already discussed some of the problems with incoming VoIP connections against NAT. Now we will look more in depth at the SIP-specific problems with incoming calls. Rosenberg and Schulzrinne [24] trace the problem back to the registration process itself. When users contact the registrar, they provide their IP address as their reachable address, and this is stored in the location server. Unfortunately, this is their private IP address. The proxy server deals only with global IP addresses, so when a message comes in for username@domain.com, it will attempt to route this call to the registered address, but in the public domain. For instance, if username@domain.com is registered to an internal IP address of 10.7.34.189, then the proxy server will attempt to forward the traffic to this address, but in the public domain. This address is unreachable for the proxy server, and the connection will be refused. The solution to this is a delicate manipulation of IP addresses and an expansion of the responsibilities of the SIP proxy server.

3.5 SIP for IM and Presence Leveraging Extensions

The lack of standards-based interoperable IM/presence systems makes it difficult for IT to control and monitor deployment of IM in addition to proprietary networks and protocols that also make it difficult for IM users to communicate with others outside their organizations. Session Initiation Protocol for IM and Presence Leveraging Extensions (SIMPLE) provides a unified protocol that enables IM/presence, just as Simple Mail Transfer Protocol (SMTP), HTTP, and Real-Time Protocol (RTP) do for e-mail, Web, and voice traffic. SIMPLE is an effort to bring interoperability to instant-messaging networks. It's based on SIP, a signaling and presence protocol used to establish Internet phone calls, multimedia conferences, chat sessions, and interactive communications. SIMPLE is an add-on to the Session Initiation Protocol (SIP) that some industry insiders predict will be the basis for a new IM and Presence Protocol (IMPP). SIP was originally developed for voice over IP (VoIP) but has since incorporated support for Web conferencing, live video, and other media. SIMPLE is backed by Microsoft, IBM, Sun, Novell, and other industry leaders.

The SIMPLE Working Group was chartered by the IETF to specify a set of profiles and extensions to SIP in order to enable IM/presence for applications. The proposed protocols have been widely implemented, and the IETF has published the general requirements for and model of IM/presence as RFCs 2778 and 2779. The SIMPLE Working Group focuses on the application of the Session Initiation Protocol (SIP, RFC 3261) to the suite of services collectively known as IM and presence (IMP). The IETF has committed to producing an interoperable standard for these services compliant to the requirements for IM outlined in RFC 2779 to include the security and privacy requirements there, as well as in the Common Presence and IM (CPIM) specification, developed within the IMPP Working Group. Since the most common services for which SIP is used share quite a bit in common with IMP, the adaptation of SIP to IMP seems a natural choice given the widespread support for the SIP standard. SIMPLE is ideally suited for integrating IM/presence with voice, data sharing, video, and other real-time collaboration features. Many of the leading manufacturers of IP and telecom equipment and most of the major IM service providers have announced support for SIMPLE, which means that there are enough SIMPLE-based offerings that it is no longer a question of whether SIMPLE will gain widespread deployment.

Instead of using the INVITE and BYE methods to start and end a call or session, SIMPLE uses data-retrieval methods such as GET and POST. SIMPLE has an additional request method, called MESSAGE, to send a one-shot IM, called pager-mode IM. The SUBSCRIBE function is used to request presence information to be sent to the requester, and NOTIFY is used to transport the presence information. INVITE and a transport protocol called Message Session Relay Protocol (MSRP) are used for signaling when participants exchange multiple messages over time from longer IM sessions. Just as SIP RTP is used to transport voice packets in an IP phone call, SIMPLE uses MSRP to transport the text of IMs. For the most part, the IM/presence infrastructure reuses SIP without change, and, just as with ordinary SIP systems, the registrar servers will process logons from endpoints. SIMPLE can enable IM interoperability across geographically distributed locations in a four-step process, as follows:

1. Clients X and Y use a SIP registrar to REGISTER their existence.
2. Client Y will SUBSCRIBE by requesting IM updates about Client X.
3. Client X will NOTIFY by reporting presence and availability to its buddy, Client Y.
4. The MESSAGE is exchanged through the IM Clients X and Y.

Figure 3.6 illustrates this four-step process.

3.6 The Future of IM Standards

Before we discuss the future of IM protocols, it is important that we go back and discuss some of the history. Just over five years ago, SIP had recently been standardized for the purposes of signaling audio and video, and using SIP to signal other kinds of real-time communication such as IM made sense, because it actually worked in this regard. Not long afterward, SIP was being used for different aspects of real-time communications but not in the holistic sense for all methods of real-time communications. For example, the Third Generation Partnership Project (3GPP), one of several

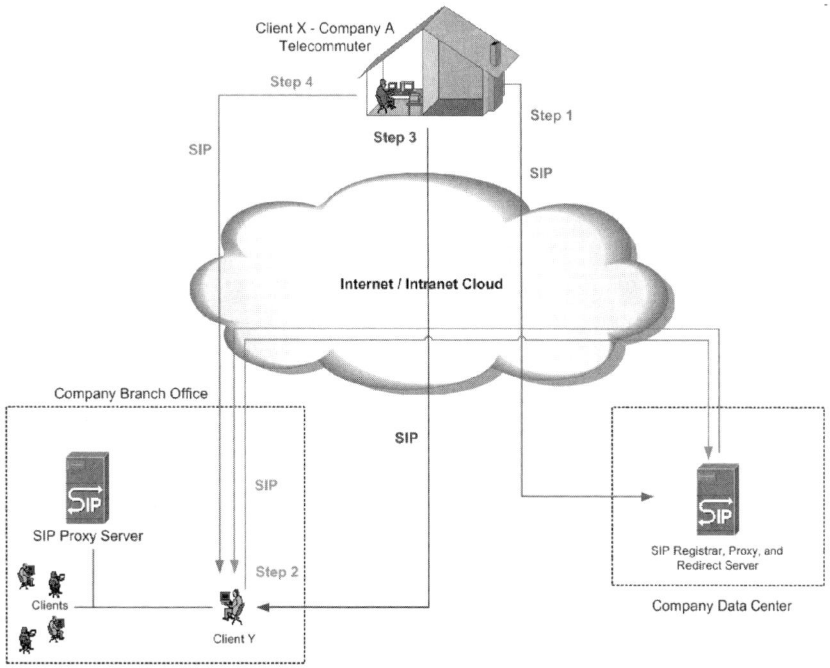

Figure 3.6 *How SIMPLE can enable IM interoperability.*

communities that tries to standardize protocols for the international mobile telephony markets, decided to standardize use of SIP for making calls on mobile phones but not for IM. In addition, Microsoft was very dedicated to the use of SIP signaling for VoIP. In a couple of years, there was a consensus building in the community that it would be a good idea to have a common signaling protocol for all of the real-time sessions that people want to use and that the protocol would also allow you to bundle those sessions together into a single audio, video, and text session. The IETF began work on presence and IM text-messaging specifications. At the time, it was thought that SIP would be the standard by which to achieve this capability; however, SIP was designed as the signaling protocol, and many claim that it really doesn't have all of the capabilities specifically needed for IM.

The SIP developers got started early in the presence game with SIP Registration being a form of presence. There were also earlier IMPP standards efforts that yielded the requirement documents for IM and presence, and the SIMPLE developers moved out from the IMPP efforts rather quickly. XMPP for IM and Jabber started a little bit later. The XMPP community began development of their own protocol. Although claimed to be "the" mature protocol for IM, there appears to have been a desperate effort to retrofit those in the form of SIP that have not been standardized yet. This is problematic, because those who are using SIP are using proprietary extensions, which is going to make it that much harder for convergence.

Twenty years ago, these standards would have just been built, and people would have thought of them as de facto in contrast to today, where the IETF requires going through proposed, draft, and then to full standard. That takes time—a lot of time, in fact. A lot of that time is getting working experience with building and deploying those protocols, and they are still in a somewhat early stage of deployment. Standards take time to develop and gain widespread acceptance. It's a layered architecture, and getting all the pieces of those architectures finalized and standardized, as with any set of standards, is going to take many, many years, especially in the more business-oriented environment of the IETF. We will most likely see a two-protocol situation that we've seen in the IETF before, both of them being discussed and worked on and subsequently deployed by ISPs; it is unlikely that there will be a consensus on a single IM protocol in the near term. There are a lot of standards dynamics, including the influence of the application writers and independent software vendors (ISVs). For the near future, we will most likely see one set of ISPs working with SIP and another set of people working in the XMPP world. As we discussed in our recent book on VoIP security [25], interoperability is king. SIP is a compelling case on the telephony side of the house, because a significant number of vendors currently have solutions today that can interoperate with the telephone network and that interoperate with each other. In this case, SIP will likely be extended the same way that XMPP has been extended over time. In the next chapter, we present a case study regarding IM security. The intent is to make the reader aware of the types of issues enterprise systems administrators and managers must contend with on a daily basis and help you to decide if IM is manageable in your enterprise.

3.7 Endnotes

1. http://www.xmpp.org/history.html
2. RFC 2327: SDP: Session Description Protocol, http://www.ietf.org/rfc/rfc2327.txt
3. RFC 3920: Extensible Messaging and Presence Protocol (XMPP): Core http://www.ietf.org/rfc/rfc3920.txt
4. RFC 3261: Session Initiation Protocol (SIP) http://www.ietf.org/rfc/rfc3261.txt

5. P. Saint-And. (October 2004). RFC 3920 - Extensible Messaging and Presence Protocol (XMPP): Core. Retrieved on January 21, 2004 from http://www.xmpp.org/specs/rfc3920.txt.
6. P. Saint-And (October 2004). RFC 3921 - Extensible Messaging and Presence Protocol (XMPP): Instant Messaging and Presence. Retrieved on January 21, 2004 from http://www.xmpp.org/specs/rfc3921.txt.
7. P. Saint-And (October 2004). RFC 3922—Mapping the Extensible Messaging and Presence Protocol (XMPP) to Common Presence and Instant Messaging (CPIM). Retrieved on January 21, 2004 from http://www.xmpp.org/specs/rfc3922.txt.
8. Note: To prevent confusion, Common Presence and IM is referred to collectively as "the CPIM specifications" whereas the Common Profile for Instant Messaging is referred to as "CPIM."
9. P. Saint-And. (October 2004). RFC 3923 - End-to-End Signing and Object Encryption for the Extensible Messaging and Presence Protocol (XMPP). Retrieved on January 21, 2004 from http://www.xmpp.org/specs/rfc3923.txt.
10. Jabber, Inc. (2005). Jabber Inc. Web site. Retrieved on January 22, 2005 from http://www.jabber.com/index.cgi?CONTENT_ID=9.
11. http://www.jabber.org/about/techover.php
12. http://www.oreillynet.com/pub/d/398
13. M. Day, S. Aggarwal, G. Moher, J. Vinncent. (February 2000). RFC 2779—Instant Messaging / Presence Protocol Requirements. Retrieved on January 21, 2004 from http://www.ietf.org/rfc/rfc2779.txt.
14. http://www.sipcenter.com/sip.nsf/html/Background
15. http://www.sipcenter.com/sip.nsf/html/What+Is+SIP+Introduction
16. J. Rosenberg, et al. (2002). SIP: Session Initiation Protocol. Retrieved July 26, 2004 from http://rfc.sunsite.dk/.
17. M. Handley, et al, (1999). RFC 2543: SIP: Session Initiation Protocol. Retrieved, July 26, 2004 from http://rfc.sunsite.dk/.
18. J. Franks, et al. (1999). RFC 2617: HTTP Authentication: Basic and Digest Access Authentication. Retrieved, July 26, 2004 from http://rfc.sunsite.dk/.

19. H. Schulzrinne, et al (1996) RFC 1889: RTP: A Transport Protocol for Real-Time Applications. Retrieved, July 26, 2004 from http://rfc.sunsite.dk/.

20. M. Handley, et al. (1998). RFC 2327: SDP: Session Description Protocol. Retrieved July 26, 2004 from http://rfc.sunsite.dk/.

21. K. Ono, S. Tachimoto. (October 20, 2003). Requirements for End-to-middle Security for the Session Initiation Protocol (SIP) draft-ietf-sipping-end2middle-security-reqs-00. Retrieved on January 30, 2005 from http://www.ietf.org/proceedings/03nov/I-D/draft-ietf-sipping-e2m-sec-reqs-00.txt

22. M. Barnes. (October 22, 2004). A Mechanism to Secure SIP information inserted by Intermediaries. Retrieved on January 30, 2005 from http://mirror.njit.edu/internet-drafts/draft-barnes-sipping-sec-inserted-info-02.txt.

23. H. Schulzrinne, S. Casner, R. Frederick, V. Jacobson. (July 2003). Network Working Group Request for Comments: 3550 (Obsoletes: 1889), Category: Standards Track, RTP: A Transport Protocol for Real-Time Applications. Retrieved July 2, 2004 from http://www.faqs.org/rfcs/rfc1889.html.

24. J. Rosenberg, H. Schulzrinne. "The Session Initiation Protocol: Providing Advanced Telephony Services across the Internet," *Bell Labs Technical Journal*, Vol. 3 , No. 4, October/December 1998, pp. 144-160

25. J. Ransome and J. Rittinghouse. (2004). *VoIP Security*, New York, Elsevier/Digital Press.

4

IM Malware

4.1 Overview

E-mail differs from IM in that IM allows users to see whether a chosen friend or coworker is connected to the Internet, and the messages are exchanged directly (almost instantly), allowing for a two-way communication in near real time. An IM service will typically alert a user if somebody on the user's contact list is online. IM is now a widespread, efficient medium for everyday business users to collaborate, organize strategy meetings, and share internal files and information.

Popular systems such as America Online's Instant Messenger and ICQ, Microsoft's MSN Messenger, and Internet Relay Chat (IRC) have changed the way we communicate with our friends, acquaintances, and now our business colleagues. Although IM is increasing in popularity in both professional and personal applications, its increasing use has led to an associated increase in the number of security risks. Companies face a difficult choice now that they are coming to understand some of the security issues associated with the use of IM in their businesses. Most of the potential problems stem from the fact that free public IM clients and networks, such as AOL Instant Messenger, Yahoo! Messenger, and MSN Messenger, do not offer security, monitoring, logging, or any other features commonly associated with corporate IT applications.

Security has taken a backseat in many IM clients. Without security mechanisms in place, IM can allow the unfettered transmission of confidential files, malicious code, and inappropriate content, for which an organization can be held liable. Managing IM use is a problem that has been identified as one of the major IT challenges facing business today. The lack of secure interoperable protocols has hindered enterprise IM, online collaboration, and unified collaboration solutions. This reduces the usefulness of the technology and makes it difficult to manage, which, in turn, makes it difficult to secure.

Although a lack of interoperability has actually prevented threats from spanning multiple networks, better interoperability will enable more businesses to adopt IM in the future and security threats will increase. Companies are faced with either blocking IM, potentially alienating employees who have come to rely on it as a communications tool, or they can take steps to manage its use. Many companies, as you might expect, in order to balance the business needs and security, are looking for ways to manage and control IM. For the most part, IT departments also have little or no control over consumer-based IM services, which can be vulnerable to hacking and incompatible with company networks. They are desperately playing catch-up with unauthorized users of IM and Peer-to-Peer (P2P) clients, who are sharing music files and videos on company time and with company resources. In fact, researchers at the Yankee Group have identified Securing IM as one of the top three priorities for IT managers in 2004. What follows are some important considerations you need to keep in mind when evaluating an IM solution for your company:

- Will IM use by employees be permitted or blocked?
- Is your company standardizing on just one IM system or will multiple choices be permitted?
- Is the IM solution a critical requirement of the business?
- Is the company subject to regulatory compliance requirements for IM?
- Is the IM solution going to be used primarily by one or two departments, or is it an enterprise-scale system to be deployed throughout the company?
- How many employees will likely be using the IM system over the next 12, 24, and 36 months?
- How many concurrent users are expected at any point in time?
- Is integration with the corporate directory and other applications, such as e-mail or CRM software, an important requirement?
- Is there a need for APIs to integrate with third-party virus scanning, file scanning, and content-filtering applications?
- Is encryption of message traffic an important feature?

- Is the ability to have company ID and namespace management important?
- Will you require a system that will continue operating and logging messages even in the event of a database failure?
- Do you require a solution that allows an IM proxy service that can be deployed in the firm's DMZ infrastructure but does not need to open inbound ports?
- Do you require an IM solution that can be deployed through existing HTTP proxies and can be used with existing infrastructure?

Certainly, finding answers to these questions before deploying any IM solution will help you to choose the solution most appropriate for your company. Simply installing and making the service available is not recommended and can only lead to trouble. Next, we will describe the specific security threats associated with IM.

4.1.1 Instant Messaging Opens New Security Holes

IM is not only used to transfer text messages but also to transfer files, which, as with e-mail, are capable of initiating a transfer of worms and other malware, and it can provide an access point for backdoor Trojan horses. IM can also be used by hackers to gain backdoor access to computers without opening a listening port, effectively bypassing desktop and perimeter firewall implementations (Figure 1.4). Unlike traditional network hacking, the hacker doesn't need to scan for unknown IP addresses. A hacker needs only to select from an updated directory of buddy lists. IM also supports peer-to-peer file sharing, where a directory or drive is shared. In this case, all the files on a computer can be shared using the IM client, leading to the spread of files that are infected with a virus or other malware.

This situation can also make the target machine vulnerable to unauthorized viewing. Viruses can be sent via file transfers, bypassing traditional gateway anti-virus security. URLs to malicious code hosted on the Internet can be pushed to users via IM, and that code can be downloaded and executed on local machines. IM's recent significant growth has resulted in many vulnerabilities, where programming flaws such as buffer overflows or boundary condition errors have been exploited to spread viruses, worms, or, in some cases, even distributed denial-of-service (DoS) attacks in popular clients such as AOL, MSN, and Yahoo! As we will see in the remainder of

Figure 4.1
A backdoor attack.

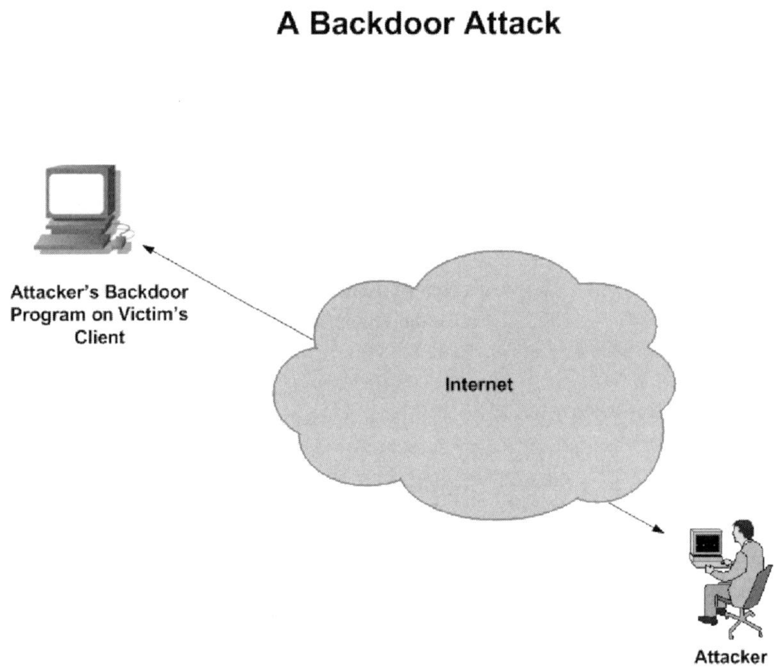

this chapter, inadequate protection for these virus and worm threats over IM is still commonplace.

A Vulnerable Architecture

Most IM systems in use today were designed to be scalable with little or no regard to security. Most current freeware IM systems lack encryption capabilities and have features to bypass traditional corporate firewalls. This makes it difficult for administrators and security personnel to control corporate users inside the organization. Many of these systems have insecure password management and are vulnerable to account spoofing and denial-of-service attacks. In addition, IM is quickly becoming ubiquitous, it provides an able communications infrastructure, and it has integrated directories that can be used to locate new targets (i.e., buddy lists). Some systems can be controlled by easy-to-write scripts, making IM an ideal platform for fast-spreading computer worms and blended threats.

The primary function of an IM client is to allow text or HTML messages to be sent to other users in near real time. Files can also be transferred between users, and a range of other services has been implemented. This includes the ability to receive e-mail notifications, stock quotes, multiplayer online game brokering, video conferencing, voice over IP, and SMS sending. Fortunately, security features continue to be added to IM clients for most of the major enterprise solutions.

IM systems generally employ a client/server architecture. The user installs the IM client on his or her local machine, and the software client communicates with an IM server in the messaging provider's infrastructure to exchange messages. IM messages are not normally sent from one user's computer directly to the message recipient. The IM message is typically sent from the first user to an IM server over the public Internet and then down to the recipient. Messages are normally sent as plainly visible (unencrypted) clear text, and they are susceptible to eavesdropping.

4.1.2 Legal Risk and Unregulated Instant Messaging

Regulatory requirements and business needs for logging IM content have emerged across several industries. Pressured by fines and threats of imprisonment for noncompliance with federal and state regulations, IT executives are cautiously deploying systems that archive their e-mail and IM communications. For example, specific language in the Sarbanes-Oxley Act of 2002 says:

> *Whoever knowingly alters, destroys, mutilates, conceals, covers up, falsifies or makes a false entry in any record, document . . . with intent to impede . . . shall be fined under this title, imprisoned not more than 20 years, or both.*

Major provisions of Sarbanes-Oxley include the following:

- Certification of financial reports by CEOs and CFOs
- Ban on personal loans to executive officers and directors
- Accelerated reporting of trades by insiders
- Prohibition on insider trades during pension fund blackout periods
- Public reporting of CEO and CFO compensation and profits
- Auditor independence, including outright bans on certain types of work and precertification by the company's Audit Committee of all other nonaudit work
- Criminal and civil penalties for securities violations

- U.S. companies are now obliged to have an internal audit function, which will need to be certified by external auditors
- Significantly longer jail sentences and larger fines for corporate executives who knowingly and willfully misstate financial statements
- Prohibition on audit firms providing extra value-added services to their clients, including actuarial services and legal and extra services (such as consulting) unrelated to their audit work
- A requirement that publicly traded companies furnish independent annual audit reports on the existence and condition (i.e., reliability) of internal controls as they relate to financial reporting

In addition to these provisions, the corporation's CEO and CFO are required to make reports in accordance with the "Internal Control over Financial Reporting and Certification of Disclosure in Exchange Act Periodic Reports" as stated in section 404 of the Sarbanes-Oxley Act of 2002. The Public Company Accounting Oversight Board[1] (PCAOB) has issued some guidelines on how management should render its opinion. The main point is that management should use a risk management approach to manage its business activities. (The approach should include specifics on how to assess the control environment, determine control objectives, perform risk assessments, and identify controls.)

Other regulations that affect public companies are the Heath Information Portability and Accountability Act of 1996 (HIPAA) and the Uniform Electronic Transactions Act, which says e-mail can be used to form contracts [2]. A variety of regulations have emerged from the Securities and Exchange Commission (SEC), NASD, and NYSE and are causing organizations to look at e-mail/IM archiving solutions that support requirements for U.S. brokerages to retain and archive all digital communications with customers for periods of up to six years. Similar regulatory issues apply to the pharmaceutical and petrochemical industries. Message logging is also a critical business requirement for call center operations and also an operational requirement for government and defense systems. The threat of a lawsuit for offensive comments or behavior for corporate wrongdoing can be a major concern for corporations.

4.2 The Use of IM as Malware

Malicious software (malware) is any type of programming intended to cause harm, such as viruses, worms, spyware, and Trojan horses [3]. The very nature of IM increases the threat from worms, viruses, and other malicious software (a.k.a., malware). Most e-mail users are aware that opening an executable file (.exe) from an unknown source is a danger, but many don't know what an IM threat looks like. IM malware can be carried in a URL from somebody in your buddy list, and users are much more likely to click on URLs embedded in IM messages or accept files without knowing they are actually accepting them. As IM interconnectivity spreads and it becomes easier to communicate between multiple IM systems, such as MSN Messenger, Yahoo! Instant Messaging, and AOL Instant Messaging, so will the threat of malware jumping from one system to another increase.

From 2002 to 2003, worms and viruses that spread via IM and peer-to-peer networks increased 400 percent, according to Symantec's Internet Security Threat Report [4]. Threats such as the the Jitux.A and Bizex worms are targeting MSN Messenger and ICQ, respectively. Jitux.A can spread itself by tapping users' IM contacts, but Bizex has more malicious intent: it sends a link to a Web site that will scan your PC for data regarding electronic payments and finances. The site was quickly shut down once the worm was discovered, but no one is sure how much data was collected before the shutdown occurred [5].

4.3 What Is Malware?

Malware (short for malicious software) is any program or file that is harmful to a computer user. Thus, malware includes computer viruses, worms, Trojan horses, and also spyware, programming that gathers information about a computer user without permission. Malware should not be confused with defective software that is intended for a legitimate purpose but has errors or bugs. Some of the more notable things that malware can do include the ability to corrupt files, alter or delete data, distribute confidential data, disable hardware, deny legitimate user access, and cause a hard drive to crash. Frequently, malware is also designed to send itself from your e-mail account to all the friends and colleagues in your address book. The results of a malware infection include wasted resources, compromised systems, lack of regulatory compliance, lost or stolen data, and the loss of user and client confidence. Malware can be classified based on how it is executed, how it spreads, and/or what it does. Common classifications of malware include viruses, worms, wabbits, Trojan horses, spyware, browser hijackers, blended threats, backdoors, exploits, and rootkits. Each will be briefly described in the following text.

4.3.1 Viruses

Viruses self-replicate within computers and across networks and alter files or data. They usually require some action on the user's part to start, most often just clicking an executable file attachment on an e-mail (although embedded programming in an e-mail message can execute a virus program). Typically, people think that the file came to them from a trusted source or is something they want to see. Not every program that copies itself is a virus or worm; for instance, backup software may copy itself to other media as part of a system backup. Viruses have utilized many types and kinds of hosts as they have evolved. Common targets are executable files that are part of application programs, documents that can contain macroscripts, and the boot sectors of floppy disks. In the case of executable files, the infection routine of the virus works such that when the host code is executed, the viral code also gets executed. Normally, the host program keeps functioning after it is infected by the virus. Some viruses overwrite other programs with copies of themselves. Viruses spread across computers when the software or document they attached themselves to is transferred from one computer to another. The difference between a virus and a worm is that a worm operates more or less independently of other files, whereas a virus depends on one or more hosts to spread itself.

4.3.2 Worms

Worms are a virus variant that can infect a computer without any user interaction. Computer worms are similar to viruses but are stand-alone software and as such do not require host files (or other types of host code) in order to spread themselves. A worm does not alter files, but resides in active memory and duplicates itself. Worms modify their host operating system to the extent that they are started as part of the boot process. To spread, worms either exploit some vulnerability of the target system or use some form of social engineering to trick users into executing them. Worms use parts of an operating system that are automatic and usually invisible to the user. It is common for worms to be noticed only when their uncontrolled replication consumes system resources, slowing or halting other tasks.

4.3.3 Wabbits

Another type of self-replicating malware is the *wabbit*. Unlike viruses, wabbits do not infect host programs or documents. Unlike worms, wabbits do

Figure 4.2
Fork bombs, easily coded in C, are a special type of wabbit.

```
#include <systypes.h>
#include <unistd.h>
int main (int argc, char *argv[])
{
  while (1)
}
fork();
{
  return 0;
}
```

not use network functionality in order to spread to other computers. Wabbits can be programmed to have (sometimes malicious) side effects in addition to the direct consequences of their quick self-replication. An example of a simple wabbit is a *fork bomb* (Figure 4.2). The fork bomb is a form of denial-of-service attack against a computer system that uses the fork function. It relies on the assumption that the number of programs and processes that may be simultaneously executed on a computer has a limit. A large number of processes will be created rapidly by the fork bomb in order to saturate the available space in the list of processes kept by the computer's operating system. The effect is devastating—no new programs can be started and the system becomes much more difficult, or even impossible, to use, because the CPU is simply overwhelmed. It can be written in one line of C source code or in a UNIX shell on any UNIX system (Figure 4.2). A fork bomb literally explodes and sucks up all available system resources by recursively spawning copies of itself (using the UNIX system call fork(2)). Eventually, it eats all the process table entries and effectively wedges the system into a locked-up state. Fortunately, fork bombs are relatively easy to spot and kill, so creating one deliberately seldom accomplishes more than to bring the just wrath of the gods down upon the perpetrator.

4.3.4 Trojan Horses

A Trojan horse program is software disguised as legitimate software containing malicious coding hidden within innocuous programming or data in such a way that it can get control and wreak its chosen form of havoc on a system. An example would be code that would ruin the file allocation table on your hard disk. A Trojan horse can be deliberately attached to otherwise useful software by a programmer, or it can be spread by tricking users into believing that it is useful. Some Trojan horses (called *droppers*) can spread or activate other malware, such as viruses. Basically, a dropper is just what the name implies: a program designed to run and install (or "drop") a virus onto your system. The program itself is not infected, nor is it a virus because it does not replicate. So, technically, a dropper should be considered a Trojan horse. Often, because the virus is hidden in the program code, a scanner will not detect the danger until after the code is dropped onto your system. It is technically possible to write a virus that also drops other viruses onto the victim's system, and several have been tried. Most are very buggy, however. It's a technical point, but there is a class of dropper that only infects the computer's memory, not the disk. These are given the name "injector" by some virus researchers. Fortunately, because of technical difficulties, droppers are hard to program and therefore are rarely distributed. In contrast to viruses or worms, Trojan horses cannot replicate themselves and may be widely redistributed in conjunction with a virus.

4.3.5 Spyware

Spyware is software that secretly collects and sends targeted information (such as browsing patterns or credit card numbers) about users to advertisers or other interested parties. The spyware products usually work and spread like Trojan horses. The category of spyware is sometimes taken to include adware of the less-than-forthcoming sort. Adware, which usually includes spyware components, can also be considered malware. Although not malicious in intent, nonmalicious spyware such as adware is often installed without your consent and even without your knowledge, as a drive-by download or as the result of clicking some option in a deceptive pop-up window.

4.3.6 Browser Hijackers

Browser hijackers are programs that alter your computer's browser settings so that you are redirected to Web sites you did not intend to visit. For example, browser hijackers can alter default home pages and search pages to those of their customers who pay for that service because of the traffic it generates. They can add bookmarks for pornographic Web sites to the users' own bookmark collections. When the browser finds its way to one of these pornographic sites, the browser is directed to begin generating pornographic pop-up windows faster than the user can click them shut. Often, hijackers will redirect users to pornographic sites when they inadvertently mistype or misspell a URL or enter a URL without the http://www. preface.

4.3.7 Blended Threats

Blended threats are becoming increasingly common, blurring the distinction between different types of malware. Blended threats combine characteristics of more than one type of malware to maximize the damage they cause and to increase the speed at which they spread. Blended threats are seen by security professionals as perhaps the single most dangerous threat they must be prepared to contend with in the treacherous computing environments of today. Though the term is new, "blended" security threats are not. These types of threats target several areas of network vulnerability simultaneously. What is new and unique, however, is what the malicious code within them is doing. In a blended threat, malicious code can take many forms and can attack your enterprise in a number of different ways. It can also do more than one kind of damage while it's in your system. You might, for example, find a piece of malicious code that can attack your company's computers through e-mail attachments, infected Web sites, or even through direct attacks on your routers and servers. Once inside your firewall, these threats can spread through everything from shared disks to internal Web servers. And they can spread to the rest of the world through e-mail/IM and file transfers.

4.3.8 Backdoors

A backdoor is a method of bypassing normal authentication or obtaining unauthorized remote access to a computer while remaining hidden to casual inspection. The backdoor may take the form of an installed program (e.g., a Trojan horse) or could be a modification to a legitimate program. Based on how they work and spread, there are two types of backdoors. The first type works much like a Trojan horse, because they are manually inserted into another piece of software, executed via their host software, and spread by their host software being installed. The second type works more like a worm in that it gets executed as part of the boot process and is usually spread by worms carrying it as their payload. A backdoor in a computer system is essentially a method of bypassing normal authentication or obtaining remote access to a computer while intended to remain hidden to casual inspection. The backdoor may take the form of an installed program (e.g., Back Orifice) or could be a modification to a legitimate program. A backdoor in a login system could take the form of a hard-coded user and password combination that gives access to the system. A famous example of this was used as a plot device in the 1983 film *WarGames,* wherein the designer of a computer system (the "WOPR") had inserted an undocumented password (named after his son) that gave the user access to the system and to undocumented aspects of its behavior (a video game–like simulation mode). An attempt to plant a backdoor in the Linux kernel, exposed in November 2003, showed how subtle such a code change could be. In this case, a two-line change took the form of an apparent typographical error, which in reality gave the caller to the *syswait* function root access to the machine.

The prevalence of backdoors in proprietary software systems is a topic of great speculation, but they have been occasionally exposed in practice. Programmers have succeeded in secretly installing even large amounts of code, known as *Easter eggs,* in programs without detection, although in these cases, there may be official forbearance, if not actual permission, to do such acts. It is also possible to create a backdoor without modifying the source code of a program or even modifying it after compilation. This can be done by rewriting the compiler so that it recognizes code during compilation that triggers inclusion of a backdoor in the compiled output. When the compromised compiler finds such code, it compiles it as normal, but also inserts a backdoor (such as a password recognition routine). When the user provides that input, he gains access to often undocumented aspects of program operation. This attack was first outlined by Ken Thompson in his famous paper "Reflections on Trusting Trust." [6] Many computer worms, such as Sobig and Mydoom, install a backdoor on the affected computer (generally a PC on broadband running insecure versions of Microsoft Windows and Microsoft Outlook). Such backdoors appear to be installed so that spammers can send junk e-mail from the machines in question.

The Ken Thompson classic "Reflections on Trusting Trust" [7] backdoor was the first major article to describe black-box backdoor issues and point out that trust is relative. It described a very clever classic backdoor mechanism based upon the fact that people only review source (human-written) code and not compiled (machine) code. A program called a compiler is used to create the second from the first, and it is trusted to do an honest job. This article described how a modified version of the UNIX C compiler could be told specifically to put an invisible backdoor in the UNIX log in command when compiled, and, as a twist, add this feature undetectably to future compiler versions upon their compilation as well.

Because the compiler itself was a compiled program, this extra functionality would never be noticed and likewise would not be noticed in software created by it.

4.3.9 Exploits

An *exploit* is a common term in the computer security community and is used to refer to a piece of software that takes advantage of a bug, glitch, or vulnerability, leading to privilege escalation or denial of service on a computer system. Exploits are not necessarily malicious in intent. They are often devised by security researchers as a way of demonstrating that a vulnerability exists.

There are several methods of classifying exploits. The most common is by how the exploit contacts the vulnerable software. A remote exploit works over a network and exploits the security vulnerability without any prior access to the vulnerable system. A local exploit requires prior access to the vulnerable system and usually increases the privileges of the person running the exploit past those granted by the system administrator. Exploits can also be classified by the type of vulnerability they attack (i.e., buffer overflows, format string attacks, race conditions, cross-site scripting errors, and cross-site request forgery). Many exploits are designed to provide root-level access to a computer system. However, it is also possible to use several exploits, first to gain low-level access and then to escalate privileges repeatedly until one reaches root. Normally, a single exploit can only take advantage of a specific software vulnerability. Often, as such an exploit is published, the vulnerability is fixed and the exploit becomes obsolete for newer versions of the software. This is the reason why some blackhat hackers do not publish their exploits but keep them private to themselves or other malicious hackers. Such exploits are referred to as "zero day" exploits, and obtaining access to these types of exploits is a primary desire of many unskilled malicious attackers (called script kiddies).

4.3.10 Rootkits

A *rootkit* is a set of tools used by hackers after cracking into a computer system. The purpose of a rootkit is to hide logins, processes, and logs altered by the hackers' presence, as well as to assist in sniffing terminals, connections, and the keyboard. Rootkits may be classified as Trojan horses. There are two types of rootkits: kernel-mode and application-level (a.k.a., user-mode) rootkits. Rootkits may also include backdoors, allowing an attacker to easily regain access to the compromised system at a later time, or they may contain exploit software that can be used to attack other systems.

Since its introduction into the intruder community, rootkit has seen widespread use, and its threat should not be taken lightly. A 1994 CIAC bulletin [8] estimated that the number of accounts compromised worldwide exceeded 100,000. By 1996, this number had become much, much larger. CERT and CIAC continue to issue periodic warnings about the popularity of sniffing user IDs and passwords. Network monitoring (sniffing) attacks represent a serious Internet threat. The typical Rootkit attack proceeds as follows: The intruders use a stolen or easily guessed password to log in to a host. They then gain unauthorized root access by exploiting known vulnerabilities in *rdist, sendmail, /bin/mail, loadmodule, rpc, lpr, or passwd*. The intruders use File Transport Protocol (FTP) to send a rootkit package to the host, unpack, compile, and install it; then they collect more username/password pairs and attack more hosts.

Rootkits, almost always allow an attacker to hide his or her presence on the victim's machine. Rootkits generally take one of two basic forms: user mode or kernel mode. User-mode rootkits modify programs and libraries, whereas kernel-mode rootkits modify the kernel. Kernel-mode Rootkits are far more efficient than user-mode Rootkits because they actually alter the kernel, changing the underlying code that all of the user programs invoke (Figure 4.3). By changing the system call table, an attacker can wield great power, planting malicious code inside the kernel and subsequently implementing execution redirection. By implementing many careful changes to the system call table, the attacker can hide processes, files, and directories, and even hide which ports are being used, thereby achieving the ultimate hidden and undetectable execution redirection attack.

In mid-1996, the only known variants of Rootkit ran on hosts running Sun OS 4.x and the Linux Slackware distribution. However, the recipe for Rootkit is quite simple. The first ingredient is a sniffer program, which can be fashioned out of *tcpdump* or *etherfind*. This sniffer program, specializing in password recording, puts the Ethernet interface into promiscuous mode and allows the reading of every packet transmitted on an Ethernet network. The second ingredient is the source code to the standard system binaries. Thus, it is quite easy to write a version of Rootkit for other Unix variants—researchers have even discovered a modified version of the Sun OS Rootkit sniffer code for Solaris Version 2.x. Additionally, you should not assume that because you don't have any workstations running Sun OS or Linux that your network is safe. Rootkit's sniffer targets every Telnet, rlogin, and FTP session regardless of system type, which includes all UNIX flavors,

Figure 4.3
An illustration of kernel-mode attack process.

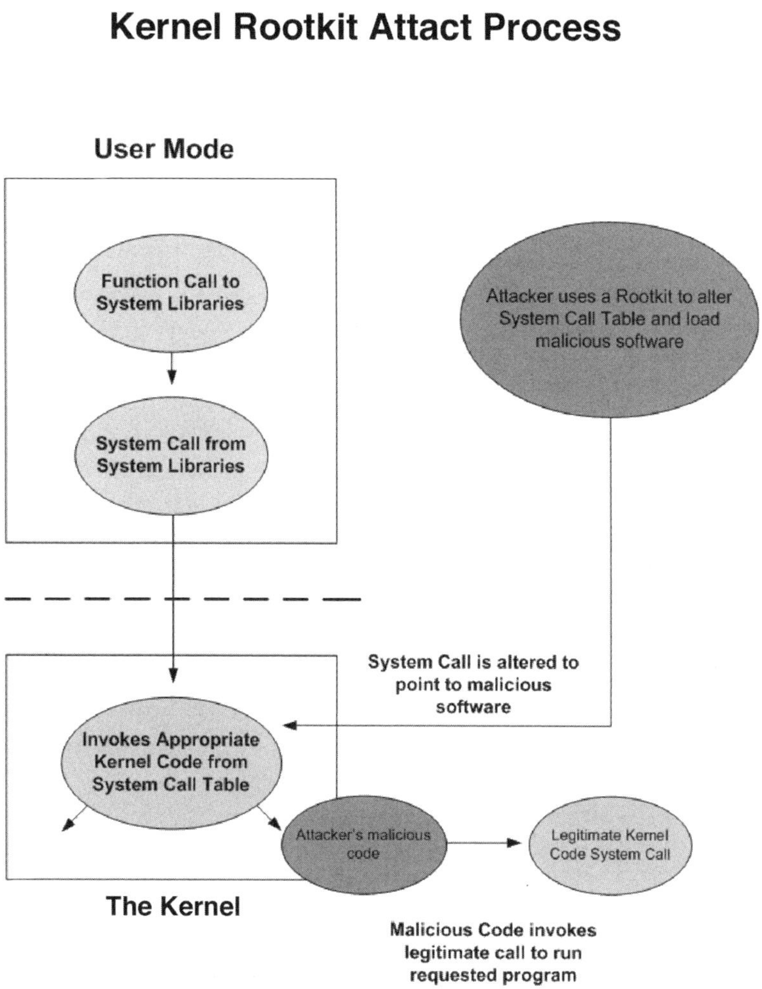

MS-DOS, VMS, and even MVS systems. This makes all your network systems highly vulnerable to attack. All it takes is one sniffer somewhere along the network path to your system to initiate the attack.

4.4 How Is IM Used as Malware?

Any Internet-enabled application is a potential carrier for worms and other malware, and IM is no exception. IM provides the ability to transfer not only text messages but also files. This means it can transfer malware and provide an access point for backdoor Trojan horses to gain access to computers without opening a listening port—thereby bypassing most firewall controls. Other functionality added to IM, such as peer-to-peer file sharing, increases the risk of falling susceptible to malware.

IM worms can utilize exposed application programming interfaces (APIs) by the vendor, enumerate windows via the Windows OS APIs to interactively send a file, send a URL link instead of a file, or patch client DLLs to send itself along with the original message to spread through an IM system. An API is a set of definitions of the ways in which one piece of computer software communicates with another.

Using a documented set of IM APIs, developers can write applications that interface with the MSN Messenger and ICQ clients to expose IM functionality that is robust enough to create IM worms. For example, using an API, a virus writer can easily create a worm that spreads using MSN Messenger. A worm can be alerted when a message is received or when a user is added to the buddy list, and then send a file to that particular user; and the worm could easily send itself to all contacts by enumerating the contact list. Many worms already exist today that utilize IM APIs. The W32.Choke.Worm is a worm that replicates using documented MSN Messenger APIs and simply sends itself in reply to any incoming text message.

4.4.1 As a Carrier

Malware is typically distributed by one of three methods:

1. By e-mail via a virus-laden attachment or code embedded in the message body
2. In an infected application
3. Through infected code on a Web site

Although e-mail attachments are currently the most frequently used method to distribute malware, infected Web sites and program downloads are having an increasing impact. Newer communications channels, such as IM and VoIP, pose a very serious threat to networks.

Viruses, Worms, and Blended Threats over IM

The discovery of vulnerabilities in network-enabled applications occurs every day. IM clients are no exception. These vulnerabilities are common coding mistakes made by programmers. At best, these vulnerabilities can cause a denial of service (DoS) and, at worst, can allow hackers unauthorized remote access. Furthermore, remotely injected code could contain classic worm replication functionality, forming an IM blended threat. This type of threat would have the potential to spread significantly faster than even CodeRed and W32/Slammer. The number of IM viruses and worms is rising steadily, but there are still no antivirus applications that directly monitor IM traffic and only a few that directly plug in to IM clients. This is partly due to the difficulty in monitoring IM traffic, as well as the constant modifications to the clients and the protocols that they use.

Antivirus software does not currently monitor IM traffic at the server or gateway level due to the difficulty in finding IM traffic, since it is often embedded inside HTTP packets. However, a few antivirus applications plug in to IM clients, scanning files as they are received. Unfortunately, this makes instant messengers an open door to the computer, as unscanned traffic will bypass most server-based security measures. If a worm starts to spread using IM, in most cases, it cannot be stopped before it reaches the user's computer. Only the antivirus product running on the computer itself can catch the worms. The way in which these worms replicate varies. Some of the worms spread via e-mail as well as IM. Others spread only via IM. However, currently, all IM worms still require user interaction for execution. None make use of an exploit to allow auto-execution upon receipt. Therefore, if IM users are more aware of the threats and how to prevent them, the success of these worms would be significantly reduced.

IM is an attractive target for those with malicious software, because it provides a robust communications channel between system users, and virtually all IM software products maintain a list of buddies with whom the user frequently interacts. These buddy lists can be leveraged like e-mail address books to serve as "hit lists" to spread a worm rapidly through the IM user base. By eliminating the need to scan for vulnerable machines, one can infect hundreds of thousands of machines in seconds rather than minutes. Furthermore, after sending itself to the buddies on the existing buddy list, an IM blended threat could also generate random buddy list names, thereby increasing its infection rate even further. Thus, an IM blended threat could infect all vulnerable machines in seconds rather than minutes or hours.

Security concerns have been heightened due to the rash of Web-based viruses that have escaped traditional, signature-based virus measures. Unlike traditional viruses, which rely on the user to spread the infected files, these new threats, often called blended threats, are automated and are always scanning the Internet and local networks for vulnerabilities and other computers to infect, meaning they spread without user interaction. In addition, script-capable or programmable IM systems provide some malicious programs targeted at these systems with an exploitable mechanism by which to spread.

It is possible to construct a blended threat that spreads without user interaction by exploiting vulnerabilities in an Internet-enabled software platform such as a Web server (i.e., CodeRed and Nimda). We will likely see similar worms or blended threats that exploit bugs or other vulnerabilities in client-side IM software. This type of threat could use a buffer overflow attack on an IM client program to gain access to a new system. Once the system is compromised, an attacker could access the user's buddy list to gain a new set of targets. CodeRed was able to attack several hundred thousand Internet servers in hours. Given the ubiquity of popular IM systems, a well-crafted IM-based worm would have the potential to hit millions or even tens of millions of home computers or wireless devices in the same amount of time. A worm that has successfully attached to a system could delete data, install backdoors, and possibly export critical data. Broadband Internet connections only exacerbate these security problems.

Scripting Instant Messaging Threats

Several IM platforms offer scripting capabilities, enabling users to write Visual Basic, JavaScript, Proprietary Script Code, and other complex programs to control various features in the messaging client. These scripting capabilities let other programs or script files (e.g., Visual Basic or JavaScript) control the client IM software via simple programming commands. Scripts such as these are able to instruct the IM client to do any number of things: contact other users, send files, change program settings, and/or execute potentially malicious actions. This functionality can provide mechanisms that enable the spread of computer worms and blended threats.

By taking advantage of such aforementioned commands, malicious code can use the IM system as a communications platform to send itself into other members of the system, change program settings, steal confidential information, and perform other potentially malicious actions. For example, there are dozens of real-world worms that are written in a scripting language provided by popular IRC client software and propagated using IRC as a communications platform. In addition to IRC worms, there now exist a number of Windows-based worms targeted at certain IM systems. These worms use scripting techniques similar to those used by the Nimda and LoveLetter and SirCam threats, to send themselves from user-to-user via IM software.

4.4.2 As a Staging Center

MSN Messenger, Yahoo! Messenger, AOL Instant Messenger, and ICQ are the four most popular IM products in use outside the commercial world; they are free and all highly vulnerable to security breaches such as worm viruses, backdoor Trojan horses, hijacking and impersonation, denial of service, and unauthorized disclosure of information, making IM an ideal staging center platform. IM enables information to be shared through file transfers and peer-to-peer file sharing among members of a messaging group, allowing users to freely transfer potentially malware-ridden files and to conduct unencrypted chat sessions that are virtually open to any reasonably knowledgeable hacker. In addition, all users in an IM group can potentially access the disks of the other members of the group, putting hard disks of unprotected IM users potentially at the disposal of any would-be hacker during an IM chat session. Security vendors have lagged behind the popularity of IM, adding to the attractiveness of IM as a staging center for malware.

Instant Messaging Server Vulnerabilities

There are two main ways messages and files are transferred between clients: server proxy and server broker. In the server proxy architecture, all IM communication is passed through the server. In this case, the IM message is sent to the server first rather than directly to each other. The server then forwards the message to the intended recipient, acting as a proxy between the users. Both clients initiate outgoing connections to the server and do not require the ability to accept incoming connections on a port that a corporate firewall may block. This is the default method that all major IM networks use today. Sending messages to the server may first incur a time delay and represent a privacy risk.

In the server broker architecture, the only packets that are sent to the server are packets requesting the server to initiate communication between two clients. The server essentially facilitates the connection between the two clients. The server provides the clients with the connection information; the clients then directly connect to one another. If attackers gain access to these servers, they could also eavesdrop on all conversations, impersonate any user, launch denial-of-service attacks, or spread malicious threats with little effort. In addition, the nonexistent or minimal use of IM traffic provides an attacker with the opportunity to control an IM server and gain access to the contents of every transmission.

Threats from File Transfers

In addition to simple text messages, all popular IM networks support file transfers between clients. Most file transfers are done via server brokering. Files transferred between clients do not pass through the server, but, instead, the server acts as a broker and informs the sender on how to find the intended recipient. The file will then be transferred directly from one client to the other. A key advantage of file transfer over IM instead of file exchanges over e-mail is that file exchanges over e-mail are dependent on the recipient's mailbox storage quota. Many corporate users find file transfer over IM a markedly more reliable way to exchange files, since file sizes continue to increase while the pressure on containing e-mail administration costs require strict limits on mailbox storage quotas. Since file transfers over IM are not scanned, IM users inadvertently expose their entire network to virus infestations, worms, and Trojan horses, as well as blended threats. IM systems also allow users to exchange files with each other in an unencrypted form.

4.4.3 As a Vehicle for General Hacking

Since most current IM systems were designed with scalability rather than security in mind, virtually all freeware IM programs lack encryption capabilities and most have features that bypass traditional firewalls. In addition, many of these systems have insecure password management and are vulnerable to account spoofing and DoS attacks. As discussed previously, IM systems have become ubiquitous, provide a communications infrastructure, have integrated directories (buddy lists), which can be used to locate new targets, and, in many cases, can be controlled by easily written scripts, which make IM systems an ideal platform for rapidly spreading malware including computer worms and blended threats.

Information Security Leaks

It is common for enterprises to have an infrastructure in place to prevent employees from sending confidential or unauthorized content beyond the firewall. This is particularly true to prevent the risk of unmonitored content leaving the corporation without the knowledge of the information security department, which can introduce both competitive and legal risk from workgroups that handle proprietary or regulatory protected information. IM file transfer is particularly useful for those trying to bypass the security and forensic capabilities of the IT and risk management departments. The lack of content filtering or archiving also makes it difficult for administrators to discover potential breaches of information security policy or to hold individuals accountable for their actions.

Eavesdropping

Since most IM systems do not encrypt network traffic, a determined third party can eavesdrop on conversations between two IM users using a packet sniffer or similar technology. This holds true for both client/server and peer-to-peer messaging models. This form of attack is among the most common and is often the preferred method of gaining access to wireless networks.

Account Hijacking

A number of IM systems are vulnerable to account hijacking or spoofing (Figure 4.4). A number of Web sites provide do-it-yourself tools or describe techniques for launching such an attack. There is also a Web site that gives detailed instructions on how to crack the password encryption scheme for one popular IM system. Password protection is very limited in most IM systems and, in some cases, unencrypted in plain text. Some IM systems store user passwords in data files on the client's PC. Such vulnerabilities allow an attacker to hijack another user's IM account and impersonate that user in conversations with others. IM users often have their passwords on the desktop computer and use the same password on multiple systems, which pro-

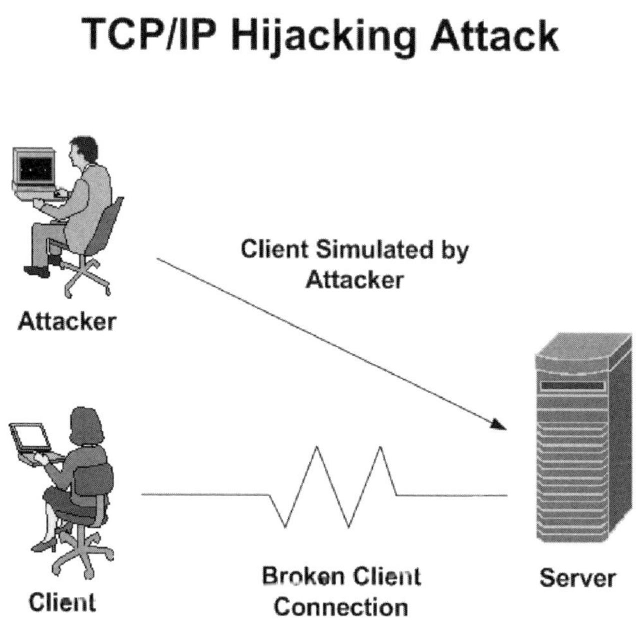

Figure 4.4 *TCP/IP hijacking attack.*

vides an attacker with the opportunity to crack the poorly secured password files and use these passwords to hack into other corporate systems. In some cases, these passwords are encrypted; in other cases, they are plainly visible.

Data Access and Modification

IM programs are no different from any other Internet-enabled software in that they can have bugs that may be exploited by attackers over the Web. Using attacks such as buffer overflows or malformed data packets, an attacker could gain access to a PC on which a vulnerable IM client is installed.

Password Exploitation and Theft

A user must first log in to the IM server before being allowed to chat with other users. One must have a preregistered username and password. A challenge-response mechanism generally verifies the password. The challenge-response method is a fairly secure method for sending a password over an insecure network connection. However, the method is only as secure as the password itself, since the algorithm for calculating the hash remains static. After a successful login, some networks will send the client a cookie. The client can use the cookie to log in to secondary servers to access other services, such as e-mail and games. The cookie will be invalidated when the user disconnects or after a predefined time period has elapsed since last receiving a packet from the client.

IM clients offer the ability to cache previously used passwords. These passwords are generally stored in an obfuscated manner in the registry or a file on the system. Recovering the plain-text password is trivial in these cases [9]. Information needed to recover the password can also be obtained without access to the actual system by sniffing network traffic. The challenge-response mechanism utilized by most IM clients requires a brute force attack. However, passwords with a length up to and including six characters could be easily broken over a weekend using a standard Pentium III 2-GHz CPU [10].

Private IM Exploits and Attacks

Private IM is designed from the ground up with security in mind. Private IM is based on the idea of taking a centralized communications system and making it decentralized. Decentralized systems are easy to abuse, so Private IM was designed from the very beginning to use strong cryptography to keep the system under control. This makes Private IM extremely secure for protecting against both impersonation and eavesdropping risks. Private IM is the most secure text chat system on the Internet. If your attacker only has access to the data traveling over the network, and you check the key signatures of the people you talk to, you can be confident that your Private IM communication is secure. However, if the attacker has not only intercepted the network communication but also has access to the file system or memory of the computer on which Private IM is being run, then Private IM is much more vulnerable to attacks. Some of the exploits and attacks that are of concern to Private IM users are described in the following paragraphs:

Traffic analysis and threats against anonymity: When you send someone a message, you send it to an object on a server that represents that person, and that object will forward it on to the actual user. When someone sends you a message, he or she sends it to an object on a server that represents you, and that object will forward it on to you. If someone has access to the code running the server, he or she can modify it to record the IP addresses of incoming messages (incoming to that server). For incoming messages (incoming for you), you don't have to worry, because you're already hiding behind your server. But if you want the outgoing messages to conceal who you are, you have to devise a system where they get relayed through another server. If you have an adversary who can view all the network traffic, then you are at risk. From the vantage point of either server, it is possible to determine the IP addresses of both people communicating.

Keyboard logger attacks: If the attacker has physical access to the machine and can install or attach a keyboard logger such as an activity monitor or spyware, the user's passphrase can be captured.

Trojan horse attacks: As discussed earlier in this chapter, if the attacker can get you to install a program on your computer, then the program can perform any of the attacks associated with Trojan horses.

Paging file attacks: If the attacker has access to the machine's hard drive and has sufficiently sophisticated knowledge, the user's private key can be recovered from the Windows virtual memory paging file in unencrypted form. This is true even if the hard drive is accessed through the network, such as a network share that is not adequately protected.

Passphrase entropy attacks: Even though Private IM never transmits your private key across the network, if an attacker can get your private key off the disk in its encrypted form, which is encrypted with your passphrase, then the attacker can try to determine the private key by guessing the passphrase, or trying all possible passphrases with a brute-force attack. The passphrase is much easier to break than the private key itself, because text entered by users will have much less entropy (randomness) than the computer-generated key.

Passphrase retrieval (on servers): The passphrase for a server is generated automatically and stored in the machine's registry. If an adversary has access to both the filesystem and the registry of the server, he or she can retrieve the server's private key.

Random number generator attacks: Private IM uses a function in Microsoft's CryptoAPI to seed its random number generator. Since Private IM is accessing its encryption library through the DLL mechanism that is part of Windows, it is possible that an attacker might insert his or her own DLL into the call sequence. This would enable an attacker to intercept all communication between Private IM and the encryption library, including all public and private keys, and passphrases.

4.4.4 As a Spy

As discussed throughout this chapter, the use of IM can put one at risk of having confidential information disclosed. A hacker can obtain passwords, system configuration information, and sensitive files via IM. This data can be stolen without a breach of the actual system and without the knowledge of the IM user. More importantly, the resultant damage due to information disclosure can outweigh the direct damage due to a malicious threat. Other threats are hijacking IM sessions, impersonating other users, maliciously proxying data, sniffing network traffic, password theft, and exporting data via IM, all important assets to a spy who wants to exploit IM.

Unauthorized Disclosure of Information

Since the data that is being transmitted over IM is typically unencrypted, it can be captured using a network sniffer. By using a sniffer, a hacker could sniff the packets from an entire IM session, which, in a corporate environment, may contain proprietary or other confidential information. Network sniffing is not the only method of retrieving sensitive data via IM. IM could also be used as a communication channel to export data found on the system; this is most easily achieved by installing a simple backdoor Trojan horse. For example, if a tool used to retrieve the system information from instant messenger users, such as an IP address retriever, were used together with a backdoor Trojan horse, the hacker could receive a message containing the IP address of an infected user each time the victim comes online. The hacker would then know the IP address of the infected user, even if the user were using dynamic IP addresses. There are many different types of data-stealing Trojan horses available for all of the different IM clients. An attacker could use good social engineering or potentially unrelated exploits to make an unsuspecting user execute the file. The data export Trojan horse finds information on the user's computer and sends it back to the hacker via the IM network. If the attacker steals the password for the user's account, the hacker can have full control over the account when the user logs out.

Identity Theft and Authentication Spoofing

Most consumer IM systems such as AOL, MSN, and Yahoo! allow individuals to create anonymous identities that do not map to e-mail addresses. For example, individuals can create IDs such as JamesRansome or James.Ransome@Elsevier.com, even if these IDs and domains are not owned by that specific individual. This spoofing of identities creates risk to the organization, as enterprise domain names and IDs may be used maliciously, outside of the control of the IT security department. Typically, companies do not have control of their .com corporate namespace on the consumer IM networks and lack enterprise authentication of public IM identities, leaving the authentication of individuals on IM networks to the traditional consumer IM services. This is a risk to companies that want their IT organizations to own their corporate namespace and control how their users are authenticated on the public IM services.

Hijacking and Impersonation

Although there are many ways for a hacker to impersonate other users, the most frequently used attack is typically the stealing of account information from an unsuspecting user. Stolen account information for any instant messenger can be very damaging. The people on the victim's buddy list will trust the hacker. Therefore, it will be easier for the hacker to convince the people on the buddy list to run files on their computers or divulge confidential information. Losing a password for an instant messenger account can therefore be dangerous for more people than just the person who lost the password. To get the account information of a user, the hacker can use a password-stealing Trojan horse. If the password for the IM client is saved on the computer, a hacker could send a Trojan horse to an unsuspecting user. The Trojan horse, when executed, would find the password for the IM account used by the victim and send it back to the hacker. The means for sending back the information to the hacker vary, including using the instant messenger itself, IRC, and e-mail.

Figure 4.5 *Man-in-the-middle attack.*

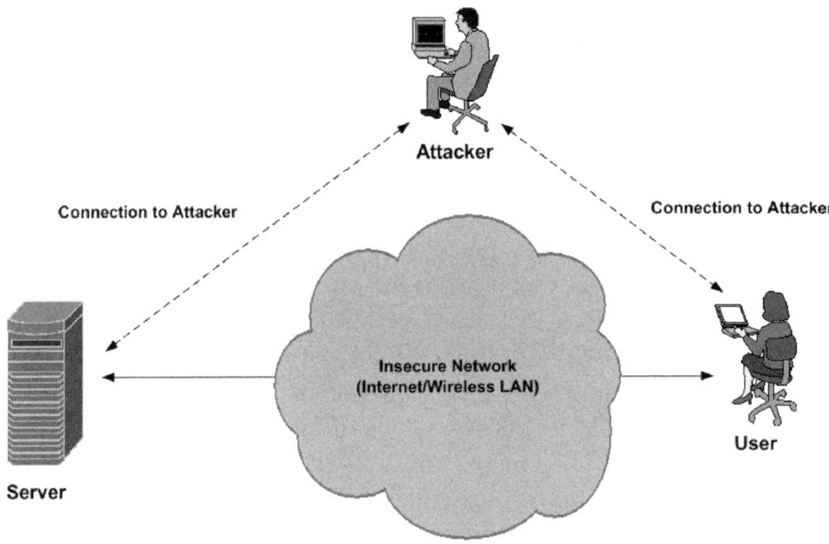

One can hijack an IM connection or impersonate other users in a variety of ways. Some methods are based on the inherently insecure nature of TCP/IP and related protocols, whereas others are specific to the design of the IM protocol. These techniques necessitate that secure IM clients utilize methods of data authentication to ensure that the data truly originates from the supposed source.

Although AIM does have an encryption mode, none of the four public IM providers typically encrypts its network traffic, making it possible to hijack connections via man-in-the-middle attacks. By inserting messages into an ongoing chat session, a hacker could impersonate one of the chatting parties. Though very difficult, one can also highjack the entire connection by using a man-in-the middle attack (Figure 4.5).

In a man-in-the-middle attack scenario, a disconnect message, which appears to come from the server, can be sent to the victim from the hacker. This will cause the client to disconnect. The hacker can also use a simple denial-of-service exploit, or other unrelated exploits, to make the client disconnect. Since the server keeps the connection open and does not know that the client has disconnected, the hacker can then impersonate the victim. Furthermore, since all data is unencrypted and unauthenticated, the hacker can use other classic man-in-the-middle attacks such as ARP spoofing. The goal of performing ARP spoofing is to send fake ARP replies to the LAN. The spoofed Ethernet frame contains an address different from the MAC address belonging to the machine sending the spoofed frame. This confuses network devices, such as switches, and, as a result, frames intended for one machine can be mistakenly sent to another, allowing the packets to be sniffed or creating an unreachable host (denial-of-service) situation.

All data between the IM server and client is unauthenticated. IM traffic is therefore vulnerable to classic TCP/IP man-in-the-middle attacks. For example, a hacker can poison the DNS cache for the user so that the user's computer believes that the hacker's computer is the IM server. When the user attempts to log in to the IM server, he or she is redirected to the hacker's system. The hacker's system simply proxies all the data to the real IM server, but is able to spy on all traffic passing through it and also inject its own messages into the message stream. The hacker effectively has full control over the session and can impersonate the hacker's system to other users and vice versa. Many IM protocols use different servers for user authentication and the actual transmission of chat messages. Such designs allow an instant messenger client to authenticate to a particular server, retrieve a session cookie, and then utilize this session cookie to log in to secondary servers, such as the messaging server. However, if this session cookie is captured via network sniffing, it can be used to impersonate the authenticated user.

4.4.5 As a Zombie Machine

Hackers might simply want to use your machine rather than to gain information on your PC. With the right program installed on your computer, hackers can use your computer to attack other machines on the Internet (i.e., distributed denial-of-service attacks). The victimized machines are called "zombies." If enough zombies are involved, the target servers will be bombarded with so much traffic that they can be slowed to a crawl. Several years ago, Yahoo! was virtually shut down by such an attack. Most people don't know their machines are part of the attack until it's too late.

Denial of Service

As with other communications systems, IM platforms are susceptible to denial-of-service (DoS) attacks. For example, an attacker could send large numbers of specially crafted TCP/IP packets to IM servers residing in the IM provider's infrastructure to prevent legitimate messages from flowing through the system. This method would be similar to the denial-of-service attacks launched on major Internet properties in the last few years. Alternatively, an attacker could send large numbers of packets to a specific user or set of users to flood them with chat or file transfer requests. These attacks may have different end results: Some DoS attacks make the IM client crash,

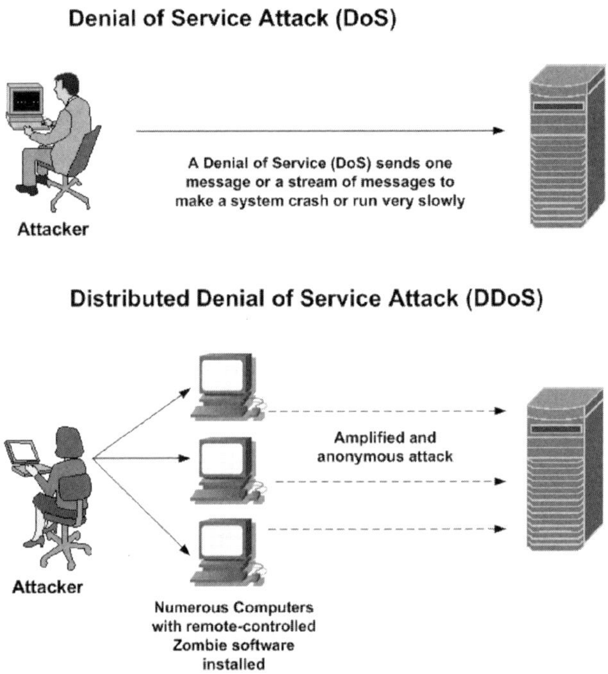

Figure 4.6 *Denial-of-service and distributed denial-of-service.*

others will make the client hang, and in some cases will consume a large amount of CPU power, causing the entire computer to become unstable.

There are many ways in which a hacker can cause a denial of service on an instant messenger client. One common type of attack is flooding a particular user with a large number of messages. Most of the popular IM clients contain protection against flood attacks by allowing the victim to ignore certain users. However, many tools allow the hacker to use many accounts simultaneously or automatically create a large number of accounts to accomplish the flood attack. Even though denial-of-service attacks are more of an annoyance than they are dangerous, they can be used in combination with other attacks, such as the hijacking of a connection (see Figure 4.6).

Backdoor Trojan Horses

A handful of Trojan horse programs target IM. Some modify configuration settings so file sharing is enabled for the entire hard drive. These types of Trojan horses pose a large threat, as they allow anyone full file access to the computer. There are also classic backdoor Trojan horses that utilize instant messengers to send messages to the author of the Trojan horse, giving the hacker information about the infected computer. This information includes things such as the IP address of the infected computer and the number of the port that has been opened. Backdoor Trojan horses that allow file access to the computer by utilizing instant messenger clients may be harder to discover than classic backdoor Trojan horses. Classic backdoor Trojan horses open a listening or outgoing port on the computer, forming a connection with a remote machine. These Trojan horses can effectively be blocked by a desktop firewall. However, if the backdoor Trojan horse operates via the IM client, it does not open a new port and thus is not blocked by traditional desktop firewall products. As a result, the user has generally already created an allow rule in his or her desktop firewall products for IM traffic to be outbound from the machine, thereby allowing the backdoor Trojan horse using the same channel to go unblocked. The number of backdoor Trojan horses utilizing instant messengers is increasing steadily.

Backdoor Trojan horses use the same techniques as those utilized by IM worms, but instead of sending themselves (replicating), backdoor Trojan horses export sensitive information or wait for specific messages to arrive, instructing them to perform a malicious action. In addition, this unauthorized remote access is not blocked by a firewall, since IM communication has already been permitted. A backdoor Trojan can modify configuration settings of the IM client, allowing unauthorized remote access, and can enable the hacker to modify settings to enable file serving on the entire drive, effectively giving the hacker remote read and write access to sensitive materials.

One can share every file on a person's computer using an instant messenger. All the popular instant messengers have file-sharing capabilities or the ability to add such functionality by applying patches or plug-ins. The benefit for a hacker using an instant messenger to access files on a remote computer instead of installing a backdoor Trojan horse is that even if the computer is using a dynamic IP address, the screen name will probably never change. Furthermore, the hacker will receive a notification each time the victim computer is online. This will make it much easier for the hacker to keep track of and access infected computers. In addition, the hacker does not need to open a new suspicious port for communication but does so via already open IM ports.

4.4.6 As an Anonymizer

IM communication normally provides complete anonymity, allowing users to hide their real identity; users can interact with and get to know people regardless of their location and without ever having to meet them in person. Most consumer IM systems such as AOL, MSN, and Yahoo! allow individuals to create anonymous identities that do not map to e-mail addresses. For example, individuals can create IDs, even if these IDs and domains are not owned by that specific individual. Enterprise domain names and IDs may also be spoofed and used maliciously, creating risk to the organization and outside of the control of the IT security department. Companies typically lack ownership and control of their corporate namespace on the consumer IM networks. This problem is exacerbated by the lack of enterprise control of the authentication of public IM identities and how their users are authenticated on the public IM services.

As a Distributed Resource

Any information a user chooses to publish to his or her peers on the Internet can be collected for other purposes. Often, users of IM on the Internet have no desire for their transactions to be identifiable or traceable and desire anonymity in their transactions. Though anonymous entities cannot participate in relationship-based network services, they can post responses to weblog entries and engage in conversations with others. This is an essential feature of any distributed IM software implementation (Figure 4.6). Operating anonymously in a social software environment does not preclude operating identifiably; however, there is no requirement that implementors of distributed IM software interfaces accommodate anonymous behavior. Although the distributed nature and anonymous communication capabilities of IM have many advantages that are discussed elsewhere in this book, they can also be advantageous for nefarious activities, such as identity spoofing, hijacking, and the anonymous staging and enhancement of distributed attacks.

SPIM (Spam over Instant Messaging)

Spam spread over IM (SPIM) is similar to e-mail spam in that it usually has a URL embedded in it for the same reasons as e-mail spam: to get the user to vist the spammer's Web site, tout pornography or fast-money schemes, and include a link to a Web site. Following a link in a SPIM message can trigger a myriad of other privacy and security problems. For example, users may get swamped with pop-up ads, spyware and Trojan horses may install themselves on their PCs, and download of destructive viruses can occur. SPIM can be even more intrusive than spam, because, just like a regular IM message, SPIM can pop up in a chat window on top of whatever you're working on at the time. Although all major IM packages let you limit or eliminate SPIM, the settings that block it require you to make some tradeoffs. Messages from people not on your contact list will be blocked.

You will still be able to add users to your buddy list, but it will take a few more mouse clicks.

Malware and SPAM/SPIM are working together in a vicious cycle. Attackers use spam to spread backdoors to machines via mass e-mailings. Unwitting users execute these e-mail attachments, thereby installing the backdoor onto their systems. Attackers then use the newly infected system as a bounce-off point to send even more SPIM while laundering their buddy lists and evading e-mail server antirelay and filter settings.

4.5 Summary

Since more people currently use e-mail than IM, it is unlikely that IM will exceed e-mail as the primary vector of malware infection in the near future. The major IM networks still use proprietary protocols, so a worm that spreads via one service, such as MSN Messenger, will not affect users of another service, such as Yahoo! Messenger. However, if clients become interoperable, or users primarily utilize one network, instant-messaging worms may become more widespread. Worms are nondiscriminate and target all computer systems of a particular network. The number of worms for IM is increasing each month, and, looking at the success of some of these worms, IM is clearly an up and coming platform for malware and other security threats, with many exploits available for the various clients. Security professionals and end users need to be aware of the security issues involved with IM. The best way to ensure the security of IM services is to educate users of the risks involved and the means of mitigating those risks, preferably before a serious incident occurs.

4.6 Endnotes

1. Akonix. (2004). "Security." Retrieved December 21, 2004 from http://www.akonix.com/solutions/security.asp.
2. http://www.pcaob.com
3. D. Connor. (November 3, 2003). "Challenges abound archiving company e-mail." Retrieved December 22, 2004 from http://www.nwfusion.com/news/2003/1103specialfocus.html
4. Wikpedia. (2004). "Malware." Retrieved on December 22, 2004 from http://en.wikipedia.org/wiki/Malware.
5. Symantec. (2003). *Symantec Internet Security Threat Report Sees Increase in Blended Threats, Vulnerabilities and Internet Attacks.*

Retrieved January 25, 2005 from http://quickstart.clari.net/qs_se/webnews/wed/bu/Bca-symantec.RFTE_DO1.html

6. L. Cassovoy. (June 2004). *Viruses Target IM*. Retrieved on December 22, 2004 from http://www.pcworld.com/reviews/article/0,aid,115837,src,ov,00.asp

7. *Communication of the ACM*, Vol. 27, No. 8, August 1984, pp. 761-763. Copyright © 1984, Association for Computing Machinery, Inc. Also appears in *ACM Turing Award Lectures: The First Twenty Years 1965-1985,* Copyright © 1987 by the ACM Press and *Computers Under Attack: Intruders, Worms, and Viruses*, Copyright © 1990 by the ACM Press.

8. Ibid.

9. *CIAC bulletin* E-12; March 18, 1994

10. N. Hinocha and E. Chien. (2003). *Malicious Threats and Vulnerabilities in Instant Messaging*. Retrieved December 22, 2004 from http://securityresponse.symantec.com/avcenter/reference/malicious.threats.instant.messaging.pdf#search='Malicious%20Threats%20and%20Vulnerabilities%20in%20Instant%20Messaging'

5

IM Security for Enterprise and Home

As discussed in the previous chapters, many of the current IM systems have inadequate security and can expose your enterprise to serious breaches. Because the adoption of IM in the enterprise accelerated through public IM networks such as AOL, MSN, and Yahoo!, IM usage has grown under the radar, unmonitored and uncontrolled. As an enterprise-class solution, however, IM must be managed and controlled as a mission-critical service, in much the same way as telecom, e-mail, and Web access. In spite of this, IM systems are rapidly working their way into corporations because of their efficiency and convenience and are now an enterprise-wide business requirement.

IT organizations are now challenged to balance IM's inherent productivity enhancements with secure management, which ensures alignment with company policy for security, corporate accountability, and regulatory compliance. Deploying an enterprise-wide IM solution to address the inherent security and legal risks associated with this form of communication is a significant challenge. The key challenge in regard to IM security is how to balance your organization's short-term needs to get IM under control with longer-term objectives of building a scalable, reliable, enterprise-class IM infrastructure that will enable you to embrace and leverage IM throughout your business (see Figure 5.1).

Many IT organizations have deployed IM management systems, such as IMlogic IM Manager, to manage, control, and secure IM usage. Leveraging integration with existing best-of-breed offerings from security, management, and compliance archiving vendors, IMlogic IM Manager enables enterprises to embrace IM as a productivity-enhancing communications tool while mitigating the management, security, and compliance risk associated with this form of communication.

The easiest way to mitigate the IM risk is just to shut down the default IM ports, which in theory will prevent users from installing and using

Figure 5.1 *Balancing business needs with security risk management.*

public IM services. As discussed previously, this is not only impractical for business reasons but also because some IM clients, such as Yahoo! Instant Messenger, for example, were designed to prevent blocking and will automatically attempt to connect to nonblocked port numbers, including port 23, which is used for Telnet and is rarely blocked. Most other public IM services allow the use of a proxy server, so chances are if an employee really wants to be able to use IM, he or she will find a way to get around blocked ports.

The use of an acceptable use policy (AUP), signed by the employee indicating that he or she agrees to the employer's stipulations about which IM service is allowed to be used, which corporate screen name should be used, and which kind of content is allowed to be shared in an IM, is another option by which to manage the security of IM in your enterprise. Violation of this policy-based management technique would be considered grounds for dismissal. This method of security presents the same compliance monitoring challenges that are currently being faced at enterprise-level Web activity AUP monitoring.

Another alternative to mitigate the risk of enterprise IM use is the deployment and management of an enterprise-class IM service. In this option, you can outsource your IM to a third-party service provider, purchasing IM software that can reside on your current communications server, or maintain a dedicated IM server. As IM usage grows, many organizations look to adopt a standardized enterprise IM system such as those available from IBM, Microsoft, and others. However, current enterprise IM systems do not interoperate with other IM systems or with the consumer IM networks. While enterprises will want to standardize on a controlled system, connectivity with customers and partners remains an important reason for the wide adoption of IM today.

Whichever solution, or combination of solutions, you choose to secure IM at the enterprise level, it must be able to secure and protect both outbound and inbound security threats. The enterprise security solution must also be cost effective to deploy and integrate seamlessly into the complex enterprise IT environment. Enterprise-class IM management has the flexibility to integrate with best-of-breed or corporate-standard security products. This requires critical security functionality, including IM security management tools that capture and deliver content to third-party solutions for logging, archiving, antivirus and antispam solutions, content filtering solutions, secure sign-on, digital signatures, and encryption, as well as providing users with the ability to log on to the system, including IM, with one user name and one password. These solutions also need to be able to leverage existing LDAP or Active Directory (AD) directories to identify and define users and groups and to create IM management policies that are then easy to administer. Automatic directory update capability ensures that the IM logging stays in sync with changes. These integration points enable IM to be run as an enterprise-level service without requiring significant new IT investment.

Even if your organization deploys an enterprise IM system internally, such as Microsoft Office Live Communications Server or IBM Lotus IM and Web Conferencing, communication across the firewall requires use of the public networks. Enterprise-class IM management supports IM on multiple platforms, including AOL, MSN, Yahoo!, and IBM, so employees can reach key business contacts regardless of network. Unfortunately, this also provides a significant threat and very attractive medium for a fast, ubiquitous, and scalable way to distribute malware across multiple organizations. IM is a conduit in and out of an organization and needs to be secured. Organizations are challenged to ensure security, compliance, and policy management through centralized deployment and management for both internal and external IM usage. We will discuss methods that enterprise-class IM management can use to protect the organization with comprehensive policy enforcement and technical solutions to stop viruses, block

SPIM (Spam over IM), filter IM content, control file transfer, and allow usage to be controlled for individuals and for groups through identity management. Identity management restricts the use of the organization's domain name to authorized employees, mapping IM identities to corporate names and preventing identity theft. We will also discuss the methods by which to secure the home use of IM. The security of home machines using IM should also be a critical piece of your security plan, not only for protection of your personal information at home but also because many home machines are also portals to a corporate network. You are only as strong as your weakest link, so it is important to address security holistically from the entire enterprise, the network edge, remote access, and to the home.

5.1 How Can IM Be Used Safely in Corporate Settings?

For the most part, IM technology had penetrated the workplace before IT and business guidelines, security, and monitoring tools could be set to monitor and regulate its use to protect the enterprise from a myriad of security risks. Whether an organization continues to employ popular free IM services or deploys a secure, corporate-focused IM solution within the company network and layers suitable security systems on top of this solution such as antivirus, firewalls, and vulnerability management, it needs to understand the associated security risks and plan appropriately. A security strategy for IM lies in leveraging the fact that the IM clients will use sophisticated techniques to establish a connection with the IM service. As we have discussed, trying to block the attempt to connect will most likely be futile, becoming an all-or-nothing situation. Assuming you have chosen to allow the use of IM as part of your corporate communications solution, you must deploy a mechanism that actually allows the IM client to connect through to the IM service. Once the connection is established, you can then control and manage the connection.

5.1.1 Understanding IM and Corporate Firewalls

Out-of-the-box firewall configurations are often not sufficient to block access to the latest generation of popular IM systems. Recent IM systems were designed with firewalls in mind, and the systems employ a number of techniques to sneak past corporate firewalls to reach their servers. To block IM clients in your corporation, you must prevent them from reaching their IM server and must add either the server address name(s) or the server IP address(es) to the firewall block list for every IM service that is to be blocked. Given that some IM systems (such as IRC) can connect to multi-

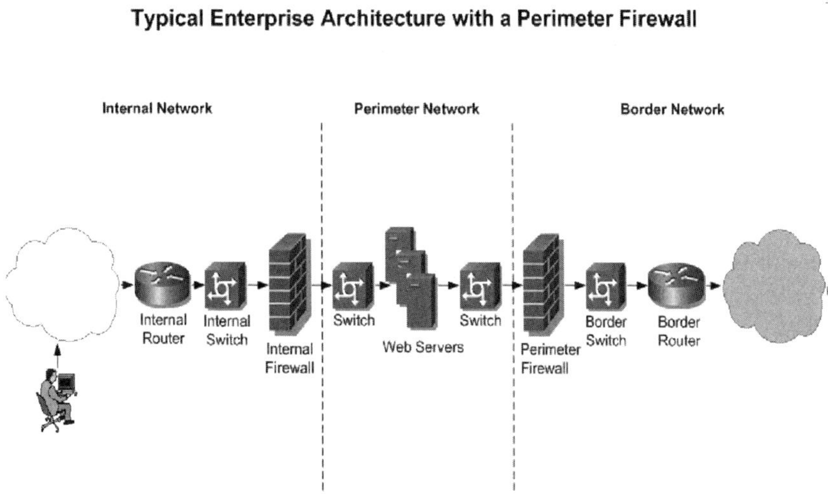

Figure 5.2 *An illustration of a typical firewall architecture in an enterprise.*

ple independent servers, blocking these systems requires a fair amount of research; however, this is the only way to achieve the desired results with any certainty.

Perimeter firewalls are used to block all nonapproved IM systems and use firewall rules to block both messaging and file transfers. Organizations can configure their perimeter firewalls to block all Internet services except for a small critical set (i.e., SMTP e-mail, HTTP Web surfing, and DNS). This limitation has led IM providers to design their IM clients to tunnel over these commonly allowed Internet services, which lets the IM client slip past the corporate firewall.

Firewall rules are used to block access to all popular IM servers and, when not feasible, the firewall is configured to block commonly used IM port numbers from all clients on the network. This will still permit properly configured IM clients to tunnel through the firewall, so you must identify the port number(s) used for peer-to-peer file transfers by each IM product and configure the firewall to block all communications over those ports to block file transfers.

Although a firewall can be very effective at blocking incoming connections and rogue outgoing connections, it can be particularly challenging because IM traffic frequently connects to commonly allowed destination ports such as HTTP (port 80). Also, popular clients will use the following default destination ports: AOL Instant Messenger (port 5190), ICQ (port 5190), MSN Messenger (port 1863), and Yahoo! Instant Messenger (port 5050). Unfortunately, if these ports are blocked, the IM clients will attempt connections on common destination ports such as telnet (23), FTP (20/21), SMTP (25), POP (110), and NNTP (119), which are typically enough to bypass a corporate firewall. By default, protocol analysis firewalls block this type of traffic, because IM traffic does not match the protocol typically utilized on that particular port (e.g., IM traffic does not resemble SMTP e-mail traffic). If a client is unable to access the IM server via a common destination port due to protocol analysis, IM traffic can instead be tunneled via HTTP (80). Typically, IM packets are embedded into an HTTP POST request and thus can bypass both types of firewalls, since the IM traffic will appear to them to be a standard POST request. To block this type of IM traffic, you have to block by domain name or IP address. For example, the following domain names are used for popular IM clients at login:

- AOL IM (login.oscar.aol.com, aimexpress.oscar.aol.com)
- ICQ (login.icq.com)
- MSN Messenger (messenger.hotmail.com, gateway.messenger.hotmail.com, login net.passport.com)
- Yahoo! IM (scs.msg.yahoo.com, scsb.msg.yahoo.com, scsc.msg.yahoo.com, scs.yahoo.com, shttp.msg.yahoo.com).

There are still more challenges to overcome, because these domains may be changed at any time and consist of a range of IP addresses; these domains may also translate into the same set of IP addresses.

Desktop firewalls must also be considered as part of the complete corporate firewall solution. The use of centrally managed desktop firewalls can effectively block IM via a "white list." Desktop firewall applications can match network traffic to the calling application, and the white list would allow certain applications, such as Internet Explorer, but would deny all other applications network access, including IM clients. Furthermore, if the client ever connects to a dispatch server, it will cache its IP address. For example, with laptops, traveling employees who connect when the machine is outside the corporate network, once they connect successfully, will have a cached IP address to connect with.

Even when a client has no direct access to the Internet, it will be able to connect to the service via HTTP. All of the popularly available IM clients have the facility to "simulate" a TCP connection to the service via HTTP,

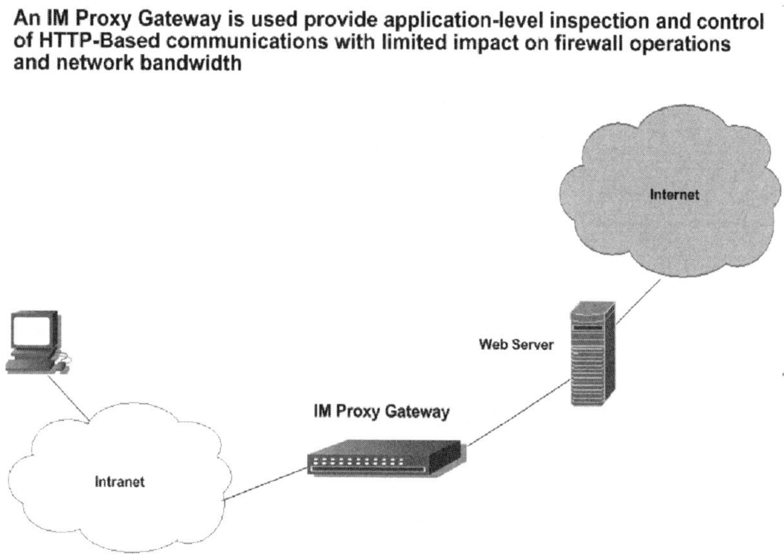

Figure 5.3 *An IM proxy.*

because enterprise desktop clients typically do not have direct access to the Internet on any port. Most desktops have access to the Web (via a Web Proxy Server) and connect to the service using HTTP (see Figure 5.3).

As a stateless protocol, HTTP poses some challenges as a replacement for a TCP connection. The service can no longer use the client's TCP session and can no longer be used by the IM service as an indicator of the client's last known presence status. For example, if the user sets presence to "available" after logging on using an HTTP message, the service has no way of knowing that the user's status has become stale and incorrect after his or her computer is turned off. In general, the service also has no way of delivering it to the client, because the client is behind a firewall and will not be reachable from the Internet. Polling is used to solve these two problems, because when a client uses HTTP to simulate TCP, it periodically refreshes the user's presence status and periodically polls the service for inbound messages.

5.1.2 Understanding IM File Transfers and Corporate Firewalls

IM services provide the easiest file transfer capability across firewalls. This causes increased vulnerability due to file transfer capabilities of IM services. A key advantage of file transfers over IM instead of file exchanges over e-mail is that file exchanges over e-mail are dependent on the recipient's mailbox storage quota. In the world of ever-increasing file sizes and the pressure on containing e-mail administration costs, which often translate to strict limits on mailbox storage quotas, many users find that file transfer over IM is a markedly more reliable way to exchange files. IM systems allow users to exchange files with each other, typically in an unencrypted form, which can cause the spread of traditional viruses, worms, and Trojan horses, as well as blended threats, since file transfers over IM are not scanned. As of this writing, no security vendor offers effective or mature gateway scanning solutions that scan IM file transfers as they pass through the corporate firewall. Therefore, the best protection against any threats spread through IM file transfers is to deploy up-to-date antivirus software on all client desktops.

5.1.3 Blocking and Proxying Instant Messaging

IM clients connect to the IM service on the Internet, but the service never needs to connect to the client. IM clients also simulate a TCP connection over HTTP by polling for presence and messages. IM clients connect to a set of servers known as dispatch servers, and their number and IP addresses grow constantly, almost on a daily basis, which makes it easy to understand why IM clients almost always manage to punch through and connect to the service on the Internet, and why it is very difficult to block IM clients from connecting to their servers. As long as access to the Web is allowed, even if via a Web Proxy Server, the typical IM client will be able to successfully connect to the service. Since the connection (whether direct or via HTTP) is made to one of a set of servers whose numbers grow and IP addresses change on a regular basis, an attempt to block IM by specifically blocking a set of URLs and IP addresses at both the firewall and HTTP servers, if implemented in isolation, will prove to be challenging.

One of the biggest challenges of managing the security of IM is that blocking has proven to be an ineffective strategy for enterprises when it comes to IM and that firewall administrators and others charged with security enforcement often end up blocking legitimate IM usage and allowing unauthorized IM usage to continue. The management of the set of URLs and IP addresses to block can be a management nightmare. If the URLs and IP addresses are for the log-in servers, the client will only go to the HTTP cloud if its other connection attempts fail in a managed environment; it will always go to the set of well-known log-in servers. The URLs and IP addresses of these servers rarely change.

An effective way to block IM is to allow the connection to go through, and then intercept and reject the user log-in packet. The rejection will appear to be a normal failed log-in to the IM client. You can also allow the login packet to go through and intercept all message packets and reject them with a warning to the user that IM use was disallowed. An application-level proxy server can be used for the function in that it allows the initial TCP connection to go through and then rejects logins/messages/file transfers and so on based on policies determined by the IT manager. An application-level proxy is also capable of scanning messages for URLs containing viruses and for scanning file transfers for viruses. IM clients will try to connect using native TCP, even if they are manually configured to use an HTTP proxy. This is because IM over native TCP is a far superior user experience than a polling-based HTTP mechanism; IM clients are designed to be extremely user friendly, so that a client on a laptop of a traveling person can be expected to be used both with and without the proxy. IM clients will try the native connection first in the event that the proxy server is not available, which is why, even if they are configured to use HTTP proxy servers, the IM client will actually end up going through IM Manager, where IM use is managed at an application level.

A knowledgeable and persistent user could force the IM client to use an HTTP proxy server by creating a hosts file on the local machine that has a bogus address for the well-known DNS names that the IM client will attempt to connect with. This could force the native TCP connection attempt by the IM client to fail and fall back to use of an HTTP proxy server. This is why the use of an IM Manager should also be combined with the blocking of a set of HTTP URLs and IP addresses that are an approved partner of the major networks. These specific URLs can then be blocked using the existing Web Proxy Servers at the enterprise.

Once you have developed a good security policy and implemented and deployed the appropriate security practices and solutions, you need to deploy an audit tool that will monitor compliance and detect if any IM traffic is leaking out without going through a management and control tool. This tool should allow the IT or security managers to monitor all network traffic and alert them to any possible attempts to bypass the security system in place. A report containing the address of the offending desktop's IP address allows the IT manager to quickly isolate the source and take corrective steps. Ideally, this tool should sniff network traffic, as opposed to introducing itself into the IP traffic route, but, when necessary, have the capability of hijacking the TCP connection used by the offending IM client and aborting it, thus blocking the IM client.

Third-party proxies are used to forward traffic to the official IM server. Even if the appropriate domains are blocked, some IM clients can still access the IM servers via an unblocked proxy. These proxy domain names

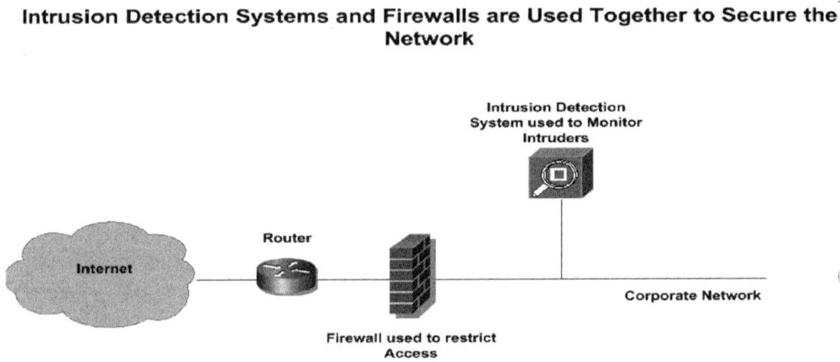

Figure 5.4 *IDS and firewall deployment.*

and IP addresses change regularly, and keeping up with them requires a great deal of vigilance in monitoring and analysis of firewall logs and appropriate blocking. To be effective, a corporate proxy will prevent access to other proxies and should be configured to block the ability to connect to the public IM servers, combined with blocking at the firewall to effectively prevent IM risks, and forcing employees to use the company proxy by blocking all other inappropriate outgoing Web traffic.

5.1.4 IM Detection Tools

Unauthorized IM traffic can be identified by network Intrusion Detection Systems (IDS). Intrusion detection signatures can detect worms, blended threats, and hacking attempts on IM clients. Network intrusion detection systems are used to detect malformed or suspicious packets as they travel through the network (see Figure 5.4).

Because the IM protocols are well understood, extraordinarily long packets or byte sequences, often used in buffer overflows, can easily be distinguished from legitimate traffic. Intrusion detection systems for use against IM threats are still relatively immature, and well-crafted exploits are less likely to be detected generically, so the detection of new exploits will often require creation of a specific signature. As with other security technology, network intrusion detection systems will mature over time to support anomaly detection specific to IM traffic.

5.2 Legal Risk and Corporate Governance

The need to comply with legal and corporate accountability standards, such as those required by the Securities and Exchange Commission (SEC), National Association of Securities Dealers (NASD), and the Health Information Portability and Accountability Act (HIPAA), is driving the search for an enterprise-class IM management solution by corporations to provide corporate governance and mitigate legal risk. For example, SEC Rules 17a-3 and 17a-4 state that instant messages are characterized as a "book or record" to be retained as an "Internet communication" [1]; NASD Rules 3010 and 2210 state that firms must maintain a "system to supervise and review" IM conversations and demonstrate compliance procedures for "electronic correspondence" [2]; and in NYSE Rules 440 and 342 in NYSE Information Memo #03-7, "IM is explicitly outlined in a type of communication that must be archived under SEC regulations" [3].

The challenges with managing IM are about more than just logging and archiving, because even industries that are not bound to regulatory compliance must provide corporate governance to conform to legal and ethical restrictions while conducting business. Another challenge is to apply, monitor, and ensure compliance of an organization's corporate communications policies to IM. IM faces the same retention requirements as e-mail and other messaging, which requires all IM to be tracked across public, hosted, and enterprise IM networks.

Financial services firms are subject to regulatory rules restricting inter-employee communications and external public communications in order to control the disclosure of inside information. For example, IM conversations in the financial services industry are generally accepted as a form of "electronic messaging" and face the same retention requirements as e-mail and other text messaging, as well as the appropriate compliance archiving and review (CAR). For example, recent regulations that highlight the need for and enforcement of a corporate communication policy for IM include the Sarbanes-Oxley Act [4], which restricts employee communications when firms undertake both "buy-side" and "sell-side" activities, and Selective Disclosure (Regulation FD), which requires that firms keep control over the communication and distribution of nonpublic information [5].

Regulatory requirements typically require audit trail systems to ensure that your compliance reviewers are satisfying compliance procedures, the generation of reports to demonstrate your "system to supervise and review" and keep a record of your compliance review, and the ability to append custom disclaimers for all IM conversations to disclose IM monitoring and archiving within your company. All of these requirements can be quite challenging to even the best-managed companies.

5.2.1 Legal Issues with Monitoring IM Traffic

There are quite a few laws that require you to protect the privacy of an individual and also maintain the proper records that can track the trail of individual transactions, such as the Health Information Portability and Accountability Act (HIPAA) and the Privacy Act. Monitoring IM usage could go against the individual's right to privacy, and the open nature and lack of controls of IM can lead to unauthorized or inadvertent exposure of controlled privacy information, which can result in monetary fines and lawsuits.

As discussed in the previous section, there are various regulatory requirements for corporations to keep logs of account activities. Insecure IM sessions, unauthorized use of IM, and the lack of log records and monitoring of IM sessions will translate into lack of such required procedures. In many cases, IM is new to an organization and the organization lacks the infrastructure to maintain and create such procedures, which could result in a lawsuit against an organization that fails to maintain such procedures. The potential of employees swapping copyrighted material over an employer's IM network also exposes the employer to copyright-related lawsuits or fines. IM has made it easy for employees to download copyrighted materials such as music from the Internet and then turn around and send the same file to a friend over IM.

5.3 Corporate IM Security Best Practices

Organizations should balance the legitimate need for IM and the dangers inherent in its use, minimizing their risk with a basic set of security policies. The single most effective method of minimizing risk is to have a corporate policy restricting the use of IM, in addition to the variety of products that can assist in minimizing the risk of infection from malicious threats or information disclosure discussed previously in this book.

You should determine whether IM is a business necessity, weighing the business necessity against the potential risk of information disclosure or infection from malicious threats before even considering the development of an IM security policy. In general, you should standardize on a particular IM client, and, if the client does not support enterprise features such as central logging and encryption, then strict rules should be enforced regarding the usage of the client. In particular, the use of IM to discuss any business matters should be prohibited. Additionally, nicknames should not reflect their association with the corporation. These requirements may make IM almost useless for pure business communication. File sharing should be blocked, and even potential incoming file transfers should be regulated. If incoming file transfers are required, users should be educated on the policies of accepting and executing unknown files that arrive via IM. A password policy should exist for complex passwords of at least eight characters in length (the longer the better) and passwords should not be cached. Finally, an IM system that can be locked down should be your first choice—in other words, a system where an administrator can install and configure the IM client according to prescribed policy. At this point, the establishment and enforcement of a corporate policy will go a long way toward minimizing the risk of IM at minimal cost.

5.3.1 Start from the Firewall

From a security perspective, the first thing you should do after establishing the need for IM in your enterprise is to evaluate IM use outside the corporate firewall (e.g., determining the extent to which employees are communicating with others outside the corporate firewall using IM). This should assess the communications requirements with customers, prospects, business partners, investors, and other constituents. As will be discussed later, other ROI business needs, strategic objectives, and requirements, such as enhancing employee productivity and improving customer communications, should be assessed during this evaluation.

5.3.2 Consider the Desktop

Desktop firewalls must be considered when developing corporate IM policy and compliance. Desktop firewalls can be configured to prevent uncertified/unapproved programs, including unapproved IM products, from communicating over the Internet and can provide far more granular protection than a perimeter firewall. The perimeter firewall can provide only a blanket policy for the entire machine, while the desktop firewall can be configured to permit or deny communications on a per-program basis; IM can be controlled as a client/server solution at the individual desktop level through the use of an IM Policy Manager. One advantage of controlling and managing IM use at the desktop is that instant messages encrypted on public network systems can only be read by IM management systems with control of the users' desktops. Tracking and searching capabilities will not be provided by proxy gateway solutions, because when the data is encrypted and captured on the gateway servers, it is not in a format that can be searched.

5.3.3 Install Patches to IM Software ASAP

IM patches and fixes should be installed by system administrators as soon as possible, especially when holes or bugs are found in corporate IM systems. CodeRed, Nimda, and even the Internet worm of 1988 used known holes to spread to new systems, for which aggressive patching or applied mitigation fixes would have significantly limited, if not stopped, the damage done by the malware.

5.3.4 Enforce Client-Side IM Settings

An IM client should be configured so that it will accept chat requests only from users specified in employees' buddy lists; only those users explicitly specified by employees should be able to contact them. In addition, the IM system should be configured to either block file transfers or allow such transfers only from users specified on the buddy list. This prevents attackers from connecting to computers on the network and sending malicious code. If this is not feasible, configure the IM software to prompt the employee before all file transfers. If supported, the IM system should also be configured to use antivirus software to scan all file transfers. To prevent unsolicited chat requests, all the IM accounts should be configured such that they are not listed on public servers and do not use any external IM system that does not employ a certified encryption system.

5.3.5 IM Proxy Gateways

A viable option to control unauthorized IM use is the implementation of a proxy gateway solution, such as IM Manager from IMlogic, Akonix Systems L7 Enterprise, or IM Director from FaceTime Communications, Inc. IM gateways allow a company's IT staff to control and manage the use of public IM systems within the organization, which means employees can continue using their current, familiar IM clients and, thus, their existing IM networks and contact lists. When a messaging infrastructure is hosted by a public network provider such as AOL, MSN, or Yahoo!, gateways can provide many of the capabilities available with in-house enterprise IM (EIM) solutions at a fraction of their cost. They act as a proxy, intercepting all IM traffic, including logons, conversations, file transfers, and logging and approving those communications. By interceding, the IM proxy is able to examine and apply controls to the IM traffic to and from that user. In this way, IM gateways can then enforce a number of additional safeguards on messaging activity, such as implementing virus scanning on received

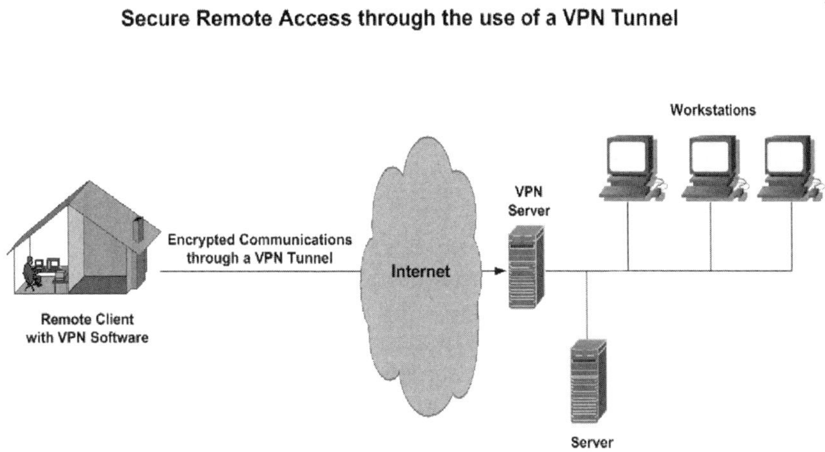

Figure 5.5 *Use of a VPN to obtain secure remote access.*

files, blocking specific users from chatting externally or at all, and even applying content filtering.

Content filtering is of special interest to enterprises concerned about compliance issues or protecting sensitive corporate information from leaving the company. IM proxies also have reporting and logging systems, allowing administrators and managers to review IM conversations and monitor productivity, violation of personal use policies, and ensure that disclosure and industry regulations are being followed. As with any other form of communications monitoring, the use of IM gateways can be invisible to the user, or the systems often can display warning notifications that users' conversations could be logged.

5.3.6 VPNs

By logging in to IM networks from lesser-protected home machines, employees make the entire corporate network more vulnerable to malicious hackers who attempt to propagate viruses and code through IM Virtual Private Networks (VPNs). If use of IM is to be selectively allowed, IM needs to be restricted to secured desktops and only authorized users. The use of IM by authorized corporate users from home desktops VPN'd in to a corporate network must be managed and controlled separately from the internal corporate network (see Figure 5.5).

5.3.7 Antivirus

Personal firewalls should be configured to prevent uncertified and unapproved programs, including unapproved IM products, from communicating over the Internet. Because America Online, Yahoo!, and Microsoft frequently change the protocols for their consumer IM products, administrators have their hands full trying to block IM traffic at the firewall. Desktop firewalls can provide more protection than a perimeter firewall, because the desktop firewall can be configured to permit or deny communications on a per-program basis. Because current corporate firewalls are unable to scan IM file transfers for computer viruses, worms, and Trojan horses, roll out up-to-date antivirus protection on all desktops, desktop antivirus protection is currently the last and only line of defense against IM-delivered malicious code.

Currently, some antivirus programs hook into popular IM clients as a plug-in. The IM client will pass files to the antivirus plug-in for scanning prior to notifying the user that the file has arrived. The antivirus program does not scan all IM traffic, but rather just the files that are transferred via IM. Thus, some types of blended threats or hack attempts will not be detected by such an antivirus plug-in. Antivirus products that scan specifically for IM threats at the gateway currently do not exist but are in development. Solutions will plug in to existing proxies that recognize IM traffic, or the antivirus solution itself will proxy IM traffic. Files and other IM traffic between users in a single corporation will often occur as a direct connection and do not pass through a gateway; therefore, antivirus protection at the client level will always be required. While IM antivirus solutions for corporate servers are still in their infancy, development in this area is ongoing and several solutions are already on the horizon. Servers currently proxy IM traffic, although transfers may still occur directly between users and are an ideal tier for antivirus scanning to take place. In the future, antivirus solutions will also plug in to enterprise IM servers scanning for potentially malicious content.

5.3.8 Set up Containment Wards

Private corporate IM servers should be deployed to isolate corporate messaging systems, with all IM clients configured to connect to these servers. The deployment of one or more IM servers within the corporate network to ensure that all internal IM communications are kept behind the corporate firewall is a valuable practice (see Figure 5.6).

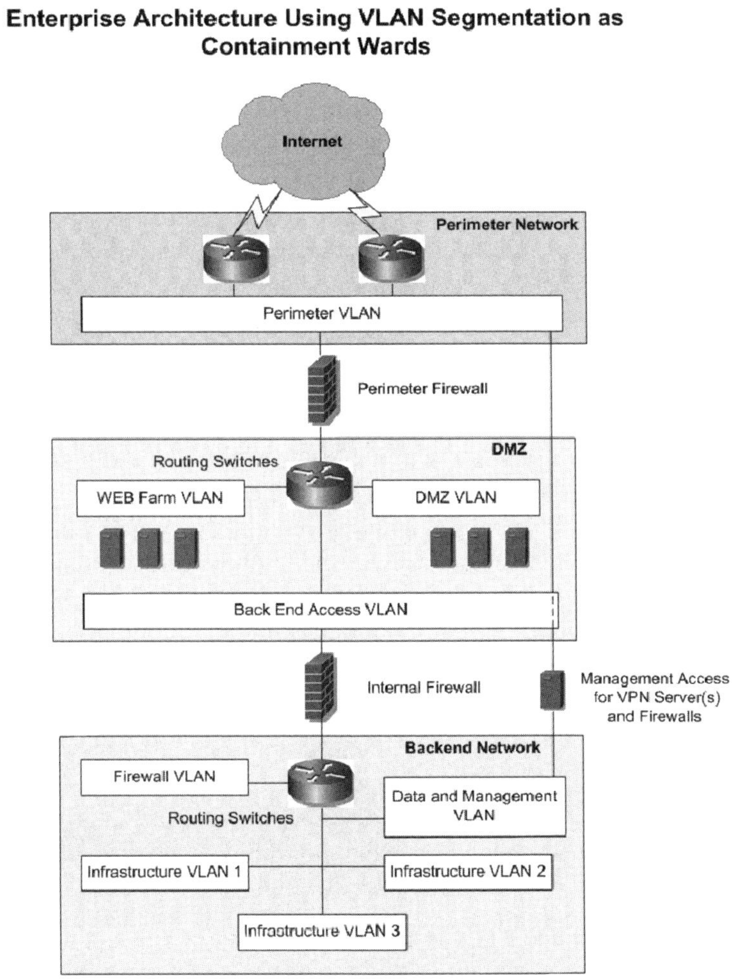

Figure 5.6 *Setting up containment wards using VLAN segmentation.*

5.3.9 Secure Information with Encryption

As discussed earlier, data encryption is a key component to successful IM security. In fact, one of the major current vulnerabilities of IM is the rare use of encryption for data transfer in IM systems. However, several companies have currently introduced business versions of IM enhanced with encryption, security, and authentication features. For example, Top Secret Messenger (TSM), by Encryption Software (www.encrsoft.com), provides a secure public-key encryption with fully integrated plug-ins for popular instant messengers and e-mail clients, such as ICQ and MSN Instant Messenger (Microsoft), and is currently working on plug-ins for Yahoo! Messenger and AIM.

5.3.10 IM System Rules, Policies, and Procedures

A corporate policy regarding IM usage is critical to good IM security practice. The responsibilities/acceptable use should be clearly stated in the corporation's security policy. At a minimum, the degree to which IM use is permitted by employees and what IM system or network(s) the company will be standardizing upon for authorized use should be defined, and the policy should clearly state that any unauthorized use of IM clients is prohibited. In order to ensure that IM does not jeopardize the security of the organization's systems, it should be clearly stated in any and all security policies that IM will be permitted only with the express knowledge and consent of the organization. Users should be prohibited from sending confidential information over public IM systems as part of the overall security policy/acceptable use policy. As with e-mail, company-provided Internet access, and telephone usage, companies should establish written procedures guiding employees on the proper use of IM. For example, if the company wishes to block outbound or inbound file attachments, a policy should be drafted and the IM technology chosen should support file blocking.

The range of possible IM solutions that meet the company's policy regarding authorized IM use will be narrower than the entire universe of available products. If more than one IM network client is going to be authorized for employee use, this must be considered when defining the policy and compliance assurance standards. Given the risks involved in using public IM systems, you should consider prohibiting the use of public IM systems entirely, or ask employees to refrain from using public IM systems for business communications.

A policy must examine security needs and existing infrastructure compatibility. You must consider how your IM vendor or service provider system handles remote workers or employees who travel and access the Internet from hotel rooms or other locations. Many IM systems based on proxy gateways cannot capture the needed information for presence awareness from computers that are off the company network.

Good IM security policy development should also evaluate the need for sending secure file attachments via IM. If personnel in one department require functionality for sending file attachments to customers or remotely located sales personnel, and other departments wish to prohibit file transfer capability completely, the right policy is one that allows for administration and control of such features at the individual user level and not at the enterprise level.

Figure 5.7 *Ensuring IM client policy compliance.*

5.3.11 Monitor to Ensure IM Client Policy Compliance

Vulnerability management solutions should be used to ensure policy compliance so that users do not change their IM client settings in a manner that violates the company policy (see Figure 5.7). These tools provide the administrator with an overall view of IM policy compliance and facilitate the process of updating those machines that violate the policy. Vulnerability management tools also help the administrator determine whether the IM software is up-to-date, whether users are running versions with security holes or buffer-overflow vulnerabilities, and whether users are running company-required antivirus and personal firewall packages; it may be necessary to facilitate the process of updating machines that violate policy.

Ideally, these tools enable a company to intelligently control the risks of unauthorized use of public IM and peer-to-peer to increase network security, optimize network resources and bandwidth consumption, reduce legal liability, and increase user productivity. They should also have the ability to block and manage leading IM protocols and block and manage file-sharing protocols. In addition, the optimal IM compliance tool should have network reporting capabilities that enable network administrators to gather and analyze data, such as usage patterns, by the type of IM and peer-to-peer communication.

5.4 Security Risks and Solutions for Specific Public IM Clients

In this section, we will take a look at four of the most widely used public IM client software products available to the general public today. These include MSN Messenger, Yahoo! Messenger, America Online Instant Messenger (AIM), and ICQ. Each of these products is easily downloaded over the Internet and can be installed onto nearly any platform that can support a browser. For each of these products, we will review their installation requirements and capabilities, protocols supported, security risks, and security solutions.

5.4.1 MSN Messenger

Windows Messenger is easy to use, delivers great voice and video quality, and enables cool, new innovation with lots of other products and services. The latest version is 7.0 (beta), and it is part of the Microsoft Windows XP Professional and Windows XP Home Edition.

Installation Requirements and Capabilities

According to the MSN Messenger Web site [6], the minimum system requirements are as follows:

- Multimedia PC
- Pentium 233-MHz processor or better (500 MHz recommended)
- Microsoft Windows 98, Windows 2000, Windows Millennium, or Windows XP operating system
- Minimum 64 MB of RAM (128 MB recommended)
- Up to 50 MB of hard disk space needed to install — after install, up to 15 MB may be needed
- 256-color VGA or higher resolution graphics card (SVGA recommended)
- Minimum 800 × 600 screen resolution
- Microsoft Internet Explorer version 5.01 or later must be installed on your computer—though it does not need to be your default browser

These requirements essentially mean that the MSN Messenger software can be run on virtually any virtually any desktop or notebook computer with an Internet connection. The product is clearly aimed at the home user market. The business-oriented client, which also uses Microsoft's .NET Messenger Service, is called MSN Messenger. There are also services to use MSN Messenger on a mobile phone. Other features that come standard with MSN Messenger include voice conversations, support for Webcams, file transfers, and built-in multiuser games. MSN Messenger version 6 supported an ability to customize the software, with personalized backgrounds, emoticons, and display pictures. There is also a large community of third-party developers that have created add-ons to extend the capabilities of the program. With the most recent version, as of December 3, 2004 (version 7.0.0425 beta), features like *winks*, which were previously only supported in a product called Three Degrees, are standard. However, the beta version has some major drawbacks, such as adverts used to sell you display pictures, emoticons, and more.

Overview of the Protocol

MSN Messenger utilizes a protocol known as the Mobile Status Notification Protocol (MSNP) over TCP. There are options to use it over HTTP in order to support use with proxies. The current version of MSNP is 11 (MSNP11), and it is the version used by MSN Messenger version 7.0 and many other third-party clients. The protocol is only partially proprietary, because Microsoft disclosed the code used in version 2 (MSNP2) to developers in 1999 in an Internet Draft document [7] but never released versions 8, 9, 10, or 11 to the general public. Since MSN servers only accept protocol versions from 8 and on, the syntax of new commands from versions above version 7 is only known by using sniffers such as Ethereal and published on the Internet [8].

The MSN Messenger protocol is an ASCII-based protocol, which makes it easy to build clients for different platforms. The protocol is documented by unofficial sources and is available on the Internet [9]. The MSN Messenger network is decentralized, so any server in the MSN Messenger network is able to authenticate clients. Currently, all MSN Messenger servers are found in a subdomain called *msgr.hotmail.com*, which is opened via port 1863. The user cannot change this port assignment. It is possible for users to proxy their MSN Messenger connection via the SOCKS 4 or 5 proxy, as well as with HTTP proxy protocols.

MSN Messenger passwords are encrypted using an MD5 hash algorithm. The MSN server generates a random seed string, which is passed to the client in a message. An example of such looks like this:

```
USR 5 MD5 S 989048851.1851 137130
```

The client appends the string **`Q1 P7W2E4J9R8U355`** to the seed string, which results in a string resembling this:

```
989048851.1851 137130Q1 P7W2E4i9R8U3S5
```

This string is hashed with the password using an MD5 algorithm and returned to the server as a string in the form of:

```
"0212eaad0876afb8505859ca75d21a78"
```

It is quite difficult to reverse-engineer this hash algorithm and retrieve the password from the seed and the hash. However, all messages other than the authentication sequence are sent in clear text, making it unnecessary for a malicious user to retrieve the password.

Security Risks

There has been at least one known instance of a propagating worm in MSN Messenger. This particular worm, known as **W32/Hello**, was not widespread and did very little, if any, actual damage. The worm relied on users accepting a download named *Hello.exe* and manually opening that file. Once this file was opened, it would send itself to others on the user's MSN Messenger contact list. The method of propagation was actually e-mail, and the worm was so poorly written that there were practically no effects from it [10]. Computer viruses can be passed around in a variety of ways: via e-mail messages, on floppy disks, and, increasingly, through messaging applications such as MSN Messenger. The Hello.exe worm is just one example of a virus that can be passed around through MSN Messenger [11]. Other notable malicious software that has recently used MSN Messenger as a vehicle includes Win32.Smbmsn.163840 (September 2003), which is a worm that spreads through MSN Messenger through a file called SMB.EXE; W32.Jitux.Worm [12] (December 2004), which is a worm written in the Visual BASIC (VB) programming language that attempts to spread through MSN Messenger and requires the VB run-time libraries for it to be executed; and Backdoor.Ducy [13] (June 2004), which is a backdoor Trojan horse that uses MSN Messenger to give an attacker access to your computer [14].

Application sharing gives a remote user access to programs installed on another computer. Optionally, a user can give control of a program to a remote user. If a user accepts the invitation to share an application, the initiating user may select which of these programs he or she wishes to share with the other user. To achieve application sharing, a direct connection is established between clients over the TCP port 1503. Obviously, before sharing an application on your local machine with a remote user, it is a good idea to be sure you know and trust that user before allowing him or her to have unfettered access to your machine.

File transfers are very similar to image transfers in that a direct connection is established. However, once the transfer process has been completed, the direct connection is closed. File transfers in MSN Messenger require a direct connection to be made between two clients. At first, the user who wishes to send a file initiates a request, passed through the MSN Messenger server, which is received by another client. If the receiving client agrees to accept the file transfer, the file will be sent. The client that initiated the file transfer listens for the response from the receiving party on TCP port 68911.

The Remote Assistance utility, found in Windows XP Professional and Home Editions, allows a remote user to control another computer. The Remote Assistance feature in MSN Messenger launches this utility. Documentation on Remote Assistance in Windows XP is available on the Internet [15].

The Webcam feature requires a direct connection to be used for Webcam broadcasts. Webcam data is transferred via UDP connections using ports 13324 and 13325. MSN Messenger can automatically detect if a Webcam is connected to your computer and will indicate to others who you have allowed to see your presence information that a video conversation is available. This notification feature can be disabled if you do not wish to take advantage of the Webcam capability.

Infected files are yet another risk users must contend with, and they come in two basic forms: Trojan horses and viruses. There have been many cases reported of users being offered files from strangers while using MSN Messenger, only to discover all too late that those files contained a Trojan or virus. Once again, the best advice regarding accepting files from strangers is to treat them as you would if a stranger just offered you a piece of candy. Beware!

Another security risk is the use of unencrypted communication when using MSN Messenger. Its protocol stack does not include a secure sockets layer. There is no encryption of any communication sent or received via MSN Messenger. Users may send sensitive data via messages or file transfers. Messages are routed from source to destination via the Internet. If transmitted documents are not encrypted, they should not be sent via MSN Messenger unless they are already a matter of public record. Users should send information over MSN Messenger with the assumption that a larger audience will have access to this data.

Copyright infringement risks are another concern to users of public IM services. Many file transfers completed through MSN Messenger violate copyright laws. It is common for users to send copyrighted software, such as MP3 files, copyrighted photos, and so on to others. Trading files over MSN Messenger eliminates file-size restrictions commonly imposed by e-mail systems and, if the recipient is known, MSN Messenger is much easier to use when compared to other software products that use FTP.

Some malicious MSN Messenger users have convinced others to divulge sensitive information such as user names, passwords, and credit card numbers. This form of *social engineering* may seem innocent enough, but it is probably one of the more common ways that sensitive information is inadvertently disclosed. Individuals trying to appear helpful or knowledgeable often provide volumes of sensitive company information to outsiders without any ill-intentioned motives.

Security risks abound when engaging in a file transfer, image transfer, voice chat, remote assistance session, or application sharing, because these actions can reveal a user's true IP address. Once an IP address is known, it is possible for a malicious user to target your system for cracking. Aside from cracking into your system, the hacker/cracker could use this information to make your computer the target of a Denial-of-Service (DoS) attack.

Perhaps the most dangerous risk of all is the theft of identity. MSN Messenger conducts its sessions in clear text. This allows a malicious user to perform a TCP hijack of an active/idle connection. This malicious user would then be able to impersonate another user in order to obtain sensitive information such as passwords, files, and so on.

Message logging is an MSN Messenger feature that records a messaging session to a text file. Malicious access to this information could be used for social engineering or to gain access to sensitive data. Additionally, such files could become evidence if litigation occurred against an employer, or they could be used as forensic evidence against individuals in situations where their machines were subject to search and seizure regulations for individuals being investigated or arrested for engaging in criminal or suspicious activities.

Security Solutions

MSN Messenger has standard port numbers associated with its features, so it is relatively easy to restrict access to some or all of the program features. To prevent file transfers, administrators can easily disable incoming and outgoing TCP sessions on port 6891. If an organization wanted to disable voice and video chat, it is very easy. Since a direct connection must be used for voice and video chat sessions, data is transferred via UDP connections on ports 13324 and 13325. To prevent voice and video conferencing, simply block UDP ports 13324 and 13325. To prevent application sharing, block the TCP port 1503. To disable MSN Messenger completely, deny access to hosts in the **msgr.hotmail.com subdomain** and block TCP port 1863. Taking these measures will prevent a user from using the MSN Messenger service, unless that user has access to the Web and configures an external proxy server to route instant messages. In this situation, a network Intrusion Detection System (IDS) may be the only sure way to detect these users.

5.4.2 Yahoo! Messenger

Installation Requirements and Capabilities

Yahoo! Messenger is a very popular IM client provided by Yahoo! [16]. Yahoo! Messenger is provided free of charge and can be downloaded and used with a generic *Yahoo! ID*. This ID also allows user access to other Yahoo! services such as Yahoo! Mail. In addition to IM and other features, similar to those offered by IM competitors ICQ and AOL Instant Messenger (AIM), Yahoo! Messenger also has some unique features [17] such as IMVironments and Yahoo! Avatars. IMVironments (IMVs) are interactive backgrounds that a user can select when talking to other users. Users can choose from many different IMVs that have been made available in Yahoo! Messenger. A Yahoo! Avatar is an image the user can create to represent him- or herself online. The user can direct the Avatar to change clothes, accessories, and hairstyles to reflect almost any desired appearance. Users often choose an Avatar to express their moods while communicating with other IM users.

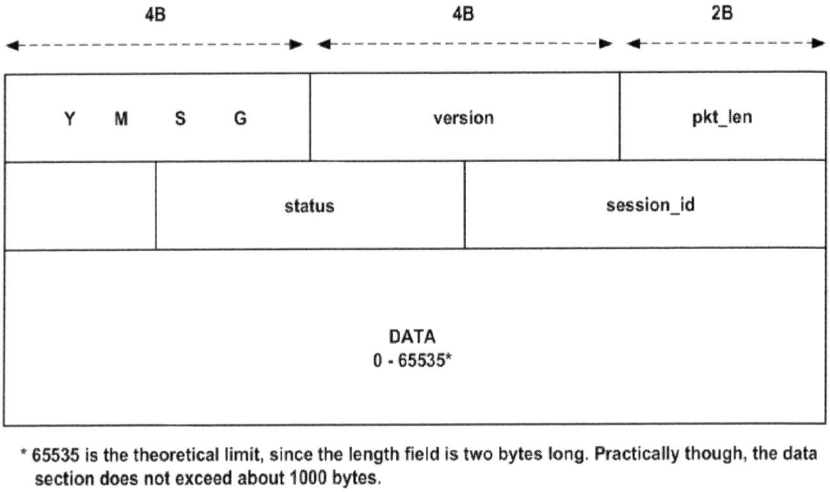

Figure 5.8 *Yahoo! YMSG packet structure.*

Overview of the Protocol

The Yahoo! Messenger protocol is an application layer protocol running most of the time over TCP. In some cases it may run over HTTP. The Yahoo! Messenger protocol is an ASCII-based protocol and utilizes two ports for its communication. The client sends information via Yahoo! servers on port 5050 and ASCII information via HTTP port 80. Most communication with other clients is handled on port 5050. Yahoo! Messenger and MSN Messenger packets share a similar structure, but Yahoo! Messenger contains some non-ASCII header information in each packet. Figure 5.8 shows what the Yahoo! Messenger Service Gateway (YMSG) protocol version 9 packet structure looks like.

All numeric fields are stored in network byte order (i.e., the most significant byte first). Here is a brief overview of each of the fields in the packet:

YMSG—The first four bytes of all YMSG packets are always YMSG: the protocol name.

version—The next four bytes are reserved for the protocol version number. For version 9, these four bytes are **0x09 0x00 0x00 0x00**. It is important to note that the last three bytes of this field may just be padding bytes.

pkt_len—A two-byte value, in network byte order, stating how many bytes are in the data section of the packet. In practice, this value does not exceed ± 1,000.

service—This is an opcode that tells the client/server what kind of service is requested/being responded to. There are 45 known services in this version.

status—In case of a response from the server, this field indicates the status of the request (success/failure/etc.). For a request, it is 0 in most cases except for packets that set the user's status (set status, typing notify, etc.). The status code is a four-byte value. Most status codes are two bytes long. The status codes (represented in decimal except for OFFLINE and TYPING) are shown below:

```
YAHOO_STATUS_AVAILABLE = 0
YAHOO_STATUS_BRB = 1
YAHOO_STATUS_BUSY =2
YAHOO_STATUS_NOTATHOME = 3
YAHOO_STATUS_NOTATDESK =4
YAHOO_STATUS_NOTINOFFICE = 5
YAHOO_STATUS_ONPHONE = 6
YAHOO_STATUS_ONVACATION = 7
YAHOO_STATUS_OUTTOLUNCH = 8
YAHOO_STATUS_STEPPEDOUT = 9
YAHOO_STATUS_INVISIBLE = 12
YAHOO_STATUS_CUSTOM = 99
YAHOO_STATUS_IDLE = 999
YAHOO_STATUS_OFFLINE = 0x5 0xa55 0xaa 0x56
YAHOO_STATUS_TYPING = 0x16
```

A user may choose either `AVAILABLE` or `INVISIBLE` as his or her initial log-in status. `TYPING` is only used when the software sends a `TYPING` notification packet.

session_id—A Yahoo! session has two states, *authentication* and *messaging*. The session starts in the authentication state. The client sends the username to the server. The server responds with a challenge string. The client responds to this challenge with two response strings. If authentication is successful, the connection goes into the messaging state. Otherwise, an error response is sent back. The server sends the *buddy list, ignore list, identity list*, and a list of cookies to the client. These might all be sent in a single packet. It then sends the list of online buddies along with their status codes.

All this is sent automatically without the client requesting anything. At this time, any offline messages are also delivered to the client. In the messaging state, a client may send/receive messages, join conferences, send/receive files, change state, and so on. Messaging state is terminated when the user goes offline by sending a `LOGOFF` packet.

DATA—The data section is **pkt_len** bytes long and consists of a series of key/value pairs. All keys are numeric strings. The packet contains their numeric values in the ASCII character set (e.g., `1 == 0x31`, `21 == 0x32`). The maximum number of digits in a key is unknown, although keys of up to three digits have been discovered. Every key and value is terminated by a two-byte sequence of `0xc0 0x80`. Some keys may even have empty values. The actual keys sent and their meanings depend on the service currently being used. The packet data needed to send an instant message looks like this:

```
0x30 0xc080 yahoo_id 0xc080 0x31 0xc080 active_id 0xc080 0x35

0xc080 recipient_id 0xc080 0x3134 0xc080 message_text 0xc080
```

The `0xc080` byte sequence is a separator. The values `0x30`, `0x31`, `0x35`, and `0x3134` are the keys. If you convert them to their ASCII equivalents, you will get 0, 1, 5, and 14.

There are 45 known services supported by Yahoo! Messenger protocol version 9, although more may exist. All known services are listed here, along with the hex values that they correspond with. Any service without a hex value is incrementally one more than the previous value (i.e., `YAHOO_SERVICE_LOGOFF=0x02` and `YAHOO_SERVICE_ISBACK =0x04`).

```
YAHOO_SERVICE_LOGON = 0x01
YAHOO_SERVICE_LOGOFF = 0x02
YAHOO_SERVICE_ISAWAY = 0x03
YAHOO_SERVICE_ISBACK = 0x04
YAHOO_SERVICE_IDLE = 0x05
YAHOO_SERVICE_MESSAGE = 0x06
YAHOO_SERVICE_IDACT = 0x07
YAHOO_SERVICE_IDDEACT = 0x08
YAHOO_SERVICE_MAILSTAT = 0x09
YAHOO_SERVICE_USERSTAT = 0x0a
YAHOO_SERVICE_NEWMAIL = 0x0b
```

```
YAHOO_SERVICE_CHATINVITE = 0x0c
YAHOO_SERVICE_CALENDAR = 0x0d
YAHOO_SERVICE_NEWPERSONALMAIL = 0x0e
YAHOO_SERVICE_NEWCONTACT = 0x0f
YAHOO_SERVICE_ADDIDENT = 0x10
YAHOO_SERVICE_ADDIGNORE = 0x11
YAHOO_SERVICE_PING = 0x12
YAHOO_SERVICE_GROUPRENAME = 0x03
YAHOO_SERVICE_SYSMESSAGE = 0x14
YAHOO_SERVICE_PASSTHROUGH2 = 0x16
YAHOO_SERVICE_CONFINVITE = 0x18
YAHOO_SERVICE_CONFLOGON = 0x19
YAHOO_SERVICE_CONFDECLINE = 0x1a
YAHOO_SERVICE_CONFLOGOFF = 0x1b
YAHOO_SERVICE_CONFADDINVITE = 0x1c
YAHOO_SERVICE_CONFMSG = 0x1d
YAHOO_SERVICE_CHATLOGON = 0x1e
YAHOO_SERVICE_CHATLOGOFF = 0x1f
YAHOO_SERVICE_CHATMSG = 0x20
YAHOO_SERVICE_GAMELOGON= 0x28
YAHOO_SERVICE_GAMELOGOFF = 0x29
YAHOO_SERVICE_GAMEMSG = 0x2a
YAHOO_SERVICE_FILETRANSFER = 0x46
YAHOO_SERVICE_VOICECHAT= 0x4a
YAHOO_SERVICE_NOTIFY = 0x4b
YAHOO_SERVICE_P2PFILEXFER = 0x4d
YAHOO_SERVICE_PEERTOPEER = 0x4f
YAHOO_SERVICE_AUTHRESP = 0x54
YAHOO_SERVICE_LIST = 0x55
YAHOO_SERVICE_AUTH = 0x57
YAHOO_SERVICE_ADDBUDDY = 0x83
YAHOO_SERVICE_REMBUDDY = 0x84
YAHOO_SERVICE_IGNORECONTACT = 0x85
YAHOO_SERVICE_REJECTCONTACT = 0x86
```

Most of the service codes should be self-explanatory. Here is a list of those that may not be so obvious:

- `IDACT/IDDEACT`—activate/deactivate an identity.
- `NOTIFY`—typing/game notification.
- `FILETRANSFER`—transfer a file using the Yahoo! filetransfer server as an intermediate.
- `P2PFILEXFER`—transfer a file between two peers; Yahoo! server not used.
- `PEERTOPEER`—check if peer-to-peer connections are possible.
- `AUTH`—send initial log-in packet (username); response contains challenge string.
- `AUTHRESP`—send response to challenge string (if received from server) or if it is a log-in failure code.
- `LOGON/LOGOFF`—a buddy logged in/out.

When a user signs on to Yahoo! Messenger, the initial authentication packet is sent via HTTP. The username and password are sent in a HTTP 1.0 GET request in clear text. The HTTP server replies with a cookie that is valid for a set amount of time. All further services use this cookie to authenticate their requests. Be aware that it is possible for users to proxy their Yahoo! connection via any SOCKS 4 proxy, SOCKS 5 proxy, or HTTP proxy protocol. Here is a list of the types of requests supported in version 9:

- Authentication
- Send message
- Send typing start/stop notification
- Set status
- Logoff
- Keep alive—sent every 20 minutes
- Add buddy
- Remove buddy
- Reject buddy add

Security Risks

Yahoo! Messenger has the weakest set of security features among the major messaging platforms. Its protocol does not encrypt usernames and passwords, making it risky to even log in to the system. Also, the usernames and passwords are sent via HTTP, which allows this information to be stored in HTTP proxy logs.

File transfers with Yahoo! Messenger require a direct connection between peers over port 80 using Indirect-TCP (ITCP). A request packet is relayed via the central Yahoo! server to another user. The sender listens on port 80 ITCP for the recipient to accept and connect back, to receive the data. The end user is able to configure the port that the Yahoo! client listens on for file transfer connections. The service uses the HTTP protocol for file transfers, so the security risks are essentially the same as with any other file transfer over the Internet.

File sharing in Yahoo! is a method that allows a user to browse a selected directory structure and to download files. While the file-sharing feature is optional, it is enabled by default when the client is set up during installation. The connection method for file sharing is the same as for a regular file transfer. The initiator sends a request packet to the target via the Yahoo! server. After the target client accepts the request, the initiator listens on port 80 (this port can also be changed in the File Sharing options dialog), and the target sends the file list information. Transfers are carried out over the same connection. A default download directory that is intended to be shared by Yahoo! Messenger is created by the installation program and is empty by default. This directory location can be changed, and, if the directory is empty, the connection attempt will fail. The three levels of user security available for file sharing are:

1. Deny all
2. Allow from all with Accept File dialog box
3. Allow file sharing only from people on the "buddy list"

Setting 3 presents the user with no dialog box—hence, no opportunity to reject a download. The program makes an automatic file transfer immediately upon request. This feature, obviously, can be quite dangerous, especially when considering the high possibility of receiving infected files such as Trojan horses and viruses. There have been many reported cases of users being offered files from strangers using Yahoo! Messenger, only to have those files turn out to be a Trojan horse or virus.

Yahoo! Messenger's protocol stack does not include a secure sockets layer. There is no encryption of any communication sent or received via Yahoo! Messenger. Users may send sensitive data via messages or file transfers. As noted before, messages (and file transfers in most cases) are routed via the Internet. If documents are not strongly encrypted, they should not be sent via Yahoo! Messenger unless they are already a matter of public record. Users should send information only with the assumption that a larger audience will have access to this data as well.

Many file transfers completed through Yahoo! Messenger also violate copyright laws. For example, it is common for users to send copyrighted software, MP3 files, copyrighted photos, and so on to other users. Trading files over Yahoo! Messenger eliminates the file-size restrictions of e-mail, and, if the recipient is known, Yahoo! Messenger is an easier solution for file transfers compared with FTP.

Social engineering is commonplace in IM environments and it constitutes a major security risk. Some malicious Yahoo! Messenger users have convinced others to divulge sensitive information, such as usernames, passwords, and credit card numbers.

As we stated previously in our discussion about MSN Messenger, file transfer or voice chat can reveal a user's true IP address. Once an IP address is known, it is possible for a malicious user to concentrate on your system for the purpose of cracking it. This information may also be obtained with the Yahoo! Messenger service and subsequently used to target the computer in a denial-of-service attack.

Yahoo! Messenger's session is based on clear text, making it possible for a malicious user to perform a TCP hijack of an active/idle connection. This malicious user would then be able to impersonate another user to obtain sensitive information such as passwords, files, and so on. Furthermore, if the initial sign-on session is captured on the network, or in HTTP proxy logs, a malicious user may simply use the clear-text password to log in to a user's account.

One Yahoo! Messenger feature called Message Logging records a messaging session to a text file. Malicious access to this information could be used for social engineering or to gain access to sensitive data. As we explained for MSN Messenger, these files can be used in evidentiary procedures.

Security Solutions

It is somewhat difficult to restrict access to Yahoo! Messenger. Since much of its communication can be routed over port 80, much of the data looks like standard HTTP Web traffic. To prevent IM, block TCP port 5050. To disable Yahoo! Messenger completely, deny access to hosts in the ***.msg.*.yahoo.com** subdomain. These measures will prevent a user from using the Yahoo! Messenger service unless that user has access to the Web and configures an external proxy server to route instant messages. In this situation, a network IDS may be the only way to detect users of this client

5.4.3 America Online Instant Messaging

Capabilities

AIM allows users to communicate instantly via text with their buddies around the world, provided they have the AIM software [18]. AIM has 195 million users [19] (January 2003), with a large proportion using Internet slang. Advocates claim that it's easy to locate these users by visiting chatrooms that AOL has set up solely for those purposes. Chat topics range from heavy metal music to current affairs. AOL also has a member directory, where AIM users can locate others online who share their interests. AIM is also noteworthy for its use of buddy icons and buddy profiles, allowing its users to construct a personal avatar and small personal information page.

Since version 2.0, AIM has included person-to-person text messaging, chatroom messaging, and the ability to share files peer-to-peer with your buddies. Somewhere in the 4.x series, the AIM client for Microsoft Windows added the ability to play games against one another. Recent versions (4.3 and later) of the client software store your contact information on AOL's servers, so you can talk to up to 200 of your buddies from any computer with Internet access. Stand-alone official AIM client software is available for free for Microsoft Windows, Mac OS, Mac OS X, Linux, Windows CE, and Palm OS. However, some users stay on the 3.0 series, because the software license agreement for 4.0 and later clients includes a clause prohibiting the user from ever using a third-party client program.

There is also a version of AIM, called AIM Express, that is implemented in DHTML and runs in a Web browser. It is intended for use by people who are unable or unwilling to install an executable client on their machines but still want to use IM. AIM Express supports many of the standard features included in the stand-alone client, but does not provide advanced features such as file transfer, audio chat, or video conferencing.

The standard protocol that AIM clients use to communicate is called OSCAR [20]. AIM Express uses another protocol called TOC. TOC has also been made available to the public, in an attempt to throw a bone to third-party client developers and lure them away from OSCAR. This scheme has not been entirely successful. AOL has continually changed the details of the OSCAR protocol [21] to keep third-party clients such as Trillian from working properly. This has resulted in a cat-and-mouse game between AOL and the client developers.

Apple Computer's iChat AV software, released in June 2003 for Mac OS X, was the first AIM-compatible client to allow for audio and video conferencing over the AIM protocol. In February 2004, AIM 5.5 was released, allowing Windows users to video conference with each other and with iChat users. However, AIM 5.5 does not allow the audio-only chats that are a feature of iChat AV. AIM software is the first to use online video streaming advertisements, via the Eyewonder protocol.

Overview of the Protocol

The AOL Instant Messenger (AIM) is a free IM computer program, published by AOL, which uses the OSCAR IM protocol and the TOC protocol [22]. The most recent software version is AIM 5.9, released in September 2004. AOL has described this technology as a means of "immediate cross-Internet communication" [23]. OSCAR is AOL's IM protocol, standing for **O**pen **S**ystem for **C**ommunic**A**tion in **R**ealtime. Despite its name, the specifications for the protocol are proprietary. AOL has gone to great lengths to keep competitors, namely Microsoft and Cerulean Studios, from implementing compatible clients for their proprietary messaging system.

All AIM commands, messages, and requests are sent through one of many central servers on its system. There are two types of servers on the AIM network: the OSCAR server and the BOS, or Basic OSCAR Service, servers. While the OSCAR server is responsible for authenticating clients, there are many BOS servers responsible for handling various features of the AIM service. Before connections are made to any of the BOS or special-purpose servers, you must first be authorized by the Authorization Server (**login.oscar.aol.com**). This will return a cookie that automatically authorizes you to connect to any of the BOS or special-purpose (e.g., Advertisement, Chat, etc.) servers. This streamlines the log-in process quite a bit. The normal steps taken to create an average AIM session are as follows:

- Connect to Authorizer and retrieve Cookie.
- Connect to the Authorizer-recommended BOS server and initiate BOS service.
- (Optional) Connect to Advertisements server and retrieve first block of ads (repeat at regular interval).
- (Optional) Connect to any other non-BOS services that may be available (AFAIK, none at this point).

The last three steps may actually be done in any order (and for the third and fourth step, probably not at all). However, authorization must always come first. OSCAR authorization follows a "single-login" concept. You log in once and get a cookie that automatically authorizes you to use any of the OSCAR-associated services, just by sending them your cookie.

The first step of the log-in process is connecting to the Authorizer. This currently resides at the DNS address **login.oscar.aol.com**. It also appears that you may connect to any port and get the same response. After the connection, the client must send the "Authorization Request" command. The server also sends a 4b+FLAP command to the client after each new connection, called the "Connection Acknowledge" command. A FLAP connection is a connection over which only FLAP packets are sent. A FLAP header makes up the first six bytes in any AIM message. It has a concept of "channels" of data and keeps a running "sequence number" for ensuring that packets are sent and received in order. Sequence numbering is also a part of TCP itself and is thus an unnecessary part of the FLAP protocol; it must, however, be followed. Everything in the AIM protocol is embodied in AIM commands. The division is not of packets, because more than one command may be sent in any one packet, depending on the transmit timing and so forth. Commands are an abstraction above packets and leads to the definition of the FLAP protocol explained in the following text. We attempt to generalize the layout of all AIM commands. The acronyms used are those used by the AIM client and the AIM division of AOL as defined in their documents [24]. Please refer to those documents if the explanations listed here are not complete enough for you.

The FLAP is the protocol that sits at the bottom of everything communicated across AIM channels. This generally makes up the first six bytes of every AIM command. If this protocol is not obeyed, the OSCAR server will disconnect the offending client immediately upon reception of a malformed command. This is not helpful for debugging, to say the least. Contained in the FLAP headers are (in order of appearance) the Command-

FLAP

`Command Start (byte: 0x2a)`
`Channel ID (byte)`
`Sequence Number (word)`
`Data Field Length (word)`

Data Field—usually SNAC Data (variable)

Start [byte] (which is always 0x2a), the Channel Identification [byte], the Sequence Number [word], and the FLAP Data Field Length [word]. This is followed immediately by an unterminated FLAP Data Field, which concludes the FLAP command. Normally, the FLAP Data Field contains a SNAC. The SNAC is the unit that sits immediately above FLAP on most commands and is the normal contents of the FLAP Data Field for channel 0x02. SNACs are only sent over channel 0x02. Data sent across other channels is not considered complete SNACs. There can be only one SNAC per FLAP command. The FLAP Data Field makes up the rest of the command (there is no FLAP-specific command terminator).

Sequence numbers are used by AOL, but specific reasons for doing so are unknown. The retransmit and data integrity standards of TCP connections make this pointless. So, they are really just there for looks, though that doesn't mean that they can be incorrect. If the server gets an out-of-order command (according to the sequence numbers, not actual receive order), the client will be disconnected. The sequence number origins are picked quite randomly. There is no connection between the sequence number set from the server and the set from the client. Sequence numbers are always incremented upward (toward 0xFFFF) for each command sent. If the seqence number does reach 0xFFFF, it will wrap to 0x0000, for obvious reasons. If you start a new connection, it is recommended that a new sequence number origin is picked for that connection, for purposes of internal coherency. Sequence numbers are independent of channels: There's a single series of sequence numbers per TCP connection (per socket).

Channels are the method used to multiplex separate paths of communication across the same TCP socket. These are analogous to TCP/UDP port numbers. Four channels are currently used by OSCAR:

```
0x01—New Connection Negotiation
0x02—SNAC Data (non-connection-oriented data)
0x03—FLAP-level Error
0x04—Close Connection Negotiation
```

After a new connection (socket) is set up using channel 0x01, data should only be transmitted on channel 0x02, until a low-level FLAP error occurs (channel 0x03) or there is planned termination, which gets "negotiated" (on channel 0x04). Most live events processed during the lifespan of the client are done over channel 0x02. SNACs are never transmitted on any channel other than 0x02.

The best way to read an incoming FLAP command is to first read only the starting 6 bytes (the FLAP headers). From these six bytes, you can determine how many more bytes you need to read to complete the command and how much memory you need to allocate to store it. Never read more or less than the number of bytes specified in the FLAP headers, or your read will result in a truncated or uninterpretable command. Because every command must follow FLAP guidelines, we recommend using a low-level routine to add the FLAP headers. This is the best way to prevent out-of-order sequence numbers from getting used.

The response to this Authorization Response contains the cookie to be used for the BOS and other connections. If the Authorization Request fails, any one of several Authorization Error codes may be returned. After you've gotten your cookie, it's safe to disconnect yourself from the Authorizer.

BOS Sign-on is the next step, and it is usually needed to connect to and initiate service with the BOS. The address of the BOS you should connect to is listed in the Authorization Response. The first step necessary to make this connection is to send the BOS Sign-on command to the server. For purposes of dispatching, it is best to wait to send this command until the Connection Acknowledge command is received from the server immediately after the connection opens (although this is optional and can be processed afterward). Normal BOS sign-on looks something like this:

- Server sends Connection Acknowledge.
- Client sends BOS Sign-on command.
- Server sends BOS Host-Ready.
- Client sends Rate Information Request.
- Server sends Rate Information Response.
- Client sends Rate Information Acknowledge.
- Client requests (in no particular order):
  - Set Privacy Flags
  - Request User Information

- Request New Service
- Optional: Request BOS Rights
- Optional: Request Buddy List Rights
- Optional: Request Locate Rights
- Optional: Request ICBM Parameter Information
- Server sends all the information requested (again, in no particular order)

- User Information Response
- BOS Rights Response
- Buddy List Rights Response
- Locate Rights Response
- ICBM Parameter Information Response
- New Service Redirect
- (Optional) Client sends a SNAC of family 0x0009, subtype 0x0004, data {0x0000, 0x001f}
- (Optional) Client sends a SNAC of family 0x0009, subtype 0x0007, no data
- Client sends buddy list using the Add Buddy to Buddy List command
- Client sends user's profile using the Set User Information command
- Client sends the Set Initial ICBM Parameter command
- Client sends the Client Ready command

At this point, you can begin processing live events, or you can use the information provided in the New Service Redirect command to connect to the Advertisements or other server.

Logging off AIM is quite simple. The abrupt way to do it is to just close the connection to the main message server. That will normally do it. Sometimes, though, the AIM client sends a small command to the server before it closes but expects no response. This "logout command" is just a FLAP without a Data Field, and the Data Field Length is set to 0x0000. Currently, OSCAR is in use for AOL's two main IM systems: ICQ and AIM. OSCAR is currently a binary protocol. Large parts of the protocol are now understood, after many undertook the process of reverse-engineering the protocol. Apple's iChat is the only officially licensed non-AOL client.

The TOC protocol or the Talk to OSCAR protocol is a legacy communications protocol used by some third-party AIM clients. AOL does not use the protocol in its own IM clients (AIM and ICQ) but provides the TOC protocol specification openly to developers in the hopes that they will use it instead of the proprietary OSCAR protocol they use themselves. TOC is an ASCII-based protocol, while OSCAR is a binary protocol. In addition, TOC contains fewer features than its OSCAR counterpart. OSCAR provides such functionality as buddy icons, file transfer, and advertising. AIM has the ability to work with proxy servers using the SOCKS 4, SOCKS 5, HTTP, and HTTPS protocols.

Security Risks

By default, all communications between the server and client happens via port 5190. However, the client is capable of connecting to an OSCAR/BOS server on any port by changing the server port number on the Connection Preferences screen. Therefore, blocking port 5190 on a firewall or other access control device might not prevent AIM clients from connecting. An AIM session begins with a sign-on process. The first FLAP packets sent to OSCAR contain an encrypted password, as well as the user's AOL screen name. The password is encrypted using weak XOR and is easily decrypted. Any packet sniffing software is able to decipher AIM passwords on the fly.

IM images are sent via a direct connection with another peer. A request is sent to the BOS server and is relayed to the target user. The request packet for direct connection contains the TCP/IP address and port information of the requester. If accepted, the target of the request listens for an incoming request on port 4443 and a conversation begins between peers. These direct connections reveal the IP address of each participant.

File transfers are very similar to image transfers in that a direct connection is established. However, once a file transfer is complete, the direct connection is closed. As in IM images, a BOS server relays a request packet to another user. When the recipient accepts the connection, a TCP port is opened to accept the incoming file. By default, this TCP port is 5190; however, it is possible for the user initiating the file transfers to select any available port by nominating it in the File Transfer options dialog. The default security option is to allow file transfers from all users after displaying an accept file dialog box. These options can be configured in File Transfer Options in Preferences.

File sharing in AIM is a method that allows a user to browse a selected directory structure and to download files. File sharing is optional and must be enabled before any sharing can take place. The connection method for file sharing is the same as for a regular file transfer. The initiator sends a request packet to the target via the BOS server. After the target client accepts the request, the initiator begins listening on port 5190 (this can be changed in the File Sharing options dialog) and the target sends the file list information. All file transfers are carried out over the same connection. If the shared directory is empty, the connection attempt will fail. The risk of obtaining infected files such as Trojan horses and viruses is the same as for the other clients mentioned previously. Any user with an AIM account has the ability to send another user a malicious or infected file.

Misconfigured file sharing is another risk AIM users have to contend with. AIM's file-sharing feature is configurable and can be set up to mistakenly share directories in which some or all of the information is sensitive or confidential. An anonymous AIM user might stumble upon sensitive data, such as company documents, system passwords, personal information, and so on.

Unencrypted communication is yet another serious risk, because AIM's protocol stack does not include a secure sockets layer. There is no encryption of any communication sent or received via AIM. Users may send sensitive data via messages or file transfers. As noted before, messages (and file transfers in most cases) are routed via the Internet. If documents are not strongly encrypted, they should not be sent via AIM unless they are already a matter of public record. Users should send information over AIM only with the assumption that a larger audience will have access to this data as well.

Copyright infringement is rampant, because many file transfers completed through AIM violate copyright laws. It is common for users to send copyrighted software, MP3 files, copyrighted photos, and so on to other users. Trading files over AIM eliminates the file-size restrictions of e-mail, and, if the recipient is known, AIM is an easier solution for file transfers compared with File Transfer Protocol (FTP).

The dangers of social engineering were explained previously, and they still exist within the AIM environment. Some malicious AIM users have convinced others to divulge sensitive information, such as user names, passwords, and credit card numbers. For example, AIM users have posed as AOL employees and asked users to verify credit card information or to verify their AOL screen names and passwords.

File transfers can reveal a user's true IP address when engaging in activities such as file transfer, image transfer, voice chat, or file sharing. Once an IP address is known, it is possible for a malicious user to concentrate on your system for the purpose of cracking it. Also, it is possible that this information can be used to make the computer a target of a denial-of-service attack.

We have discussed the extreme consequences that a theft of identity situation can cause. Identity theft can occur due to social engineering or from a malicious user with the ability to intercept an AIM user's password. Several utilities can be used to decrypt AIM passwords, which would enable a malicious user to impersonate another user on AIM. This can also lead to more serious social engineering issues, where a user can mistakenly trust a malicious user and provide sensitive and confidential information.

Security Solutions

AIM was designed to be flexible and is able to work around firewalls and proxies; it can be configured on different ports. Even if traffic for the default AIM ports is blocked, the user has the ability to configure incoming and outgoing TCP sessions on different ports for many of AIM's services. To prevent file transfers and file sharing, disable incoming and outgoing TCP sessions on port 5190. This port can be reconfigured via the AIM client to communicate over a different port. To disable IM images, block incoming and outgoing TCP sessions on port 4443. This port cannot be reconfigured via the AIM client. To disable AIM completely, access to the host **login.oscar.aol.com** must be denied on ALL ports. This prevents users from authenticating with an OSCAR server, therefore preventing these users from utilizing all of AIM's services. These measures will prevent a user from using the AIM service unless a user has access to the Web and configures an external proxy server to route instant messages. In this situation, a network IDS may be the only way to detect users of this client.

5.4.4 ICQ

ICQ is the first IM computer program created by start-up Israeli company Mirabilis and first released in November 1996 [25]. The name ICQ is a play on the phrase "I seek you." In June 2004, ICQ celebrated its 300-millionth download from download.com, where it remained the number one most popular download for seven consecutive years. ICQ was founded by Yair Goldfinger, Arik Vardi, Sefi Vigiser, and Amnon Amir and managed by Ariel Yarnitsky.

ICQ allows the sending of text messages, URLs, multiuser chats, file transfers, greeting cards, and more. ICQ users are identified by numbers called UIN, distributed in sequential order (though it is rumored there are gaps in the sequence). New users are now given a UIN of well over

100,000,000, and low numbers (six digits or less) have been auctioned on eBay by users who signed up in ICQ's early days. AOL acquired Mirabilis and ICQ in 1998. ICQ 5 is to be released soon; however, the exact date or month is unknown at present. ICQ's main features are IM, voice and video chat, file transfers, and file sharing.

Capabilities

According to the ICQ Web site [26], with ICQ Instant Messenger you can video/audio chat, send e-mail, SMS, and wireless-pager messages, as well as transfer files and URLs. If you're away from your personal computer, you can still chat with friends and contacts, even where the ICQ client is not installed, by using the Web-based ICQ2Go that works from any computer. With ICQ version 4, you can customize your ICQ to be exactly what you need and always up-to-date by adding shortcuts to your favorite features in order to launch them directly from your ICQ. This means that you can send your friends and contacts greeting cards and invitations to games, multichats, video sessions, and more directly from your client and/or the message window. In the message window you can also choose to display your photo or one of ICQ's unique, animated devils. ICQphone incorporates IP telephony functions, enabling you to engage in PC-to-PC and PC-to-phone calls. Used in multiple-user mode, groups can conduct conferences or play games with ICQ. In fact, ICQ supports a variety of popular Internet applications and serves as a universal platform from which you can launch peer-to-peer applications. Basically, ICQ brings together the most widely used methods of communication in the simplest way.

Overview of the Protocol

The ICQ protocol is a binary command-based protocol. It has been reverse-engineered and is well documented at many Internet sites. Most of the communication between ICQ users occurs via one or more of the ICQ servers. These servers are reached on port 5190. The log-in server is known as **login.icq.com**, and, while the port number is the same as AIM, the server does not allow the remote user to choose any port, as AIM does.

When users sign on to the ICQ network, their UIN (User Identification Number) is sent along with their password in a packet encrypted with a proprietary algorithm, which has since been reverse-engineered. It is possible for users to proxy their ICQ connection via any one of the SOCKS 4 proxy, SOCKS 5 proxy, HTTP proxy, or HTTPS proxy protocols.

Security Risks

IM is simply the passing of HTML clear-text messages from one user to another. The message is not encrypted and is always routed over the Internet. Messages are sent via TCP port 3570. For voice and video chat services, a direct connection must be used. This data is transferred via a UDP connection to port 6701. File transfers require that a direct connection be established. However, once a file transfer is complete, the direct connection is closed. To begin the file transfer, a request packet is sent via the standard instant message method to another user. After the user accepts the connection, the receiving client opens a TCP port on 3574 to accept the incoming file. The remote user must accept all file transfers by clicking Accept in a file transfer request dialog.

File sharing in ICQ is a method that allows a user to browse a selected directory structure and to download files from that directory structure. File sharing is disabled by default. It must be enabled before any sharing can take place. The connection method is similar to a regular file transfer. The initiator will send a request packet to the target. The target does not need to accept this request as long as the initiator is on its ICQ list. The initiator then connects to the remote system's TCP port 7320 and the target sends the file list information. All file transfers are carried out on separate connections, which seem to happen on randomly selected TCP ports. The default directory to be shared is created by the ICQ installation program and may be changed. The ICQ protocol is known for its lack of strong authentication, lack of encryption, and simplicity. Apart from protocol weaknesses, ICQ has been the target of many DoS bugs and at least one remote buffer overflow.

As a result of the aforementioned security weaknesses, many types of infected files such as Trojan horses and viruses have been sent across the ICQ network. There have been many reported cases of users being offered files from strangers using ICQ, only to have those files turn out to be a Trojan horse or virus. Many a user has fallen victim to such insidious methods of attack.

ICQ does not include a strong encryption model. There is no encryption of any communication sent or received via ICQ. Users may send sensitive data via messages or file transfers. As noted before, messages (and file transfers in most cases) are routed via the Internet. If documents are not strongly encrypted, they should not be sent via ICQ unless they are already a matter of public record. Users should send information over ICQ only with the assumption that a larger audience will have access to this data as well.

Many file transfers completed through ICQ violate copyright laws. It is common for users to send copyrighted software, MP3 files, copyrighted photos, and so on to other users. Trading files over ICQ eliminates the file size restrictions of e-mail, and, if the recipient is known, ICQ is an easier solution for file transfers compared with FTP.

Social engineering attacks are commonplace in this type of environment. Some malicious ICQ users have convinced others to divulge sensitive information, such as user names, passwords, and credit card numbers. When an attacker intends to conduct theft activities, he or she often starts by obtaining the true IP address of the proposed victim. Because file transfers reveal IP addresses, when a client is busy engaging in file transfer, voice chat, or activating the file-sharing service, this process has a vulnerability that can reveal a user's true IP address. Once an IP address is known, it is possible for a malicious user to crack the user's system. It is also possible that this information can be used to make the computer a target of a denial-of-service attack. Most often, however, malicious users' motives are financial, and theft of identity is their true purpose. A malicious person with the ability to intercept an ICQ user's password can decipher the password and would then be able to impersonate another user to obtain sensitive information such as passwords, files, and so forth.

Message logging is another feature of ICQ that is present in all of the other systems discussed in this chapter. The ability to record a messaging session to a text file can cause serious risks to your security. If a malicious user gains access to this file, this information could be used for social engineering or to gain access to sensitive data.

Security Solutions

To prevent access to ICQ from a network, proper access controls are needed. To prevent stand-alone file transfers, block TCP sessions on port 3574. To disable file-sharing images, block TCP port 7320. To disable ICQ completely, deny access to the host login.icq.com on TCP port 5190. These measures will prevent a user from using the ICQ service unless a user has access to the Web and configures an external proxy server to route instant messages. In this situation, a network IDS may be the only way to detect users of this client.

5.4.5 Beware of IM Third-Party Clients and Services

Over time, we may see the 100 or so third-party IM clients and services reduced to a fraction of the number that currently exists because the major players such as Microsoft and Yahoo! simply don't want third-party clients using its network without some form of compensation [27]. Third-party IM add-in applications or services may also cause degradation of performance and varying degrees of unstable operation; they can add additional security risk. AOL is concerned that third-party applications such as Trillian may compromise the security of AOL's own network by storing users' screen names and passwords beyond AOL's control [28].

From a security perspective, probably the most intriguing freeware third-party application is Trillian. Trillian is a multiprotocol IM application for Windows created by Cerulean Studios that can connect to multiple IM programs from one client, such as AIM, ICQ, MSN Messenger, Yahoo! Messenger, IRC, Novell Rendezvous, and Jabber networks. Trillian Pro allows for and can be extended by plug-ins. Plug-ins are available for free and are hosted at the main Trillian Web site but will only work with the Pro version of Trillian. Trillian's creators have promised to continue to support and maintain a free version of Trillian, yet it remains a closed-source application. Trillian mirrors the features of each IM service on its client. However, one of its more popular features is its ability to encrypt messaging sessions between Trillian clients when using AIM or ICQ messaging sessions. This feature is called SecurelM, is exclusive to Trillian, and is responsible for a great deal of its popularity. Trillian is able to encrypt IM traffic by making a SecurelM request to another Trillian user. Once this SecurelM connection is accepted, a random key is generated and stored in memory (this is done every time a new SecurelM connection is made). Trillian then uses an asymmetric or Diffie-Hellman key exchange process to swap keys during the transfer. The resulting authenticated connection is then encrypted with a 128-bit Blowfish cipher. Blowfish is a symmetric block cipher that can be used as a drop-in replacement for DES or IDEA. It takes a variable-length key, from 32 bits to 448 bits, making it ideal for both domestic and exportable use. Blowfish was designed in 1993 by Bruce Schneier as a fast, free alternative to existing encryption algorithms. Since then, it has been analyzed considerably, and it is slowly gaining acceptance as a strong encryption algorithm. Blowfish is unpatented and license free and is available free for all uses [29].

Another feature (as well as security risk) is Trillian's ability to record any messaging session to a text file. Although useful for many legitimate purposes, if a malicious user gains access to this file, this information could be used for social engineering or to gain access to sensitive data. Since Trillian relies on other networks for its functionality, all security risks for individual IM clients (detailed previously) may apply to this client. There are several known security issues with older Trillian clients. However, users generally upgrade to newer versions of the Trillian client due to connectivity issues with network owners.

As time goes on, there will more than likely be more and more attractive third-party products that can be used to provide or enhance security for both public and enterprise IM clients, such as IMLogic (http://www.imlogic.com), Akonix (http://www.akonix.com/), Websense (http://ww2.Websense.com/global/en/), and Internet Security Systems (http://www.iss.net/). In regard to nonsecurity third-party solutions and services, unless it is an absolutely necessary business need, it is better to uninstall third-party add-in applications or services that you have installed and that may be causing issues; report these issues to the third-party application vendors.

5.5 Home IM Security Best Practices

Just as with corporate IM use, there are risks associated with the use of IM in the home. Since all authentication information and content passed using IM is unencrypted, your user name, password, and data could be viewed by anyone. Of course, you may ask why anyone would want to break into your system at home? Rather than wanting to gain access to and misuse information concerning your identity, financial information, or blackmail you for your Web usage habits, an attacker may want to gain control of your computer so he or she can use it to launch attacks on other computer systems. Gaining control of your computer gives an attacker the ability to hide his or her true location as attacks are launched, often against high-profile computer systems such as government or financial systems. An attacker can also watch all your actions on the computer or cause damage to your computer by reformatting your hard drive or changing your data. Even if you have a computer connected to the Internet only to play the latest games or to send e-mail to friends and family, your computer may be a target.

If you use your computer to gain remote access to your company's network, you are also at risk of an attacker exploiting any IM vulnerabilities you have on your machine to gain the same access and rights you have to your company network. If you work from a home computer and require remote access to the corporate network, you should always consult your system support personnel. If you use your broadband access to connect to your employer's network via a Virtual Private Network (VPN) or other means, your employer may have policies or procedures relating to the security of your home network. Be sure to consult with your employer's support personnel, as appropriate, before following any of the steps outlined in this chapter.

As a general rule, IM should not be used for sending or receiving sensitive, confidential, personal, protected, or privileged information. You should also avoid using IM to authorize, confirm, approve, or initiate any business action involving personal, financial, or property assets.

Offers for software downloads or files over IM should also be rejected, as they are frequently a means by which viruses or malicious code is spread. Although you may not consider your IM communications "sensitive," you probably do not want unauthorized parties reading your e-mail or IM message, using your computer to attack other systems, sending forged e-mail from your computer, or examining personal information stored on your computer such as financial statements or Web surfing logs.

Antivirus software should be used on all Internet-connected computers, in particular those used for IM. Your antivirus software should always be kept up-to-date and you should use automatic updates of virus definitions, when available. We also strongly recommend the use of some type of firewall product, such as a network appliance or a personal firewall software package. Attackers are constantly scanning home user systems for known vulnerabilities, which is particularly problematic for those users with cable modems or DSL. As a reminder, no firewall can detect or stop all attacks, so it's not sufficient to install a firewall and then ignore all other security measures discussed in this section.

Before opening any IM attachments, be sure you know the source of the attachment. It is not enough that the mail originated from an address you recognize. The Melissa virus spread precisely because it originated from a familiar address. Malicious code might be distributed in amusing or enticing programs. Bottom line, don't open unknown IM attachments. However, if you must open before you verify the source, you should make sure your virus definitions are up-to-date, save the file to your hard disk, scan the file using your antivirus software before you open the file, and, for added protection, disconnect your computer's network connection before opening the file. This is not a failsafe method by which to open an attachment from an unknown source, but it will substantially reduce the risk.

You should never run a program unless you know it to be authored by a person or company that you trust. Programs of unknown origin should also not be sent to your friends or coworkers, simply because they might contain a Trojan horse program. Windows operating systems contain an option to "Hide file extensions for known file types." Although this option is enabled by default, you should disable it in order to have file extensions displayed by Windows. Even though you disable hidden filenames, some file extensions will continue to remain hidden by default. For example, the ".LNK" extension associated with Windows shortcuts remains hidden even after a user has turned off the option to hide extensions. Specific instructions for disabling hidden filename extensions can be found on the Internet [30].

As stated previously, IM patches and fixes should be installed by system administrators as soon as possible. Vendors will usually release patches for their software when a vulnerability has been discovered. Most product documentation offers a method to get updates and patches. You should be able to obtain updates from the vendor's Web site. Read the manuals or browse the vendor's Web site for more information. If no automated notification mechanism is offered, you may need to check periodically for updates. Another good security practice is to turn off your computer or disconnect it from the network when not in use. An intruder cannot attack your computer if it is powered off or otherwise completely disconnected from the network.

If possible, you should also disable Java, JavaScript, and ActiveX, because of the risks involved in the use of "mobile code." A malicious Web developer can attach a script to something sent to a Web site, such as a URL, an element in a form, or a database inquiry, so that when the Web site responds to you, the malicious script is transferred to your browser. This vulnerability can be avoided completely by disabling all scripting language options to keep you from being vulnerable to malicious scripts, but it will limit the interaction you can have with some Web sites and may degrade the functionality you have with these sites. Detailed instructions for disabling browser scripting languages can be found on the CERT Web site.

Another risk mitigation technique is to make regular backups of critical data and store the backup media somewhere away from the computer. This will provide the ability to restore your data in the event that it is successfully destroyed or modified by malicious activity. Backups should be made to a medium that can be stored offline, such as a CD-RW device, tape device, or other offline storage devices.

As stated earlier, you should never download, install, or run programs of unknown origin. Never open or use a program unless you know it to be authored by a person or company that you trust. This is a commonly used method among intruders attempting to build networks of DDoS agents by exploiting users of IRC and IM services. Intruders are using automated tools to post messages to unsuspecting users of IRC or IM services that typically offer the opportunity to download software of some value to the user, including improved music downloads, antivirus protection, or pornography. If users download and execute the malicious software, their system is co-opted by the attacker for use as an agent in a distributed DDoS network. Trojan horse and backdoor programs are being propagated via similar techniques. If systems are compromised by users running untrusted software, attackers may exercise remote control, expose confidential data, install other malicious software, change files, delete files, or install DDoS agents. Sites that are infected by DDoS agents or undergo a DDoS attack may experience unusually heavy traffic volumes or high packet rates, resulting in degradation of services or loss of connectivity altogether.

5.6 Summary

In summary, we recommend that you always use a best practices approach to mitigate IM security threats. Some of the critical IM security best practices that we recommend are to establish a corporate IM usage policy; encourage users not to send confidential information over public IM systems; properly configure corporate firewalls to block unapproved IM traffic; deploy private corporate IM servers if possible to isolate your corporate messaging systems from the outside world; enforce client-side IM settings (e.g., refuse file transfers by default); install patches to IM software as soon as possible; and use vulnerability management solutions to ensure IM client policy compliance. Both corporations and home users should deploy a desktop firewall or an integrated antivirus/firewall on all desktops. Such a firewall can help block usage of unapproved IM programs and potentially prevent attacks to and from these systems.

See URL http://www.cert.org/incident_notes/IN-2000-07.html.

5.7 Endnotes

1. U.S. Securities and Exchange Commission. (2002). "Final Rule: Applicability of CFTC and SEC Customer Protection, Recordkeeping, Reporting, and Bankruptcy Rules and the Securities Investor Protection Act of 1970 to Accounts Holding Security Futures Products." Retrieved December 29, 2004 from http://www.sec.gov/rules/final/34-46473.htm.

2. NASD. (2004). "NASD Manual Online: NASD Rules." Retrieved December 29, 2004 from http://complianceintl.com/

nasd/nasdviewer.asp?SelectedNode=3&FileName=/nasd/nasd_rules/RulesoftheAssociation_mg.xml.

3. Highlander. (2004). "Frequently Asked Questions About Meeting Compliance Requirements with IM Manager." Retrieved December 29, 2004 from http://www.vbxtras.co.uk/software_topnav/imlogic/financial-services-compliance-faq.cfm.

4. Sarbanes-Oxley Act of 2004. (2004). "Sarbanes-Oxley Act." Retrieved December 29, 2004 from http://www.sarbanes-oxley.com/.

5. U.S. Securities and Exchange Commission. (2000). "Final Rule: Selective Disclosure and Insider Trading." Retrieved December 29, 2004 from http://www.sec.gov/rules/final/33-7881.htm.

6. http://messenger.msn.com/SysReq.aspx. Retrieved January 30, 2005.

7. R. Movva, et al. "Instant Messaging and Presence Protocol—MSN Messenger Service 1.0 Protocol," IETF Draft August 1999, http://www.hypothetic.org/docs/msn/ietf_draft.txt. Retrieved January 20, 2005.

8. http://www.hypothetic.org/docs/msn/ietf_draft.txt. Retrieved January 30, 2005.

9. Ibid.

10. Symantec. (April 25, 2001). "W32.FunnyFiles.Worm." Retrieved January 31, 2005 from http://www.symantec.com/avcenter/venc/data/w32.funnyfiles.worm.html.

11. R. Konrad. (May 1, 2001). "Worm crawls into MSN Messenger." Retrieved January 31, 2005 from http://news.com.com/2100-1023-256816.html?legacy=cnet.

12. Symantec. (December 31, 2003). "W32.Jitux.Worm." Retrieved January 31, 2005 from http://securityresponse.symantec.com/avcenter/venc/data/w32.jitux.worm.html.

13. Symantec. (June 6, 2004). "Backdoor.Ducy." Retrieved January 31, 2005 from http://securityresponse.symantec.com/avcenter/venc/data/backdoor.ducy.html.

14. Market Wire. (September 26, 2003). "Virus Alert: Global Hauri Issues Medium Warning for 'SMB Worm' Spreading Through

MSN Messenger." Retrieved January 31, 2005 from http://www.marketwire.com/mw/release_html_b1?release_id=57978.

15. http://support.microsoft.com/default.aspx?scid=kb;en-us;Q300546.
16. Wikpedia. (2005). "Yahoo! Messenger." Retrieved January 30, 2005 from http://en.wikipedia.org/wiki/Yahoo%21_Messenger.
17. http://messenger.yahoo.com/features.php.
18. Wikpedia. (2005). "AOL Instant Messenger." Retrieved January 30, 2005 from http://en.wikipedia.org/wiki/AOL_Instant_Messenger.
19. ITworld.com. (February 3, 2003). "AOL, IBM work on corporate IM integration." Retrieved January 31, 2005 from http://www.itworld.com/App/300/030203aolibm/.
20. A. Fritzler. (1998). "AIM/Oscar Protocol Specification: Section 3: Connection Management." Retrieved January 30, 2005 from http://iserverd.khstu.ru/docum_ext/aim_proto/section3.htm.
21. Wikpedia. (2005). "Oscar Protocol." Retrieved January 30, 2005 from http://en.wikipedia.org/wiki/OSCAR_protocol.
22. Wikpedia. (2005). "TOC Protocol." Retrieved January 30, 2005 from http://en.wikipedia.org/wiki/OSCAR_protocol.
23. CNET Download.com. (2005). "AOL Instant Messenger (AIM) 5.9.369." Retrieved January 30, 2005 from http://joust.kano.net/wiki/oscar/moin.cgi/FlapConnection.
24. http://www.aim.aol.com/javadev/terminology.html.
25. Wikpedia. (2005). "ICQ." Retrieved January 30, 2005 from http://en.wikipedia.org/wiki/ICQ.
26. http://www.icq.com/products/whatisicq.html.
27. J. Evers. (2003). "Yahoo Messenger Update Will Boot Trillian: Instant Messaging services buck interoperability, reserve their networks to customers." Retrieved January 31, 2005 from http://www.pcworld.com/news/article/0%2Caid%2C112511%2C00.asp.
28. Washingtonpost.com. (2002). "Instant messaging: Tear Down the Walls." Retrieved January 31, 2005 from http://kalscy.com/2002/02/aol_im_bs.

29. http://www.schneier.com/blowfish.html.
Retrieved on February 15, 2005.

30. http://www.cert.org/tech_tips/malicious_code_FAQ.html.

6

IM Security Risk Management

In many companies, IM is used for contact between project team members, between customers and vendors on a project, and between employees and their families (even if not officially sanctioned by corporate management or the IT department). Many departments or subgroups are using IM, because it is easily downloaded for free and works in many corporate network environments without any special request to the IT department. These factors only increase the security challenges associated with IM. Although there are risks and challenges associated with private-enterprise IM, the use of free, consumer-grade IM products in a corporate environment exposes the company network to several security risks, because there are few security features in the free products. Unfortunately, there is no permanent remedy for IM security. A continuous process of adaptation is necessary, and it is a tradeoff between the proactive costs of security technology versus the tangible (and intangible) costs of security breaches. This process is called risk management. We have covered the technical risks of IM in detail and, in this chapter, we will start by putting IM risk in perspective in comparison to e-mail and other business records, and then describe the various regulatory requirements that will also drive the need for risk mitigation in your enterprise. Finally, we will try to define the general requirements for an IM Risk Management program.

6.1 IM Is a Form of E-mail

IM is a form of e-mail combining all the features of e-mail with the real-time convenience and conferencing capabilities of the telephone. As discussed earlier in the book, IM matches e-mail feature for feature and then some. It is important that IM is rapidly being held to the same regulatory, legal, business records, risk auditing, business requirements, and performance standards as e-mail.

6.2 IM Security and the Law

Regulations imposed by the Securities Exchange Commission (SEC), the Freedom of Information Act, and the Sarbanes-Oxley Act make no distinction between public instant-messaging clients provided by AOL, MSN, ICQ, and Yahoo! and the enterprise-messaging systems provided by Microsoft Live Communications Server and IBM Lotus Instant Messaging. No matter which platform they are using, financial institutions that fail to meet security compliance mandates can face significant financial and legal liabilities. Perhaps two of the most notable events that have recently transpired in the area of IM regulatory and legal issues are the NASD Notice to Members 03-33 [1] relating to compliance issues surrounding the use of IM and the recent case of *Zubulake v. UBS Warburg* [2], a court decision relating to a party's right to obtain e-mails in litigation. Corporate employees should understand what the securities rules and the law expect and require, not only of e-mail communications but also for IM.

The National Association of Securities Dealers (NASD) informed its roughly 5,300 brokerage firm members on June 18, 2005, that they must retain their IM records for at least three years. Under federal law, every securities firm doing business with the U.S. public must be a member of NASD [3]. NASD 3010 requires that member firms establish and maintain a system to "supervise" the activities of each registered representative, including transactions and correspondence with the public (see Figure 6.1). "Supervision," as defined by the NASD, includes implementing a formalized review process of incoming and outgoing electronic correspondence relating to its investment banking or securities business. In addition, NASD Rule 3010 requires that member firms additionally implement a retention program for all correspondence involving registered representatives. Members are required to retain correspondence of registered representatives in accordance with Rule 3110 [4].

The general rules and regulations promulgated under the Securities Exchange Act of 1934, Rule 17a-4, outlines the records to be preserved by certain exchange members, brokers, and dealers. Although traditionally covering only written agreements and guarantees, the rule has expanded its presence over the last five years to include new communication technologies, such as e-mail, the Internet, and IM. The recording requirements as dictated by the SEC generally include both internal/intrafirm communications as well as correspondence between brokers/dealers and their clients. Rule 17a-3 additionally outlines record-keeping requirements and specifications for brokers/dealers [5].

Figure 6.1
New rules require corporate employees to be educated about e-mail and IM retention policies.

The SEC has recently launched an information inquiry regarding electronic storage and archiving to members of the NYSE and NASD as it pertains to Rule 17a-4. It is generally accepted that the majority of member firms are not compliant at present and are making "best efforts" toward upholding the letter of the law. The 1997 amendments to Rule 17a-4 outline the specific requirements of brokers-dealers for using electronic storage media systems to store records they are required to retain. Brokers-dealers may use automatic electronic message archiving and record retrieval service for the bulk of the records retention needs as required by the SEC and NASD. Under SEC and NASD regulation, IM is generally treated as electronic messaging communication and faces the same recording requirements as e-mail or other text messaging. Rule 17a-4 and NASD Rule 3010 dictate how electronic messages should be retained supervised/reviewed. The amended rules [6] of these governing bodies include additional requirements for brokers-dealers who intend to rely on electronic storage media to comply with record-keeping and auditing requirements [7].

In July 2004, the Federal Deposit Insurance Corporation (FDIC) issued its 5,300 member banks and financial institutions a warning about unmanaged IM access. Its "Guidance on IM" warned that using popular consumer IM clients, such as Yahoo! Instant Messenger, Microsoft's MSN Messenger, and AOL's Instant Messenger can expose companies to security, privacy, and legal liability risks [8].

One of the key findings of Ferris Research's new report entitled "Sarbanes-Oxley and the Messaging Manager" [9] notes that SOX is really about process, and, in particular, it regulates the process of assembling financial reports. If messaging systems are used in that process, as they surely are in any modern enterprise, certain things must be done to ensure the integrity of those communications. In particular, senders and recipients of messages must be identified and authenticated in some meaningful way. Messaging systems have to maintain an adequate log of messages received and sent. Messages must be secure during transmission and storage. The requirements are achievable with most e-mail and collaboration systems, but public IM systems allows virtually anonymous messaging, which makes compliance using them almost impossible to achieve [10]. Perhaps the most stringent of the regulations involves storing electronic messages. This can cause unique problems, because e-mail and messaging clients are not typically integrated into one common application.

Included in these risks are viruses and worms, illegal downloading of copyrighted material, loss of confidential information, and identity theft. According to the FDIC recommendations, members should protect themselves against these vulnerabilities by establishing policies and implementing solutions to allow, restrict, or deny IM use based on the individual needs of the enterprise. The FDIC requires financial institutions to design and implement a comprehensive written information security program. The security program should include appropriate controls and training to address the risks posed by the use of public IM [11].

In a recent well-known corporate case, the Federal Energy Regulatory Commission (FERC), during its investigation of Enron on charges it manipulated energy prices in California and other western states, revealed potential legal issues with the e-mail and IM content observed as a result of the investigation. The investigation revealed tens of thousands of Enron messages, 4 percent of all of those released by the FERC, that contained inappropriate content ranging from porn to racial comments, which could have led to lawsuits. Another 8 percent included personal content, such as messages about medications and ailments. [12]

Congress passed the Health Insurance Portability and Accountability Act of 1996 (HIPAA) to ensure the security and privacy of patient records. These laws mandate that all healthcare institutions take the necessary steps to protect patient information, especially electronic data, for administrative and financial functions. The HIPAA Privacy Rule, which took effect in April 2003, requires all organizations that handle protected or patient health information (PHI) to put in place administrative, physical, and technical safeguards for PHI in all forms, including electronic media. The recently published Security Rule focuses on electronic PHI or "e-PHI" to further stress the importance of protecting health information. Any occurrence of an unauthorized leak of information from an individual's medical record is a breach of these rules. Hospitals and healthcare organizations are working to meet the HIPAA security and privacy regulations. However, a report issued on May 28, 2003 [13] found that the efforts of these organizations may be at risk by allowing peer-to-peer (P2P) and instant messenger (IM) applications to run on their networks. The report concluded that by failing to control P2P and IM, hospitals and other healthcare organizations risk compromising patient health information and are at an increased exposure to lawsuits.

FDA Regulation 21 CFR Part 11 states that records can be audited by the agency and, according to Section 11.10 (e), "*audit records shall be available for agency reviews and copying* [14]." This regulation includes IM as well as e-mail. Even attorneys and their support staff who are monitoring legal issues are using IM. West Publishing's President Mike Wilens recently indicated his support for West's support personnel (who are called "reference attorneys") to use IM to provide support to law students who use the computerized legal research service Westlaw, and, according to Wilens, West has gone from providing 100 percent of its law student support through phone service to only 20 percent. West now provides 80 percent of its support to law students by way of IM [15].

Companies are not only faced with setting up standards that will meet regulatory compliance but also with contending with a mixed IM client and multiplatform environment. Investing in an IT system that automatically monitors, logs, purges, retains, and archives IM according to the organization's policies and federal and state regulators' guidelines is essential to good business practice that maximizes ROI while reducing risk.

6.3 Cybersecurity and the Law

With the rash of cyberincidents that have taken a huge financial toll on governments and businesses within the last decade, legislators began to see that laws needed to be enacted to control the "Wild West" environment that existed in cyberspace. Laws have been enacted to protect privacy, infrastructure, people, companies, and just about anything that uses a computer or any form of computer technology. We will discuss the most significant of those laws and how they impact corporate operations in the remainder of this chapter.

6.3.1 The 1996 National Information Infrastructure Protection Act

In 1996, when this law was passed, legislators were presented with some startling statistics. For example, the Computer Emergency and Response Team (CERT) at Carnegie-Mellon University reported *a 498 percent increase in the number of computer intrusions and a 702 percent rise in the number of sites affected with such intrusions* in the three-year period from 1991 through 1994 [16]. During 1994, approximately 40,000 Internet computers were attacked in 2,460 incidents. Similarly, the FBI's National Computer Crime Squad opened over 200 hacker cases from 1991 to 1994 [17].

Before passing this law, legislators realized there are two ways, conceptually, to address the growing computer crime problem. The first would be to comb through the entire United States Code, identifying and amending every statute potentially affected by the implementation of new computer and telecommunications technologies. The second would be to focus substantive amendments on the *Computer Fraud and Abuse Act* to specifically address new abuses that spring from the misuse of new technologies. The new legislation adopted the latter approach for a host of reasons, but the net effect on this approach was a revamp of our laws to address computer-related criminal activity. The full text of the legislative analysis can be found at the following Web address:

```
http://www.usdoj.gov/criminal/cybercrime/1030_anal.html
```

With these changes, the United States stepped into the forefront of rethinking how information technology crimes must be addressed—simultaneously protecting the confidentiality, integrity, and availability of data and systems. And by choosing this path, the hope was to encourage other countries to adopt a similar framework, thus creating a more uniform approach to addressing computer crime in the existing global information infrastructure.

6.3.2 President's Executive Order on Critical Infrastructure Protection

Following the terrorist attack on the World Trade Center and Pentagon that occurred on the morning of September 11, 2001, there was a growing realization in our government and across industry sectors that our national infrastructure was very vulnerable and that we had become (almost completely) dependent on such critical elements that they needed specific protection. On October 16, 2001, President George W. Bush issued an Executive Order [18] to ensure protection of information systems for critical infrastructures, including emergency preparedness communications, and the physical assets that support such systems.

The President's Executive Order established policy that reflects the fact that the information technology revolution has changed the way business is transacted, government operates, and national defense is conducted. Those three functions now depend (almost wholly) on an interdependent network of critical information infrastructures. The protection program authorized by this Executive Order requires continuous efforts to secure information systems for critical infrastructure. Protection of these systems is essential to the telecommunications, energy, financial services, manufacturing, water, transportation, healthcare, and emergency services sectors. The official statement of policy, excerpted from the Executive Order, follows:

> *It is the policy of the United States to protect against disruption of the operation of information systems for critical infrastructure and thereby help to protect the people, economy, essential human and government services, and national security of the United States, and to ensure that any disruptions that occur are infrequent, of minimal duration, and manageable, and cause the least damage possible. The implementation of this policy shall include a voluntary public-private partnership, involving corporate and non-governmental organizations.*

Ten days after this Executive Order was issued, the 107th Congress of the United States of America passed H.R. 3162, which became Public Law 107-56, the USA Patriot Act of 2001 [19].

6.3.3 The USA Patriot Act of 2001

Public Law 107-56, formally titled as *"Uniting and Strengthening America by Providing Appropriate Tools Required to Intercept and Obstruct Terrorism (USA PATRIOT ACT) Act of 2001,"* was enacted on October 26, 2001. A result of the terrorist attacks against the United States on September 11, 2001, carried out by members of Osama Bin Laden's Al Qaeda organization, this legislation made broad and sweeping changes that created a federal antiterrorism fund and directed law enforcement, military, and various government agencies to collectively develop a national network of electronic crime task forces throughout the United States. These task forces were designed to prevent, detect, and investigate various forms of electronic crimes, including potential terrorist attacks against critical infrastructure and financial payment systems.

Title II of this bill amends the federal criminal code to authorize the interception of wire, oral, and electronic communications for the production of evidence of (1) specified chemical weapons or terrorism offenses and (2) computer fraud and abuse.

This section of the law authorizes law enforcement and government personnel who have obtained knowledge of the contents of any wire, oral, or electronic communication or evidence derived therefrom, by authorized means, to disclose contents to such officials to the extent that such contents include foreign intelligence or counterintelligence.

Title III of this law amends existing federal law governing monetary transactions. The amended document prescribes procedural guidelines under which the Secretary of the Treasury may require domestic financial institutions and agencies to take specified measures if there are reasonable grounds for concluding that jurisdictions, financial institutions, types of accounts, or transactions operating outside or within the United States are part of a primary money-laundering concern. The intent of this section is to prevent terroristic concerns from using money-laundering techniques to fund operations that are destructive to national interests.

Title IV is targeted at tightening the control of our borders and immigration laws. In addition to waiving certain restrictions and personnel caps, it directs the Attorney General and the Secretary of State to develop a technology standard to identify visa and admissions applicants. This standard is meant to be the basis for an electronic system of law enforcement and intelligence sharing that will be made available to consular, law enforcement, intelligence, and federal border inspection personnel. Among the many provisions of the Immigration and Naturalization Service changes, this section of the law includes within the definition of "terrorist activity" the use of any weapon or dangerous device. The law redefines the term "engage in terrorist activity" to mean, in an individual capacity or as a member of an organization, to:

1. Commit or to incite to commit, under circumstances indicating an intention to cause death or serious bodily injury, a terrorist activity.
2. Prepare or plan a terrorist activity.

3. Gather information on potential targets for terrorist activity.
4. Solicit funds or other things of value for a terrorist activity or a terrorist organization (with an exception for lack of knowledge).
5. Solicit any individual to engage in prohibited conduct or for terrorist organization membership (with an exception for lack of knowledge).
6. Commit an act that the actor knows, or reasonably should know, affords material support, including a safe house, transportation, communications, funds, transfer of funds or other material financial benefit, false documentation or identification, weapons (including chemical, biological, or radiological weapons), explosives, or training for the commission of a terrorist activity, to any individual who the actor knows or reasonably should know has committed or plans to commit a terrorist activity, or to a terrorist organization (with an exception for lack of knowledge).

Title IV of this law also defines "terrorist organization" as a group designated under the Immigration and Nationality Act or by the Secretary of State; or a group of two or more individuals, whether related or not, that engages in terrorist-related activities.

It also provides for the retroactive application of amendments under this Act and stipulates that an alien shall not be considered inadmissible or deportable because of a relationship to an organization that was not designated as a terrorist organization prior to enactment of this Act. A provision is included to account for situations when the Secretary of State may have identified an organization as a threat and has deemed it necessary to formally designate that organization as a "terroristic organization." This law directs the Secretary of State to notify specified congressional leaders seven days prior to formally making such a designation.

In Title V, "*Removing Obstacles to Investigating Terrorism*," the law authorizes the Attorney General to pay rewards from available funds pursuant to public advertisements for assistance to the U.S. Department of Justice (DOJ) to combat terrorism and defend the nation against terrorist acts, in accordance with procedures and regulations established or issued by the Attorney General, subject to specified conditions, including a prohibition against any such reward of $250,000 or more from being made or offered without the personal approval of either the Attorney General or the President.

Title VII, "*Increased Information Sharing for Critical Infrastructure Protection,*" amends the Omnibus Crime Control and Safe Streets Act of 1968 to extend Bureau of Justice assistance regional information-sharing system grants to systems that enhance the investigation and prosecution abilities of participating federal, state, and local law enforcement agencies in addressing multijurisdictional terrorist conspiracies and activities. It also revised the *Victims of Crime Act of 1984* with provisions regarding the allocation of funds for compensation and assistance, location of compensable crime, and the relationship of crime victim compensation to means-tested federal benefit programs and to the September 11th victim compensation fund. It established an antiterrorism emergency reserve in the *Victims of Crime Fund.*

Title VIII, "*Strengthening the Criminal Laws against Terrorism,*" amends the federal criminal code to prohibit specific terrorist acts or otherwise destructive, disruptive, or violent acts against mass transportation vehicles, ferries, providers, employees, passengers, or operating systems. It amends the federal criminal code to revise the definition of "international terrorism" to include activities that appear to be intended to affect the conduct of government by mass destruction; and define "domestic terrorism" as activities that occur primarily within U.S. jurisdiction, that involve criminal acts dangerous to human life, and that appear to be intended to intimidate or coerce a civilian population, to influence government policy by intimidation or coercion, or to affect government conduct by mass destruction, assassination, or kidnaping.

The specific issue of information sharing that came up in many discussions of the "talking heads" around the Washington, D.C., area after the September 11 attacks is addressed in Title IX, "Improved Intelligence." Herein, amendments to the National Security Act of 1947 require the Director of Central Intelligence (DCI) to establish requirements and priorities for foreign intelligence collected under the Foreign Intelligence Surveillance Act of 1978 and to provide assistance to the Attorney General (AG) to ensure that information derived from electronic surveillance or physical searches is disseminated for efficient and effective foreign intelligence purposes. It also requires the inclusion of international terrorist activities within the scope of foreign intelligence under such Act.

Part of this section expresses the sense of Congress that officers and employees of the intelligence community should establish and maintain intelligence relationships to acquire information on terrorists and terrorist organizations. The law requires the Attorney General or the head of any other federal department or agency with law enforcement responsibilities to expeditiously disclose to the Director of Central Intelligence any foreign intelligence acquired in the course of a criminal investigation.

By now, it should be abundantly clear that the 107th Congress viewed the threat of terroristic activities as a huge security concern. Steps taken to close loopholes in money transaction processes, immigration and border control changes, and the hundreds of other specifics found in Public Law 107-56 reflect the determination of a nation victimized by terrorism to prevent reoccurrences using any means necessary and available. Citizens of the United States rallied around a cause like few other times in history, and the will of the people was reflected in these congressional actions.

6.3.4 The Homeland Security Act of 2002

Nine months after the terrorist attack on September 11, 2001, President George W. Bush proposed creation of a cabinet-level Department of Homeland Security which, was formed to unite essential agencies to work more closely together. The affected agencies consisted of the Coast Guard, the Border Patrol, the Customs Service, immigration officials, the Transportation Security Administration, and the Federal Emergency Management Agency. Employees of the Department of Homeland Security would be charged with completing four primary tasks:

1. To control our borders and prevent terrorists and explosives from entering our country
2. To work with state and local authorities to respond quickly and effectively to emergencies
3. To bring together our best scientists to develop technologies that detect biological, chemical, and nuclear weapons and to discover the drugs and treatments to best protect our citizens
4. To review intelligence and law enforcement information from all agencies of government, and produce a single daily picture of threats against our homeland. Analysts will be responsible for imagining the worst and planning to counter it.

On November 25, 2002, President George W. Bush signed the *Homeland Security Act of 2002* into law. The Act restructures and strengthens the executive branch of the federal government to better meet the threat to our homeland posed by terrorism. In establishing a new Department of Homeland Security, the Act created a federal department whose primary mission will be to help prevent, protect against, and respond to acts of terrorism on our soil. The creation of this new cabinet-level department was a historic event in American history, and it will have long-lasting repercussions on the global community as well. For security professionals, it adds yet another dimension to the complexity of securing infrastructure from malcontents.

Since the tragic events of September 11, 2001, the U.S. Congress has enacted legislation in the USA Patriot Act that has strengthened or amended many of the laws relating to computer crime and electronic evidence. In this section, we will review some of the more important changes that have been made to the laws [20] of the United States, and we will discuss the topics of investigations and ethics.

Authority to Intercept Voice Communications

Under previous law, investigators could not obtain a wiretap order to intercept wire communications (those involving the human voice) for violations of the Computer Fraud and Abuse Act (18 U.S.C. §1030). For example, in several investigations, hackers have stolen teleconferencing services from a telephone company and used this mode of communication to plan and execute hacking attacks. The new amendment changed this by adding felony violations of the Fraud and Abuse Act (18 U.S.C. §1030) to the list of offenses for which a wiretap could be obtained. However, this provision will sunset by December 31, 2005, unless Congress mandates otherwise.

Obtaining Voice-mail and Other Stored Voice Communications

The Electronic Communications Privacy Act (ECPA) granted law enforcement access to stored electronic communications (such as e-mail) but not to stored wire communications (such as voice-mail). Instead, the wiretap statute governed such access because the legal definition of "wire communication" included stored communications, requiring law enforcement to use a wiretap order (rather than a search warrant) to obtain unopened voice communications. Thus, law enforcement authorities were forced to use a wiretap order to obtain voice communications stored with a third-party provider, but they could use a search warrant if that same information were stored on an answering machine inside a criminal's home. This created an unnecessary burden for criminal investigations. Stored voice communications possess few of the sensitivities associated with real-time interception of telephones, making the extremely burdensome process of obtaining a wiretap order unreasonable.

Moreover, in large part, the statutory framework envisions a world in which technology-mediated voice communications (such as telephone calls) are conceptually distinct from nonvoice communications (such as faxes, pager messages, and e-mail). To the limited extent that Congress acknowledged that data and voice might coexist in a single transaction, it did not anticipate the convergence of these two kinds of communications typical of today's telecommunications networks. With the advent of Multipurpose Internet Mail Extensions (MIME) and similar features, an e-mail may include one or more "attachments," consisting of any type of data, including voice recordings. As a result, a law enforcement officer seeking to obtain a suspect's unopened e-mail from an ISP by means of a search warrant had no way of knowing whether the inbox messages included voice attachments (i.e., wire communications), which could not be optained using a search warrant. This necessitated that changes be made to the existing wiretap procedures.

Changes to Wiretapping Procedures

An amendment was written that altered the way in which the wiretap statute and the ECPA apply to stored voice communications. The amendment deleted "electronic storage" of wire communications from the definition of "wire communication" and inserted language to ensure that stored wire communications are covered under the same rules as stored electronic communications. Thus, law enforcement can now obtain such communications using the procedures set out in section 2703 (such as a search warrant) rather than those in the wiretap statute (such as a wiretap order). This provision will sunset by December 31, 2005, unless Congress mandates otherwise.

Scope of Subpoenas for Electronic Evidence

The government must use a subpoena to compel a limited class of information, such as a customer's name, address, length of service, and means of payment, under existing law. Prior to the amendments enacted with the USA Patriot Act, however, the list of records investigators could obtain with a subpoena did *not* include certain records (such as credit card number or other form of payment for the communication service) relevant to determining a customer's true identity. In many cases, users register with Internet service providers using false names. In order to hold these individuals responsible for criminal acts committed online, the method of payment is an essential means of determining true identity. Moreover, many of the definitions used within were technology specific, relating primarily to telephone communications. For example, the list included "local and long-distance telephone toll billing records," but did not include parallel terms for communications on computer networks, such as "records of session times and durations." Similarly, the previous list allowed the government to use a subpoena to obtain the customer's "telephone number or other subscriber number or identity" but did not define what that phrase meant in the context of Internet communications.

Amendments to existing law expanded the narrow list of records that law enforcement authorities could obtain with a subpoena. The new law includes "records of session times and durations," as well as "any temporarily assigned network address." In the Internet context, such records include the Internet Protocol (IP) address assigned by the provider to the customer or subscriber for a particular session, as well as the remote IP address from which a customer connects to the provider. Obtaining such records will make the process of identifying computer criminals and tracing their Internet communications faster and easier.

Moreover, the amendments clarify that investigators may use a subpoena to obtain the "means and source of payment" that a customer uses to pay for his or her account with a communications provider, "including any credit card or bank account number." While generally helpful, this information will prove particularly valuable in identifying users of Internet services where a company does not verify its users' biographical information.

Clarifying the Scope of the Cable Act

Previously, the law contained several different sets of rules regarding privacy protection of communications and their disclosure to law enforcement: one governing cable service [21], one applying to the use of telephone service and Internet access [22], and one called the pen register and trap and trace statute [23]. Prior to the amendments enacted, the Cable Act set out an extremely restrictive system of rules governing law enforcement access to most records possessed by a cable company. For example, the Cable Act did not allow the use of subpoenas or even search warrants to obtain such records. Instead, the cable company had to provide prior notice to the customer (*even if he or she were the target of the investigation*), and the government had to allow the customer to appear in court with an attorney and then justify to the court the investigative need to obtain the records. The court could then order disclosure of the records only if it found by "clear and convincing evidence"—a standard greater than probable cause or even a preponderance of the evidence—that the subscriber was "reasonably suspected" of engaging in criminal activity. This procedure was completely unworkable for virtually any criminal investigation.

The restrictive nature of the Cable Act caused grave difficulties in criminal investigations because today, unlike in 1984 when Congress passed the Cable Act, many cable companies offer not only traditional cable programming services but also Internet access and telephone service. In recent years, some cable companies have refused to accept subpoenas and court orders pursuant to the pen/trap statute and ECPA, noting the seeming inconsistency of these statutes with the Cable Act's harsh restrictions. Treating identical records differently depending on the technology used to access the Internet made little sense. Moreover, these complications at times delayed or even ended important investigations.

When this restrictive legislation was amended in the USA Patriot Act, it clarified the matter, stating that the ECPA, the wiretap statute, and the pen/trap and trace statute all govern disclosures by cable companies that relate to the provision of communication services such as telephone and Internet service. The amendment preserves the Cable Act's primacy with respect to records revealing which ordinary cable television programming a customer chooses to purchase, such as particular premium channels or "pay per view" shows. Thus, in a case where a customer receives both Internet access and conventional cable television service from a single cable provider, a government entity can use legal process under ECPA to compel the provider to disclose only those customer records relating to Internet service but could not compel the cable company to disclose those records relating to viewer television usage of premium channels or "adult" channels and so on.

Emergency Disclosures by Communications Providers

Previous law relating to voluntary disclosures by communication service providers was inadequate for law enforcement purposes in two respects. First, it contained no special provision allowing communications providers to disclose customer records or communications in emergencies. If, for example, an Internet Service Provider (ISP) independently learned that one of its customers was part of a conspiracy to commit an imminent terrorist attack, prompt disclosure of the account information to law enforcement could save lives. Since providing this information did not fall within one of the statutory exceptions, however, an ISP making such a disclosure could be sued in civil courts. Second, prior to the USA Patriot Act, the law did not expressly permit a provider to voluntarily disclose noncontent records (such as a subscriber's log-in records) to law enforcement for purposes of self-protection, even though providers could disclose the content of communications for this reason. Moreover, as a practical matter, communications service providers must have the right to disclose to law enforcement the facts surrounding attacks on their systems. For example, when an ISP's customer hacks into the ISP's network, gains complete control over an e-mail server, and reads or modifies the e-mail of other customers, the provider must have the legal ability to report the complete details of the crime to law enforcement.

The USA Patriot Act corrected both of these inadequacies. The law was changed to permit, but not require, a service provider to disclose to law enforcement either content or noncontent customer records in emergencies involving an immediate risk of death or serious physical injury to any person. This voluntary disclosure, however, does not create an affirmative obligation to review customer communications in search of such imminent dangers. The amendment here also changed the ECPA to allow providers to disclose information to protect their rights and property. All of these changes are scheduled to sunset December 31, 2005, unless Congress mandates otherwise.

Pen Register and Trap and Trace Statute

The pen register and trap and trace statute (the "pen/trap" statute) governs the prospective collection of noncontent traffic information associated with communications, such as the phone numbers dialed by a particular telephone. Section 216 of the USA Patriot Act updates the pen/trap statute in three important ways: (1) The amendments clarify that law enforcement may use pen/trap orders to trace communications on the Internet and other computer networks; (2) Pen/trap orders issued by federal courts now have *nationwide* effect; and (3) Law enforcement authorities must file a special report with the court whenever they use a pen/trap order to install their own monitoring device on computers belonging to a public provider.

Intercepting Communications of Computer Trespassers

Under prior law, the wiretap statute allowed computer owners to monitor the activity on their machines to protect their rights and property. This changed when Section 217 of the USA Patriot Act was enacted. It was unclear whether computer owners could obtain the assistance of law enforcement in conducting such monitoring. This lack of clarity prevented law enforcement from assisting victims to take the natural and reasonable steps in their own defense that would be entirely legal in the physical world. In the physical world, burglary victims may invite the police into their homes to help them catch burglars in the act of committing their crimes. The wiretap statute should not block investigators from responding to similar requests in the computer context simply because the means of committing the burglary happen to fall within the definition of a "wire or electronic communication" according to the wiretap statute.

Because providers often lack the expertise, equipment, or financial resources required to monitor attacks themselves, they commonly have no effective way to exercise their rights to protect themselves from unauthorized attackers. This anomaly in the law created, as one commentator has noted, a "*bizarre result*," in which a "*computer hacker's undeserved statutory privacy right trumps the legitimate privacy rights of the hacker's victims*." To correct this problem, the amendments in Section 217 of the USA Patriot Act allow victims of computer attacks to authorize persons "acting under color of law" to monitor trespassers on their computer systems. Also added was a provision where law enforcement may intercept the communications of a computer trespasser transmitted to, through, or from a protected computer. Before monitoring can occur, however, four requirements must be met:

1. The owner or operator of the protected computer must authorize the interception of the trespasser's communications.
2. The person who intercepts the communication must be lawfully engaged in an ongoing investigation. Both criminal and intelligence investigations qualify, but the authority to intercept ceases at the conclusion of the investigation.
3. The person acting under color of law has reasonable grounds to believe that the contents of the communication to be intercepted will be relevant to the ongoing investigation.
4. Investigators intercept only the communications sent or received by trespassers. Thus, this section would only apply where the configuration of the computer system allows the interception of communications to and from the trespasser and not the interception of nonconsenting users authorized to use the computer.

The USA Patriot Act created a definition of a "computer trespasser." Such trespassers include any person who accesses a protected computer without authorization. In addition, the definition explicitly *excludes* any person "known by the owner or operator of the protected computer to have an existing contractual relationship with the owner or operator for access to all or part of the computer." For example, certain Internet service providers do not allow their customers to send bulk unsolicited e-mails (spam). Customers who send spam would be in violation of the provider's terms of service, but would *not* qualify as trespassers, because they are authorized users and because they have an existing contractual relationship with the provider. These provisions will sunset December 31, 2005, unless Congress mandates otherwise.

Nationwide Search Warrants for E-mail

Previous law required the government to use a search warrant to compel a communications or Internet service provider to disclose unopened e-mail less than six months old. Rule 41 of the Federal Rules of Criminal Procedure required that the "*property*" (the e-mails) to be obtained must be "*within the district*" of jurisdiction of the issuing court. For this reason, some courts had declined to issue warrants for e-mail located in other districts. Unfortunately, this refusal placed an enormous administrative burden on districts where major ISPs are located, such as the Eastern District of Virginia and the Northern District of California, even though these districts had no relationship with the criminal acts being investigated. In addition, requiring investigators to obtain warrants in distant jurisdictions slowed time-sensitive investigations.

The amendment added in the USA Patriot Act has changed this situation in order to allow investigators to use warrants to compel records outside of the district in which the court is located, just as they use federal grand jury subpoenas and orders. This change enables courts with jurisdiction over investigations to obtain evidence directly, without requiring the intervention of agents, prosecutors, and judges in the districts where major ISPs are located. This provision will sunset December 31, 2005, unless Congress mandates otherwise.

Deterrence and Prevention of Cyberterrorism

There were a number of changes made in Section 814 of the USA Patriot Act that improve the Computer Fraud and Abuse Act. This section increases penalties for hackers who damage protected computers (from a maximum of 10 years to a maximum of 20 years). It clarifies the *mens rea* required for such offenses to make explicit that a hacker need only *intend* damage, not necessarily inflict a particular type of damage. It also adds a new offense for damaging computers used for national security or criminal justice and expands the coverage of the statute to include computers in foreign countries so long as there is an *effect* on U.S. interstate or foreign commerce. It now counts state convictions as "prior offenses" for the purpose of recidivist sentencing enhancements and it allows losses to several computers from a hacker's course of conduct to be aggregated for purposes of meeting the $5,000 jurisdictional threshold. We discuss the most significant of these changes in the following text.

Raising Maximum Penalty for Hackers

Under previous law, first-time offenders could be punished by no more than five years' imprisonment, while repeat offenders could receive up to ten years. Certain offenders, however, can cause such severe damage to protected computers that this five-year maximum did not adequately take into account the seriousness of their crimes. For example, David Smith pled guilty to releasing the Melissa virus that damaged thousands of computers across the Internet. Although Smith agreed, as part of his plea, that his conduct caused over $80 million worth of loss (the maximum dollar figure contained in the sentencing guidelines), experts estimate that the real loss was as much as ten times that amount. Had the new laws been in effect at the time of Smith's sentencing, he would most likely have received a much harsher sentence.

Eliminating Mandatory Minimum Sentences

Previous law set a mandatory sentencing guideline of a minimum of six months' imprisonment for any violation of the Computer Fraud and Abuse Act, as well as for accessing a protected computer with the intent to defraud. Under new amendments in the USA Patriot Act, the maximum penalty for violations for damaging a protected computer increased to 10 years for first offenders and 20 years for repeat offenders. Congress chose, however, to eliminate all mandatory minimum guidelines sentencing for section 1030 (Computer Fraud and Abuse Act) violations.

Hacker's Intent versus Degree of Damages

Under previous law, an offender had to "intentionally [cause] damage without authorization." Section 1030 of the Computer Fraud and Abuse Act defined "*damage*" as impairment to the integrity or availability of data, a program, a system, or information that met the following criteria:

1. Caused loss of at least $5,000
2. Modified or impaired medical treatment
3. Caused physical injury
4. Threatened public health or safety

The question arose, however, whether an offender must intend the $5,000 loss or other special harm, or whether a violation occurs if the person only intends to damage the computer, which in fact ends up causing the $5,000 loss or harming the individuals. Congress never intended that the language contained in the definition of "*damage*" would create additional elements of proof of the actor's mental state. Moreover, in most cases, it would be almost impossible to prove this additional intent. Now, under the new law, hackers need only intend to cause damage, not inflict a particular consequence or degree of damage. The new law defines "*damage*" to mean "any impairment to the integrity or availability of data, a program, a system, or information." Under this clarified structure, in order for the government to prove a violation, it must show that the actor caused damage to a protected computer and that the actor's conduct caused *either* loss exceeding $5,000, impairment of medical records, harm to a person, or threat to public safety.

Aggregating Damage Caused by a Hacker

Previous law was unclear about whether the government could aggregate the loss resulting from damage an individual caused to different protected computers in seeking to meet the jurisdictional threshold of $5,000 in loss. For example, an individual could unlawfully access five computers on a network on 10 different dates—*as part of a related course of conduct*—but cause only $1,000 loss to each computer during each intrusion.

If previous law were interpreted not to allow aggregation, then that person would not have committed a federal crime at all, since he or she had not caused over $5,000 to any particular computer. Under the new law, the government may now aggregate "*loss resulting from a related course of conduct affecting one or more other protected computers*" that occurs within a one-year period in proving the $5,000 jurisdictional threshold for damaging a protected computer.

Damaging Computers Used for National Security or Criminal Justice Purposes

Previously, there were no special provision in the Computer Fraud and Abuse Act that would enhance punishment for hackers who damage computers used in furtherance of the administration of justice, national defense, or national security. Thus, federal investigators and prosecutors did not have jurisdiction over efforts to damage criminal justice and military computers where the attack did not cause over $5,000 loss (or meet one of the other special requirements). Yet these systems serve critical functions and merit felony prosecutions even when the damage is relatively slight. Furthermore, an attack on computers used in the national defense that occurs during periods of active military engagement are particularly serious—even if they do not cause extensive damage or disrupt the war-fighting capabilities of the military—because they divert time and attention away from the military's proper objectives. Similarly, disruption of court computer systems and data could seriously impair the integrity of the criminal justice system. Under new provisions, a hacker violates federal law by damaging a computer "*used by or for a government entity in furtherance of the administration of justice, national defense, or national security,*" even if that damage does not result in provable loss over $5,000.

"Protected Computer" and Computers in Foreign Countries

Before the law was changed, "protected computer" was defined as a computer used by the federal government or a financial institution, or one "that is used in interstate or foreign commerce." The definition did not explicitly include computers outside the United States. Because of the interdependency and availability of global computer networks, hackers from within the United States are increasingly targeting systems located entirely outside of this country. The old statute did not explicitly allow for prosecution of such hackers. In addition, individuals in foreign countries frequently route communications through the United States, even as they hack from one foreign country to another. In such cases, their hope may be that the lack of any U.S. victim would either prevent or discourage U.S. law enforcement agencies from assisting in any foreign investigation or prosecution.

The USA Patriot Act amends the definition of "protected computer" to make clear this term includes computers outside of the United States so long as they affect "*interstate or foreign commerce or communication of the United States.*" By clarifying the fact that a domestic offense exists, the United States can now use speedier domestic procedures to join in international hacker investigations. Since these crimes often involve investigators and victims in more than one country, fostering international law enforcement cooperation is essential. In addition, the amendment creates the option of prosecuting such criminals in the United States. Since the United States is urging other countries to ensure they can vindicate the interests of U.S. victims for computer crimes that originate in their nations, this provision will allow the United States to reciprocate in kind.

Counting State Convictions as Prior Offenses

Under previous law, the court at sentencing could, of course, consider the offender's prior convictions for state computer crime offenses. State convictions, however, did not trigger the recidivist sentencing provisions of the Computer Fraud and Abuse Act, which double the maximum penalties available under the statute. The new law alters the definition of "conviction" so that it includes convictions for serious computer hacking crimes under state law—i.e., state felonies where an element of the offense is "*unauthorized access, or exceeding authorized access, to a computer.*"

Definition of Loss

Calculating "loss" is important where the government seeks to prove that an individual caused over a $5,000 loss in order to meet the jurisdictional requirements found in the Computer Fraud and Abuse Act. Yet existing law had no definition of "loss." The only court to address the scope of the definition of loss adopted an inclusive reading of which costs the government may include. In *United States v. Middleton*, 231 F.3d 1207, 1210-11 (9th Cir. 2000), the court held that the definition of loss includes a wide range of harms typically suffered by the victims of computer crimes, including costs of responding to the offense, conducting a damage assessment, restoring the system and data to their condition prior to the offense, and any lost revenue or costs incurred because of interruption of service. In the new law, the definition used in the Middleton case was adopted.

Development of Cybersecurity Forensic Capabilities

The USA Patriot Act requires the U.S. Attorney General to establish such regional computer forensic laboratories as is considered appropriate, and to provide support for existing computer forensic laboratories, to enable them to provide certain forensic and training capabilities. The provision also authorizes the spending of money to support those laboratories.

Investigations

During the conduct of any investigation following a bona fide incident, a specific sequence of events is recommended. This sequence of events should generally be followed as a matter of good practice for all incidents unless special circumstances warrant intervention by law enforcement personnel. This section is meant to provide an overview of the process taken when an investigation is needed. The sequence of events for investigations is as follows:

- Investigate report
- Determine crime committed
- Inform senior management
- Determine crime status
- Identify company elements involved
- Review security/audit policies and procedures
- Determine need for law enforcement
- Protect chain of evidence
- Assist law enforcement as necessary
- Prosecute

Ethics

Internet RFC 1087 [24], "Ethics and the Internet," may have been the first document that addressed ethical behavior for access to and use of the Internet. It stated that it is a privilege and should be treated as such by all users. An excerpt from the RFC follows:

> The IAB strongly endorses the view of the Division Advisory Panel of the National Science Foundation Division of Network, Communications Research and Infrastructure, that, in paraphrase, characterized as unethical and unacceptable any activity which purposely: (a) seeks to gain unauthorized access to the resources of the Internet, (b) disrupts the intended use of the Internet, (c) wastes resources (people, capacity, computer) through such actions, (d) destroys the integrity of computer-based information, and/or (e) compromises the privacy of users. The Internet exists in the general research milieu. Portions of it continue to be used to support research and experimentation on networking. Because experimentation on the Internet has the potential to affect all of its components and users, researchers have the responsibility to exercise great caution in the conduct of their work. Negligence in the conduct of Internet-wide experiments is both irresponsible and unacceptable. The IAB plans to take whatever actions it can, in concert with federal agencies and other interested parties, to identify and to set up technical and procedural mechanisms to make the Internet more resistant to disruption. Such security, however, may be extremely expensive and may be counterproductive if it inhibits the free flow of information that makes the Internet so valuable. In

> the final analysis, the health and well-being of the Internet is the responsibility of its users who must, uniformly, guard against abuses that disrupt the system and threaten its long-term viability.

Since the wide acceptance and use of the Internet, the blending of technologies has made it a bit harder to distinguish the "research-based" Internet of 1989 from the intra/extra/Internet businesses in use today. With such evolved networks come evolved ideas of how to behave. In the next section, we extend the security realm to coverage of wireless issues and discuss the ramifications of setting up WLANs in your business environment.

6.4 IM Must Be Managed as a Business Record

We have addressed the potentially costly business and legal challenges IM brings to the workplace with new legal and regulatory issues, challenges management must pursue to reevaluate security, technology, and employee productivity. Thanks to IM, employers now face even greater electronic communications problems than they do with e-mail and its risks and regulatory requirements. As IM increases in popularity, employers, lawyers, compliance officers, and information technology professionals wrestle to define and manage it in light of myriad business, security, technology, legal, and regulatory concerns. IM is defined more formally as a type of e-mail, an electronic communication that produces a written record that may be discoverable in the course of an audit, an investigation, or a litigation than as the latest fad nuisance to work productivity.

As can be seen from the discussion of the various IM regulatory processes in the previous section, industry and government regulators have helped the financial services industry, healthcare providers, and others clarify that IM is a form of written correspondence that creates a written business record from the standpoint of content and retention, just as e-mail. As such, IM is a written business record that can be subpoenaed and used as evidence in litigation or regulatory investigations requiring adherence to a strategic IM management program, complete with written rules and policies, as a legal and business necessity for any organization that expects its employees and the corporation to meet the current regulatory requirements of IM. Employers and their employees who fail to manage IM today, as they do other controllable business records, will tomorrow face legal and regulatory challenges and will have to make decisions that impact employee productivity and company security, and those are potentially expensive decisions. Of course, you should always seek the advice of competent legal,

IT, records management, and compliance experts before implementing your organization's IM system, rules, policies, and procedures.

6.5 IM Risk Management

Risk management challenges associated with the use of IM include revealing confidential information over an unsecured delivery channel, spreading viruses and worms, and exposing the network to backdoor Trojan horses, which are hidden programs on a system that perform a specific function once users are tricked into running them. IM is also vulnerable to denial-of-service attacks, hijacking sessions, and legal liability resulting from downloading copyrighted files. The numerous vulnerabilities inherent in IM dictate that senior management perform a risk assessment on the business benefit of allowing the use of public IM on corporate networks. Corporations should consider the following practices regarding IM as part of an effective information security program:

- Establish a policy to restrict public IM usage and require employees to sign an acknowledgment of receipt of the policy.
- Include the vulnerabilities of public IM in information security awareness training.
- Ensure a strong virus protection program.
- Ensure a strong patch (software update) management program.
- Create firewall rules to block IM delivery and file sharing.
- Consider blocking specific IM vendors.
- Implement an intrusion detection system to identify IM traffic.
- Assess the need for other IM security products.

IM risks can be mitigated through an effective risk management program. As discussed in previous chapters, IM may be used by employees both officially and unofficially in work environments and may also be used at home to contact and interface with employees in their normal work environment. The use of IM may also expose corporations to security, privacy, and legal liability risks because of the ability to download copyrighted files. Technology vendors have released enterprise IM products for corporate use that authenticate, encrypt, audit, log, and monitor IM communication and provide an alternative to public IM solutions used in a corporate environment. These new corporate enterprise products help corporations use IM technology in a more secure environment and assist in compliance with applicable laws and regulations. Risk management considerations for IM include antivirus, privacy, antihijacking, firewall, intrusion detection, and other risk mitigation controls and practices. Although these controls and practices have been discussed in detail in previous chapters, we will touch on them briefly in the following paragraphs in relation to key IM risk management practices—in particular, how they relate to public IM.

Viruses and worms can spread quickly in an environment where there is a lack of built-in security, the ability to download files, and the built-in buddy list of IM recipients. Public IM does not travel through a central server, where traditional corporate antivirus protection software is located; this provides additional risks, and public IM products available on the Internet are unofficially used in many organizations. IM products can enter the workplace in two ways: The first is referred to as Server Proxy, in which messages pass through the IM vendor's computer and are forwarded to the user, and the second is by Server Broker, in which messages are passed to the IM vendor only to initiate the communication between users, who then communicate directly with each other. As discussed previously, Server Broker and Server Proxy IM virus protection should include network desktop and laptop solutions to handle both methods of IM delivery. Virus protection specifically for IM is still being developed, so senior management will need a comprehensive antivirus program to detect the many blended threats that currently exist with the technology.

Firewalls are configured to block incoming and outgoing public IM traffic. Although known Web sites that broadcast nuisance material such as SPIM should also be blocked, this can be difficult to manage, because Internet names and addresses may change and senior management may have other legitimate reasons for allowing activity based upon legitimate business purposes. For example, although default destination ports for the major IM vendors include ports 5190, 1863, 5050, and other well-known ports such as Telnet (port 23), File Transfer Protocol (port 20), and Simple Mail Transfer Protocol (port 25), it is difficult to block all IM at the firewall because IM has a "port crawling" or "port agile" feature, which allows messages to travel through legitimate open ports if others are unavailable. It is also possible for IM to use Hypertext Transfer Protocol (port 80) in an attempt to bypass the firewall.

Corporate IM risk management should also use Intrusion Detection Systems (IDS) to detect the unauthorized use of IM by preventing, detecting, and responding to threats. This can be achieved by installing IDS software on primary computer systems that actively search for and monitor Internet traffic. For the most part, information on the Internet may be accessed by anyone. Since Public IM transmits unencrypted information, it should never be used for sensitive or confidential information. In addition, IM file sharing may expose the user's IP address and increases the risk that unauthorized parties could gain access to the computer. If information received by IM is not authenticated, you have no way to verify that a message really originated from the sender with whom the recipient believes he or she is communicating during the session. This provides the opportunity for chat sessions where users can be impersonated and hijacked. Corporations should be, and in some cases are required to design and implement a comprehensive written information security program in the form of enforceable policies and guidelines; these should include appropriate controls and training to address the risks posed by the use of public IM.

6.6 Summary

It is now widely accepted that IT security risk management is as much a business issue as it is a technical issue. Even security reviews have become business related and result in cost-justified solutions and recommendations. It is now expected that companies will explore and adopt new approaches to the traditional constraints of lack of expertise, time, and budget. Organizations must also seek better and more visible return on their security budgets. In order to justify an IM budget, you must assess the ROI of your solution to include the cost to secure it. In the next chapter, we will discuss the business value and the ROI assessment of corporate IM solutions.

6.7 Endnotes

1. S. Pruitt. (2003). "Financial IM to be stored for three years." Retrieved January 30, 2005 from http://www.nwfusion.com/news/2003/0619finanimto.html.

2. United States District Court Southern District of New York. (2003). "United States District Court Southern District of New York: Laura Zubulake (Plantiff)–against–US Warburg LLC, UBS Warburg, and UBS AG (Defendents)." Retrieved January 30, 2005 from http://www.malsm.org/zubulake.pdf#search='Zubulake%20v.%20UBS%20Warburg'.

3. S. Pruitt. (2003). "Financial IM to be stored for three years." Retrieved January 30, 2005 from http://www.nwfusion.com/news/2003/0619finanimto.html.

4. U.S. SEC. (2004). "Self-Regulatory Organizations; Notice of Filing of Proposed Rule Change and Amendment Nos. 1 and 2 thereto by the National Association of Securities Dealers, Inc. Relating to Proposed New Uniform Definition of "Branch Office" under NASD Rule 3010(g)(2)." Retrieved January 30, 2005 from http://www.csboston.com/exhibitors/imlogic1.pdf#search='SEC,%20instant%20messaging%20regulations'.

5. U.S. SEC. (2002). "Final Rule: Applicability of CFTC and SEC Customer Protection, Recordkeeping, Reporting, and Bankruptcy Rules and the Securities Investor Protection Act of 1970 to Accounts Holding Security Futures Products." Retrieved January 30, 2005, from http://www.sec.gov/rules/final/34-46473.htm.

6. U.S. SEC. (2004). "Self-Regulatory Organizations; Notice of Filing of Proposed Rule Change and Amendment Nos. 1 and 2 thereto by the National Association of Securities Dealers, Inc. Relating to Proposed New Uniform Definition of "Branch Office" under NASD Rule 3010(g)(2)." Retrieved January 30, 2005 from http://www.csboston.com/exhibitors/imlogic1.pdf#search='SEC,%20instant%20messaging%20regulations'.

7. U.S. SEC. (2002). "Final Rule: Applicability of CFTC and SEC Customer Protection, Recordkeeping, Reporting, and Bankruptcy Rules and the Securities Investor Protection Act of 1970 to Accounts Holding Security Futures Products." Retrieved January 30, 2005, from http://www.sec.gov/rules/final/34-46473.htm.

8. J. Germain. (2004). "E-mail and Instant Messaging Face Compliance Challenges." Retrieved January 30, 2005 from http://www.technewsworld.com/story/E-mail-and-Instant-Messaging-Face-Compliance-Challenges-36797.html.

9. Ferris Research. (October 2004). "Sarbanes-Oxley and the Messaging Manager Report." Retrieved January 30, 2005 from http://www.ferris.com/view_content.php?o=E-mail&id=691.

10. J. Dickinson. (November 5, 2004). "SOX Makes E-mail Archiving Serious Business." Retrieved January 30, 2005 from http://nwc.advancedippipeline.com/showArticle.jhtml?articleID=52200242.

11. FDIC. (July 21, 2004). "Financial Institution Letters—Guidance on Instant Messaging." Retrieved on January 30, 2005 from http://www.fdic.gov/news/news/financial/2004/fil8404a.html.

12. TechWeb News. (November 17, 2004). "Analysis of Enron E-mail Shows Liability Nightmare." Retrieved January 30, 2005 from http://www.systemmanagementpipeline.com/53700437

13. D. Jacobson, and M. Glowacki. (2003). "Hidden Threats to HIPAA: HIPAA Privacy Rule." Retrieved January 30, 2005 from http://www.palisadesys.com/news&events/HIPAAstudy.pdf.

14. U.S. Department of Health and Human Services—Food and Drug Administration. (1997). "Part II: Department of Health and Human Services—Food and Drug Administration—21 CFR Part 11—Electronic Records; Electronic Signatures; Final Rule Electronic Submissions; Establishment of Public Docket; Notice." Retrieved January 30, 2005 from http://www.fda.gov/ora/compliance_ref/part11/FRs/background/pt11finr.pdf.

15. Ernie the Attorney. (April 29, 2004). "Instant Messaging—A Corporate tool?" Retrieved January 30, 2005 from http://www.ernietheattorney.net/ernie_the_attorney/2004/04/instant_messagi.html.

16. CERT Coordination Center. (1994). CERT Coordination Center Web document, http://www.cert.org/, also see CERT Annual Report to ARPA for further information.

17. United States Dept. of Justice, Web page entitled "The National Information Infrastructure Protection Act of 1996 Legislative Analysis," Web document at: http://www.usdoj.gov/criminal/cybercrime/1030_anal.html.

18. United States of America Executive Order issued October 16, 2001 by President George Bush. URL reference is http://www.whitehouse.gov.

19. Public Law 107-56, electronic document available from the Library of Congress, ref: H.R. 3162, URL reference is http://www.thomas.loc.gov .

20. More information on these changes can be found at the U.S. Department of Justice Web site, http://usdoj.gov.

21. Known as the "Cable Act," 47 U.S.C. § 551.

22. Known as the wiretap statute, 18 U.S.C. § 2510 et seq.; ECPA, 18 U.S.C. § 2701 et seq.

23. Known as the "pen/trap" statute, 18 U.S.C. § 3121 et seq.

24. FC 1087, "Ethics and the Internet", Internet Activities Board, January 1989, available at http://www.ietf.org.

7

The Business Value of IM

This chapter has been contributed by Terry L. Dalby, CISM, CISSP, who has over 30 years' experience in network operations, performance management, and security operations—specifically in the telecommunications industry and with large service providers in the United States and Europe. He has been responsible for the design, installation, and operations of extremely large heterogeneous networks, including traditional IP elements as well as fiber and RF systems that provided backbone and distribution for converged voice, video, and data traffic. His publishing credits include *Computer Interfacing: A Practical Approach to Data Acquisition and Control*, as well as multiple magazine articles relating to security management. He is currently a Principal Information Security Engineer at Qwest Communications.

7.1 Ubiquitous Presence and Workflow

IM isn't just another question facing businesses today, it is arguably *the* question. As stated previously, it isn't whether or not to employ IM in the enterprise but rather, how do we control it? IM offers businesses significant benefits in enhanced workgroup communications that are easier and quicker in many cases than the e-mail and voice alternatives, but IM brings risk.

Recent studies have found that more than 90 percent of companies surveyed have IM traffic in their networks while as few as 18 percent of Fortune 500 companies have officially deployed IM [1]. Most of the adopters are in the communications and high-tech sectors. This disparity between *ad hoc* use and official use is typical across the board and makes the formal acceptance of IM a difficult issue to address. As with most problems, IM adoption is a multidimensional issue. Business communication can be formal or informal, person-to-person or group, planned or impromptu, quick and easy or complicated. Culture plays a role in the decision as well. Businesses must consider all of these factors when deciding how to proceed with a potential IM deployment.

Just like a three-legged chair, whether a company deploys IM or not is often a balancing act between employee productivity, scalability, and security. Remove any one of the three legs and it falls. The problem with IM in the business world is that it wasn't designed for the business world. IM has been available to home users for quite some time, and it is likely that in many business environments IM was introduced by users and not as part of a planned deployment. When any technology has its roots in the user base—that is, when IM is translated from home use to the workplace by the same user—then adoption and acceptance are obviously high. But since IM does not have security in mind from conception, and since this type of grass-roots deployment does not consider the enterprise and its pressures, this type of deployment will likely fail to meet the company's needs.

IM is a client-driven rather than a server-driven service. Any user can download a client, configure a user account, and be up and running in minutes. He or she can use the same account and access the same buddy list when at home, at work, or on the road, from any computer he or she has access to. In contrast to IM, e-mail is a server-driven resource. It requires an e-mail server, which must be configured with the user's account information. This server is almost always under the control of the company's IT department and is, therefore, subject to the company's specific policies. The user must rely on system administrators to configure and ultimately "allow" communications. Frequently, this access is not allowed from outside the network or, at the very least, it is tightly controlled. The ease with which users have begun adopting IM has led to a bottom-up spread of IM.

The fact that IM is here to stay is obvious. IT departments can address the IM issue and, in the process, they can spend resources in three ways when it comes to IM:

- Reacting to security events generated by ad hoc use of IM
- Trying (probably unsuccessfully) to prevent the use of IM
- Controlling and developing the benefits of IM

When a company is ready to address the IM problem, controlling and developing the benefits of IM will be the best use of time, manpower, and money.

IM users point to several reasons for the quick adoption of this form of communications. These reasons include ease of use, fast transfer of information, and IM's ability to fit the multitasking work style of employees. But because IM comes form the home user community, some managers consider it a toy and feel it takes away from the productivity of employees. And, certainly, there is potential for abuse in the same way the telephone on employees' desks or their corporate e-mails could be abused.

As with any technology, the Return on Investment (ROI) depends on how the tool is planned, deployed, and controlled. IM offers significant improvement for certain types of communications. Employees at companies that have deployed IM have found it helped them to spend less time on the telephone and on relying on e-mail; it helped them to rapidly identify coworkers, clients, resources available to them for immediate tactical activities, and avoid unproductive phone calls. They have found that IM is faster than e-mail and less intrusive than a phone call, less intrusive for the sender as well as the recipient. IM allows employees to ask a quick question of a co-worker and immediately turn their attention to something else while they wait for the response.

For most users, IM is simply another communication method that complements their existing telephone and e-mail communication. Most users had adopted IM because it was quicker and more convenient than telephone or e-mail—and its use did not represent a significant portion of their workday. IM offers several advantages to both employers and employees. IM provides:

1. *Phone costs savings:* In geographically dispersed environments, IM can be used as an alternative to routine, short-duration phone calls, and in the process eliminate some expenses. Presence information, whether or not the person you are calling is there or not, can also be used to eliminate telephone tag. IM enables users to determine when others are in the office and available. Most business phone calls end up in voice mail, and presence information can help eliminate that. Arranging a quick team conference meeting through IM can be far simpler then trying to set up a telephone conference and far less expensive if multiple continents are involved. A typical office worker may make dozens of calls a day.
2. *Back-channel communications:* IM can also be used to augment other communication channels. For example, if your team has a conference call with a vendor, supplier, or potential client, IM can

be used to clarify points, plan strategy, or share other private information in the background. Similarly, IM can also be used to create a parallel communication channel when you are hosting a Web conference or when a subgroup wants to break out and pursue a particular point without putting the meeting off track.

3. *Immediate communications:* In the last five years, e-mail has emerged as the communication system of choice for most users, but e-mail has its drawbacks. Critical, time-sensitive messages may languish in the recipient's inbox or get lost among the daily flood of communications. IM allows users to cut through the "noise" of all that e-mail and communications clutter and get an immediate response. This has proven invaluable in time-sensitive business processes such as customer service, regulatory issues, crisis management, and problem resolution. For example, a company may choose to use IM as part of its help-desk support solution so that users' issues can be addressed more quickly. Some help-desk problems can be easily resolved by telling the user where to find the resource or how to change a setting. IM would allow this to be done, saving the user valuable time. Similarly, investment professionals can use customer presence information to determine availability to rapidly communicate important news.

4. *Emergency communications channel:* IM has many strengths that allow it to be a communication channel for rapidly disseminating critical information. This communication can be sent to an individual or to multiple groups and is particularly well suited to emergency response, whether your emergency is a natural catastrophe, a health issue, a network outage, or a schedule change. Obviously, if the emergency involves an outage of the telephone or e-mail systems, IM may be your only alternative if the data network remains operational.

5. *Team bonding:* Often, one of the most difficult issues to overcome for people who work in dispersed workgroups is the lack of interpersonal interaction that occurs when a worker idly stops by the office of a colleague. This interpersonal interaction hopefully translates to team building, but isolated workers don't get to participate in this and their feeling of isolation grows. IM can provide a substitute for these quick, not directly related to work encounters and allows users to be more comfortable reaching out to dispersed coworkers throughout the organization. These ad

hoc contacts facilitate workflow and increase productivity by allowing each user to quickly add other team members to his or her workgroup. In this case, IM fosters the "virtual office" and helps users with quality-of-life issues by getting them personally connected to their team.

6. *Find-me-wherever-I-am service:* IM-to-SMS gateway services are becoming more common for routing instant messages to cell phones, creating an inexpensive but reliable multiplatform communication infrastructure that has found favor in help-desk/service-desk operations. Now the recipient doesn't have to be at his or her computer to be contacted, nor does he or she have to carry a Blackberry or similar expensive device.
7. *Expertise on demand:* Similar to the help-desk support example, IM systems can help users quickly reach out to subject matter experts for instant consultations or for surveying multiple experts at one time. Web transactions can be enhanced if they make a sales expert available when a customer faces a problem on the Web site. IM allows users to maintain context by not forcing them to switch to the phone or to e-mail. This fact alone could have a major impact on online sales.
8. *Self-service:* IM applications can allow person-to-machine queries. These machine recipients are virtual agents that resemble their human support staff counterparts. The request can be for information on how to complete an application or to enable salespeople to gain access to sales information.

These items are powerful reasons to include IM as part of a company's communications infrastructure. But IM comes with some concerns as well. Employee productivity has already been mentioned, but just as importantly is how IM assumes its place in the IT infrastructure. Three major issues arise when considering IM in your enterprise: name control, security, and auditing. If IM is deployed from the user community and not controlled, the corporation has no control over user identities. Because IM user identities are independent of the corporate directory, two important ramifications arise:

- IM operations independent of the corporate directory may not reflect the company's naming policies.

- When an IM user leaves the company, there is no way to prevent the continued use of that user name. This can introduce significant liability for the employer.

Security is another issue IM use poses. The home-user or consumer-grade IM systems, clients, and their associated networks do not provide end-to-end encryption, local routing, or other secure messaging capabilities. Because these clients can often penetrate corporate firewalls, enterprises are at risk of receiving viruses, worms, rogue protocols, and other malicious content through their IM infrastructure, not to mention the lack of protection for sensitive content transmitted via IM.

Auditing and logging is another problem for consumer-grade IM clients. The fact that these clients operate completely independent of the infrastructure means they typically do not provide any sort of logging of IM conversations—when the parties to an IM conversation leave the session, the content of their conversation is lost unless the text thread is manually copied and saved. This can result in significant problems for an enterprise that archives employees' electronic communication. Further, it leaves an enterprise vulnerable if the archived content of an IM conversation is modified after the fact.

These issues don't mean that IM is not a viable tool for the enterprise, but they do present problems that need to be addressed. As IM matures and managers come to understand its implications, capabilities, and limitations, they are becoming more open to IM's presence and use in the enterprise. A company's infrastructure is an investment, and IM will likely be a part of that investment, whether it is a planned investment or not. It is important for management to address any issues with IM before problems arise. Maximizing the ROI for IM hinges on identified goals, proper planning, and IM management.

7.2 It's All about Culture

The decision whether or not to deploy IM (or any other service for that matter) should be based on a measurable ROI—at least in a perfect world. Is IM right for your organization? That depends on several factors. If your company is struggling to enforce a "no personal calls or e-mails" policy today, or if personal communication is becoming an issue, then IM may not be a good strategy. IM's value to a company depends on how it is used and managed. That, in turn, depends on your corporate culture.

If your business is like many others, you have employees working remotely, some from their homes perhaps, but certainly in other offices across town or across the country. One feature that managers find interesting is the "presence" that IM affords. As soon as you become an IM user you understand what "presence" is. It is that feature of IM that allows you to know who is online and whether they are active or not. A company that employs IM as part of its telecommuting solution can also employ "presence." If the employee is not at his or her computer and actively using the computer, the IM detects this idleness and displays it. Some may feel that this is an invasion of privacy, while others just see the improved communications capability of IM.

Organizations where change is the rule of the day and time is always of the essence may find IM enables employees to more rapidly respond to those changes and build teams and identify experts and resources who are ready to attack the problem. This allows them to save valuable time and be more responsive to their customers. Conversely, if your company is located at one facility or works strictly by department and committee, the advantages of IM and presence awareness to coworkers and resources is diminished. It is also important to remember to consider how management interacts with staff members today. If e-mail is the method that managers use to communicate both to subordinates and to their managers, then IM can be the natural complement to such communications. IM will allow faster management notification and will provide a feedback path when issues arrive. However, if your environment is a more formal or hierarchical environment, IM may not be the way to go. One size doesn't have to fit all.

So far, this discussion has focused on text-based communications, but IM offers enriched alternatives, including voice, video, file transfer, and application sharing. This enables "virtual presentations," where a company's message can be conveyed in powerful and effective ways without sending a team to the customer's location. It wasn't that long ago that companies had to maintain expensive travel budgets, because that was how they delivered their message, demonstrated their product, or built business relationships, but business culture has changed and is becoming more accepting of doing business virtually through electronic media.

Vendors are responding to this change. Microsoft, Yahoo!, and other IM vendors are beginning to look beyond mere text messaging, responding to the users' demand for next-generation services such as video conferencing and Voice-over-IP (VoIP). Microsoft's Live Communication Server 2003 ships with support for both features, and many other IM solutions offer some degree of support for these services. It's difficult to see clearly all the possibilities for IM, but even the hacking community has seen the power of using IM for automated, system-level communications. Other next-generation usages may include building IM interfaces onto existing applications so that users can query these applications for information. The rapid growth and obvious acceptance of IM shows that users are growing more and more comfortable with IM as an interface, and this will lead to the use of this IM interface to interact with other applications, especially if existing systems can be retrofitted. Imagine including your most frequently used applications in your buddy list so that you would have nearly instant access to data and information. That way, if you want to query an inventory management system, you can find out how many of your best-selling products are available just by using IM to connect to the master database.

As stated previously, IM users have driven much of the growth and functional improvement of the technology. Vendors are responding to such growth and demand as well. It is the competition among vendors that is fueling much of the functional growth of IM. Microsoft, Yahoo!, AOL, and several other vendors are all vying for what they see as an exploding market. Vendors clearly recognize the impact that IM will likely have on daily work styles, and they are rushing to deliver new value-added features to the IM market to help differentiate themselves from their competitors. Just look at Yahoo!'s partnership with Web conferencing provider WebEx Communications to add Web conferencing to its Yahoo! Business Messenger product as an example. As stated earlier in this section, the decision to implement IM in your infrastructure should be based on a measurable ROI. You may ask yourself if it is possible to calculate an accurate ROI. Let's take a look.

7.3 Overall ROI for IM

The basic approach to determining the ROI for something is to calculate the cost of the old technology and subtract the cost of deploying the new technology. If the result is a positive number, then the company has saved money, and, in such a case, the new technology (IM) would likely improve the efficiency of operations within the organization. For example, using this simple model, let's start with a company with 5,000 employees with an average burdened salary of $80,000 per year or approximately $39.00 per hour. If our ROI study concludes that if IM is deployed, each employee would save 30 minutes per day, on average, through more efficient communications and multitasking while communicating, we could calculate an ROI starting point. This example company would save $19.50 per employee per day. That adds up to $25,350,000 per year in increased productivity, but this is just the first dart thrown at determining an ROI. Our calculation doesn't include the savings obtained from fewer long-distance phone calls or the incremental savings obtained from reduced load on e-mail servers. This calculation also overlooks the cost of deploying IM, operating the IM infrastructure, and, just as importantly, securing IM. The problem with putting too much credence in this simple approach is that the real-world problem we are trying to solve isn't simple.

When e-mail started to become widely accepted in the corporate world in the early 1990s, IT organizations spent considerable time trying to calculate the ROI prior to large-scale investments. These ROI studies began with the overall mailroom expenses, the cost of routing interoffice memos, and fax machines and associated telephone lines. If e-mail was going to increase communications efficiency, then these costs should be higher than the cost of deploying e-mail. However, most organizations were unable to generate a positive ROI model. One reason for this was that they failed to begin with the actual value of their existing communications systems. They compared the operating costs of the old system to the deployment and operating costs of the new e-mail system. This was hardly an apples-to-apples comparison.

Of course, e-mail didn't end there. It has been an unparalleled success, and most businesses employ e-mail to some degree. In fact, practically all users now favor e-mail communication over telephone use and certainly over the traditional postal mail system. A similar phenomenon is occurring with IM. The core value of IM, rapid information dissemination, is nearly impossible to quantify. As in the e-mail example, it is nearly impossible to put a dollar figure on quality of service. What is the value of being able to rapidly respond to customer needs? How much is it worth to be able to quickly pass the word about a competitor's latest move to a product team or to fine-tune a bid at the last minute? The problem is that much of the value of a support system is related to the quality of the service delivered by that system plus the "forgotten" costs of the original deployment. Thus, calculating an ROI specifically related to these factors is difficult, unless the merit of that information or interaction can be valued in some concrete, tangible way.

The second major benefit of IM, that of knowing the presence status of another user, which might be used to make an in-person visit or a phone call, is also difficult to quantify. Even though the initial investment required to deploy and run IM systems is considerably lower than e-mail, with the exception of the archival/record management costs, there are still substantial costs involved. There are license-acquisition costs, though they may be waived as part of a proprietary system's maintenance fees, and there are the costs of hardware to factor into the equation. Even given lower costs, firms attempting to build a business case for IM based simply on traditional ROI approaches are probably going to miscalculate its value.

Instead, a potentially better approach would be for organizations to look at business processes and determine where in the firm investment strategy IM will pay off. Start by looking at processes characterized by volatility, time sensitivity, geographic dispersal, and those without significant records management and compliance issues. These make good candidates for IM. After these potential candidates are identified, a pilot program should be run to test the assumption. As with any proof of concept or pilot program, this initial IM deployment should be carefully monitored for success/failure, and a "lessons learned" or postmortem case study should be written to convey why the program failed or succeeded. It is extremely important to somehow quantify success, maybe not in dollars saved but in improved quality of service. This improved quality of service might be reflected in improved process times, increased customer satisfaction, or faster task delegation. If the pilot was determined to be a success, then this limited rollout could be extended to additional areas in the firm that are likely to benefit from IM. Alternatively, the company could decide to deploy IM throughout the enterprise. Either way, the real challenge will be in convincing management of the soft benefits of IM versus hard ROI.

7.4 The Choice Is Yours

IM has become a necessary piece of business infrastructure for many organizations. Much of IM's use is uncontrolled, but it still exists in the enterprise. The important challenge one must face is how to deal with IM. Policies that forbid IM use are difficult to enforce, and simply ignoring IM neglects the potential security risks that are associated with its unmanaged use. Perhaps the best approach is to accept it officially but also control it, manage it, and secure it. There are products available that allow administrators to control IM traffic—much like an Internet proxy controls access to the World Wide Web. These IM proxies can filter content and help improve the secure use of IM. At the same time, controls can be put in place that protect the company by integrating IM with the directory services infrastructure, thereby maintaining standardized naming conventions and user identity.

The direction for all IM systems is clear—more robust clients with text, voice, application-sharing, and presentation capabilities. The functions provided by these messaging platforms will continue to grow, but this additional functionality will come at the price of increased demand placed on the network infrastructure. It's not hard to imagine a day, none too soon, when the IM platform will hold the same level of importance in the enterprise that the e-mail system occupies today. However, that won't come as a result of hard ROI figures. Just like e-mail, IM is here to stay. Bottom line: Deal with it now or pay a steep price later.

7.5 Endnotes

1. Nucleus Research. (2004). "Instant Messaging: Breaking the Bad ROI Rap." Retrieved December 29, 2004 from http://www.nucleusresearch.com/research/e109.pdf.

8

The Future of IM

This chapter has been contributed by Tony Dubendorf, who has enjoyed a long and distinguished career in the computer industry. Tony has over 30 years of experience in the security and wireless communications industry, starting with his ventures into amateur radio in the early 1970s. Tony has authored several books and papers, including *Wireless Data Technologies*, published by John Wiley & Sons. During his technical career, Tony has worked heavily in the design and deployment of metropolitan area MESH networks for Corpus Christi, Texas; Chaska, Minnesota; Jamestown, New York; and St. Cloud, Florida, to name just a few. Tony led the infrastructure design, implementation, and security audits for several global corporations, such as Nokia, Mitsubishi Heavy Industries, and the Atlantis Resort on Paradise Island, Bahamas, as well as for several government organizations. Tony's professional background includes management, wireless technologies and security consulting, business development, and participation in the full range of enterprise program and project management activities, with specific emphasis on wireless and information security technologies.

IM (as defined by www.dictionary.com [1]) is "a *computer application that allows for communications in real time, a live chat, and e-mail service.*" A student text on computing essentials [2] defines IM as a "*communication and collaboration tool for direct, live, connections over the Internet.*"

Regardless of which definition you use regardless of text, voice, or video over media such as the local network or the Internet, via PDA, cell phone, or by WiFi; whichever means you choose, IM is affecting the communication skills/habits/tactics of most people we know under age 50 in the workplace. People are getting used to writing much shorter, terse messages now; you do not type out a formal memo or even use full sentences when your IM buddy is impatiently waiting for a live response on the other end. In one century, we have gone from flowery, polite, even long-winded Edwardian-style business letters to telegraphic (or, one might say, telecryptic) instant messages.

Consider where IM is right now: on your computers, PDAs, mobile phones, on your network, across the Internet, literally everywhere around the globe. It is considered the heartbeat of the Internet now, and it is growing at approximately 40 percent annually by some estimates. It is expected to be in use by 85 percent of all companies by the end of 2005. By the end of 2005, it's expected to surpass e-mail as the primary online communications tool. IM is evolving at a fast and furious pace. It is becoming a core communications engine for voice, peer-to-peer file transfers, secure messaging, applications sharing, person-to-machine communications, and machine-to-machine communications.

IM is the first "killer application" of presence awareness, and presence awareness is going to continue beyond person-to-person text messaging and will include linking people to applications, applications to applications, applications to machines, and machines to machines. Let us remember how presence awareness is really defined. Presence awareness is the messaging technology that lets users or devices quickly find each other, no matter where their physical location may be at the moment. RFC 2779, which defines some presence requirements, says:

> *Presence is a means for finding, retrieving, and subscribing to changes in the presence information (e.g. online or offline) of other users.*

An example of just such a presence system is the AOL Instant Messenger or Lotus Sametime. In a typical presence network, a central server (or servers) keeps track of users as they log into and out of the network. Presence awareness has rapidly become one of the most compelling features of IM applications. Never before in the history of communications have we been able to tell whether the person we want to communicate with can actually be reached before we try to engage with him or her. The promise of presence technology is that users can reach others instantly, regardless of the location of either party, over a variety of media, including chat, video, and wireless or traditional voice. Also possible will be technologies such as spontaneous audio and video conferences.

Person-to-application IM is already an offering available from software giant IBM. It extends the value of the buddy list to nearly any application. Examples of person-to-application IM include gaining access to directory records, interacting with applications, and searching for experts. Application-to-person, server-initiated IM, in which an application is aware of a person's online presence, can significantly speed workflow and business processes.

It is expected that in the future the capabilities of application-to-application IM through Web services will truly leverage the advantages of real-time presence. I see the most interesting trend going forward to be the migration from person-to-person IM to having presence capabilities pervasive on the network and the ability to be leveraged by any IM-enabled application. With this, you can thread presence awareness throughout an entire enterprise in both applications and systems.

With literally billions of messages sent every day, IM is the world's second most popular online communication medium behind e-mail. Its extension into the mobile ubiquitous network space has made a significant impact on our personal and business lives.

8.1 The Pervasive Network

An unstoppable trend is growing toward ubiquitous computing. The pervasive network is being deployed now and is available in many areas around the world. It is a reality creating the need for intelligent agents to process information anytime and anywhere. This leap from tethered computing to the world of wireless and mobile solutions jumpstarts a new science, one rapidly growing in prominence, that we mentioned earlier: Presence Awareness (PA).

The majority of successful companies have obtained a competitive edge by enabling their employees to work anytime and anywhere. Enabling technologies such as Bluetooth, IP, Java, Jini, WML, WiFi, and XML/Voice make it possible to build applications that can be accessed by employees from any location around the globe—even from the Space Station. Consumers are benefitting by building in-home networks and enjoying gaming on their wireless handheld devices. Pervasive technologies go far beyond wireless voice and data connectivity by providing enterprises with connectivity for CRM, ERP, and SFA processes on a ubiquitous basis, resulting in employees who are more efficient and thereby creating a more profitable company. Carriers, both traditional and wireless, play a crucial role in bringing pervasive technologies to the market through broadband networks, IP-based messaging and conferencing services, 3G Cellular, WiFi hotspots, metropolitan area wireless networks, and enterprise consulting services.

Services from pervasive networks will enhance our way of life by providing the right information for the right context. First, pervasive services will enable easy access to information from the workplace or home in a secure fashion. The pervasive network will be able to adapt to the kind of device the user has at hand to connect to the network. The network will be connected to the user's presence, enabling a connection with that user on the device of his or her choice.

Wireless networks provide mobility, and mobile computing offers anytime, anywhere connectivity to the Internet and to other users—though, in both cases, users still must initiate access to the network. With pervasive networks and pervasive computing, numerous landline and wireless systems will integrate seamlessly and will be on all the time. When the IM system is part of an integrated communications platform, presence awareness can become more sophisticated. It can notify others when a user is online, willing to accept phone calls at a home or office number, or if that user has a mobile phone turned on. Users can even set presence messages, so others trying to contact them will know that they have stepped out for lunch and will return at a certain time.

When the element of mobility is added to IM, it introduces a new level of presence awareness, letting others know where a user is based on where the user logs in to the system or location information provided by the wireless network. For example, if User A wanted to set a meeting with User B but noticed when accessing the messaging system that User B was out of town, User A would not even have to contact User B to learn that the user was unavailable. This level of presence awareness does bring up some issues, particularly that of privacy. Just as even the basic messaging systems of today allow users to make themselves invisible to other users when they are online or to block communication from certain users, more advanced messaging systems will have to provide a certain degree of control over presence awareness. Only the most trusted users would have access to location information, for example, so users would not be broadcasting to the world at large that they are away from home. There can be certain degrees of presence information made available, from appearing totally invisible online to complete strangers, to "away from the office" messages to business colleagues, and full presence information to immediate family.

8.2 Peer-to-Peer Instant Messaging

Providing effective and cost-efficient services is also about achieving time-sensitive communications: getting the right message to the right people at the right time to enable the right decision.

Innovations in technology during the last century, most notably the telephone and, of late, e-mail, have played a huge role in the enabling of true international commerce, making the business world a smaller, more accessible place. However, as e-mail becomes clogged with spam and viruses, and the cost of regular international calls remains high, technology has again come to the rescue. IM and Peer-to-Peer (P2P) networking represent the next generation of powerful communication technologies, delivering messaging and content in real-time, while breaking cost barriers and increasing employee productivity.

IM is now everywhere. According to International Data Corporation (IDC), the rapid consumer adoption of Public IM networks makes it the fastest growing communication channel in history. Studies suggest that P2P applications can be found installed in a massive 77 percent of organizations with between 10 and 45,000 employees. In firms employing over 500 people, this figure rises to 100 percent. Business users have discovered the following values of IM:

- Having virtual conferences
- Collaborating on projects
- Augmenting phone conversations
- Exchanging transaction instructions

8.3 Peer-to-Application (the Human-Computer Interface)

The Internet is a communications device. As such, it enables anyone or any application to access anyone or any application at almost anytime. The peer-to-application (P2A) world is not the exclusive domain of the Web. BOTS, applications or utilities that have their interface as a projection of a persona into the online chat world, are a great and fun way to bring people and applications together in a conversational way.

Peer-to-application IM, which IBM currently offers through its same-time BOTS technology, extends the value of the buddy list to nearly any application. Examples of peer-to-application IM include gaining access to corporate directory records, interacting with applications, and searching for experts. Application-to-person, server-initiated IM, in which an application is aware of a person's online presence, can speed workflow and greatly improve the business process. In the future, application-to-application messaging through Web services will truly leverage the advantages of real-time presence. The most interesting trend we see going forward is the migration from person-to-person IM to having presence capabilities pervasive on the network and (able to be) leveraged by any application. You can thread presence awareness throughout the enterprise, including embedding it in applications and systems.

8.4 Machine-to-Machine (Application-to-Application)

The evolution of the Web and the desktop shows a definite trend toward applications becoming peers and having conversations with other applications, services, and even people. The predominant common language of conversations in both media, as we will see in the following section on Jabber, has become XML. As a way of providing a hierarchical structure and a meaningful context for data, XML is being heavily adopted throughout the world as the de facto language for moving this data between disparate applications.

When applications talk to each other, they are typically going to use a push process instead of a pull process. In other words, rather than sending a request and waiting patiently for it to respond, they are going to send a message (push a message to the other application) and service queues that the other application will use to send messages back. There are three basic reasons why I believe that only in a few cases will the applications ever synchronously invoke each other:

1. *Applications are not always available 24 hours a day, or 7 days a week, or even 365 days a year.* Without a doubt in anyone's mind, all applications are down at some point in time. There are times when they may appear to be down, and in essence if they are unreachable, they are down, but they are executing batch processes and aren't prepared to provide interactive services. In an ideal world, a program will not hold the memory for a thread and

block processes for any significant period of time, which is what the requesting applications would have to do in this case. It becomes a single risk point for failure. It's one thing when people are waiting for their browsers to load, but when applications are waiting, they are mindless and will often patiently retry over and over again every 10 seconds, which just queues up more and more requesting threads to the unresponsive application.

2. *Applications were not written for unpredictable load, but enabling any application on the Net or on other devices to invoke them invites exactly that.* Most applications have been written assuming some limited number of humans within some enterprise would invoke them. They can only scale so far. If the load surges during peak periods and each request is a synchronous request/response, either the server will deny the request (which means that the requesting application will either fail or retry, which will make things worse), or it will try to handle more requests than is good for it and will bog down and ultimately start to thrash. We saw this in the early days of the Web. It was called firestorms or Web-storms and typically resulted from naive programmers queuing up more threads as more demands came in rather than recognizing that there was/is a native limit to the throughput of a processor. There are also Quality of Service (QOS) issues involved. Some requests matter more than others.

   eBay, for example, wants to service requests to add goods to an auction at a much higher priority than requests to return the results of a query about which goods arc available at a given price/type. Trading systems want important clients to get faster feedback than nickel and dime ones. There are no good mechanisms for doing this if all invocations result in synchronous threads in the serving application. There are if all invocations result in queued requests. It is called intelligent dequeuing.

3. *Last, but certainly not least, most applications in the real world involve people, process, and time.* Ask a bank for my credit history. A person in a workflow may have to authenticate and approve this request. Ask a papermill to make you paper and to let you know when the paper is ready and weeks may elapse. Ask a financial application to compute a hedging strategy and an analyst may have to work it out by hand. Even ask a database a sufficiently hard and/or expensive question (say, some assay of oil drilling results or genome analysis) and the answer may be slow in com-

ing. All of these delays are best handled, if a robust, reliable, scalable architecture is desired, with messaging. Then the programming model fits the reality. It understands that long periods of time may elapse between the request and the response (or responses for things where status messages are expected).

8.5 Jabber

To fully realize the potential for unifying the conversations ranging throughout the Internet today, and enabling applications and services to run on top of a common platform, a community of developers worldwide has developed a set of technologies collectively known as Jabber (http://jabber.org). Jabber was designed for peer conversations, both P2P and particularly application-to-application, and for real-time as well as asynchronous/offline conversations. Jabber is fully distributed, while allowing a corporation or service to manage its own namespace. Its design is a response to the popularity of the closed IM services. We are trying to create a simple and manageable platform that offers the conversational traits described earlier in this chapter, traits that none of the existing systems comes close to providing in full.

Jabber began in early 1998 out of a desire to create a truly open, distributed platform for IM and to break free from the centralized, commercial IM services. The design began with XML, which we exploited for its extensibility and for its ability to encapsulate data, which lowers the barrier to accessing it. The use of XML is pervasive across Jabber, allowing new protocols to be transparently implemented on top of a deployed network of servers and applications. XML is used for the native protocol, translated to other formats as necessary in order to communicate between Jabber applications and other messaging protocols.

The Jabber project emerged from that early open collaboration of numerous individuals and companies worldwide. The name Jabber symbolizes its existence as numerous independent projects sharing common goals, each building a part of the overall architecture. These projects include:

- A modular open-source server written in C
- Numerous open-source and commercial clients for nearly every platform
- Gateways to most IM services and Internet messaging protocols

- Libraries for nearly every programming language
- Specialized agents and services such as RSS and language translations

Jabber is simply a set of common technologies that all of these projects agree on collaboratively when building tools for peer-to-peer systems. One important focus of Jabber is to empower conversations between both people and applications.

The Jabber team hopes to create an open medium in which the user has choice and flexibility in the software used to manage conversations, instead of being hindered by the features provided by a closed, commercial service. We hope to accelerate the development of peer applications built on an open foundation, by enabling them to have intelligent conversations with other people and applications and by providing a common underlying foundation that facilitates conversations and the accessibility of dynamic data from different services.

8.6 Security and Government Compliance

In order to provide you with a better understanding of what makes an IM client so powerful (and so dangerous), the following is a list of the typical capabilities offered by the big three IM client packages: AOL Instant Messenger, Microsoft .NET Messenger, and Yahoo! Messenger:

- Basic text-mode messaging between users
- Voice over IP conversations
- Video over IP sessions
- File transfers
- Application sharing
- Group chat in chatrooms, similar to IRC

While all three of the IM clients, have some (or all) of these features, not all of the IM clients have all of these features. For this reason, you may find that users will often make use of two or perhaps even three clients on their machines.

Most organizations are using IM whether they like it or not. Unless blocked at the firewall, end users frequently use outside IM services such as AOL IM/ICQ or MSN Messenger for business purposes, without central

IT group authorization. With the growth of IM and peer-to-peer (P2P) technologies, businesses are increasingly facing security and management challenges. Simply denying service to employees is not the answer, and IT departments should learn not to fear P2P networks but rather embrace these channels as the future of person-to-person messaging.

The organizational security risks of IM and P2P deployment stem not from malicious viruses, unauthorized breaks of copyright, or IM's apparent unaccountability. The real problem is much closer to home and much easier to solve. The root problem is the lack of awareness of IM and P2P usage within business.

While it would be inaccurate to suggest that there are no risks to IM and P2P deployments, properly managed, such risks are very simply negated and stem from the following points:

1. Applications are selected, downloaded, and installed by employees without IT involvement—bottom-up technology adoption.
2. IM and P2P applications are designed to work around existing security mechanisms such as firewalls.
3. The rapid increase in the installed base of these applications makes them a natural target for exploitation by hackers and virus propagation.
4. IT organizations have little chance of detecting the presence of these applications, how they are being used, and how these applications bypass security mechanisms, including breaching firewalls through random port crawling, intrusion detection systems, and perimeter antivirus scanners.
5. Organizations have no means of logging and monitoring the content crossing the corporate boundaries by means of IM and P2P. Confidential or inappropriate information could be leaving the company. Illegal transfer of copyrighted material—music, video—onto a corporate network could leave organizations liable to the bodies such as the Recording Industry Artists Association (RIAA) or the Motion Picture Association of America (MPAA).

Having a clear understanding of these technologies and their most common use is the starting point to protecting an organization and extracting the benefits from appropriate usage. Enterprises must now create a set of best practices and usage policies that act as a framework for the adoption and uptake of these applications. A typical organization might decide to support the following simple policy:

1. All users can use internal IM.
2. A subset of users can use IM externally—but only if conversations are monitored and controlled.
3. No users can transfer files using IM or P2P applications.
4. Implement suitable policies for authorized users:
   - For example, it's essential in any organization to be able to dynamically map IM user or screen names to corporate identities.
   - Should conversations be recorded?
   - Do you need to provide disclaimers or usage terms and conditions within an IM conversation?
   - Ensure that unauthorized activity is blocked completely (at a protocol level—IM and P2P applications port-crawl and use different and often changing IPs for access).

8.7 The Business Impact

Winning in business is about achieving time-sensitive communications—getting the right message to the right people at the right time to enable the right business decision. Innovations in technology during the 20th century, most notably the telephone and e-mail, have played a huge role in this, enabling true international commerce, making the business world a smaller, more accessible place. However, as e-mail becomes clogged with spam and virus technology again comes to the rescue, IM and P2P networking represent the next generation of powerful communication technologies, delivering messaging and content in real-time while breaking cost barriers and increasing employee productivity.

The motivation for the adoption of IM in business is the need to communicate and multitask in real-time. Business users have discovered the value of IM—having virtual conferences, collaborating on projects, augmenting phone conversations, and exchanging transaction instructions. IM advocates benefit from reduced telephony costs, more accuracy in communications, and faster and more efficient activity in time-sensitive markets.

Many organizations simply do not know whether IM and P2P are being used, which employees are using them, or, what they are being used for. Once businesses are confident about their ability to manage and control IM and P2P behavior, they should start to explore how other processes could be made more productive by the adoption of real-time technologies. Many businesses are failing to "see the woods for the trees." Once organizations come to understand the reality of IM and P2P, these once-threatening communications channels become truly transparent and are found to offer very clear cost and efficiency benefits.

8.8 Endnotes

1. http://dictionary.reference.com/search?q=Instant%20Messaging.
2. T. O'Leary and L. O'Leary, *Computing Essentials*, New York, McGraw-Hill, 2002.

A

General Network Security

Regardless of whether computer and network data is transmitted on a wired or wireless medium, the basic security concepts remain much the same. A solid foundation of security understanding is required before we cover the elements of network security common to both wired and wireless environments. This appendix is intended for those requiring a general knowledge of network security before jumping in to our chapters on IM security risks and best practices because knowledge without preparation does us very little good. Some of the content presented in this appendix has been excerpted from our *Wireless Operational Security* [1] book with the permission of Digital Press, an imprint of Elsevier.

For those among us who are tasked with managing business, and for those ever-shrinking number of Information Technology (IT) professionals who are not directly involved in the daily struggles of coping with cyber-security issues, one might be tempted to ask: What is the big deal about cybersecurity, really? How does it affect our company infrastructure? How does it affect users in our organization? Is it something our management team should worry about?

These are all legitimate questions. More and more today, IT professionals face an ever-growing and daunting task. Attacks occur *every* single day [2]. The only question to be asked in today's modern computing environment is: Are we prepared to deal with an attack? This appendix will provide guidance on how to prepare for such assaults against the organizational infrastructure. It will help network and systems administrators prepare to answer these types of questions and provide compelling information that can help even the most reluctant manager or administrator come to terms with the changed, threatening computing environment we face today.

A.1 Threats to Personal Privacy

Vast data stores in myriad organizations hold personal information about each of us. The accumulation of such large amounts of electronic information, combined with the increased ability of computers to monitor, process, and aggregate this information about people creates a massive threat to our individual privacy. The reality of today is that all of this information and technology now available can be electronically linked together, allowing unknown entities unabated access to even our most private information. This situation should give us reason to pause and ask ourselves if we have not created a modern information age with an unwanted byproduct some have often referred to as "Big Brother."

While the magnitude and cost of the threat to our personal privacy is very difficult to determine, it is readily apparent that information technology is becoming powerful enough to warrant fears of the emergence of both government and corporate "Big Brothers." More awareness of the situation is needed at the organizational and personal level. With the increased accessibility of such information, we have created an ever-growing vulnerability that someone, such as a cyberterrorist, is likely to exploit. Another consideration of late, the recently legislated Privacy Acts that many different countries have enacted in order to try to protect the data assets of their citizenries, has become an ever-growing part of this modern information age. All companies using computing resources today now need to be keenly aware of both these threats and the legal ramifications that ensue when they attempt to monitor, prevent, or provide access to their information resources.

A.2 Fraud and Theft

Computer systems can be exploited for the purpose of conducting fraudulent activities and for outright theft. Such criminal acts are accomplished by "automating" traditional methods of fraud and by inventing and using new methods that are constantly being created by enterprising criminal minds. For example, individuals carrying out such criminal activity may use computers to transfer a company's proprietary customer data to computer systems that reside outside the company premises, or they may try to use or sell this valuable customer data to that company's competitors. Their motives may be for profit, they may be for inflicting damage to the victimized company to compensate for some perceived injustice, or it may just be an act of malicious behavior for their entertainment or bragging rights. Computer fraud and theft can be committed by both company insiders and outsiders, but studies have shown that most corporate fraud is committed by company insiders [3].

In addition to the use of technology to commit fraud, computer hardware and software resources may be vulnerable to theft. Actual examples include the theft of unreleased software and storage of customer data in insecure places such as anonymous FTP accounts so that it can be accessed and stolen by outsiders. Data being exposed to these threats generates a secondary threat for a company: the loss of credibility and possible liability for damages as a result of premature release of information, exposure or loss of information, and so on. Preventative measures that should be taken here are quite simple but are often overlooked. Implementation of efficient access control methodologies, periodic auditing, and firewall usage can, in most cases, prevent fraud from occurring or at least make it more easily detected.

A.3 Internet Fraud

The meteoric rise in fraud perpetrated over the Internet has brought about the classification of nine types of fraud, developed from the data reported to the Internet Fraud Complaint Center [4] (IFCC). Analysts at the IFCC determine a fraud type for each Internet fraud complaint received. IFCC analysts sort complaints into one of the following nine fraud categories:

1. *Financial Institution Fraud*—Knowingly misrepresenting the truth or concealment of a material fact by a person to induce a business, organization, or other entity that manages money, credit, or capital to perform a fraudulent activity [5]. Credit/debit card fraud is an example of financial institution fraud that ranks among the most commonly reported offenses to the IFCC. Identity theft also falls into this category; cases classified under this heading tend to be those where the perpetrator possesses the complainant's true name identification (in the form of a Social Security card, driver's license, or birth certificate), but there has not been a credit or debit card fraud committed.
2. *Gaming Fraud*—To risk something of value, especially money, for a chance to win a prize when there is a misrepresentation of the odds or events [6]. Sports tampering and claiming false bets are two examples of gaming fraud.
3. *Communications Fraud*—A fraudulent act or process in which information is exchanged using different forms of media. Thefts of wireless, satellite, or landline services are examples of communications fraud.
4. *Utility Fraud*—When an individual or company misrepresents or knowingly intends to harm by defrauding a government-regulated entity that performs an essential public service, such as the supply of water or electrical services [7].
5. *Insurance Fraud*—A misrepresentation by the provider or the insured in the indemnity against loss. Insurance fraud includes the "padding" or inflating of actual claims, misrepresenting facts

on an insurance application, submitting claims for injuries or damage that never occurred, and "staging" accidents [8].

6. *Government Fraud*—A knowing misrepresentation of the truth or concealment of a material fact to induce the government to act to its own detriment [9]. Examples of government fraud include tax evasion, welfare fraud, and counterfeit currency.

7. *Investment Fraud*—Deceptive practices involving the use of capital to create more money, either through income-producing vehicles or through more risk-oriented ventures designed to result in capital gains [10]. Ponzi/Pyramid schemes and market manipulation are two types of investment fraud.

8. *Business Fraud*—When a corporation or business knowingly misrepresents the truth or conceals a material fact [11]. Examples of business fraud include bankruptcy fraud and copyright infringement.

9. *Confidence Fraud*—The reliance on another's discretion and/or a breach in a relationship of trust resulting in financial loss. A knowing misrepresentation of the truth or concealment of a material fact to induce another to act to his or her detriment [12]. Auction fraud and nondelivery of payment or merchandise are both types of confidence fraud and are the most reported offenses to the IFCC. The Nigerian Letter Scam is another offense classified under confidence fraud. The Nigerian Letter Scam [13] has been around since the early 1980s. The scam is effected when a correspondence outlining an opportunity to receive nonexistent government funds from alleged dignitaries is sent to a "victim," but there is a catch. The scam letter is designed to collect advance fees from the victim. This most often requires that payoff money be sent from the victim to the "dignitary" in order to bribe government officials. While other countries may be mentioned, the correspondence typically indicates "The Government of Nigeria" as the nation of origin. This scam is also referred to as "419 Fraud," after the relevant section of the Criminal Code of Nigeria, as well as "Advance Fee Fraud."

Because of this scam, the country of Nigeria ranks second for total complaints reported at the IFCC on businesses by country. The IFCC has a policy of forwarding all Nigerian Letter Scam complaints to the U.S. Secret Service. The scam works as follows:

1. A letter, e-mail, or fax is sent from an alleged official representing a foreign government or agency.
2. The letter presents a business proposal to transfer millions of dollars in overinvoiced contract funds into your personal bank account. You are offered a certain percentage of the funds for your help.
3. The letter encourages you to travel overseas to complete the details.
4. The letter also asks you to provide blank company letterhead forms, banking account information, and telephone numbers.
5. Next, you receive various documents with official-looking stamps, seals, and logos testifying to the authenticity of the proposal.
6. Finally, they ask for up-front or advance fees for various taxes, processing fees, license fees, registration fees, attorney fees, and so on.

A.4 Employee Sabotage

Probably the easiest form of employee sabotage known to all system administrators would be "accidental" spillage. The act of intentionally spilling coffee or soda on a keyboard for the purpose of making the computer unusable for some time is a criminal offense. Proving the spillage was deliberate, however, is next to impossible, without the aid of hidden cameras or other surveillance techniques. Some administrators have even experienced severe cases where servers have been turned off over a weekend, resulting in unavailability, data loss, and the incurred but needless cost of hours of troubleshooting. Employees are the people who are most familiar with their employer's computers and applications. They know which actions can cause damage, mischief, or sabotage. The number of incidents of employee sabotage is believed to be much smaller than the instances of theft, but the cost of such incidents can be quite high [14].

As long as people feel unjustly treated, cheated, bored, harassed, endangered, or betrayed at work, sabotage will be used as a method of achieving revenge or a twisted sense of job satisfaction. We will show how serious sabotage acts can be prevented by implementing methods of strict access control.

A.5 Infrastructure Attacks

Devastating results can occur from the loss of supporting infrastructure. This infrastructure loss can include power failures (outages, spikes, and brownouts), loss of communications, water outages and leaks, sewer problems, lack of transportation services, fire, flood, civil unrest, and strikes. A loss of infrastructure often results in system downtime, sometimes in the most unexpected ways. Countermeasures against loss of physical and infrastructure support include the addition of redundant systems and establishment of recurring backup processes. Because of the damage these types of threats can cause, the Critical Infrastructure Protection Act was enacted.

A.6 Malicious Hackers

The term *malicious hacker* refers to those who break into computers without authorization. They can include both outsiders and insiders. The hacker threat should be considered in terms of past and potential future damage. Although current losses due to hacker attacks are significantly smaller than losses due to insider theft and sabotage, the hacker problem is widespread and serious. One example of malicious hacker activity is that directed against the public telephone system (which is, by the way, quite common, and the targets are usually employee voice-mailboxes or special "internal only" numbers allowing free calls to company insiders). Another common method is for hackers to attempt to gather information about internal systems by using port scanners and sniffers, password attacks, denial-of-service attacks, and various other attempts to break publicly exposed systems such as File Transfer Protocol (FTP) and World Wide Web (WWW) servers. By implementing efficient firewalls and auditing/

alerting mechanisms, external hackers can be thwarted. Internal hackers are extremely difficult to contend with since they have already been granted access. However, conducting internal audits on a frequent and recurring basis will help organizations detect these activities.

A.7 Malicious Coders

Malicious code refers to viruses, worms, Trojan horses, logic bombs, and other "uninvited" software. Sometimes mistakenly associated just with personal computers, such types of malicious code can attack other platforms. The actual costs that have been attributed to the presence of malicious code most often include the cost of system outages and the cost of staff time for those who are involved in finding the malware and repairing the systems. Frequently, these costs are quite significant.

Today, we are subject to a vast number of virus incidents. This has generated much discussion on the issues of organizational liability and must be taken into account. Viruses are the most common case of malicious code. In today's modern computing platform, some form of antivirus software must be included in order to cope with this threat. To do otherwise can be extremely costly. In 1999, a virus named Melissa was released with devastating results [15]. The Melissa virus caused an estimated $80 million in damage and disrupted computer and network operations worldwide.

Melissa was especially damaging as viruses go, because its author had deliberately created the virus to purposely evade existing antivirus software and to exploit specific weaknesses in corporate and personal e-mail software, as well as server and desktop operating systems software. Melissa infected e-mail and propagated itself in that infected state to 50 other e-mail addresses it obtained from the existing e-mail address book it found on the victim's machine. It immediately began sending out these infectious e-mails from every machine it touched. The Melissa infection spread across the Internet at an exponential rate. Systems were literally brought down from overload as a result of exponential propagation.

A.8 Industrial Espionage

A company might be subject to industrial espionage simply because competitors share some level of sensitive customer information that might be worth millions for interested parties, ranging from governments to corporate and private entities. It is not only the press that would be willing to pay for information. This situation might be encouraging enough for many hackers to tempt fate and attempt to obtain such information. Internal staff might consider the risk minimal and give away such information. There could be active attempts to retrieve information without authorization by hacking, sniffing, and other measures. A case of espionage can have serious consequences for a company, in terms of incurring the cost of lawsuits and resulting damage awards. This situation can also devastate a company's reputation in the marketplace.

Formally defined, industrial espionage is the act of gathering proprietary data from private companies or governments for the purpose of aiding others. Industrial espionage can be perpetrated either by companies seeking to improve their competitive advantage or by governments seeking to aid their domestic industries. Foreign industrial espionage carried out by a government is often referred to as economic espionage. Since information is processed and stored on computer systems, computer security can help protect against such threats; it can do little, however, to reduce the threat of authorized employees selling that information.

Cases of industrial espionage are on the rise, especially after the end of the cold war when many intelligence agencies changed their orientation toward industrial targets. A 1992 study sponsored by the American Society for Industrial Security (ASIS) found that proprietary business information theft had increased 260 percent since 1985. The data indicated 30 percent of the reported losses in 1991 and 1992 had foreign involvement. The study also found that 58 percent of thefts were perpetrated by current or former employees. The three most damaging types of stolen information were pricing information, manufacturing process information, and product development and specification information. Other types of information stolen included customer lists, basic research, sales data, personnel data, compensation data, cost data, proposals, and strategic plans.

Within the area of economic espionage, the Central Intelligence Agency has stated that the main objective is obtaining information related to technology, but that information on U.S. government policy deliberations concerning foreign affairs and information on commodities, interest rates, and other economic factors are also a target. The Federal Bureau of Investigation concurs that technology-related information is the main target but also lists corporate proprietary information, such as negotiating positions and other contracting data, as a target.

Because of the increasing rise in economic and industrial espionage cases over the last decade, the Economic and Espionage Act of 1996 was passed by the U.S. government. This law, coded as 18 U.S.C. §1832, provides:

1. Whoever, with intent to convert a trade secret, that is related to or included in a product that is produced for or placed in interstate or foreign commerce, to the economic benefit of anyone other than the owner thereof, and intending or knowing that the offense will injure any owner of that trade secret, knowingly:

    a. Steals, or without authorization appropriates, takes, carries away, or conceals, or by fraud, artifice, or deception obtains such information

    b. Without authorization copies, duplicates, sketches, draws, photographs, downloads, uploads, alters, destroys, photocopies, replicates, transmits, delivers, sends, mails, communicates, or conveys such information

    c. Receives, buys, or possesses such information, knowing the same to have been stolen or appropriated, obtained, or converted without authorization

    d. Attempts to commit any offense described in paragraphs (a) through (c)

    e. Conspires with one or more other persons to commit any offense described in paragraphs (a) through (c), and one or more of such persons do any act to effect the object of the conspiracy, shall, except as provided in subsection (2), be fined under this title or imprisoned not more than 10 years, or both

2. Any organization that commits any offense described in subsection (1) shall be fined not more than $5,000,000

In a recent case [16], conviction was upheld against violators of 18 U.S.C. §1832 in an appeal of Mr. Pin-Yen Yang and his daughter Hwei Chen Yang (Sally) for industrial espionage, among other crimes. Mr. Yang owned the Four Pillars Enterprise Company, Ltd., based in Taiwan. This company specialized in the manufacture of adhesives. Mr. Yang and his daughter conspired to illegally obtain trade secrets from their chief U.S. competitor, Avery Dennison Corporation, by hiring an ex-employee of Avery Dennison, a Dr. Lee. Lee was retained as a consultant by Yang, and the group conspired to pass confidential trade secrets from Avery to Four Pillars. When the FBI confronted Lee on the matter, he agreed to be videotaped in a meeting with Mr. Yang and his daughter. During the meeting, enough evidence was gathered to effect a conviction [17].

Measures against industrial espionage consist of the same measures that are taken by companies to counter hackers, with the added security obtained by using data encryption technology. Where this is not possible due to government regulations (France, for example), proprietary compression or hashing algorithms can be used, which results in the same effect as encryption but with a higher chance of being broken by a determined adversary. Legal protections exist, of course, but were once very difficult to dissect from the vast amount of legislation in Title 18 of the United States Code. Congress amended the many laws dotted throughout Title 18 into a comprehensive set of laws known as the 1996 National Information Infrastructure Protection Act.

A.9 Social Engineering

The weakest link in security will always be people, and the easiest way to break into a system is to engineer your way into a system through the human interface. Most every hacker group has engaged in some form of social engineering over the years and, in combination with other activities, these groups have been able to break into many corporations as a result of these types of activities. In this type of attack, the attacker chooses a mark that he or she can scam to gain a password, user ID, or other usable information. Because most administrators and employees of companies are more concerned with providing efficiency and helping users, they may be unaware that the person they are speaking to is not a legitimate user. And because there are no formal procedures for establishing whether an end user is legitimate, the attacker often gains a tremendous amount of information in a very short amount of time, and often with no way to trace the information leak back to the attacker.

Social engineering begins with a goal of obtaining information about a person or business and can range in activities from dumpster diving through cold calls or impersonations. As acknowledged in the movies, many hackers and criminals have realized that a wealth of valuable information often is to be found in the trash bins waiting to be emptied by a disposal company. Most corporations do not adequately dispose of information, and trash bins often contain information that may identify employees or customers. This information is not secured and is available to anyone willing to dive into the dumpster at night and look for it—hence, the term dumpster diving.

Other information is readily available via deception. Most corporations do not contain security measures that adequately address deception. What happens when the protocol is adhered to properly but the person being admitted is not who he or she really is? Many groups utilize members of their group in a fashion that would violate protocols so as to gather information about what a corporate admittance policy is. Often the multiperson attack will result in gaining admittance to the company and ultimately obtaining the information desired. Using the bathroom or going for a drink of water is always a great excuse for exiting from a meeting and often you will not have an escort. Most corporations do not have terminal locking policies, and this is another way that an attacker can gain access or load software that may pierce the company's firewall. So long as the person entering the corporation can act according to the role he or she has defined for access and he or she looks the part, it is unlikely the person will be detected.

Remotely, social engineering actually becomes less challenging. There are no visual expectations to meet, and people are very willing to participate with a little coaxing. As is often the case, giving away something free can always be a method for entry. Many social engineering situations involve sending along a free piece of software or something of value for free. Embedded within free software, Trojan horses, viruses, and worms can go undetected and can bypass system and network security. Since most security that protects the local machine has a hard time differentiating between real and fake software, it is often not risky for the attacker to deliver a keylogger or Trojan horse to the victim's machine. Also equally effective, the customer support or employee support personnel can be duped into aiding a needy user with their passwords and access to information they do not necessarily know about.

A.9.1 Educate Staff and Security Personnel

According to NIST Publication SP800-12 [18], the purpose of computer security awareness, training, and education is to enhance security by:

- Improving awareness of the need to protect system resources
- Developing skills and knowledge so computer users can perform their jobs more securely
- Building in-depth knowledge, as needed, to design, implement, or operate security programs for organizations and systems

By making computer system users aware of their security responsibilities and teaching them correct practices, it helps users change their behavior. It also supports individual accountability, which is one of the most important ways to improve computer security. Without knowing the necessary security measures (and how to use them), users cannot be truly accountable for their actions. The importance of this training is emphasized in the Computer Security Act, which requires training for those involved with the management, use, and operation of federal computer systems.

Awareness stimulates and motivates those being trained to care about security and to remind them of important security practices. Explaining what happens to an organization, its mission, customers, and employees when security fails, often motivates people to take security more seriously. Awareness can take on different forms for particular audiences. Appropriate awareness for management officials might stress management's pivotal role in establishing organizational attitudes toward security. Appropriate awareness for other groups, such as system programmers or information analysts, should address the need for security as it relates to their jobs. In today's systems environment, almost everyone in an organization may have access to system resources and therefore may have the potential to cause harm.

Both dissemination and enforcement of policy are critical issues that are implemented and strengthened through training programs. Employees cannot be expected to follow policies and procedures of which they are unaware. In addition, enforcing penalties may be difficult if users can claim ignorance when caught doing something wrong. Training employees may also be necessary to show that a standard of due care has been taken in protecting information. Simply issuing policy, with no follow-up to implement that policy, may not suffice. Many organizations use acknowledgment statements, which state that employees have read and understand computer security requirements.

Awareness is used to reinforce the fact that security supports the mission of the organization by protecting valuable resources. If employees view security as just bothersome rules and procedures, they are more likely to ignore them. In addition, they may not make needed suggestions about improving security or recognize and report security threats and vulnerabilities. Awareness is also used to remind people of basic security practices, such as logging off a computer system or locking doors. A security awareness program can use many teaching methods, including videotapes, newsletters, posters, bulletin boards, flyers, demonstrations, briefings, short reminder notices at logon, talks, or lectures. Awareness is often incorporated into basic security training and can use any method that can change employees' attitudes. Effective security awareness programs need to be designed with the recognition that people tend to practice a tuning-out process (also known as *acclimation*). For example, after a while, a security poster, no matter how well designed, will be ignored; it will, in effect, simply blend into the environment. For this reason, awareness techniques should be creative and frequently changed.

Security education is more in-depth than security training and is targeted for security professionals and those whose jobs require expertise in security. Security education is normally outside the scope of most organization awareness and training programs. It is more appropriately a part of employee career development. Security education is obtained through college or graduate classes or through specialized training programs. Because of this, most computer security programs focus primarily on awareness. An effective Computer Security Awareness and Training (CSAT) program requires proper planning, implementation, maintenance, and periodic evaluation. The following seven steps constitute one approach for developing a CSAT program:

Step 1: Identify program scope, goals, and objectives.

Step 2: Identify training staff.

Step 3: Identify target audiences.

Step 4: Motivate management and employees.

Step 5: Administer the program.

Step 6: Maintain the program.

Step 7: Evaluate the program.

A.9.2 Crafting Corporate Social Engineering Policy

When you begin the process of building a corporate policy for social engineering, several important considerations need to be included in the policy. Ensure that employees are aware of the data they are making available to others and what hackers might do with the knowledge they gain from that data. Train end users in the proper handling of social engineering tactics, such as:

- Dumpster diving
- Phone calls
- E-mail
- IM
- On-site visits

A.9.3 Prevention

Teach employees how to prevent intrusion attempts by verifying identification, using secure communications methods, reporting suspicious activity, establishing procedures, and shredding corporate documents. It is important to define a simple, concise set of established procedures for employees to report or respond to when they encounter any of these types of attacks.

A.9.4 Audits

It is a good idea to periodically employ external consultants to perform audits and social engineering attempts to test employees and the network security readiness of your organization. Define the regularity of audits conducted by external consultants in a manner that cannot become predictable, such as a rotation of the month in each quarter an audit would occur. For example, if your external audits are conducted semiannually, the first audit of the year may occur in month one of quarter one. The next audit may occur in month three of quarter three. Then, when the next year comes around, you have rotated to another month or even changed to quarters two and four. The point is not in which months and quarters the audits are done but that they are done in a nonpredictable fashion that only you and your trusted few will know.

A.9.5 Privacy Standards and Regulations

There has been a lot of activity on the national legislative front over the last couple of years, specifically regarding the protection of information that is unique to the individual. This type of information is regarded as a basic element of our right to privacy, and companies are being required to take (sometimes costly and arduous) steps to protect it. Failure to do so can have serious repercussions. Insurance companies, healthcare providers, financial institutions, service providers, retailers, telemarketing organizations, communications providers, and so on all have a part to play in protecting an individual's right to privacy. The next few sections will highlight some of the more relevant changes made in the last few years.

A.9.6 NAIC Model Act

Beginning in the early 1980s, the National Association of Insurance Companies [19] (NAIC) recognized the importance of protecting the privacy of its customers. With the adoption of the *Insurance Information and Privacy Protection Model Act,* the NAIC established a standard for disclosure of insurance consumers' personal information, including financial and health information. Currently, 13 states have laws based on this 1982 Model Act. The NAIC believes that the state laws based on this Act are generally more protective of consumer privacy than the privacy provisions of the Gramm-Leach-Bliley Act (GLBA), discussed in the next section.

In 1998, the NAIC turned its focus specifically to the privacy of personal health information. The Health Information Privacy Model Act was developed primarily to give guidance to Congress and the U.S. Department of Health and Human Services, both of which were considering health information privacy protections under the Health Insurance Portability and Accountability Act (HIPAA).

In February 2000, the NAIC established the Privacy Issues Working Group in order to give guidance to state insurance regulators in response to the enactment of the Gramm-Leach-Bliley Act (GLBA), which required state insurance regulators to promulgate regulations enforcing the consumer privacy protection laws. On September 26, 2000, the Privacy of Consumer Financial and Health Information Model regulation was adopted by the NAIC.

In 2001, the NAIC reconvened the Privacy Issues Working Group. This group was tasked to increase dialog among regulators and interested parties who were concerned about privacy standards and regulations, since they deeply affected the conduct of operations for these insurance carriers.

One of the principal missions of the Privacy Issues Working Group was to serve as a forum for regulators, industry, and individual consumers. This forum allowed participants to discuss questions and issues that arose as the states interpreted and began enforcement of their privacy protections. In order to stay abreast with the states' efforts and to be consistent in their approaches to privacy protection, the Privacy Issues Working Group established a goal to agree on uniform responses to such questions, because many of these issues would be repeated in multiple states. The Privacy Issues Working Group's analysis of particular issues and responses to questions has served as guidance to all NAIC members.

In March 2002, the Privacy Issues Working Group adopted a document entitled *Informal Procedures for Consideration of Privacy Questions*. These procedures were developed as part of an effort to be responsive to interested party concerns about the drafting and adoption of Q&A documents among NAIC members. The informal procedures are a reflection of the evolving efforts of the Privacy Issues Working Group to ensure that members and other interested parties are well informed of the process for consideration of privacy issues.

In early 2002, content found within financial institutions' privacy notices and the degree to which consumers are opting out from disclosure received a great deal of attention. In an effort to make these privacy notices worthwhile for consumers and industry, and to realize the intent of Congress and the regulators who put these protections in place, the NAIC formed a subgroup, the Privacy Notice Subgroup, whose task was to draft a "plain language" model for privacy notices. The Privacy Notice Subgroup has begun working closely with interested parties to draft samples that make privacy notices more understandable for consumers while ensuring a high degree of uniformity and compliance with the requirements of the NAIC model privacy regulation for industry.

In the latter part of 2002, the NAIC reestablished the former subgroup called the Privacy Notice Subgroup. This group completed a draft report outlining specific suggestions to improve privacy notices. The changes include use of simpler sentences, clearer terminology, and easy-to-read formatting. At an annual meeting held in the fall of 2002, the Privacy Notice Subgroup distributed a draft report to the Privacy Issues Working Group and urged recipients to examine the report and submit comments to NAIC staff for inclusion in the final report. The NAIC has been a vanguard in establishment of privacy protections and will continue to do so for some time.

A.9.7 Gramm-Leach-Bliley Act

The Gramm-Leach-Bliley Act [20] (GLBA) was enacted as Public Law 106-102 on November 12, 1999. This law was intended to enhance competition in the financial services industry by providing a prudential framework for the affiliation of banks, securities firms, insurance companies, and other financial service providers. The GLBA is enforced by several different agencies, depending on the type of financial business involved. Most depository institutions, such as banks and savings and loans, are regulated by either the Office of the Comptroller of Currency (OCC), the Federal Reserve, the Federal Deposit Insurance Corporation (FDIC), or the Office of Thrift Supervision (OTS). These four agencies have enacted joint regulations that became effective July 1, 2001, under 12 CFR part 30 et al., to guide audit and compliance certification processes.

There are also many other nondepository institutions that are regulated by the Federal Trade Commission (FTC), which specifically claims authority over financial institutions "not otherwise subject to the enforcement authority of another regulator" 16 CFR part 313.1 (b). The FTC information security requirements were published on May 23, 2002, as 16 CFR part 314, and are available from the FTC. Finally, the Office for Regulatory Audits and Compliance (OFRAC) is an Atlanta-based organization set up to conduct compliance surveys and audits for regulations affecting businesses regulated by the GLBA; Department of Transportation (DOT); HIPAA; HHS; CFR 42, 49, 67, USA PATRIOT ACT; and the Public Health Security and Bioterrorism Preparedness Response Act of 2002 (HR 3448). Their services are designed to meet the testing requirements of both GLBA and HIPAA. This is extremely important, as the penalties for not complying with the aforementioned laws are quite severe. Individuals failing to fully comply with the regulations are subject to a $250,000 fine, and any other person (facility or organization) failing to follow the regulations is subject to a fine of $500,000. Prison terms can be up to five years for each violation. As you can see, privacy security has become a very serious issue that mandates business attention at the risk of huge penalties.

A.9.8 HIPAA

The Health Insurance Portability and Accountability Act [21] (HIPAA) was enacted in order to accomplish several goals. These goals intended to:

1. Improve portability and continuity of health insurance coverage in group and individual markets
2. Combat waste, fraud, and abuse in health insurance and health care delivery
3. Promote the use of medical savings accounts
4. Improve access to long-term care services and coverage
5. Simplify the administration of health insurance

In order to comprehend the total impact of HIPAA, it is important to understand the protections it created for millions of working Americans and their families. HIPAA includes provisions that may increase people's ability to get health coverage for themselves and their dependents if they start a new job. HIPAA can lower an individual's chance of losing existing healthcare coverage, regardless of whether he or she has that coverage through a job or through individual health insurance. HIPAA can help people maintain continuous health coverage for themselves and their dependents when they change jobs. HIPAA also can help a person buy health insurance coverage on his or her own if coverage under an employer's group health plan is lost and no other health coverage is available. Among its specific protections, HIPAA limits the use of preexisting condition exclusions and prohibits group health plans from discriminating by denying someone coverage or charging extra for coverage based on a covered member's past or present poor health. HIPAA guarantees certain small employers, and certain individuals who lose job-related coverage, the right to purchase health insurance, and it guarantees (in most cases) that employers or individuals who purchase health insurance can renew the coverage regardless of any health conditions of individuals covered under the insurance policy. In short, HIPAA may lower an individual's chance of losing existing coverage, ease an individual's ability to switch health plans, and/or help him or her to buy coverage if coverage under an employer's plan is lost and no other coverage is available.

In setting out to achieve each of the aforementioned goals, the final bill that was enacted can be summarized in five areas where action was mandated. These are discussed in the following text:

1. *Standards for electronic health information transactions*. Within 18 months of enactment, the Secretary of Health and Human Services was required to adopt standards from among those already approved by private standards developing organizations (such as NAIC) for certain electronic health transactions, including claims, enrollment, eligibility, payment, and coordination of benefits. *These standards were required to address the security of electronic health information systems.* This last sentence is of particular concern to security professionals who must enable organizations to enforce such privacy rules.
2. *Mandate on providers and health plans, and timetable*. Providers and health plans were *required to use the standards for the specified electronic transactions* 24 months after they were adopted. Plans and providers were given the option to comply directly or to use a healthcare clearinghouse. Certain health plans, in particular worker's compensation, were not covered.
3. *Privacy.* The Secretary of HHS was required to recommend privacy standards for health information to Congress 12 months after HIPA was enacted. There was a provision that stated that if Congress did not enact privacy legislation within three years of HIPA enactment, the Secretary of HHS shall promulgate privacy regulations for individually identifiable electronic health information.
4. *Preemption of state law.* The HIPA bill superceded state laws, except where the Secretary of HHS determined that the state law is necessary to prevent fraud and abuse or to ensure the appropriate regulation of insurance or health plans, as well as address concerns about the use of controlled substances. If the Secretary promulgates privacy regulations, those regulations could not preempt state laws that imposed more stringent requirements. These

provisions did not limit a state's ability to require health plan reporting or audits.

5. *Penalties*. The bill imposed civil monetary penalties and prison for certain violations. Individuals failing to fully comply with the regulations are subject to a $250,000 fine, and any other person (facility or organization) failing to follow the regulations is subject to a fine of $500,000. Prison terms can be up to five years for *each* violation.

As you can see, items 1, 2, and 3 have specific provisions for protection of electronic data. This is the area of HIPAA where cybersecurity is most concerned. The preceding sections have concentrated on standards, laws, and enforcement issues related to security and privacy. In the actual implementation of security measures needed to comply with such regulatory guidance, a security professional relies on adoption of good practices that have been evaluated and adopted as "best practices" across the industry.

A.10 Summary

Most people rarely think of security when they use IM; however, the amount of potentially confidential information that is transmitted by IM clients every day is staggering. Security vulnerabilities on both wired and wireless networks can be exploited. This appendix is intended to give the reader an overview of the network security issues and why they must be addressed as part of an overall IM security program.

A.11 Endnotes

1. J. Rittinghouse and F. Ransome. *Wireless Operational Security*, 1st ed. New York, Digital Press, 2004.
2. http://isc.sans.org/trends.html.
3. Computer Security Institute. (2002). "2002 CSI/FBI Computer Crime and Security Survey," Richard Power. http://www.gocsi.com.
4. Internet Fraud Complaint Center report titled "IFCC Annual Internet Fraud Report, January 1, 2001 to December 31, 2001." http://www1.ifccfbi.gov/strategy/statistics.asp.
5. *Black's Law Dictionary*, 7th ed., 1999.
6. Ibid.
7. Ibid.
8. *Fraud Examiners Manual*, 3rd ed., Vol. 1, 1998.
9. Black's Law Dictionary, 7th ed., 1999; *The Merriam Webster Dictionary*, Home and Office ed., 1995.
10. *Barron's Dictionary of Finance and Investment Terms*, 5th ed., 1998.
11. *Black's Law Dictionary*, 7th ed., 1999.
12. Ibid.
13. Internet Fraud Complaint Center report titled "IFCC Annual Internet Fraud Report, January 1, 2001 to December 31, 2001," http://www1.ifccfbi.gov.
14. U.S. Department of Justice, Press Release of February 26, 2002, "Former Computer Network Administrator at New Jersey High-Tech Firm Sentenced to 41 Months for Unleashing $10 Million Computer Time Bomb. http://www.usdoj.gov/criminal/cybercrime/lloydSent.htm.
15. U.S. Deptartment of Justice, Press Release of May 1, 2001, "Creator of Melissa Virus Sentenced to 20 Months in Federal Prison," http://www.usdoj.gov/criminal/cybercrime/MelissaSent.htm .

16. U.S. Deptartment of Justice, Electronic Citation: 2002 FED App. 0062P (6th Cir.), File Name: 02a0062p.06, decided and filed 20 Feb 2002 http://www.usdoj.gov/criminal/cybercrime/4Pillars_6thCir.htm.

17. The full text of this rendering can be reviewed at http://www.usdoj.gov/criminal/cybercrime/4Pillars_6thCir.htm.

18. IST SP 800-12, *Computer Security Handbook*, author unknown, February 1996, US Department of Commerce.

19. http://www.naic.org.

20. Public Law 106-102, electronic document available from the Library of Congress, ref: S.900, http://www.thomas.loc.gov.

21. Public Law 104-191,aug. 21, 1996 "Health Insurance Portability and Accountability Act of 1996," http://www.thomas.loc.gov .

B

Managing Access

Access control is a key element of a good IM security program. As in Appendix A, our intent is to give those requiring general knowledge of access control the necessary background to enhance their reading experience with our chapters that cover IM security risks and best practices. In this appendix, we will cover the essential elements every security administrator needs to know about access control and management of passwords. Some of the content presented in this appendix has been excerpted from our *Wireless Operational Security* [1] book with the permission of Digital Press, an imprint of Elsevier.

B.1 Access Control

According to the ISSA [2], "*access control is the collection of mechanisms for limiting, controlling, and monitoring system access to certain items of information, or to certain features based on a user's identity and his or her membership in various predefined groups.*" In this section, we will explore the major building blocks that comprise the field of access control as it applies to organizational entities and the information systems these entities are trying to protect from compromising situations.

B.1.1 Purpose of Access Control

"*What are some reasons why we should have access control?*" Access control is necessary for several reasons. Information proprietary to a business may need to be kept confidential, so there is a confidentiality issue that provides a purpose for having access controls. The information that an organization keeps confidential also needs to be protected from tampering or misuse.

The organization must ensure the integrity of this data for it to be useful. Having internal data integrity also provides a purpose to having access controls. When employees of the organization show up for work, it is important that they have access to the data they need to perform their jobs. The data must be available to the employees for work to continue or the organization becomes crippled and loses money. It is essential that data availability be maintained. Access controls provide yet another purpose in maintaining a reasonable level of assurance that the data is available and usable to the organization. Therefore, the answer to the previous question is that there are three very good reasons for having access controls:

- Confidentiality
- Data integrity
- Data availability

B.1.2 Access Control Entities

In any discussion of access control, some common elements need to be understood by all parties. These elements comprise a common body of terminology so everyone working on security access issues is talking about the same thing. For our purposes, there are four primary elements we will discuss:

1. The subject, who is an active user or process that requests access to a resource
2. The object, which is a resource that contains information (can be interchanged with the word *resource*)
3. The domain, which is a set of objects that the subject can access
4. Groups, collections of subjects and objects that are categorized into groups based on their shared characteristics (i.e., membership in a company department, sharing a common job title, etc.)

B.1.3 Fundamental Concepts of Access Control

There are three concepts basic to implementation of access control in any organization. These concepts are establishment of a security policy, accountability, and assurance. We discuss each of these concepts in the following test.

Establishment of a Security Policy

Security policy for an organization consists of the development and maintenance of a set of directives that publicly state the overall goals of an organization and recommend prescribed actions for various situations that an organization's information systems and personnel may encounter. Policy is fundamental to enabling a continuity of operations. When something happens and the one person who knows the answer is on vacation, what is to be done? When policies are in place, administrators know what to do.

Accountability

For any information systems that process sensitive data or maintain privacy information, the organization must ensure that procedures are in place to maintain individual accountability for user actions on that system and also for their use of that sensitive data. There have been cases in industry where individuals who were employees of an organization committed criminal acts, such as theft of credit card data, theft of personal information for resale to mailing lists, theft of software or data for resale on eBay, and so on, and those people who committed these criminal acts compromised the integrity of the information system. Such criminal actions cause huge problems for organizations, ranging from embarrassment to legal action. When these criminals have been caught, it has been because there were procedures in place to ensure the accountability of their actions on the data. These procedures could be in the form of log files, audit trails for actions taken within an application, or even keystroke monitoring in some instances.

Assurance

As discussed previously, information systems must be able to guarantee correct and accurate interpretation of security policy. For example, if sensitive data exists on Machine A and that machine has been reviewed, inspected, and cleared for processing data of that particular level of sensitivity, when

Joe takes the data from Machine A and copies it to his laptop to work on when traveling on an airplane, that data has most likely become compromised unless Joe's laptop has been reviewed, inspected, and cleared for processing of that particular level of data sensitivity. If his machine has not been cleared, there is no assurance that the data has *not* been compromised. The policies in place at Joe's organization must be known to Joe in order to be effective, and they must be enforced in order to remain effective.

B.1.4 Access Control Criteria

When implementing security access controls, five common criteria that are used to determine whether access is to be granted or denied. These five criteria are location, identity, time, transaction, and role (LITTR). *Location* refers to the physical or logical place where the user attempts access. *Identity* refers to the process that is used to uniquely identify an individual or program in a system. *Time* parameters can be control factors that are used to control resource use (e.g., contractors are not allowed access to system resources after 8:00 P.M. Monday through Friday, and not at all on weekends). *Transaction* criteria are program checks that can be performed to protect information from unauthorized use, such as validating whether or not a database query against payroll records that is coming from a user identified as belonging to the HR department is valid. Finally, a *role* defines which computer-related functions can be performed by a properly identified user with an exclusive set of privileges specific to that role. All of these criteria are implemented in varying degrees across the depth and breadth of a security plan. The policies and procedures used by an organization to make the plan effective determine the interplay among these criteria.

B.1.5 Access Control Models

When an organization begins to implement access control procedures, there are three basic implementation models from which an administrator can choose. These three models are mandatory, discretionary, and nondiscretionary. Each has its particular strengths and weaknesses, and the implementer must decide which model is most appropriate for a given environment or situation. It is important to point out that most operating, network, and application systems security software in use today provide administrators with the capability to perform data categorization, discretionary access control, identity-based access control, user-discretionary access control, and nondiscretionary access control. This section will provide an overview of each type of access control model. Armed with this information, implementers of access controls will be able to make better decisions about which model is most appropriate for their purposes.

Mandatory Access Control Model

Mandatory access control occurs when both the resource owner and the system grant access based on a resource security label. A security label is a designation assigned to a resource [3] (such as a file). According to the *NIST Handbook*:

> *Security labels are used for various purposes, including controlling access, specifying protective measures, or indicating additional handling instructions. In many implementations, once this designator has been set, it cannot be changed (except perhaps under carefully controlled conditions that are subject to auditing).*
>
> *When used for access control, labels are also assigned to user sessions. Users are permitted to initiate sessions with specific labels only. For example, a file bearing the label "Organization Proprietary Information" would not be accessible (readable) except during user sessions with the corresponding label. Moreover, only a restricted set of users would be able to initiate such sessions. The labels of the session and those of the files accessed during the session are used, in turn, to label output from the session. This ensures that information is uniformly protected throughout its life on the system.*

Security labels are a very strong form of access control. Because they are costly and difficult to administer, security labels are best suited for information systems that have very strict security requirements (such as those used by government, financial, and R&D organizations that handle classified information or information whose loss would severely or critically degrade the financial viability of the organization). Security labels are an excellent means for consistent enforcement of access restrictions; however, their administration and highly inflexible characteristics can be a significant deterrent to their use.

Security labels generally cannot be changed, because they are permanently linked to specific information. For this reason, user-accessible data cannot be disclosed as a result of a user copying information and changing the access rights on a file in an attempt to make that information more accessible than the document owner originally intended. This feature eliminates most types of human errors and malicious software problems that compromise data. The drawback to using security labels is that sometimes the very feature that protects user data also prevents legitimate use of some information. As an example, it is impossible to cut and paste information from documents having different access levels assigned to their respective labels.

Data Categorization

One method used to ease the burden necessary for administration of security labeling is categorizing data by similar protection requirements (data categorization). As an example, a label could be developed specifically for "Company Proprietary Data." This label would mark information that can be disclosed only to the organization's employees. Another label, "General Release Data," could be used to mark information that is available to anyone.

When considering the implementation of mandatory access controls with security labels, one must decide between using a rule-based approach, where access is granted based on resource rules, or using an administratively directed approach, where access is granted by an administrator who oversees the resources. Using a rule-based approach is most often preferred, because members of a group can be granted access simply by validating their membership in that group. Access levels are assigned at a group level so all members of the group share a minimum level of access. All files that are created or edited by any one of the members of that group are equally accessible to any other member because the security labels that are instituted have all members of the group sharing equal access to the group resources. Trust is extended to the membership as a whole simply because membership in the group without having proper access *would not be allowed*.

This approach is less administratively intensive than using the approach where an administrator manually oversees resources, granting or withdrawing access on an individual case-by-case basis. There are some instances where this approach is preferable, however. Consider a scenario where there are only a few members who need access to extremely sensitive information. The owner of this information may choose to manually oversee security label application simply to maintain a personal level of control over the access to highly sensitive materials.

Discretionary Access Control Model

According to a document [4] published in 1987 by the National Computer Security Center, discretionary access control is defined as:

> *A means of restricting access to objects based on the identity of subjects and/or groups to which they belong. The controls are discretionary in the sense that a subject with a certain access permission is capable of passing that permission (perhaps indirectly) on to any other subject.*

Discretionary access controls restrict a user's access to resources on the system. The user may also be restricted to a subset of the possible *access types* available for those protected resources. Access types are the operations a user is allowed to perform on a particular resource (e.g., read, write, execute). Typically, for each resource, a particular user or group of users has the authority to distribute and revoke access to that resource. Users may grant or rescind access to the resources they control based on need to know, job-essential, or some other criteria. Discretionary access control mechanisms grant or deny access based entirely on the identities of users and resources. This is known as *identity-based discretionary access control.*

Knowing the identity of the users is key to discretionary access control. This concept is relatively straightforward in that an *access control matrix* contains the names of users on the rows and the names of resources on the columns. Each entry in the matrix represents an access type held by that user to that resource. Determining access rights is a simple process of looking up a user in the matrix row and traversing the resource columns to find out which rights are allowed for a given resource.

A variant of this is user-directed discretionary access control. Here, an end user can grant or deny access to particular resources based on restrictions he or she decides, irrespective of corporate policy, management guidance, and so on. With an ability to inject the human factor into this equation, you can surmise that the level of protection for an organization becomes dependent upon the specific actions of those individuals tasked to protect information. One drawback to the discretionary access control model is that it is administratively intense and highly dependent on user behavior for success in protecting resources. This has led to the creation of *hybrid access control* implementations that grant or deny access based on both an identity-based model and the use of user-directed controls.

Nondiscretionary Access Control Model

This access control model removes a user's *discretionary ability* and implements mechanisms whereby resource access is granted or denied based on policies and control objectives. There are three common variants of this approach: (1) role-based, where access is based on users' responsibilities; (2) task-based, where access is based on users' job duties; and (3) lattice-based, where access is based on a framework of security labels consisting of resource labels, which hold a security classification, and a user label, which contains security clearance information. The most common of these approaches is Role-Based Access Control (RBAC). The basic concept of RBAC is that users are assigned to roles, permissions are assigned to roles, and users acquire permissions by being members of roles. David Ferraiolo et al., of the National Institute of Standards, drafted the "*Proposed NIST Standard for Role-Based Access Controls*" [5] which states:

> *Core RBAC includes requirements that user-role and permission-role assignment can be many-to-many. Thus, the same user can be assigned to many roles and a single role can have many users. Similarly, for permissions, a single permission can be assigned to many roles and a single role can be assigned to many permissions. Core RBAC includes requirements for user-role review, whereby the roles assigned to a specific user can be determined as well as users assigned to a specific role. A similar requirement for permission-role review is imposed as an advanced review function. Core RBAC also includes the concept of user sessions, which allows selective activation and deactivation of roles.*

As an example, Joe is an accountant and serves as the manager of payroll operations at ABC Company. His role in the company as manager of payroll would, in RBAC, allow Joe to see all materials necessary for successful conduct of payroll operations. He is also a member of the whole accounting group at ABC Company. In that role, as a member of accounting, he is given access to all of the general accounting resources that are made available to the accounting group, but he does not have access to specific files that belong to the accounts payable, accounts receivable, or expense processing teams. If the expense processing team decided to make an internal document available to the general accounting group, then Joe would be able to see that document because of his membership in the accounting group.

The distinction between role-based and task-based access is subtle but distinctly different. The previous scenario was built around Joe's area of responsibility and his membership in a group. In the task-based access control scenario, Joe would only see documents in accounting that were determined by company workflow procedures as necessary for Joe to successfully manage payroll operations. Based on Joe's current job duties, it is not "job necessary" for Joe to see what is produced by the expense department, accounts payable, or accounts receivable, *even if* Joe is a member of the accounting group. For many, this subtle distinction is more trouble than it is worth, since the RBAC model can be more easily implemented with the newer computing platforms of today.

In the lattice-based model, Joe's access is based on a framework of security labels. The documents Joe would need to perform his job would have to have their resource labels checked to see which security classification ("*general release*" or "*company proprietary*," for example) that resource has, and a user label that contains security clearance information would be checked to ensure that Joe is entitled, or "*cleared*," to access that company proprietary-level information. In a government scenario, working with classified material, this model is much more prevalent than it is in industry. Substitute the words *unclassified, confidential, secret*, or *top secret* for the words *company proprietary* or *general release* and you will get the idea.

B.1.6 Uses of Access Control

There are seven general uses for access controls. They are as follows:

1. *Corrective,* which is used to remedy acts that have already occurred
2. *Detective,* used to investigate an act that has already occurred
3. *Deterrent,* which is for discouraging an act from occurring
4. *Recovery,* used to restore a resource to a state of operation prior to when an act has occurred
5. *Management,* who dictates the policies, procedures, and accountability to control system use
6. *Operational,* where personnel procedures set by management are used to protect the system
7. *Technical,* where software and hardware controls are used to automate system protection

Ideally, *management* policies and procedures would dictate *operational* activities that implement *technical* solutions that *deter* unauthorized access and, when that fails, *detects* such access in a manner that allows for rapid *recovery* using *corrective* actions. There, I said it! As simplistic as that sentence sounds, it embodies the very essence of the many uses of access control in an organization. Why make it more complicated?

B.1.7 Access Control Administration Models

Centralized Administration Model

The centralized administration model is based on the designation of a single office location or single individual as the responsible party tasked with setting proper access controls. The advantage to using this approach is that it enforces strict controls and uniformity of access. This is because the ability to make changes to access settings resides with very few individuals in a centralized administration model. When an organization's information processing needs change, personnel having access to that information can have their access modified but only through the centralized location. Most of the time, these types of requests require an approval by the appropriate manager before such changes are made. Each user's account can be centrally monitored, and closing all accesses for any user can be easily accomplished if that individual leaves the organization. Because the process is managed by a few centralized resources in an organization, standard, consistent procedures are fairly easy to enforce. The most obvious drawback to a centralized model approach is the time it takes to make changes when they must be coordinated and approved before being made. Sometimes, when there are many people in an organization, these requests can become backlogged. However, most of the time, the tradeoff between having strict enforcement and standardized processes is worth enduring the hassle of going through a little bureaucracy to get something done. An example of a centralized access model would be the use of a Remote Authentication Dial-in User Service (RADIUS) server, which is a centralized server used for a single point of network authentication for all users needing access to the network resources. Another example would be a Terminal Access Controller Access Control System (TACACS) server, which is a centralized database of accounts that are used for granting authorization for data requests against a data store or subsystem (e.g., a company-owned CRM product).

Decentralized Administration Model

Using the decentralized administration model, all access is controlled by the specific document or file originator. This allows control to remain with those who are responsible for the information. The belief is that these people are best suited to make a determination of who needs access to a document and which type of access they need. However, there is great opportunity to suffer the consequences of a lack of consistency among document originators over procedures and criteria that are used for making user access decisions. Also, with the decentralized administration model, it is difficult to get a composite view of all user accesses on the system at any given time. These inconsistencies can create an environment where different applications or data owners may inadvertently implement access combinations that create conflicts of interest or jeopardize the organization's best interests. Another disadvantage is that the decentralized administration model needs to be used in conjunction with other procedures to ensure that accesses are properly terminated when an individual leaves the company or is moved to another team within the organization. An example of common use of the decentralized administration model is a domain where all file shares are accessible in read-only mode, but each file share owner would determine if a user could perform write or execute activities in the file share. In a domain with a few hundred file shares, this lack of uniformity and standardization quickly becomes apparent.

Hybrid Administration Model

The hybrid administration model combines the centralized and decentralized administration models into a single approach. An example would be use of a RADIUS server (centralized login/authentication) for gaining basic access to the network and having resources distributed across the network, where each domain on the network is controlled by a different administrator. This is a typical corporate model, where the central administration part is responsible for the broadest and most basic of accesses, that of gaining entry to the network, and the decentralized part, where the system owners and their users (the creators of the files) specify the types of access implemented for those files that are under their control. The main disadvantage to a hybrid approach is the haggle over what should and should not be centralized.

B.1.8 Access Control Mechanisms

Many mechanisms have been developed to provide internal and external access controls, and they vary significantly in terms of precision, sophistication, and cost. These methods are not mutually exclusive and are often employed in combination. Managers need to analyze their organization's protection requirements to select the most appropriate, cost-effective logical access controls. Logical access controls are differentiated into internal and external access controls. Internal access controls are a logical means of separating what defined users (or user groups) can or cannot do with system resources.

B.1.9 Internal Access Controls

We will cover four methods of internal access control in this section: Passwords, Encryption, Access Control Lists, and Constrained User Interfaces. Each of these four methods of internal access are discussed next.

Passwords

Passwords are most often associated with user authentication. However, they are also used to protect data and applications on many systems, including PCs. For instance, an accounting application may require a password to access certain financial data or to invoke a restricted application. The use of passwords as a means of access control can result in a proliferation of passwords, which can reduce overall security. Password-based access control is often inexpensive, because it is already included in a large variety of applications. However, users may find it difficult to remember additional application passwords, which, if written down or poorly chosen, can lead to their compromise. Password-based access controls for PC applications are often easy to circumvent if the user has access to the operating system (and knowledge of what to do).

Encryption

Another mechanism that can be used for logical access control is encryption. Encrypted information can only be decrypted by those possessing the appropriate cryptographic key. This is especially useful if strong physical access controls cannot be provided, such as for laptops or floppy diskettes. Thus, for example, if information is encrypted on a laptop computer, and the laptop is stolen, the information cannot be accessed. While encryption can provide strong access control, it is accompanied by the need for strong key management. Use of encryption may also affect availability. For example, lost or stolen keys or read/write errors may prevent the decryption of the information.

Access Control Lists

Access Control Lists (ACLs) refer to a matrix of users (often represented as rows in the matrix, that include groups, machines, processes) who have been given permission to use a particular system resource, as well as the types of access they have been permitted (usually represented in the matrix as columns). ACLs can vary widely. Also, more advanced ACLs can be used to explicitly deny access to a particular individual or group. With more advanced ACLs, access can be at the discretion of the policymaker (and implemented by the security administrator) or individual user, depending upon how the controls are technically implemented.

Elementary ACLs

The following brief discussion of ACLs is excerpted from the *NIST Handbook* [6]. Elementary ACLs (e.g., "permission bits") are a widely available means of providing access control on multiuser systems. Elementary ACLs are based on the concept of owner, group, and world permissions. These preset groups are used to define all permissions (typically chosen from read, write, execute, and delete access modes) for all resources in this scheme. They usually consist of a short, predefined list of the access rights each entity has to files or other system resources.

The owner is usually the file creator, although in some cases, ownership of resources may be automatically assigned to project administrators, regardless of the identity of the creator. File owners often have all privileges for their resources. In addition to the privileges assigned to the owner, each resource is associated with a named group of users. Users who are members of the group can be granted modes of access distinct from nonmembers, who belong to the rest of the world, which includes all of the system's users. User groups may be arranged according to departments, projects, or other ways appropriate for the particular organization.

Example of Elementary ACL for the file "payroll":

Owner: PAYMANAGER
Access: Read, Write, Execute, Delete

Group: COMPENSATION-OFFICE
Access: Read, Write, Execute, Delete

"World"
Access: None

Advanced ACLs

Advanced ACLs provide a form of access control based upon a logical registry. They do, however, provide finer precision in control. Advanced ACLs can be very useful in many complex information-sharing situations. They provide a great deal of flexibility in implementing system-specific policy and allow for customization to meet the security requirements of functional managers. Their flexibility also makes them more of a challenge to manage. The rules for determining access in the face of apparently conflicting ACL entries are not uniform across all implementations and can be confusing to security administrators. When such systems are introduced, they should be coupled with training to ensure their correct use.

Example of Advanced ACL for the file "payroll"

PAYMGR:	R,	W,	E,	D
J. Anderson:	R,	W,	E,	-
L. Carnahan:	-,	-,	-,	-
B. Guttman:	R,	W,	E,	-
E. Roback:	R,	W,	E,	-
H. Smith:	,	-,	-,	-
PAY-OFFICE:	R,	-,	-,	-
WORLD:	-,	-,	-,	-

Constrained User Interfaces

Interfaces that restrict users' access to specific functions by never allowing them to request the use of information, functions, or other specific system resources for which they do not have access are known as constrained user interfaces. They are often used in conjunction with ACLs. There are three major types of constrained user interfaces: menu-driven systems, database views, and physically constrained user interfaces.

Menu-driven systems are a common constrained user interface, where different users are provided different menus on the same system. Constrained user interfaces can provide a form of access control that closely models how an organization operates. Many systems allow administrators to restrict users' abilities to use the operating system or application system directly. Users can only execute commands that are provided by the administrator, typically in the form of a menu. Another means of restricting users is through restricted shells, which limit the system commands the user can invoke. The use of menus and shells can often make the system easier to use and can help reduce errors.

Database views are a mechanism for restricting user access to data contained in a database. It may be necessary to allow a user to access a database, but that user may not need access to all the data in the database (e.g., not all fields of a record or all records in the database). Views can be used to enforce complex access requirements that are often needed in database situations, such as those based on the content of a field. For example, consider the situation where clerks maintain personnel records in a database. Clerks are assigned a range of clients based upon last name (e.g., A–C, D–G). Instead of granting a user access to all records, the view can grant the user access to the record based upon the first letter of the last name field.

Physically constrained user interfaces can also limit users' abilities. A common example is an ATM, which provides only a limited number of physical buttons to select options; usually, no alphabetic keyboard is present.

External Access Controls

External access controls are comprised of a variety of methods used for managing interactions between a system and external users, systems, and services. External access controls employ many methods, sometimes including a separate physical device placed between the system being protected and a network. Examples include port protection devices, secure gateways, and host-based authentication.

Port Protection Devices

These devices are physically connected to a communications port on a host computer. A port protection device (PPD) authorizes all access to the port to which it is attached. This is done prior to and independently of the computer's access control functions. A PPD can be a separate device in the communications stream, or it can be incorporated into a communications device (e.g., a modem). PPDs typically require a separate authenticator, such as a password, in order to access the communications port.

Secure Gateways/Firewalls

Often called firewalls, secure gateways block and/or filter access between two networks. They are most often employed between a private network and a larger, more public network such as the Internet. Secure gateways allow network users to connect to external networks and simultaneously they prevent malicious hackers from compromising the internal systems. Some secure gateways allow all traffic to pass through *except* for specific traffic that has known or suspected vulnerabilities or security problems, such as remote log-in services. Other secure gateways are set up to disallow all traffic *except* for specific types, such as e-mail. Some secure gateways can make access-control decisions based on the location of the requester. There are several technical approaches and mechanisms used to support secure gateways.

Types of Secure Gateways

There are various types of secure gateways on the market today. These include packet filtering (or screening) routers, proxy hosts, bastion hosts, dual-homed gateways, and screened-host gateways. Because these secure gateways provide security to an organization by restricting services or traffic that passes through their control mechanisms, they can greatly affect system usage in the organization. This fact reemphasizes the need for the establishment of security policy so management can decide how the organization will balance its operational needs against the security costs incurred.

Secure gateways benefit an organization by helping to reduce internal system security overhead. This is because they allow an organization to concentrate security efforts on a few machines instead of on all machines. Secure gateways allow for a centralization of services. They provide a central point for services such as advanced authentication, e-mail, or public dissemination of information. This can reduce system overhead and improve service in an organization.

Host-Based Authentication

The Network File System (NFS) is an example of a host-based authentication system. It allows a server to make resources available to specific machines. Host-based authentication grants access based upon the *identity of the host* originating the request rather than authenticating the identity of the user. There are many network applications in use today that employ host-based authentication mechanisms in order to determine whether or not access is allowed to a given resource. Such host-based authentication schemes are not invulnerable to attack. Under certain circumstances, it is fairly easy for a hacker to masquerade as a legitimate host and fool the system into granting access. Security measures used to protect against the misuse of some host-based authentication systems are often available but require special steps or additional configuration actions before they can be used. An example would be enabling DES encryption when using remote procedure calls.

B.1.10 Techniques Used to Bypass Access Controls

In the realm of security, the use of common terms enables all parties to understand exactly what is meant when discussing security issues. When talking about attacks, four terms are quite common: vulnerability, threat, risk, and exposure. A *vulnerability* is a flaw or weakness that may allow harm to an information system. A *threat* is an activity with the potential for causing harm to an information system. *Risk* is defined as a combination of the chance that threat will occur and the severity of its impact. *Exposure* is a specific instance of weakness that could cause losses to occur from a threat event.

There are several common methods hackers use to bypass access controls and gain unauthorized access to information, principally brute force, denial of service, social engineering, and spoofing. The brute-force method consists of a persistent series of attacks, often trying multiple approaches, in an attempt to break into a computer system. A Denial of Service (DoS) occurs when someone attempts to overload a system through an online connection in order to force it to shut down. Social engineering occurs when someone employs deception techniques against organizational personnel in order to gain unauthorized access. This is the most common method of attack known. Finally, spoofing occurs when a hacker is masquerading an ID in order to gain unauthorized access to a system.

B.2 Password Management

When granting access to a computer system, such access can be restricted by means of controls based on various kinds of identification and authorization techniques. Identification is a two-step function: to identify the user and to authenticate (validate) the identity of the user. The most basic systems rely on passwords only. These techniques do provide some measure of protection against casual browsing of information, but they rarely stop a determined criminal. A computer password is much like a key to a computer. Allowing several people to use the same password is like allowing everyone to use the same key. More sophisticated systems today use SmartCards and/or biometric evaluation techniques in combination with password usage to increase the difficulty in circumventing password protections. Use of the password methodology is built on the premise that something you know could be compromised by someone getting unauthorized access to the password. A system built on something you know (i.e., a password) combined with something you possess (i.e., a SmartCard) is a much stronger system. The combination of knowing and possessing, combined with being (biometrics) provides an even stronger layer of protection. Without having all three elements, even if someone could obtain your password, it is useless without the card and the right biometrics (fingerprint, retinal scan, etc.).

B.2.1 SmartCards

In general, there are two categories of SmartCards. The first is a magnetic strip card and the second is a chipcard. As its name suggests, the magnetic strip card has a magnetic strip containing some encoded confidential information destined to be used in combination with the cardholder's personal code or password. The ChipCard uses a built-in microchip instead of a magnetic strip. The simplest type of ChipCard has a memory chip containing information, but it has no processing capability. The more effective type of ChipCard is the SmartCard, which contains a microchip with both memory to store some information and a processor to process it. Hence, the term SmartCard. Such cards are often used in combination with cryptographic techniques to provide even stronger protection.

B.2.2 Biometric Systems

Biometric systems use specific personal characteristics (biometrics) of an individual (e.g., a fingerprint, a voiceprint, keystroke characteristics, or the pattern of the retina). Biometric systems are still considered an expensive solution for the most part, and, as a result of the cost, they are not yet in common use today. However, even these sophisticated techniques are not infallible. The adage that "*if someone wants it bad enough, he or she will find a way to break in and take it*" still holds true.

B.2.3 Characteristics of Good Passwords

Passwords should be issued to an individual and kept confidential. They should not be shared with anyone. When a temporary user needs access to a system, it is usually fairly simple to add him or her to the list of authorized users. Once the temporary user has finished his or her work, the user-ID must be deleted from the system. All passwords should be distinctly different from the user-ID, and, ideally, they should be alphanumeric and at least six characters in length. Administrators should require that passwords be changed regularly, at least every 30 days. It is possible to warn the user automatically when his or her password expires. To ensure that users enter a new password, they should be restricted in their ability to enter the system after the expiration date, although they may be allowed a limited number of grace-period log-ins.

Passwords must be properly managed. This entails using a password history list, which maintains a list of all of the passwords that have been used in the past 6 to 12 months. New passwords should be checked against the list and not accepted if they have already been used. It is good security practice for administrators to make a list of frequently used forbidden passwords, such as names, product brands, and other words that are easy to guess and therefore not suitable as passwords. This list will be used in the same way as the history list. Only the system manager should be able to change the password history and forbidden lists. In today's modern computing environments, most operating systems conform to these standards and generate passwords automatically. Passwords should be removed immediately if an employee leaves the organization or gives his or her notice of leaving. Finally, it is important to note that extreme care should be taken with the password used by network and systems administrators for remote maintenance. Standard passwords, which are often used to get access to different systems for maintenance purposes, should always be avoided.

B.2.4 Password Cracking

Data gathered from security experts across industry, government, and academia cite weak passwords as one of the most critical Internet security threats. While many administrators recognize the danger of passwords based on common family or pet names, sexual positions, and so on, far fewer administrators recognize that even the most savvy users expose networks to risk due to use of inadequate passwords. Data gathered and reported at one of the largest technology companies in the world [7] where internal security policy required that passwords exceed eight characters, mix cases, and include numbers or symbols, revealed the following startling data:

- L0phtCrack obtained 18 percent of the user passwords in only 10 minutes.
- Within 48 hours, 90 percent of all the passwords were recovered using L0phtCrack running on a very modest Pentium II/300 system.
- Administrator and most domain admin passwords were also cracked.

Password cracking refers to the act of attempting penetration of a network, system, or resource with or without using tools to unlock a resource secured with a password. Crack-resistant passwords are achievable and practical, but password auditing is the only sure way to identify user accounts with weak passwords. The L0phtCrack software (now called LC4, described in the following text) offers this capability.

B.2.5 Windows NT L0phtCrack (LC4)

LC4 is the latest version of the password auditing and recovery application, L0phtCrack. LC4 provides two critical capabilities to Windows network administrators:

1. It helps systems administrators secure Windows-authenticated networks through comprehensive auditing of Windows NT and Windows 2000 user account passwords.
2. It recovers Windows user account passwords to streamline migration of users to another authentication system or to access accounts whose passwords are lost.

LC4 supports a wide variety of audit approaches. It can retrieve encrypted passwords from stand-alone Windows NT and 2000 workstations, networked servers, primary domain controllers, or Active Directory, with or without SYSKEY installed. The software is capable of sniffing encrypted passwords from the challenge/response exchanged when one machine authenticates to another over the network. This software allows administrators to match the rigor of their password audit to their particular needs by choosing from three different types of cracking methods: dictionary, hybrid, and brute-force analysis. These methods will be discussed in the next section. Finally, using a distributed processing approach, LC4 provides administrators with the capability to perform time-consuming audits by breaking them into parts that can be run simultaneously on multiple machines.

B.2.6 Password Cracking for Self-Defense

Using a tool such as LC4 internally enables an organization's password auditor to get a quantitative comparison of password strength. This is done by reviewing LC4's report on the time required to crack each password. A "Hide" feature even allows administrators the option of knowing whether or not a password was cracked without knowing what the password was. Password results can be exported to a tab-delimited file for sorting, formatting, or further manipulation in applications such as Microsoft Excel. LC4 makes password auditing accessible to less-experienced password auditors by using an optional wizard, which walks new users through the process of configuring and running their password audit, letting them choose from preset configurations. As mentioned previously, when performing the cracking process, three cracking methods (dictionary, hybrid, and brute-force analysis) are used. In his Web-based article [8], "*Hacking Techniques—Introduction to Password Cracking,*" Rob Shimonski provides an excellent description of these three methods. They are as follows:

Dictionary Attack

A simple dictionary attack is by far the fastest way to break into a machine. A dictionary file (a text file full of dictionary words) is loaded into a cracking application (such as L0phtCrack), which is run against user accounts located by the application. Because the majority of passwords are often simplistic, running a dictionary attack is often sufficient to do the job.

Hybrid Attack

Another well-known form of attack is the hybrid attack. A hybrid attack will add numbers or symbols to the filename to successfully crack a password. Many people change their passwords by simply adding a number to the end of their current passwords. The pattern usually takes this form: first month password is "cat"; second month password is "cat1"; third month password is "cat2"; and so on.

Brute-force Attack

A brute-force attack is the most comprehensive form of attack, though it may often take a long time to work, depending on the complexity of the password. Some brute-force attacks can take a week depending on the complexity of the password. L0phtCrack can also be used in a brute-force attack.

B.2.7 UNIX Crack

Crack is a password guessing program that is designed to quickly locate insecurities in UNIX password files by scanning the contents of a password file, looking for users who have misguidedly chosen a weak log-in password. This program checks UNIX operating system user passwords for "guessable" values. It works by encrypting a list of the most likely passwords and checking to see if the result matches any of the system user's encrypted passwords. It is surprisingly effective. The most recent version of Crack is version 5.0.

Crack v5.0 is a relatively smart program. It comes preconfigured to expect a variety of crypt() algorithms that are available for cracking in any particular environment. Specifically, it supports "libdes" as shipped, Michael Glad's "UFC" in either of its incarnations (as "ufc" and as GNU's stdlib crypt), and whatever crypt() algorithm is in your standard C library. Crack v5.0 takes an approach where the word guesser sits between two software interfaces: the Standard Password Format (SPF) and the External Library Crypt Interface Definition (ELCID).

When Crack is invoked, it first translates whatever password file is presented to it into SPF; this is achieved by a invoking a utility program called "xxx2spf." The SPF input is then filtered to remove data that has been cracked previously, is sorted, and then passed to the cracker, which starts generating guesses and tries them through the ELCID interface, which contains a certain amount of flexibility to support salt collisions (which are detected by the SPF translator) and parallel or vector computation.

B.2.8 John the Ripper

John the Ripper is a password cracker. Its primary purpose is to detect weak UNIX passwords. It has been tested with many UNIX-based operating systems and has proven to be very effective at cracking passwords. Ports of this software product to DOS and Windows environments also exist. To run John the Ripper, you must supply it with some password files and, optionally, specify a cracking mode. Cracked passwords will be printed to the terminal and saved in a file called `/user_homedirectory/john.pot`. John the Ripper is designed to be both powerful and fast. It combines several cracking modes in one program and is fully configurable for your particular needs. John is available for several different platforms, which enables you to use the same cracker everywhere. Out of the box, John the Ripper supports the following ciphertext formats:

- Standard and double-length DES-based format
- BSDI's extended DES-based format
- MD5-based format (FreeBSD among others)
- OpenBSD's Blowfish-based format

With just one extra command, John the Ripper can crack AFS passwords and WinNT LM hashes. Unlike other crackers, John does not use a crypt(3)-style routine. Instead, it has its own highly optimized modules for different ciphertext formats and architectures. Some of the algorithms used could not be implemented in a crypt(3)-style routine, because they require a more powerful interface (bitslice DES is an example of such an algorithm).

B.2.9 Password Attack Countermeasures

An important recommendation for self-defense against password cracking is to perform frequent recurring audits of passwords. It is often a good idea to physically review workstations to see if passwords are placed on sticky notes, hidden under a keyboard, tacked on a bulletin board, and so on. You should set up dummy accounts and remove the administrator account. The administrator account is sometimes left as bait for tracking someone when detected attempting to use it. Finally, set local security policy to use strong passwords and change them frequently.

B.3 Physical Access

Access control must also be concerned with physical access to the machine, because even the most secure of systems is vulnerable to compromise if anyone can just walk in, pick up the computer, and walk out with it. Physical prevention measures must be used in conjunction with information security measures to create a total solution. Many people go to great lengths to secure their networks from the outside so that intruders cannot get in, but they are often incredibly lax about ensuring that data system equipment is safe from direct attacks by people physically at the machine. Physical security is important for securing the data center, the network and equipment used by IM, and the environment around the equipment. Unless the IM network is encrypted, anyone with physical access to the office LAN could potentially connect network monitoring tools and tap into IM communications. Even if encryption is used, physical access to IM servers and gateways may allow an attacker to monitor network traffic or compromise the system in a matter of minutes. If the proper physical countermeasures, such as insertion of sniffers or other network monitoring devices, are not in place to mitigate some of the biggest risks, then the installation of a sniffer could result in not just data but all IM voice and video communications being intercepted. Therefore, it is important to ensure that adequate physical security measures are in place. Barriers, locks, access control systems, and guards are typically the first line of defense.

B.4 Summary

As discussed previously, many of the IM vulnerabilities are due to weak or nonexistent access controls. Strong authentication of each user and administrator should be performed to be certain that they really are who they say they are. Stringent access controls should be enforced, especially for those who access and transfer sensitive data as part of their jobs. Access policies must be clearly and consistently applied to include which objects each person is allowed to read, write, modify, create, or delete; consistent access controls across all systems; auditing of changes to the validation, authentication, and access control; and the checking of data integrity. Good password policies, guidelines, controls, and auditing must also be used as part of good access control security management. Access control must also be concerned with physical access to the machine. This appendix is intended to give you an overview of the access control issues and why they must be addressed as part of an overall IM security program.

B.5 Endnotes

1. J. Rittinghouse and F. Ransome. *Wireless Operational Security*, 1st ed. New York, Digital Press, 2004.
2. Information Systems Security Association, Inc., CISSP Review Course 2002, Domain 1 "Access Control Systems and Methodology" PowerPoint presentation August 10, 1999, slide 3.
3. U.S. Department of Commerce Special Publication 800-12, "An Introduction to Computer Security—The NIST Handbook," undated, ref: ch. 17, pp 204.
4. National Computer Security Center publication NCSC-TG-003, "A Guide to Understanding Discretionary Access Control in Trusted Systems," September 30, 1987.
5. F. Ferraiolo, et. al. "*Proposed NIST Standard for Role-Based Access Control*," November 2002, NIST, 100 Bureau Drive, Stop 8930, Gaithersburg, MD 20899-8930.
6. National Institute of Standards and Technology. "*An Introduction to Computer Security: The NIST Handbook*." Special Publication 800-12, undated.
7. Data obtained from public Web site of @stake, Inc., http://www.atstake.com/research/lc/index.html.
8. Shimonski, Rob, "Hacking Techniques—Introduction to Password Cracking," July 2002, http://www-106.ibm.com/developerworks/security/library/s-crack/

C

Security Management Issues

Security managers must cope daily with the possibility that electronic information could be lost, corrupted, diverted, or misused. These types of issues represent a real threat to an organization's business performance. Today, companies are more dependent than ever on information technology. Information systems have transitioned from merely being an important asset in a business to being the single most essential, mission-critical factor in the performance of a business mission. However, even as corporate dependence on information technology has grown, so too has the vulnerability of this technology and the range of external threats to it. IM has become a critical part of the the IT communications structure, and as such, the security management issues related to its vulnerabilities should be addressed as aggressively as any other general IT security practice.

As a result of such vulnerabilities, considerable effort has been expended by hundreds, if not thousands, of security experts in creating the applicable policies that attempt to mitigate the risks these vulnerabilities pose. The U.S. government has moved to keep abreast of such changes, enacting various laws that impose severe penalties for perpetrators of cybercrimes. Furthermore, laws placing specific obligations on corporate entities have also been passed to enable or assist law enforcement in pursuing these cybercriminals. A "get-tough" attitude toward hackers and cybercriminals has become pervasive since the 09/11 disaster.

No corporate or government entity wants to take chances that expose it to greater risk these days. Security teams must now operate within a highly complex legal and security policy landscape to ensure the resources they are tasked to protect remain safe. Providing security for IT resources is a difficult technical challenge, one that needs to be managed properly and have support from the top echelons of an organization. IT and network security is also highly dependent on the behavior of human beings. To this end, formal management of both the technology aspects and the human aspects of a security organization are addressed in this appendix.

C.1 Organizational Security Management

The exact needs for a security organization can vary widely. Small organizations with little to no presence on the Internet may not require an organization at all, getting by with a knowledgeable systems administrator and decent HR policies. However, the vast majority of business entities today fall outside that category and need to have a team of dedicated, well-trained security professionals in their organizations. What should the composition of such a team look like? Who should the team report to? What are the team's roles and responsibilities? In the next several sections, we will try to answer all of these questions.

C.1.1 Perceptions of Security

"Those security guys are holding up development team progress. We need to forget their recommendations and get this product out the door." Sound familiar? It is not easy to be the voice of dissent when hype is thrown at you during a meeting. However, many companies have learned the hard way, sometimes at extraordinary cost, that it is far cheaper to take security precautions early on in a development process rather than deal with the issues caused by ignoring them completely. From an individual perspective, some people feel the use of security tools on their equipment is an invasion of privacy. For others, the security teams are lifesavers, coming to the rescue every time they are called. They are the "White-Hatted Rangers of Cyberspace," saving the day whenever a distress signal is heard. It all depends on who is asking and is being asked. Perception is transient. Advocation of strong security measures, in the form of policies and adequate enforcement of such, should remain persistent.

C.1.2 Placement of a Security Group in the Organization

Where does security fit in an organization? Does it belong to the CIO or should it report to the CEO directly? Should there be a centralized function or should security be distributed across the organization? These are difficult questions to answer. Much of the data needed to answer these types of questions needs to come from an introspective look at the organization itself. It is necessary to determine which level of management attention the security team should have. That should help with the reporting structure. If security is a big issue, for which internal reason, then perhaps the CEO will want the security team to report directly to him or her. In very large organizations, security may be distributed in a regional model, with each regional security management leader reporting to a regional business leader or president. Our recommendation, is to place the security organization high enough up the corporate ladder to enable it to effect positive change. It must operate with a high degree of autonomy, and it must be led by someone who is respected by the management team as an effective role model with a high degree of integrity. Once a company comes to terms with who the security team should report to, the next issue is to figure out what the team should look like.

C.1.3 Security Organizational Structure

Before putting a security organization in place, a couple of considerations must be addressed. First, is security something that will likely be a public or private issue for your organization most of the time? If the vast majority of security issues in your organization are never raised to the public, then your security team is likely also going to be a low-profile operation. However, for most companies, this is not the case. Any publicly traded company is more likely to fit in the high-profile category than the low-profile category. That being the case, the security team is going to have to be structured to respond to issues that can limit exposure of risk and contain that risk in such a manner that all legal requirements are met and the public at large can feel satisfied that the management team is adequately protecting the assets with which they have been entrusted.

Structural issues now must look at basic elements of security, such as incident response, policy development, forensics, training and awareness, perimeter security measures, intrusion detection, secure remote access, and so on. There are many, many distinct areas that have to be addressed in a security plan. How the organization is structured is also a reflection of what specifically is emphasized in this site security plan. The security manager entrusted with running this organization must decide where to place his or her resources to get the most bang for the buck. Speaking of which, that brings up the point that an adequate budget must be set aside for the security team. How much? Once again, it depends on what the structure of the organization will look like and what needs to be emphasized for the particular needs of each organization. There is no "one size fits all" answer to this question. Suffice it to say, the security team needs to have enough budget to succeed *every* time and with *every* issue it will encounter. The CEO or CFO and the security manager should work together to derive a realistic working budget that is flexible enough to accommodate an ever-changing environment.

C.1.4 Convincing Management of the Need

Only a couple of years ago, business interruption and the extra expense as a result of computer virus or malicious destruction of the data inside the computer system were viewed in terms of cost. However, with the advent of new, major federal and state laws impacting information access and protection, security professionals are obliged to know how to determine which laws and jurisdictions apply to information security. They must be aware of which types of information their companies are required to protect. They have specific legal obligations concerning the use and handling of personal information and protection of the rights of employers and employees concerning e-mail and other information.

C.1.5 Legal Responsibilities for Data Protection

No business that is connected to a network or the Internet today is completely secure from the danger hackers pose. Hackers can destroy data, release information to competitors, or make the computer system unusable. Liability for losses caused by fraudulent and malicious acts committed by either employees or third parties against a company's computer systems, electronic computer programs, electronic data and media, and computer virus attacks is becoming the responsibility of the business management team. Executives and directors are becoming more and more accountable for their actions when they allow their organizations to remain exposed to preventable risks. Companies now face liability exposure for any failure of their management to meet legal restrictions and requirements recently enacted. Liability considerations facing corporate security managers include the following:

- *Media liability*: Protection for claims arising out of the content placed on a Web site. This includes trademark, copyright, defamation, privacy, libel, and slander issues. It is also known as "contextual liability" in the insurance world.
- *Unauthorized access and/or denial of service*: A hacker, cracker, disgruntled employee(s), competitor, terrorist, or prank by an Internet "gangster" can cause this claim to be made by bringing your ability to respond to customers' requests to a halt.
- *Loss of income from business interruption*: Income from a Web site can be interrupted due to various technology perils, such as electrical outage without backup equipment being operational, earthquake, data center floods, and so on.
- *CyberExtortion*: There have been numerous extortion events demanding payment to avoid proprietary information, credit cards, and other information from being released to the general public.
- *Data and software destruction*: Reestablishment of the content of the Web site: the cost associated with rebuilding the total Web site.
- *Cybertheft of money, securities, and other property*: The unauthorized theft of money; securities; and other information, including trade secrets, client lists, proprietary information, and so on.

C.1.6 DHS Office of Private Sector Liaison

To emphasize the importance of security in recent months, consider the fact that the U.S. government created a new cabinet-level office, which, in February 2003, started operations in earnest as the Department of Homeland Security (DHS). Part of the mission Secretary Tom Ridge took on when he assumed the position was to ensure that the DHS will provide America's business community with a direct line of communication to government. The office will work directly with individual businesses and through trade associations and other nongovernment organizations to foster dialog between the private sector and the DHS on the full range of issues and challenges faced by America's business sector in the post-9/11 world. The office will be organized to specifically deal with America's critical industry sectors as outlined in the President's National Strategy for Homeland Security, as well as general business matters and concerns related to the DHS. The office will serve America's business community as the focal point of contact with the DHS. The DHS will also give the private sector one primary contact, instead of many, for coordinating protection activities with the federal government, including vulnerability assessments, strategic planning efforts, and exercises.

> Let us take things as we find them: let us not attempt to distort them into what they are not. We cannot make facts. All our wishing cannot change them. We must use them.
>
> —John Henry Cardinal Newman (1801 - 1890)

C.2 Security Management Areas of Responsibility

This section covers the basic areas that should be addressed as part of any security plan for any organization. It does not go into details about how to configure equipment or develop scripts and so on. It is strictly a management perspective of the coverage areas that need to be addressed to ensure that adequate organizational protections are in place. These areas are generally implemented by establishing policy. Consider these areas the basic requirements, policy is used to implement the requirements, and the security team is there to enforce the requirements and adjust as needed to ensure currency with changing business conditions.

When putting together a site security plan, it is important to build a strategy that satisfies the needs of the organization. To accomplish this, you must first determine what the organization's needs are by conducting a needs assessment. The results of this assessment will aid in defining the security program appropriate for your organization. Review the program with senior staff to ensure you have their buy-in on implementing the programs and set up a process to periodically review these programs to ensure they meet the business needs. The next step is to develop an awareness and training plan, identify the various audiences (or constituency as some prefer to call it), and begin training. Let's discuss this program in a bit more detail.

C.2.1 Awareness Programs

Successful computer security programs are highly dependent on the effectiveness of an organization's security awareness and training program. If employees are not informed of applicable organizational policies and procedures, they cannot be expected to properly secure computer resources. The dissemination and enforcement of the security policy is a critical issue, which can be addressed through local security awareness and training programs. Employees cannot be expected to follow policies and procedures of which they are unaware. In addition, enforcing penalties may be difficult if users can claim ignorance when caught doing something wrong.

Training employees can also show that a standard of due care has been taken in protecting information. Simply issuing policy without follow-through to implement that policy is not enough to get the job done right. Many organizations use acknowledgment statements to verify that employees have read and understand computer security requirements. New hires are an especially important audience for security awareness training. It is critical that any new employee receive training on the security policies in place at an organization within the first week or two of employment.

Many employees regard computer security as an obstacle to their job productivity. To help motivate employees to be security aware, awareness should emphasize how security can contribute to productivity. The consequences of poor security should be explained without using fear and intimidation tactics employees often associate with security. Awareness helps reinforce the fact that security supports the mission of the organization by protecting valuable resources. If employees view security measures as bothersome rules and procedures, they are likely to ignore them. Managers are responsible for ensuring that their personnel are briefed and understand the role they play in supporting security efforts. By informing all personnel of the statutes and policies surrounding IT security, and by conducting periodic security awareness briefings, managers can accomplish this task.

Security training is most effective when targeted to a specific audience. This enables the training to focus on security-related job skills and knowledge that people need performing their duties. Divide the audiences into groups according to their level of security awareness. Individuals may be separated into groups according to their current level of awareness. This may require research to determine how well employees follow computer security procedures or understand how computer security fits into their jobs. Training groups can be segmented according to general job task or function, specific job category, or their level of competence and understanding of general computer knowledge.

C.2.2 Risk Analysis

A prime consideration for creating a computer security policy is to ensure that the effort spent on developing and implementing the security policy will yield cost-effective benefits. It is important for a security manager to understand where the most obvious "quick wins" in security will be found. While there is a great deal of information in the press about intruders hacking into computer systems, most security surveys reveal the actual loss from insiders is a far greater risk.

Risk analysis involves determining what you need to protect, what you need to protect it from, and how you need to protect it. Risk analysis is the process of examining all of the potential risks you may face, then rank ordering those risks by level of severity. This process will involve choosing cost-effective solutions on what you want to protect and how it is to be protected. It is important to balance the value of the asset that needs protection against the cost of providing that protection. For example, if you spend $500,000 to protect reproducible code assets that originally only cost $180,000, it is not likely a sound security investment. Always consider the cost-versus-worth scenario when selecting your security solutions.

Identify Assets

For each asset, the basic goals of security are availability, confidentiality, and integrity. A risk analysis process requires the identification of all assets that need to be protected. For each asset, try to determine what potential threats exist for that particular asset. A list of asset categories suggested by Pfleeger [1] includes the following:

- *Hardware*: Keyboards, monitors, laptops, personal computers, printers, disk drives, communication lines, terminal servers, routers
- *Software*: Source programs, object programs, utilities, diagnostic programs, operating systems, communication programs
- *Data*: Used during execution, stored online, archived offline, backups, audit logs, databases, in transit over communication media
- *People*: Users, administrators, hardware maintainers
- *Documentation*: On programs, hardware, systems, local administrative procedures
- *Supplies*: Paper, forms, paperclips, ink cartridges, ribbons, magnetic media

Identifying the Threats

Once the assets have been identified, it is necessary to determine the potential threats to those assets. Threats can then be examined to determine a loss potential. Loss potential helps rank the asset and threat against other items in your list. The following are classic threats that should be considered:

unauthorized access, unintended disclosure of information, and denial of service. Depending on your organization, more specific threats should be identified and addressed.

C.2.3 Incident Handling

In this section, we cover the process of establishing the incident handling function in an organization. A security manager must consider serveral key issues when establishing an incident response group. What are the goals the group needs to accomplish? What should this team be relied upon to do in a consistent and professional manner? Who should the team provide this service to (i.e., what is the incident handling group's constituency)? It is important to understand the constituency, because what is provided for one audience may be inadequate for another. For example, if your constituency is a distributed data center operation, its incident response needs will be quite different from those of a retail Web site selling t-shirts and such.

Once the constituency is known, the next step is to begin determining what the structure of the incident response group will look like. Should it be a centralized organization or a decentralized, distributed organization? This decision greatly affects the staffing and funding requirements. Once you have determined the structure best suited to the needs of a constituency, your organization's management team must support the decision and agree to the funding requirements. As you begin to set up the operation, a centralized mechanism needs to be put in place for the constituency to report incidents or potential incidents. A team must be assembled to respond to those incidents, and the team should operate from a high-level "guidebook" or charter. Creating a charter for the team will get everyone on the team working toward achieving the same goals. How the team goes about achieving those goals is defined by process and procedures, usually put in place by creating an *Incident Response Group Operations Handbook*. This handbook is considered the starting point for handling all incidents, and the team members must be instructed to update and make it a living document as environmental conditions change. Finally, when an incident is reported, investigated, and resolved, a management reporting function needs to be in place to let management understand what happened and the impact it had on the organization.

C.2.4 Alerts and Advisories

Alerts and advisories are released (almost daily) that detail newly discovered vulnerabilities and other security information. This information may require immediate action on the part of the system administrators, the incident response group, or the users. Advisories come from a variety of sources, such as vendors and product manufacturers. There are also places like the CERT Coordination Center (CERT/CC) and the Federal Computer Incident Response Capability (FEDCIRC), now both a part of the new "National Strategy to Protect Infrastructure." To help develop ways to better protect our critical infrastructures and to help minimize vulnerabilities, the U.S. Department of Homeland Security has established Information Sharing and Analysis Centers, or ISACs, to allow critical sectors to share information and work together to help better protect the economy. The IT-ISAC is a forum for sharing information about network vulnerabilities, as well as effective solutions [2]. It is also a forum for sharing threat-related information and ways to protect against those threats. The operations center is intended to help in achieving a higher level of critical infrastructure protection through sharing of key security solutions.

Regardless of which source agency sends out an advisory, upon receipt of any alerts and advisories requiring action, ensure compliance with the required action. If compliance cannot occur for any reason, obtain a statement of waiver with reasons that the actions cannot be implemented. For any compliance or waiver actions needed, ensure they are reported to the CSO or security manager for briefing to other senior management.

C.2.5 Warning Banners

It is good security practice for all systems to display warning banners upon connection to a given system. These banners should display a warning informing the user logging in that the system is for legitimate use only, is subject to monitoring, and carries no expectation of privacy. The use of warning banners provides legal notice to anyone accessing the system that he or she is using a system that is subject to monitoring. Users should also be notified of the possible sanctions, such as loss of privileges, employment, or even prosecution, if they misuse or access the network without authorization. System administrators can install the banners quite easily, and the information contained in the banners should be approved by the organization's legal staff. A sample of banner wording is as follows:

```
This is a proprietary computer system that is "FOR INTERNAL
USE ONLY." This system is subject to monitoring. Therefore, no
expectation of privacy is to be assumed. Individuals found
performing unauthorized activities are subject to
disciplinary action including criminal prosecution.
```

C.2.6 Employee Termination Procedures

Unfortunately, termination often leads to a security incident. This sad fact of life must be dealt with by businesses every day. Security teams have routinely become involved in termination processing to ensure that disgruntled employees cannot take actions detrimental to the company. The termination procedure encompasses those activities that occur when an employee terminates his or her employment with the organization or is terminated by the organization. It is good business practice to require the Chief People Officer (CPO) or VP of Human Resources to provide the Chief Information Officer (CIO) and Chief Information Security Officer (CISO) or equivalent with a list of terminated employees on a weekly or monthly basis.

C.2.7 Training

All authorized users should be required to attend training on how to fulfill their security responsibilities within 30 days of employment. They should also be required to participate in periodic recurring training in information system security awareness and accepted information system security practices, as appropriate to their job functions and responsibilities. Users having access to multiple applications should be encouraged to attend training on each application and in all general support systems. The system security plan should specify the type and frequency of training required in such circumstances.

IT and security managers should plan and prepare for two types of training, one for users and the other for system administrators. Users should be required to participate in certain training activities, such as awareness training, and various application training classes, which may be offered periodically. The second type of training, for the System Administrators (SAs) should be in security competency. It is the manager's responsibility to ensure that the system administrators have been provided with all the security training needed to fulfill the security requirements for which they are responsible.

C.2.8 Personnel Security

Personnel security involves training users to be aware of their responsibilities and the consequences of any failure to abide by security policies for using the computer automation assets. Personnel security should be a part of the overall security training plan. Supervisors should be responsible for coordinating and arranging system access requests for all new or transferring employees and for verifying an individual's need to gain access to any sensitive information in an organization.

Regardless of their position or job function, personnel who have access to the network should read and sign an acceptable-use policy. They should attend periodic recurring security training. Users usually only need to sign the acceptable-use agreement once, when their e-mail account is issued by the organization. After that, they should be briefed at least annually on any updates to the acceptable-use policy. New procedures should be covered and awareness of security concerns addressed.

Quite often, an organization will provide all employees with a *Personnel Security Handbook*, which describes the responsibilities of employees. All persons accessing sensitive computer systems should have a background check prior to being granted access. The handbook should describe minimum requirements for any background investigations. Contractors who design, operate, test, maintain, or monitor systems should be required to have background checks as well.

C.2.9 Internet Use

It is a good idea for an organization to require all employees and contractors who use company-provided information systems in their jobs to sign an Internet use policy. Employees and contractors should be prohibited from accessing systems that are not necessary for the performance of their duties. They should also be restricted from performing tasks on systems they are authorized to access but are not related to their job responsibilities. For example, a help-desk agent may have access to a payroll computer, but that does not give him or her the right to go in and use the payroll computer for any purpose. System administrators have the ability to audit network logs and perform periodic checks for misuse and should do so on a regular basis. This practice will help ensure compliance among the masses.

C.2.10 E-mail

It is a primary responsibility of the IT group and/or the security team to ensure the appropriate use of e-mail systems. Various technical measures can assist in this goal. First, e-mail should be used primarily for official business. People using company systems for sending e-mail should make the same provisions to ensure confidentiality as those that would be made for sending hard-copy correspondence. All activities on a company's information systems are subject to monitoring. Users should have no expectations of privacy. By using a company's e-mail system, users implicitly agree to be governed by that company's acceptable-use policy regarding e-mail.

C.2.11 Sensitive Information

All organizational personnel are responsible for the safeguarding and appropriate handling of sensitive corporate information. Sensitive corporate information is defined as information that is critical to the operation of the business and information for which public release is inappropriate. Ensure that your users are trained and briefed on how to handle sensitive corporate information. Maintain adequate access controls and accountability of information. Set specific policies for the use and handling of sensitive information.

C.2.12 System Security

Providing for adequate system security requires advanced planning and effort. Ensure that system administrators have adequate resources to establish and maintain system security levels. The following list includes the basic areas security managers should be concerned with for ensuring that adequate security measures are in place.

Hardening systems: No system should ever be placed on the network without a security configuration setup. "*Hardening*" refers to the process of disabling unnecessary services, installing all the latest fixes and patches, installing adequate security software, tuning the operating system for security rather than performance, and documenting the system on the network. All of this work takes a great deal of effort to accomplish but should not be taken lightly. It takes only one incorrectly configured system to allow an intruder into your network.

Network architecture: The way systems (nodes) are placed on a network affects the level of security for that network. It is good practice to keep the internal network separate from the publicly accessible network. Publicly accessible portions include things such as Web servers and mail systems. The way administrators go about segregating the two sections of the network varies. In many cases, a firewall is used to create a demilitarized zone. This is a separate area of the network, where the Web servers and other publicly accessible systems are placed.

User authentication and identification: All systems should incorporate proper user authentication and identification methodologies. This includes authentication based on user ID and password, tokens, or biometrics. To protect systems and data, companies should require outside entities needing access to their systems (whether contractors or other agencies) to use access controls commensurate with those used by the organization. Additionally, these systems should undergo a periodic review of user access privileges to ensure that no accounts exist where users are no longer working on the system (not to exceed semiannually). All such "ghost" accounts should be deleted.

C.2.13 Physical Security

Physical security involves safekeeping the systems from theft or physical damage and preventing unauthorized access to those systems. If unauthorized users are given physical access to a system, it is a simple matter for them to break in and then gain access to important business data. All employees and contractors should be held responsible (and accountable) for taking every reasonable precaution to ensure the physical security of their IT hardware and related peripherals, including mobile devices, from theft, abuse, avoidable hazards, or unauthorized use. Company servers, routers, and other communication hardware essential for maintaining the operability of the systems and their connectivity to the Internet should be placed in a controlled-access location (i.e., behind locked doors).

Managers must ensure that the nodes that comprise the network (such as file servers, Web servers, mail servers, and any other equipment that forms the basis of the network) will be secured in an area where access is controlled. Only authorized personnel will have access to network equipment. Ensure that users' systems are as secure as is practical. This includes securing the systems from casual use by installing password-protected screensavers. Provide the ability for users to lock the workstations when they leave their areas. The responsibility to safeguard IT assets should not include having company employees or contractors endangering themselves or others by attempting to physically prevent the unauthorized removal or destruction of IT hardware, accessories, or supplies.

C.3 Security Policies

A good starting point for understanding the development of security policy is RFC 2196 [3], "Site Security Handbook." Much of the information toward policy development has evolved from the original RFC 1244, which was obsoleted by RFC 2196. The purpose herein is to provide practical guidance to administrators trying to secure their information and services as they pertain to their "site." For the purposes of this book, a "site" is any organization that has computers or network-related resources. These resources may include host servers, routers, application and database servers, PCs and PDAs, or other devices that have access to the Internet.

C.4 Basic Approach to Policy Development

One generally accepted approach to development of site policy is that suggested by Fites [4], which recommends one take the following steps:

1. Identify what you are trying to protect.
2. Determine what you are trying to protect it from.
3. Determine how likely the threats are.
4. Implement measures that will protect your assets in a cost-effective manner.
5. Review the process continuously; make improvements each time a weakness is found.

Most organizations will concentrate their efforts on item 4, but if an effective security plan is to be established at your site, the other steps cannot be avoided. An axiom to remember is that the cost of protecting yourself against a threat should be less than the cost of recovering if the threat were to strike you. Cost in this context should factor in losses expressed in dollars, reputation, trustworthiness, and other less-obvious measures. Without reasonable knowledge of what you are protecting and what the likely threats are, following this rule could be difficult. We will briefly review each of the five items in the preceding list.

C.4.1 Identify What Needs Protection and Why

These two steps are initially accomplished in the risk analysis phase described at the beginning of this appendix. The list of categories suggested by Pfleeger [5] is worth mentioning again. The specific items in the list are less relevant than the categories themselves. For every organization, the inventoried assets will be different, but most will fall into one of the previous categories. Conduct your asset inventory, listing every item, grouped by category. This may help you determine potential threats for an entire group of assets versus an item-by-item approach. For example, mandating that all disposable supplies should be locked in a cabinet may be more cost effective and equally effective as having separate procedures for ribbons, paper, and so on. Once the assets requiring protection have been identified, an organization should take steps to identify corresponding potential threats for those assets. These threats can subsequently be evaluated to determine if any potential for loss may exist.

C.4.2 Determine Likelihood of Threats

A computer security policy is generally created to ensure that efforts spent on security yield cost-effective benefits. Most surveys of computer security show that, for most organizations, the actual loss from insiders is a much greater risk than attack by an outsider. We have discussed a process that involves determining what a site needs to protect, what a site needs to protect it from, and how to actually protect it. The process of examining all of the risks associated with each of these three items, including ranking those risks by level of severity, is what we mean by determining the likelihood of a threat. This process involves making cost-effective decisions on what you want to protect. After all, it does not make good business sense to spend more to protect something than it is actually worth.

C.4.3 Implement Protective Measures

The security-related decisions you make, or fail to make, largely determine how secure your network is. However, you cannot make good decisions about security without first determining which security goals need to be set for your organization. Until you determine what your security goals are, you cannot make effective use of any collection of security tools, because you simply won't know what to check for and which restrictions to impose. Your goals will be largely determined by the following key tradeoffs:

1. *Services offered versus security provided*—Each service offered to users carries its own security risks. For some services the risk outweighs the benefit of the service, and the administrator may choose to eliminate the service rather than try to secure it.
2. *Ease of use versus security*—The easiest system to use would allow open access to any user and require no passwords. Of course, there would be no security. Requiring passwords makes the system a little less convenient but more secure. Requiring device-generated, one-time passwords makes the system even more difficult to use but much more secure.
3. *Cost of security versus risk of loss*—There are many different costs to security: monetary, performance, and ease of use, to name a few. There are also many levels of risk: loss of privacy, loss of data, and the loss of service. Each type of cost must be weighed against each type of loss.

Goals should be communicated to all users, operations staff, and managers through a set of security rules, called a "security policy."

Definition of a Security Policy

A security policy is a formal body of the rules by which people who are given access to an organization's technology and information assets must abide. It is part of an overall organizational site security plan. Its purpose is to inform members of the organization of their responsibilities under certain circumstances that could pose potential risk to the company.

Purposes of a Security Policy

The main purpose of a security policy is to inform users, staff, and managers of their obligatory requirements for protecting technology and information assets. The policy should specify the mechanisms put in place to meet these requirements. Another purpose is to provide a baseline from which to acquire, configure, and audit computer systems and networks for compliance with the policy. An Acceptable Use Policy (AUP) should be part of any security policy. The AUP should spell out what users shall and shall not do on the various components of the system, including the type of traffic allowed on the networks. The AUP should be as explicit as possible to avoid any ambiguity or misunderstanding.

C.4.4 What Makes a Good Security Policy?

Characteristics of a good security policy are that it must be implementable through system administration procedures, publishing of acceptable use guidelines, or other appropriate methods. It must be enforceable using security tools, where appropriate, and sanctions, where actual prevention is not technically feasible. Finally, it must clearly define the areas of responsibility for the users, administrators, and management. These three characteristics form the basis of any sound security policy. Additionally, there must be buy-in from Legal, the CIO, and HR for the policies developed. Otherwise, they are not worth the paper they are printed on.

Components of a Good Security Policy

Which elements make up a good security policy? What needs to be in the policy to make it effective without overloading users on hundreds of security-related items? This section has identified eight key areas that should be addressed in security policies. The following list shows these areas, which are discussed next.

- Access
- Authentication
- Accountability
- Privacy

- Availability
- Systems and networking maintenance
- Acquisition guidelines
- Violations reporting

The access policy is used to define access rights and privileges necessary to protect company assets from loss or disclosure by specifying acceptable use guidelines for users, staff, and management. The access policy should provide specific guidelines for use of external connections, data communications, connecting user-owned devices to a network, and adding new software to systems. It should also specify any required banner messages.

The authentication policy is used to establish trust through use of an effective password policy. It also is used for setting guidelines for remote location authentication and use of various authentication devices. It should outline minimum requirements for access to all resources.

An accountability policy defines the responsibilities of users, staff, and management. It should specify a periodic, recurring audit capability and provide basic incident handling guidelines.

The privacy policy defines reasonable expectations of privacy regarding such issues as monitoring of electronic mail, logging of keystrokes, and access to user files.

Availability statements are used to set expectations for the availability of resources. This statement should address redundancy and recovery issues. It should also be used to specify operating hours and maintenance downtime periods. It is important to include contact information for reporting system and network failures as a part of this document.

The information technology system and network maintenance policy describes how both internal and external maintenance people are allowed to handle and access technology for routine tasks such as system backup, equipment maintenance, application of upgrades, patches, and so on. One important topic to be addressed here is whether remote maintenance is allowed and how such access is controlled.

Another area for consideration is outsourcing and how it is managed. Computer technology purchasing guidelines should be used to specify required, or preferred, security features. These guidelines should supplement existing purchasing policies and guidelines.

The Violations Reporting Policy indicates which types of violations (e.g., privacy and security, internal and external) must be reported and to whom the reports are made. A nonthreatening atmosphere and the possibility of anonymous reporting will result in a greater probability that a violation will be reported if it is detected.

It is a good idea to also provide supporting information that can provide users contact information for each type of policy violation encountered. Specific guidelines on how to handle outside queries about a security incident, or information that may be considered confidential or proprietary, are a good idea. Include cross-references to security procedures and related information, such as company policies. There may be regulatory requirements that affect some aspects of your security policy (e.g., line monitoring). The policy should be reviewed by legal counsel before being put into effect. Once your security policy has been established, it should be clearly communicated to users, staff, and management. Having all personnel sign a statement indicating that they have read, understood, and agreed to abide by the policy is an important part of the process.

C.4.5 Review and Assess Regularly

Security managers must ensure that the organizational security policy is reviewed on a regular basis (*semiannually is our recommended review frequency*) to see if it is successfully supporting your security needs. Adapt the plan to meet any changed conditions and distribute change notices to the constituency as needed. Ensure that training plans are updated with the changed material and that managers brief their personnel on all security changes.

It is equally important to assess the adequacy of measures implemented by the policies. Ensure that the measures taken not only solve the problem, but help prevent it from reoccurring. Have security and IT staff independently evaluate the effectiveness if possible. Sometimes, it is even a good idea to bring in third-party organizations to perform independent assessments of your processes and procedures. If you make changes here, be sure to go back and update the policy book accordingly.

C.5 Security Personnel

C.5.1 Coping with Insider Threats

According to a Gigalaw by Andrew Handelsmann report [6], an internal security breach occurs when an employee of a company uses the company's information system without authorization or uses it in such a way that exceeds his or her valid authorization. The author states that in 2001, the American Computer Security Institute surveyed a large number of corporations, medical institutes, and government agencies about serious security breaches of their computer systems, such as the theft of proprietary information, financial fraud, denial-of-service attacks, and sabotage of data or networks. The findings were startling. More than 70 percent of respondents reported these kinds of attacks as having occurred from inside the company, while only 25 percent reported system penetration from outsiders.

Employees, who often occupy positions of trust, have the greatest access to information within the organization. They have the greatest potential to exploit information sources or sabotage computer systems for personal gain. Insider acts involve unauthorized viewing or use of information and the unauthorized entry or alteration of data to produce false transactions and tamper with information systems. Handlesmann advocates that "employers must acknowledge the risks of unauthorized access and computer fraud by employees and put in place monitoring systems and preventative measures that address these risks."

While an employee who commits an attack will often face criminal prosecution, the employee's company may also find itself the subject of a civil lawsuit. A significant danger exists in regard to insider e-security breaches. If an employee misuses a company's data systems to commit electronic fraud or cause damage or loss to third parties, it may be held (vicariously) liable for the acts of its employee. The standard test for vicarious liability is that the employee's action must have been committed in the course and scope of the employment. It is important to note that "in the course and scope of employment" is a broad term for which there is no absolute legal definition. However, case law (in Australia) has established a few guiding principles. Handlesmann cites the following:

- Where an employer authorizes an act but it is performed in an improper or unauthorized manner, the employer will still be held liable.
- It does not matter that an employee is unauthorized to perform an act, and the mere fact that an act is illegal does not bring it outside the scope of employment.
- Even though unauthorized access or computer fraud by an employee is an act that lies outside the employee's scope of employment, this does not automatically exclude the employer from vicarious liability.
- It is not necessarily an answer to a claim against an employer that the wrong done by the employee was for the employee's own benefit.

Much of the computer fraud committed by employees can be averted if employers implement an effective security policy that puts in place measures targeted at prevention, ongoing monitoring, and recovery strategies in the case of breach. Monitoring may detect problems in progress and allow the possibility of aborting a process before any serious damage is done.

C.5.2 How to Identify Competent Security Professionals

It is always a good idea to understand which areas and applications of security are most in demand when trying to find competent staff. Some of these areas include perimeter management, intrusion detection, forensics, firewalls and VPNs, and internal information security. Sounds like all the basic areas of security, right? Well, it is! Security is a diverse field and it covers a lot of territory. When looking for people for your organization's needs, you need to know as much as possible about the organization before you go headhunting. Then, and only then, will you know what to look for in finding competent people. To find these people, you need to ask yourself, "What are the basic things people seeking information security jobs should know?"

When hiring entry-level or nonsenior security engineers, education and training play a much bigger role. This indicates a strong level of effort to stand out from the crowd and hone skills in a particular area. Look for certifications and similar indicators of professional training and qualification. However, once you get past the six to eight years of experience level, when looking for management-level security professionals, certifications are less important than experience. This does not mean to ignore certifications, but they should be considered as a secondary factor. For example, would you rather have a security engineer with certification of less than a year and less than six years of industry experience, or someone without the certification but 12 years of hands-on, in-the-dirt security consulting experience? It is your call, but we encourage looking at the whole person and not focusing on one specific credential or certification. If someone with eight to ten years of experience also has the certifications, all the better. It is but one factor in the decision-making process.

Security managers should have broad security experience. They should know how to manage and implement data security controls and understand architecture and strategies. They should possess in-depth knowledge and understanding of international, national, and local legislation affecting information security and be able to develop and implement business plans and policies. That is what you should look for. Other considerations may include (in no particular order) background checks, credit checks, drug screening, membership in hacker groups, and references from the last job.

When hiring a security professional, be sure to have a job description prepared prior to advertising the position. This helps identify your firm's needs and the skills candidates must offer. Determine the salary range your firm is willing to pay and check around to make sure it is competitive. In the security realm, it is true that you get what you pay for. Candidates with in-depth experience supported by formal training and a college degree command top salaries. Those with only on-the-job training may not be as costly. In addition to IT and functional departments, let their future colleagues interview candidates. Plan an interview process using several people employing questions in diverse areas and compare notes when the interview is over. Security isn't just technology; it's a process requiring effective communication. Insist on a background check as a condition of employment.

In this specialty professional, qualifications should include a problem-free personal background.

C.5.3 How to Train and Certify Security Professionals

The Value of Certifications

We are often asked if security certifications are required to get ahead in security. The answer is no, but they certainly help. Certification isn't mandatory, but it exposes a professional to key concepts, policies, and procedures for practicing security. If two equal candidates, in terms of experience, are competing for the same job, the one with certification will most likely have the upper hand. It indicates a level of effort expended to stand out in the crowd and perform the job better. To be sure, certification will help anyone break into the security field, but it will not carry him or her through it.

Types of Security Certifications Available

Which security certifications are the most worthwhile? The answer depends on an individual's background and career interests. Those with an interest in firewalls should look at the Check Point Certified Security Administrator (CCSA) certification. CCSA is a foundation-level certification, which validates a candidate's ability to configure and manage fundamental implementations of Check Point's flagship product, FireWall-1, as an enterprise level Internet security solution to protect corporate networks [7]. As a CCSA, security professionals possess the requisite skills to define and configure security policies that enable secure access to information across corporate networks. In addition to these essential skills, CCSAs also have the ability to monitor network security activity and implement measures to block intruder access to networks. For people more interested in auditing and monitoring, perhaps the Certified Information Systems Auditor (CISA) is more appropriate. The CISA certification is awarded to those individuals with an interest in information systems auditing, control, and security, who meet stringent requirements, including the successful completion of the CISA examination, certified information systems auditing, control or security experience, adherence to a code of professional ethics, participation in a continuing education program, and demonstrated understanding of information systems auditing standards.

More experienced security management professionals may choose to get a Certified Information System Security Professional (CISSP) certification. This is a stringent certification process reflecting the qualifications of information systems security practitioners. The CISSP examination consists of 250 multiple-choice questions, covering topics such as access control systems, cryptography, and security management practices, and is administered by the International Information Systems Security Certification Consortium or (ISC)2. (ISC)2 promotes the CISSP exam as an aid to evaluating personnel performing information security functions.

The Global Information Assurance Certification (GIAC) Certified Security Expert (CSE) is a comprehensive, technically oriented certification for security professionals. This certification is rare, and to date only a very few candidates (less than five at the time of this writing, according to the GIAC Web site [8]) have been considered for inclusion in this elite group. The exam for a GIAC/CSE certification consists of 10 different parts. Four sections of the exam consist of hands-on assessment and reporting about four distinctly different business plans and network designs implemented in a simulated production environment. Four other sections will test the knowledge and the ability of the candidate to gather information and interpret it through 30 to 40 in-depth essay questions and 90 accompanying multiple-choice questions on various focus areas; that's about 130 questions per section! The candidates are also required to deliver a one-hour (or longer) technical presentation to demonstrate their ability to relate technical information to others. The remaining portion of the exam requires the candidate to take a business plan, recommend changes, and implement those changes into a simulated production network, which will then be assessed by the staff and the other candidates. Certainly, someone who possesses this qualification would be considered at the very top tier of qualifications in security.

A more common GIAC certification is the Security Essentials Certification (GSEC). This is a basic- to intermediate-level professional certification, which is targeted to security professionals who want to fill the gaps in their understanding of technical information security. It is a good certification for systems, security, and network administrators who want to understand the pragmatic applications of a common body of knowledge. Managers who want to understand information security beyond simple terminology and concepts may also attain this certification. It is also a good certification for anyone who is new to the field of information security with some background in information systems and networking. GIAC certification graduates have the knowledge, skills, and abilities that businesses need to incorporate good information security practice into any organization. The GSEC tests the essential knowledge and skills required of any individual with security responsibilities within an organization.

GIAC also offers certifications in firewalls, intrusion analysis, incident handling, and more. For security managers, it may be a good idea for an organization to have their designee attend the GIAC Information Security Officer (GISO) Certification program. It is a basic-level program designed for newly appointed information security officers who need to hit the ground running and need an overview of Information Assurance. It is specifically for managers, information security officers, and system administrators, who need an overview of risk management and defense-in-depth techniques. It can be useful to anyone who writes, implements, or must adhere to security policies. People involved in shaping the decisions an organization makes regarding the use of emerging and changing information technology would be well served by this program.

Currently, the broader, more policy-focused CISSP (for managers) and the in-depth, hands-on certifications from SANS/GIAC tend to pay the best dividends for professional development, and some employers will often pay extra for them. As your security organization develops, you may find it useful to track the number of certifications held by members of your team. I have even seen organizations strive to attain 100 percent completion levels for certain types of security certifications. Not only does it pay dividends to the organization in terms of having highly qualified, skill-certified practitioners, but it can provide a means to assure customers of the competency provided by the company. Very few companies can brag that their security team is 100 percent staffed by certified professionals.

C.5.4 Security-Related Job Descriptions

The following job descriptions are actual postings taken from corporate career sites. Each security position, as you will see, has several common threads required by all employers. The job postings also tell you that employers expect a lot from their security personnel. Often, they list 20 or more specific technologies that a security professional must be familiar with and demonstrate competency in for the job to be awarded. It is a tough career field, because the expectations are very high and it takes a huge amount of dedication to attain the level of professional skills employers demand. The rewards, of course, can be very good, but they do not come before security professionals have earned them, both in the trenches and the classroom. Now, let's look at some job descriptions.

Senior Security Consultant

Overview:

As a key technical architect, you will work with a top-notch security-focused team in a lead role analyzing and conceptualizing technical and business requirements for enterprise security. Successful candidates will perform duties as a subject-matter expert in network vulnerability and hacker exploits; will design enterprise solutions involving intrusion detection, vulnerability assessment, and event management; will also consult on methodologies, practices, and tools in a development team environment; will undertake mentoring responsibilities, evaluate leading-edge technologies, and keep current on industry knowledge.

Job Responsibilities:

- Drafting and updating security policy
- Supervising the implementation of security policy and maintaining related available knowledge
- Maintaining internal and external contacts in this context
- Serving as a project manager in security and development projects
- Coordinating information security with current projects in the organization

- Executing and initiating risk analyses and small-scale internal audits
- Organizing and participating in an information security coordinating committee
- Establishing criteria, norms, and standards for the implementation of a security policy and coordinating the activities of people, departments, and agencies involved in this implementation
- Collecting and registering information regarding current security measures
- Developing security plans with respect to security measures and providing support
- Providing advice (solicited or not) to the management of the organization
- Organizing and coordinating internal training sessions on information security for personnel
- Stimulating security awareness and creating, implementing, and maintaining a communication plan
- Dealing with security incidents and taking measures to prevent the recurrence of similar incidents
- Reporting to the management of the organization about the implemented policy with respect to information security, the progress of the implementation of new measures, the occurrence of incidents, actions taken, study results, and control results
- Staying ahead of new developments regarding security, operating systems, and open source concerned

Required Skills:

Bachelor's degree in computer science, network engineering, or related degree; 3+ years of experience in security-related architecture/design/development that address at least one of the following security areas:

- Vulnerability assessment

- Penetration assessment
- Incident/intrusion detection
- Firewall and VPN event management

Must possess UNIX essentials and must have business strategy exposure. Experience in standards-based security architecture necessary. Experience with vulnerability assessments pertaining to information technology, including IP hijacking, offset fragment attacks, OS fingerprinting, malformed header attacks, heap overflows, format string attacks, and buffer overflows. Must be knowledgeable in C/C++, UNIX-based operating systems; fluent in the standard encryption technologies (i.e., DES, 3DES, CAST, RC2, SKIP, ISAKMP/Oakley, SSL, and so on); and have basic knowledge of network attack methods.

Desired Skills:

Certifications a plus (CISSP, GSEC)

Information Security Engineer Job Description

Overview:

The Incident Response Team (IRT) is an established world-class and efficient incident response and penetration testing capability for the Federal Reserve System (FRS) and the U.S. Treasury. The IRT is charged with ensuring that the risks associated with FRS's use of the Internet and its associated Web-enabled technologies are identified and that protection measures are in place.

Job Responsibilities:

Performs one or more tasks of the Computer Emergency Response Team (CERT) operations, including intrusion detection, new incident tracking, documentation, analytical investigation, problem closure, and/or future security configuration threat countermeasures. Other responsibilities include:

- Assists in developing, testing, and implementing security plans, products, control techniques, security policy, and procedures of national network security oversight, intrusion response tracking

- Provides and analyzes security data in the event of an investigation, and implements recommended corrective actions for data security incidents
- Provides technical expertise and support to client, IT management, and staffs in the performance of risk assessments and the implementation of appropriate data security procedures
- Maintains an awareness of existing and proposed security standard setting groups, state and federal legislation, and regulations pertaining to information security
- Maintains awareness of up-to-date threat and vulnerability profiles, including respective countermeasures
- Performs related duties as assigned or requested in compliance with ISO 9001; automates any manual process using software development
- Enhance IRT supporting IT infrastructure

Job Requirements:

Bachelor's degree in computer science, engineering, or a related discipline and two to four years of technical experience in security aspects of multiple platforms, operating systems, software communications, and network protocols, or an equivalent combination of education and work experience.

Other Requirements:

- Demonstrated experience in server management and software development using Java, JSP, and ASP
- Proven experience in database development using MSSQL or Oracle
- Experience in configuration/administration/management in the following areas: Windows (95, 98, NT, 2000), database, Sun Solaris, routers and switches, firewalls, proxy servers, Web server, intrusion detection system
- Good analytical ability, consultative and communication skills, and the proven ability to work effectively with clients, IT management and staff, vendors, and consultants
- CISSP certified/qualified or ability to work actively toward obtaining the certification as soon as eligibility requirements are met

- Ability to obtain National Security Clearance
- Infosec Assessment Methodology (IAM) certified or the ability to achieve certification within one year

Applications Security Engineer Job Description

Job Responsibilities:

Participate in research of new information security technologies (in the areas of application and application infrastructure components) and propose ideas for new security service development. Participate in all aspects of new security service development projects including the following project phases: business case development, requirements gathering, architecture development, product/service selection and procurement, functional and QA testing, detailed technical design, technology infrastructure implementation and deployment, migration from existing services, operational process and procedure documentation, operations staff training, internal marketing material development.

Advise and consult internal clients on appropriate application of existing security services to solve their problems or enable new business opportunities. Deliver previously developed information security services in support of client needs, including: requirements gathering, technical design, service deployment and integration, migration, operational transition, end-user documentation, user training.

In support of various enterprise IT initiatives, sell/recommend, customize, implement, document, and transition to operations reusable technical security service components, including firewall systems, intrusion detection systems, authentication systems, authorization systems, audit trail management systems, virus detection and prevention systems, cryptographic systems, and many others.

Research and implement new security technologies to be used as point solutions for IT initiatives unable to take advantage of or needing greater functionality than reusable enterprise security services. Based on accumulated knowledge of project-specific security implementations, recommend new security service development ideas to the security technology R&D process.

Serve as the subject-matter expert on a number of production security technologies and fulfill corresponding vendor relationship and product/service acquisition, support, and maintenance contract management. Provide fourth-level (technical architecture design and vendor management issues) support for a number of production security technologies.

Qualifications:

In-depth, hands-on experience *in as many of the following technologies* as possible:

- Development languages: C, C++, Java, UML, XML, XSLT, applied in Object Oriented (OO) n-tier application development environment
- Application frameworks and their built-in security services and APIs: Sun J2EE, MS COM+, MS .NET, OMG CORBA or others
- General application security APIs and protocols: GSS-API, MS CryptoAPI, PAM, Kerberos, DCE Security Service, SSL/TLS, SAML, S/MIME, PKCS API's, or others
- Application Authentication and Authorization Systems: Netegrity SiteMinder, RSA ClearTrust, Entrust GetAccess, Oblix NetPoint, or others
- Cryptographic tool kits for application development: RSA BSAFE, Certicom Security Builder, or others
- Built-in security functions and services of application infrastructure components: Oracle, DB2/UDB, MS IIS, MS BizTalk Server, MS Integration Server, IBM WebSphere, iPlanet Directory, MS Active Directory, SAP R/3, Vitria BusinessWare, IBM MQSeries, MSMQ, MS Exchange, BEA WebLogic, or others
- Application-layer Intrusion Detection Systems: Sanctum AppShield, or others
- PKI systems: Entrust Authority CA, RSA Keon, or others
- In-depth hands-on experience in complex enterprise architectures lockdowns
- Inner workings and security aspects of variety of Application Servers, Web Servers, Media/Content Servers, Messaging Servers, Database Servers, Integration Servers, and such

- Minimum of six years' experience in information security solution engineering and security service delivery
- Stellar technical writing, documentation development, process mapping, and visual communication skills
- Experience in managing several (two to four) concurrent large-scale enterprise-wide information technology capability development projects
- Excellent interpersonal and verbal communication skills

Just look at how many technologies these job descriptions require. It is amazing! There is no other professional technology field I know of that demands more. Security professionals are considered the cream of the crop in the information technology arena and have to work very hard to meet such demanding requirements. Is it any wonder they are so very hard to find?

C.6 Management of Security Professionals

Managing an information security program in an organization presents significant challenges. Information is typically collected, stored, and processed in all departments and locations of the organization. Diverse types of media, systems, and networks are used for the storage and transmission of confidential information. The confidentiality, integrity, and availability of such information must be protected with consistent, effective measures. Staff members and others who may have access must be informed of the importance of protecting the information and about their specific responsibilities for such information protection. Appropriate techniques and mechanisms to protect the information must be provided and communicated to all users of information.

The information security manager must be alert to continual changes in the organization and the business environment. Legal and accreditation requirements for protecting an individual's privacy are rapidly changing. Security technology is also evolving rapidly. The security manager's job of evaluating risks, determining system and network security requirements, and implementing appropriate controls is challenging, to say the least.

The information security manager must be prepared to implement measures for information protection in an environment where these measures are sometimes incorrectly perceived as an impediment to business functions.

The information security manager serves as the focal point for the overall coordination of security policy and procedures for the organization. This responsibility is shared with management and all other information and system users. The information security manager identifies potential exposures and risks to the confidentiality, integrity, and availability of information and makes recommendations to management to mitigate the risks. It is the responsibility of the information security manager to identify the impact on the information security program of changes in the business and computer systems environments. Based on an awareness of the industry and organizational needs, the information security manager should direct and modify (as needed) the information security program. The scope of this responsibility encompasses the organization's information in its entirety.

C.6.1 Organizational Infrastructure

Depending upon the size and complexity of the organization, the information security function may range from a part-time assignment for one person to a unit with a full-time information security manager and multiple information security staff members. The information security unit is typically assigned to the Chief Information Officer but may be assigned to any senior manager in the organization if that manager will provide the most effective reporting arrangement. The information security function should be perceived to be an organization-wide function and not an entity that is limited to a specific department or person. Therefore, except for system security functions that can be successfully managed by the information systems organization with advice from the information security manager, many of the security administration functions will be distributed throughout the organization. An information security advisory group should be formed to provide advice and support to the information security manager. Typical functions of this group include reviewing proposed policies, standards, procedures, and education programs. Membership in an information security advisory group should include:

- Chief Information Officer
- Risk Manager
- Finance and Accounting Manager
- Human Resources Manager
- Quality Assurance Manager
- Legal Counsel

C.6.2 Reporting Relationships

The Information Security Manager often reports to the Chief Information Officer, having dotted-line reporting relationships to Legal, HR, or even a CTO. The dotted-line relationship allows a degree of independence needed to ensure that the Security Manager can make decisions that are best for the company and, sometimes, these decisions may not be agreeable to all parties involved. The scope of the position should be organization-wide and should involve information on all types of media and in all forms. The Information Security Manager maintains an allegiance to the goals and objectives of the organization's information security program rather than to a specific manager or department. It is important that the Security Manager be given latitude to make decisions in the absence of the CIO or other executive management. These types of decisions usually revolve around incident containment and management. The CIO and the Security Manager should work out a plan on how to allow such decisions to be made if an incident occurs and the CIO cannot be reached.

C.6.3 Working Relationships

The Information Security Manager must maintain strong working relationships with key representatives from all functional areas of the organization. These areas include:

- Chief Executive Officer—provide status reports, advice, apprise of serious incidents, and recommend policy
- Chief Information Officer—direct reporting relationship as well as support for implementation of information security controls in systems and networks

- Senior management—foster awareness, determine responsibility for protection of information assets, and provide advice and ongoing education
- Internal and external auditors—report on status of information security measures as requested and respond to audit findings on information security issues
- Consultants and vendors—convey information security requirements

C.6.4 Accountability

The Information Security Manager is accountable for successful implementation of the information security program. Therefore, the Information Security Manager must:

- Maintain technical knowledge about systems, networks, and telecommunications
- Maintain technical knowledge about information security technology
- Effectively manage staffing and budget
- Ensure competent, motivated, and knowledgeable staff
- Be able to function effectively in a dynamic environment
- Provide prompt information security support to all users of the systems and networks
- Maintain effective communications with all departments
- Maintain good relationships with appropriate vendor and industry personnel
- Participate in industry events and maintain currency in security skills

C.7 Summary

We have taken a look at what is required to put together an effective security function in an organization. Management of a security function requires planning and a deep understanding of the concept of risk management. The interface between the CSO/CISO, HR, and legal counsel cannot be emphasized enough. Their partnership is key to successful implementation of a site security plan. The basic precepts of security, such as incident response, forensics, training, and awareness; and perimeter security measures; intrusion detection; secure remote access; and so on have been discussed in terms of establishing functions devoted to those functional areas. Policy development and the role such policies play in an organization's risk management and site security plans have also been covered. We looked at issues regarding staffing and hiring security personnel, and we reviewed the items a security manager should be held responsible and accountable for in performance of his or her duties in an organization. While this appendix does not cover specific policies per se, it has covered the reasons why they are important.

C.8 Endnotes

1. C. Pfleeger. *Security in Computing*, Englewood Cliffs, NJ, Prentice-Hall 1989.
2. https://www.it-isac.org.
3. RFC 2196, "*Site Security Handbook*," September 1997, ed. B. Fraser, IETF NWG, http://www.ietf.org.
4. M. Fites, P. Kratz, and A. Brebner. "*Control and Security of Computer Information Systems*," Computer Science Press, 1989.
5. C. Pfleeger. *Security in Computing*, Englewood Cliffs, NJ, Prentice-Hall, 1989.
6. Report entitled "*Insider Threats to E-Security*," Andrew Handelsmann, December 2001, http://www.gigalaw.com.
7. http://www.checkpoint.com/services/education/certification/certifications/ccsa.html
8. http://www.giac.org

D

IM Policy Essentials

IM in the enterprise has become a standard communication tool, which must be managed just like any other communications tool in the network, and written rules and policies must be in place that will enforce your IM security management plan. You must be very careful to ensure that what you have written can also be enforced; otherwise, all you have created is a "paper tiger," which doesn't have teeth and also degrades the credibility of any other policy that you want to enforce. To date, millions of dollars have been spent by corporations defending against lawsuits and regulatory litigation for the improper use of e-mail and the Internet, and the use of IM will be no different. The first step in mitigating the legal risk of IM use in your environment is the development, implementation, and enforcement of rules and policies that govern IM and other forms of electronic communication in your corporation. To maximize the limitation of liability, communication policies typically address personal use, content, retention, deletion, monitoring, compliance, and other such issues. The basic policies that cover the use of IM in an organization are typically the organization's acceptable-use policy, with more detailed policies for the use of IM covered in the e-mail use and e-mail retention policy, for which we have provided templates for your use in developing your own policies.

D.1 ABC Inc. Information Security Acceptable Use Policy

Policy No. 1

Effective date: Month / Day / Year

Implement by: Month / Day / Year

1.0 Overview

Information Systems Security's intentions for publishing an acceptable, use policy are not to impose restrictions that are contrary to ABC Inc.'s established culture of openness, trust, and integrity. Information System Security is committed to protecting ABC Inc.'s employees, partners, and the company from illegal or damaging actions by individuals, either knowingly or unknowingly.

Internet/intranet/extranet-related systems, including, but not limited to computer equipment, software, operating systems, storage media, network accounts providing electronic mail, WWW browsing, and FTP are the property of ABC Inc. These systems are to be used for business purposes in serving the interests of the company and of our clients and customers in the course of normal operations. Please review HR policies <Insert Link> for further details.

Effective security is a team effort involving the participation and support of every ABC Inc. employee and affiliate who deals with information and/or information systems. It is the responsibility of every computer user to know these guidelines and to conduct his or her activities accordingly.

2.0 Purpose

The purpose of this policy is to outline the acceptable use of computer equipment at ABC Inc. These rules are in place to protect the employee and ABC Inc. Inappropriate use exposes ABC Inc. to risks, including virus attacks, compromise of network systems and services, and legal issues.

3.0 Scope

This policy applies to employees, contractors, consultants, temporaries, and other workers at ABC Inc., including all personnel affiliated with third parties. This policy applies to all equipment that is owned or leased by ABC Inc.

4.0 Policy

4.1 General Use and Ownership

While ABC Inc.'s network administration desires to provide a reasonable level of privacy, users should be aware that the data they create on the corporate systems remains the property of ABC Inc. Because of the need to protect ABC Inc.'s network, management cannot guarantee the confidentiality of information stored on any network device belonging to ABC Inc.

Employees are responsible for exercising good judgment regarding the reasonableness of personal use. Individual departments are responsible for creating guidelines concerning personal use of Internet/intranet/extranet systems. In the absence of such policies, employees should be guided by departmental policies on personal use, and if there is any uncertainty, employees should consult their supervisor or manager. The ABC Information System Security Group recommends that any information that users consider sensitive or vulnerable be encrypted.

For security and network maintenance purposes, authorized individuals within ABC Inc. may monitor equipment, systems, and network traffic at any time, per Information System Security's Audit Policy. ABC Inc. reserves the right to audit networks and systems on a periodic basis to ensure compliance with this policy.

4.2 Security and Proprietary Information

The user interface for information contained on Internet/intranet/extranet-related systems should be classified as either confidential or not confidential, as defined by corporate confidentiality guidelines <Insert Link>, details of which can be found in HR policies. Examples of confidential information include, but are not limited to, company private, corporate strategies, competitor sensitive, trade secrets, specifications, customer lists, employee personal data, employee job data, and research data. Employees should take all necessary steps to prevent unauthorized access to this information. Keep passwords secure and do not share accounts. Authorized users are responsible for the security of their passwords and accounts.

All PCs, laptops, and workstations should be secured with a password-protected screensaver with the automatic activation feature set at 10 minutes or less, or by locking access to the computer (control-alt-delete for Windows platform users) when the host will be unattended.

Because information contained on portable computers is especially vulnerable, special care should be exercised. Protect laptops in accordance with the laptop security guidelines policy.

Postings by employees from an ABC Inc. e-mail address to newsgroups are prohibited unless the posting is in the course of business duties.

All hosts used by the employee that are connected to the ABC Inc. Internet/intranet/extranet, whether owned by the employee or ABC Inc., shall be continually executing approved virus-scanning software with a current virus database, unless overridden by department or group policy. Employees must use extreme caution when opening e-mail attachments received from unknown senders, which may contain viruses, e-mail bombs, or Trojan horse code.

4.3 Unacceptable Use

1. The following activities are, in general, prohibited. Employees may be exempted from these restrictions during the course of their legitimate job responsibilities (e.g., systems administration staff may have a need to disable the network access of a host if that host is disrupting production services).
2. Under no circumstances is an employee of ABC Inc. authorized to engage in any activity that is illegal under local, state, federal, or international law while utilizing ABC Inc.–owned resources.
3. The following lists are by no means exhaustive but attempt to provide a framework for activities that fall into the category of unacceptable use.

4.4 System and Network Activities

The following activities are strictly prohibited, with no exceptions:

- Violations of the rights of any person or company protected by copyright, trade secret, patent or other intellectual property, or similar laws or regulations, including, but not limited to, the installation or distribution of "pirated" or other software products that are not appropriately licensed for use by ABC Inc.
- Unauthorized copying of copyrighted material, including, but not limited to, digitization and distribution of photographs from magazines, books, other copyrighted sources, copyrighted music, and the installation of any copyrighted software for which ABC Inc. or the end user does not have an active license is strictly prohibited.
- Exporting software, technical information, encryption software, or technology, in violation of international or regional export control laws, is illegal. The appropriate management should be consulted prior to export of any material that is in question.
- Introduction of malicious programs into the network or server (e.g., viruses, worms, Trojan horses, e-mail bombs, etc.).
- Revealing your account password to others or allowing use of your account by others. This includes family and other household members when work is being done at home.
- Using ABC Inc.'s computing assets to actively engage in procuring or transmitting material that is in violation of sexual harassment or hostile workplace laws in the user's local jurisdiction.
- Making fraudulent offers of products, items, or services originating from any ABC Inc. account.
- Making statements about warranty, expressly or implied, unless it is a part of normal job duties.
- Effecting security breaches or disruptions of network communication. Security breaches include, but are not limited to, accessing data of which the employee is not an intended recipient or logging in to a server or account that the employee is not expressly authorized to access, unless these duties are within the scope of regular duties. For purposes of this section, "disruption" includes, but is not limited to, network sniffing, ping floods, packet spoofing, denial of service, and forged routing information for malicious purposes.
- Port scanning or security scanning is expressly prohibited unless prior notification to Information System Security is made.

- Executing any form of network monitoring, which will intercept data not intended for the employee's host, unless this activity is a part of the employee's normal job/duty.
- Circumventing user authentication or security of any host, network, or account.
- Interfering with or denying service to any user other than the employee's host (e.g., denial-of-service attack).
- Using any program/script/command, or sending messages of any kind, with the intent to interfere with, or disable, a user's terminal session, via any means, locally or via the Internet/intranet/extranet.
- Providing information about, or lists of, ABC Inc. employees to parties outside ABC Inc.

4.5 E-mail and Communications Activities

- Sending unsolicited e-mail messages, including the sending of junk mail or other advertising material to individuals who did not specifically request such material (e-mail spam).
- Any form of harassment via e-mail, telephone, or paging, whether through language, frequency, or size of messages.
- Unauthorized use, or forging, of e-mail header information.
- Solicitation of e-mail for any other e-mail address, other than that of the poster's account, with the intent to harass or to collect replies.
- Creating or forwarding chain letters, Ponzi, or other pyramid schemes of any type.
- Use of unsolicited e-mail originating from within ABC Inc.'s networks of other Internet/intranet/extranet service providers on behalf of, or to advertise, any service hosted by ABC Inc. or connected via ABC Inc.'s network.
- Posting the same or similar non-business-related messages to large numbers of Usenet newsgroups (newsgroup spam).
- Posting of ABC Inc.'s confidential information by employees is prohibited unless the posting is in the course of business duties.
- Transmission of ABC Inc.'s confidential information to unauthorized recipients (internal or external) by employees is prohibited unless the posting is in the course of business duties.

5.0 Enforcement

Any employee found to have violated this policy may be subject to disciplinary action, up to and including termination of employment.

6.0 Definitions

Spam—Unauthorized and/or unsolicited electronic mass mailings.

Junk Mail—Unsolicited e-mail. It is also another term for Spam.

7.0 Exceptions

Exceptions to Information System Security's policies exist in rare instances, where a risk assessment examining the implications of being out of compliance has been performed, where a policy exception form <Insert Link> has been prepared by the data owner or management, and where this form has been approved by both the director of Information Systems Security and the Chief Information Officer (CIO).

7.0 Revision History

Date: ___/____/_____

Version: ______________________________

Author: ______________________________

Summary: ____________________________

D.2 ABC Inc. E-mail/IM Use Policy

Policy No. 2

Effective date: Month / Day / Year

Implement by: Month / Day / Year

1.0 Purpose

To prevent tarnishing the public image of ABC Inc. When e-mail or IM goes out from ABC Inc., the general public will view that message as an official policy statement from ABC Inc.

2.0 Scope

This policy covers appropriate use of any e-mail/IM sent from an ABC Inc. e-mail/IM address and applies to all employees, vendors, and agents operating on behalf of ABC Inc.

3.0 Policy

3.1 Prohibited Use

The ABC Inc. e-mail/IM system shall not to be used for the creation or distribution of any disruptive or offensive messages, including offensive comments about race, gender, hair color, disabilities, age, sexual orientation, pornography, religious beliefs and practice, political beliefs, or national origin. Employees who receive any e-mail/IMs with this content from any ABC Inc. employee should report the matter to their supervisor immediately.

3.2 Personal Use

Using a reasonable amount of ABC Inc. resources for personal e-mail/IMs is acceptable, but non-work-related e-mail/IM shall be saved in a separate folder from work-related e-mail/IM. Sending chain letters or joke e-mail/IMs from an ABC Inc. e-mail/IM account is prohibited. Virus or other malware warnings and mass mailings from ABC Inc. shall be approved by

ABC Inc. VP operations before sending. These restrictions also apply to the forwarding of mail received by an ABC Inc. employee.

3.3 Monitoring

ABC Inc. employees shall have no expectation of privacy in anything they store, send, or receive on the company's e-mail/IM system. ABC Inc. may monitor messages without prior notice. ABC Inc. is not obliged to monitor e-mail/IM messages.

4.0 Enforcement

Any employee found to have violated this policy may be subject to disciplinary action, up to and including termination of employment.

5.0 Definitions

Terms and definitions:

E-mail/IM—The electronic transmission of information through a mail protocol such as SMTP or IMAP. Typical e-mail clients include Eudora and Microsoft Outlook. Typical IM clients include MSN Messenger and Yahoo! Messenger.

Forwarded e-mail/IM—E-mail/IM resent from an internal network to an outside point.

Chain e-mail/IM or letter—E-mail/IM sent to successive people. Typically the body of the note has direction to send out multiple copies of the note and promises good luck or money if the direction is followed.

Sensitive information—Information is considered sensitive if it can be damaging to ABC Inc. or its customers' reputation or market standing.

Virus warning—E-mail/IM containing warnings about virus or malware. The overwhelming majority of these e-mail/IMs turn out to be a hoax and contain bogus information usually intent only on frightening or misleading users.

Unauthorized Disclosure—The intentional or unintentional revealing of restricted information to people, both inside and outside ABC Inc., who do not have a need to know that information.

6.0 Revision History

Date: ___/____/_____

Version: ______________________________

Author: ______________________________

Summary: ____________________________

D.3 ABC Inc. E-mail/IM Retention Policy

1.0 Purpose

The e-mail/IM retention policy is intended to help employees determine which information sent or received by e-mail/IM should be retained and for how long. The information covered in these guidelines includes, but is not limited to, information that is either stored or shared via electronic mail or IM technologies. All employees should familiarize themselves with the e-mail/IM retention topic areas that follow this introduction. Questions about the proper classification of a specific piece of information should be addressed to your manager. Questions about these guidelines should be addressed to the director of Information Systems Security.

2.0 Scope

This e-mail/IM retention policy is secondary to ABC Inc.'s policy on freedom of information and business record keeping. Any e-mail/IM that contains information in the scope of the business record keeping policy should be treated in that manner. All ABC Inc.'s e-mail/IM information is categorized into four main classifications with retention guidelines:

- Administrative Correspondence (4 years)
- Fiscal Correspondence (4 years)
- General Correspondence (1 year)
- Ephemeral Correspondence (Retain until read, destroy)

3.0 Policy

3.1 Administrative Correspondence

ABC Inc.'s administrative correspondence includes, but is not limited to, clarification of established company policy, including holidays, time card information, dress code, workplace behavior, and any legal issues such as intellectual property violations. All e-mail/IM with the information sensitivity label "Management Only" shall be treated as administrative correspondence. To ensure that administrative correspondence is retained, a mailbox, admin@ABC Inc., has been created; if you copy (cc) this address when you send e-mail/IM, retention will be administered by the IT department.

3.2 Fiscal Correspondence

ABC Inc.'s fiscal correspondence is all information related to revenue and expense for the company. To ensure that fiscal correspondence is retained, a mailbox, fiscal@ABC Inc., has been created; if you copy (cc) this address when you send e-mail/IM, retention will be administered by the IT department.

3.3 General Correspondence

ABC Inc.'s general correspondence covers information that relates to customer interaction and the operational decisions of the business. The individual employee is responsible for e-mail/IM retention of general correspondence.

3.4 Ephemeral Correspondence

ABC Inc.'s ephemeral correspondence is by far the largest category and includes personal e-mail/IM, requests for recommendations or review, e-mail/IM related to product development, updates, and status reports.

3.5 Instant Messenger Correspondence

ABC Inc.'s Instant Messenger general correspondence may be saved with logging function of Instant Messenger or copied into a file and saved. Instant Messenger conversations that are administrative or fiscal in nature should be copied into an e-mail/IM message and sent to the appropriate e-mail/IM retention address.

3.6 Encrypted Communications

ABC Inc.'s encrypted communications should be stored in a manner consistent with ABC Inc.'s information sensitivity policy, but in general, information should be stored in a decrypted format.

3.7 Recovering Deleted E-mail/IM via Backup Media

ABC Inc. maintains backup tapes from the e-mail/IM server, and once a quarter a set of tapes is taken out of the rotation and moved off-site. No effort will be made to remove e-mail/IM from the off-site backup tapes.

4.0 Enforcement

Any employee found to have violated this policy may be subject to disciplinary action, up to and including termination of employment.

5.0 Definitions

Approved Electronic Mail—Includes all mail systems supported by the IT Support Team. These include, but are not necessarily limited to, [insert corporate supported mailers here...]. If you have a business need to use other mailers contact the appropriate support organization.

Approved Encrypted e-mail and files—Techniques include the use of DES and PGP. DES encryption is available via many different public domain packages on all platforms. PGP use within ABC Inc. is done via a license. Please contact the appropriate support organization if you require a license.

Approved Instant Messenger—The <Fill in> IM Client is the only IM that is approved for use on ABC Inc.'s computers.

Individual Access Controls—Individual Access Controls are methods of electronically protecting files from being accessed by people other than those specifically designated by the owner. On UNIX machines, this is accomplished by careful use of the **chmod** command (use man **chmod** to find out more about it). On PC's and Mac's, this includes using passwords on screen savers.

Insecure Internet Links—Insecure Internet Links are all network links that originate from a locale or travel over lines that are not totally under the control of ABC Inc.

Encryption—Secure ABC Inc. Sensitive information in accordance with the Acceptable Encryption Policy. International issues regarding encryption are complex. Follow corporate guidelines on export controls on cryptography, and consult your manager and/or corporate legal services for further guidance.

6.0 Revision History

Date: ___/____/_____

Version: ______________________________

Author: ______________________________

Summary: ____________________________

E

Glossary, References, and Policy Issues

E.1 IM Specific Glossary

Access Rules—These rules serve as constraints on how a PRESENCE SERVICE makes PRESENCE INFORMATION available to WATCHERS. For each PRESENTITY'S PRESENCE INFORMATION, the applicable ACCESS RULES are manipulated by the PRESENCE USER AGENT of a PRINCIPAL that controls the PRESENTITY.

ADMINISTRATOR—A PRINCIPAL with authority over local computer and network resources, who manages local DOMAINS or FIREWALLS. For security and other purposes, an ADMINISTRATOR often needs or wants to impose restrictions on network usage based on traffic type, content, volume, or endpoints. A PRINCIPAL'S ADMINISTRATOR has authority over some or all of that PRINCIPAL'S computer and network resources.

Closed—A distinguished value of the STATUS marker. In the context of INSTANT MESSAGES, this value means that the associated INSTANT INBOX ADDRESS, if any, corresponds to an INSTANT INBOX that is unable to accept an INSTANT MESSAGE. This value may have an analogous meaning for other COMMUNICATION MEANS, but any such meaning is not defined by this model. Contrast with OPEN.

Communication Address—Consists of COMMUNICATION MEANS and CONTACT ADDRESS.

Communication Means—Indicates a method whereby communication can take place. INSTANT MESSAGE SERVICE is one example of a COMMUNICATION MEANS.

Contact Address—A specific point of contact via some COMMUNICATION MEANS. When using an INSTANT MESSAGE SERVICE, the CONTACT ADDRESS is an INSTANT INBOX ADDRESS.

Delivery Rules—Constraints on how an INSTANT MESSAGE SERVICE delivers received INSTANT MESSAGES to INSTANT INBOXES. For each INSTANT INBOX, the applicable DELIVERY RULES are manipulated by the INBOX USER AGENT of a PRINCIPAL that controls the INSTANT INBOX. Motivation: We need a way of talking about filtering instant messages.

DOMAIN—A portion of a NAMESPACE.

ENTITY—A PRESENTITY, SUBSCRIBER, FETCHER, POLLER, or WATCHER.

Fetcher—A form of WATCHER that has asked the PRESENCE SERVICE for the PRESENCE INFORMATION of one or more PRESENTITIES, but has not asked for a SUBSCRIPTION to be created.

FIREWALL—A point of administrative control over connectivity. Depending on the policies being enforced, parties may need to take unusual measures to establish communications through the FIREWALL.

IDENTIFIER—A means of indicating a point of contact, intended for public use such as on a business card. Telephone numbers, email/IM addresses, and typical home page URLs are all examples of IDENTIFIERS in other systems. Numeric IP addresses like 10.0.0.26 are not, and neither are URLs containing numerous CGI parameters or long arbitrary identifiers.

Inbox User Agent—Means for a PRINCIPAL to manipulate zero or more INSTANT INBOXES controlled by that PRINCIPAL. This is intended to isolate the core functionality of an INSTANT INBOX from how it might appear to be manipulated by a product. This manipulation includes fetching messages, deleting messages, and setting DELIVERY RULES. The protocol does not specify whether the INBOX USER AGENT, INSTANT INBOX, and INSTANT MESSAGE SERVICE are collocated or distributed across machines.

Instant Inbox—A receptacle for INSTANT MESSAGES intended to be read by the INSTANT INBOX'S PRINCIPAL.

Instant Inbox Address—Indicates whether and how the PRESENTITY'S PRINCIPAL can receive an INSTANT MESSAGE in an INSTANT INBOX. The STATUS and INSTANT INBOX ADDRESS information are sufficient to determine whether the PRINCIPAL appears ready to accept the INSTANT MESSAGE.

Instant Message—An identifiable unit of data, of small size, to be sent to an INSTANT INBOX. The term "small" is undefined in the protocol, but an attempt was made to avoid the possibility of transporting an arbitrary-length stream labeled as an "*instant message.*"

Instant Message Protocol—The messages that can be exchanged between a SENDER USER AGENT and an INSTANT MESSAGE SERVICE, or between an INSTANT MESSAGE SERVICE and an INSTANT INBOX.

Instant Message Service—Accepts and delivers INSTANT MESSAGES. May require authentication of SENDER USER AGENTS and/or INSTANT INBOXES. May have different authentication requirements for different INSTANT INBOXES, and may also have different authentication requirements for different INSTANT INBOXES controlled by a single PRINCIPAL. May have an internal structure involving multiple SERVERS and/or PROXIES. There may be complex patterns of redirection and/or proxying while retaining logical connectivity to a single INSTANT MESSAGE SERVICE. Note that an INSTANT MESSAGE SERVICE does not require having a distinct SERVER—the service may be implemented as direct communication between SENDER and INSTANT INBOX. An INSTANT MESSAGE SERVICE may have an internal structure involving other INSTANT MESSAGE SERVICES, which may be independently accessible in their own right as well as being reachable through the initial INSTANT MESSAGE SERVICE.

INTENDED RECIPIENT—The PRINCIPAL to whom the sender of an INSTANT MESSAGE is sending it.

NAMESPACE—The system that maps from a name of an ENTITY to the concrete implementation of that ENTITY. A NAMESPACE may be composed of a number of distinct DOMAINS.

Notification—A message sent from the PRESENCE SERVICE to a SUBSCRIBER when there is a change in the PRESENCE INFORMATION of some PRESENTITY of interest, as recorded in one or more SUBSCRIPTIONS.

Open—A distinguished value of the STATUS marker. In the context of INSTANT MESSAGES, this value means that the associated INSTANT INBOX ADDRESS, if any, corresponds to an INSTANT INBOX that is ready to accept an INSTANT MESSAGE. This value may have an analogous meaning for other COMMUNICATION MEANS, but any such meaning is not defined by this model. Contrast with CLOSED.

Other Presence Markup—Any additional information included in the PRESENCE INFORMATION of a PRESENTITY.

OUT OF CONTACT—A situation in which some ENTITY and the PRESENCE SERVICE cannot communicate.

Poller—A FETCHER that requests PRESENCE INFORMATION on a regular basis

Presence Information—Consists of one or more PRESENCE TUPLES.

Presence Protocol—The messages that can be exchanged between a PRESENTITY and a PRESENCE SERVICE, or a WATCHER and a PRESENCE SERVICE.

Presence Service—Accepts, stores, and distributes PRESENCE INFORMATION. May require authentication of PRESENTITIES and/or WATCHERS. May have different authentication requirements for different PRESENTITIES. May have different authentication requirements for different WATCHERS, and may also have different authentication requirements for different PRESENTITIES being watched by a single WATCHER. May have an internal structure involving multiple SERVERS and/or PROXIES. There may be complex patterns of redirection and/or proxying while retaining logical connectivity to a single PRESENCE SERVICE. Note that a PRESENCE SERVICE does not require having a distinct SERVER—the service may be implemented as direct communication among PRESENTITY and WATCHERS. May have an internal structure involving other PRESENCE SERVICES, which may be independently accessible in their own right as well as being reachable through the initial PRESENCE SERVICE.

Presence Tuple—Consists of a STATUS, an optional COMMUNICATION ADDRESS, and optional OTHER PRESENCE MARKUP.

Presence User Agent—Means for a PRINCIPAL to manipulate zero or more PRESENTITIES. Motivation: This is essentially a "model/view" distinction: the PRESENTITY is the model of the presence being exposed, and is independent of its manifestation in any user interface. In addition, the protocol does not specify whether the PRESENCE USER AGENT, PRESENTITY, and PRESENCE SERVICE are collocated or distributed across machines.

Presentity—(*presence entity*) Provides PRESENCE INFORMATION to a PRESENCE SERVICE. The presentity represents an unambiguous term for the entity of interest to a presence service. Note that the presentity is not (usually) located in the presence service. The presence service only has a recent version of the presentity's presence information. The presentity initiates changes in the presence information to be distributed by the presence service.

Principal—A human, program, or collection of humans and/or programs that choose to appear to the PRESENCE SERVICE as a single actor, distinct from all other PRINCIPALS.

Proxy—A SERVER that communicates PRESENCE INFORMATION, INSTANT MESSAGES, SUBSCRIPTIONS, and/or NOTIFICATIONS to another SERVER. Sometimes a PROXY acts on behalf of a PRESENTITY, WATCHER, or INSTANT INBOX.

Sender—The source of INSTANT MESSAGES to be delivered by the INSTANT MESSAGE SERVICE.

Sender User Agent—A means for a PRINCIPAL to manipulate zero or more SENDERS.

Server—An indivisible unit of a PRESENCE SERVICE or INSTANT MESSAGE SERVICE.

SPAM/SPIM—Unwanted INSTANT MESSAGES.

Spoofing—A PRINCIPAL improperly imitating another PRINCIPAL.

Stalking—Using PRESENCE INFORMATION to infer the whereabouts of a PRINCIPAL, especially for malicious or illegal purposes.

Status—A distinguished part of the PRESENCE INFORMATION of a PRESENTITY. STATUS has at least the mutually exclusive values OPEN and CLOSED, which have meaning for the acceptance of INSTANT MESSAGES, and may have meaning for other COMMUNICATION MEANS. There may be other values of STATUS that do not imply anything about INSTANT MESSAGE acceptance. These other values of STATUS may be combined with OPEN and CLOSED or they may be mutually exclusive with those values. Some implementations may combine STATUS with other entities. For example, an implementation might make an INSTANT INBOX ADDRESS visible only when the INSTANT INBOX can accept an INSTANT MESSAGE. Then, the existence of an INSTANT INBOX ADDRESS implies OPEN, while its absence implies CLOSED.

Subscriber—A form of WATCHER that has asked the PRESENCE SERVICE to notify it immediately of changes in the PRESENCE INFORMATION of one or more PRESENTITIES.

Subscription—The information kept by the PRESENCE SERVICE about a SUBSCRIBER'S request to be notified of changes in the PRESENCE INFORMATION of one or more PRESENTITIES.

SUCCESSFUL DELIVERY—A situation in which an INSTANT MESSAGE was transmitted to an INSTANT INBOX for the INTENDED RECIPIENT, and the INSTANT INBOX acknowledged its receipt. SUCCESSFUL DELIVERY usually also implies that an INBOX USER AGENT has handled the message in a way chosen by the PRINCIPAL. However, SUCCESSFUL DELIVERY does not imply that the message was actually seen by that PRINCIPAL.

Visibility Rules—Constraints on how a PRESENCE SERVICE makes WATCHER INFORMATION available to WATCHERS. For each WATCHER'S WATCHER INFORMATION, the applicable VISIBILITY RULES are manipulated by the WATCHER USER AGENT of a PRINCIPAL that controls the WATCHER.

Watcher—Requests PRESENCE INFORMATION about a PRESENTITY, or WATCHER INFORMATION about a WATCHER, from the PRESENCE SERVICE. Special types of WATCHER are FETCHER, POLLER, and SUBSCRIBER.

Watcher Information—Information about WATCHERS that have received PRESENCE INFORMATION about a particular PRESENTITY within a particular recent span of time. WATCHER INFORMATION is maintained by the PRESENCE SERVICE, which may choose to present it in the same form as PRESENCE INFORMATION. The service may choose to make WATCHERS look like a special form of PRESENTITY. If a PRESENTITY wants to know who knows about it, it is not enough to examine only information about SUBSCRIPTIONS. A WATCHER might repeatedly fetch information without ever subscribing. Alternately, a WATCHER might repeatedly subscribe, then cancel the SUBSCRIPTION. Such WATCHERS should be visible to the PRESENTITY if the PRESENCE SERVICE offers WATCHER INFORMATION, but will not be appropriately visible if the WATCHER INFORMATION includes only SUBSCRIPTIONS.

Watcher User Agent—A means for a PRINCIPAL to manipulate zero or more WATCHERS controlled by that PRINCIPAL. As with PRESENCE USER

AGENT and PRESENTITY, the distinction is made to isolate the core functionality of a WATCHER from how it might appear to be manipulated by a product. The protocol does not specify whether the WATCHER USER AGENT, WATCHER, and PRESENCE SERVICE are colocated or distributed across machines.

E.2 General Security Glossary

NOTE: Some of the material presented herein was taken from the *Cybersecurity Operations Handbook* by Dr. John W. Rittinghouse and Dr. William M. Hancock, Digital Press, New York 2003. Reprinted with permission.

Access Control Lists (ACLs)—Data typically comprised of a list of principals, a list of resources, and a list of permissions.

ACL-based Authorization—A scheme where the authorization agent consults an ACL to grant or deny access to a principal. *See centralized authorization.*

Address spoofing—A type of attack in which the attacker steals a legitimate network address of a system and uses it to impersonate the system that owns the address.

Administrator—A person responsible for the day-to-day operation of system and network resources. This is most often a number of individuals or an organization.

Advanced Mobile Phone Service (AMPS)—The standard system for analog cellular telephone service in the United States AMPS allocates frequency ranges within the 800–900 MHz spectrum to cellular telephones. Signals cover an area called a *cell.* Signals are passed into adjacent cells as the user moves to another cell. The analog service of AMPS has been updated to include digital service.

Agent—A program used in DDoS attacks that sends malicious traffic to hosts based on the instructions of a handler.

Alert— Notification that a specific attack has been directed at the information system of an organization.

Anonymity—Anonymity is the fact of being anonymous. To provide anonymity, a system will use a security service that prevents the disclosure of information that leads to the identification of the end users. An example is anonymous e-mail that has been directed to a recipient through a third-party server that does not identify the originator of the message.

Application Program Interface (API)—An API is the specific method prescribed by a computer operating system or by an application program by which a programmer writing an application program can make requests of the operating system or another application. An API can be a set of standard software interrupts, calls, and data formats that application programs use to initiate contact with network services, mainframe communications programs, telephone equipment, or program-to-program communications.

Application-level firewall—A firewall system in which service is provided by processes that maintain complete TCP connection state and sequencing; application-level firewalls often readdress traffic so that outgoing traffic appears to have originated from the firewall, rather than the internal host. In contrast to packet filtering firewalls, this firewall must have knowledge of the application data transfer protocol and often has rules about what may be transmitted and what may not.

Application gateway firewall—A type of firewall system that runs an application, called a proxy, that acts like the server to the Internet client. The proxy takes all requests from the Internet client and, if allowed, forwards them to the intranet server. Application gateways are used to make certain that the Internet client and the intranet server are using the proper application protocol for communicating. Popular proxies include Telnet, FTP, and HTTP. Building proxies requires knowledge of the application protocol.

Application proxy—An application that forwards application traffic through a firewall. Proxies tend to be specific to the protocol they are designed to forward, and may provide increased access control or audit.

Assurance—A measure of confidence that the security features and architecture of a secured site correctly mediate and enforce the security policy in place for that site.

Asymmetric algorithm—An encryption algorithm that requires two different keys for encryption and decryption. These keys are commonly referred to as the public and private keys. Asymmetric algorithms are slower than symmetric algorithms. Furthermore, speed of encryption may be different than the speed of decryption. Generally asymmetric algorithms are either used to exchange symmetric session keys or to digitally sign a message. RSA, RPK, and ECC are examples of asymmetric algorithms.

Asynchronous Transfer Mode (ATM)—ATM (asynchronous transfer mode) A fast cell-switched technology based on a fixed-length 53-byte cell. All broadband transmissions (whether audio, data, imaging or video) are divided into a series of cells and routed across an ATM network consisting of links connected by ATM switches.

Attack—Intentional action taken to bypass one or more computer security controls.

Attribution—A determination based on evidence of probable responsibility for a computer network attack, intrusion, or other unauthorized activity. Responsibility can include planning, executing, or directing the unauthorized activity.

Audit—(1) A service that keeps a detailed record of events. (2) The independent review of data records and processes to ensure compliance with established controls, policy, and operational procedures. Followed up with formal recommendations for improvements in controls, policy, or procedures.

Authenticate—To verify the identity of a user, user device, or other entity, or the integrity of data stored, transmitted, or otherwise exposed to unauthorized modification in an information system, or to establish the validity of a transmission.

Authentication—A secure process used to establish the validity of a transmission, message, message sender, or an individual's authorization to gain access to or receive specific information.

Authentication Header (AH)—An IP device used to provide connectionless integrity and data origin authentication for IP datagrams.

Authentication token—*See token.*

Authorization—The process of determining what a given principal can do.

Availability—The timely access to data and information services for authorized users.

Backdoor—A hidden mechanism in software or hardware that is used to circumvent security controls (*a.k.a. trap door*).

Baselining—Monitoring resources to determine typical utilization patterns so that significant deviations can be detected.

Bastion host—A host system that is a "strong point" in the network's security perimeter. Bastion hosts should be configured to be particularly resistant to attack. In a host-based firewall, the bastion host is the platform on which the firewall software is run. Bastion hosts are also referred to as gateway hosts.

Biometrics—A method of generating unique, replicable authentication data by digitizing measurements of physical characteristics of a person, such as their fingerprint, hand size and shape, retinal pattern, voiceprint, or handwriting *(a.k.a. biometric authentication)*.

Blended attack—Malicious code that uses multiple methods to spread.

Boot sector virus—A virus that plants itself in a system's boot sector and infects the master boot record.

Breach—Detected circumvention of established security controls that result in penetration of the system.

Buffer overflow—A condition that occurs when data is put into a buffer or holding area that exceeds the capacity the buffer can handle. This condition often results in system crashes or the creation of a back door leading to system access.

Centralized authorization—A scheme in which a central, third-party authorization agent is consulted for access control. All access control rules are defined in the database of the central authorization agent.

CERT (Computer Emergency Response Team)—A federally funded research and development center at Carnegie-Mellon University. They focus on Internet security vulnerabilities, provide incident response services to sites that have been the victims of attack, publish security alerts, research security and survivability in wide-area-networked computing, and develop site security information. They can be found at http://www.cert.org.

Certification Authority (CA)—A trusted agent that issues digital certificates to principals. Certification authorities may themselves have a certificate that is issued to them by other certification authorities. The highest certification authority is called the Root CA.

Code Division Multiple Access (CDMA)—CDMA refers to any of several protocols used in wireless communications. As the term implies, CDMA is a form of multiplexing, which allows numerous signals to occupy a single transmission channel, optimizing the use of available bandwidth. The technology is used in ultra-high-frequency (UHF) cellular telephone systems in the 800-MHz and 1.9-GHz bands.

Common Criteria (CC)—The Common Criteria represents the outcome of a series of efforts to develop criteria for evaluation of IT security that are broadly useful within the international community. The Common Criteria is an International Standard (IS 15408) and is a catalog of security functionality and assurance requirements.

Compromise—A situation where secured information is disclosed to unauthorized persons in either an intentional or unintentional manner.

Compromised Key List (CKL)—A list with the Key Material Identifier (KMID) of every user with compromised key material; key material is compromised when a card and its personal identification number (PIN) are uncontrolled or the user has become a threat to the security of the system.

Computer Security Incident Response Team (CSIRT)—A capability set up to assist in responding to computer security-related incidents; also called a Computer Incident Response Team (CIRT) or a CIRC (Computer Incident Response Center, Computer Incident Response Capability).

Computer forensics—The practice of gathering and retaining computer-related data in a manner that makes the data admissible in a court of law.

Computer intrusion—An incident of unauthorized access to data or an Automated Information System (AIS).

Computer security incident—*See incident.*

Countermeasures—An intentional action taken to reduce the vulnerability of an information system to compromise.

Credential—A credential is what one principal presents to another to authenticate itself. For mutual authentication, both parties exchange credentials. Credentials are issued by an authentication agent or a certification authority. Depending on the model for authentication, credentials may only be valid for a session, or they may have longer validity periods. Digital certificates are credentials that typically last for a year or two. Tickets are credentials that are only good for a session, which typically does not last more than several hours.

Critical Infrastructures—Those physical and cyber-based systems necessary for the continued maintenance of a minimum level of operations supporting the economy and government.

Cryptographic Application Program Interface (CryptoAPI)—A standardized interface to cryptographic functionality. *Also see API.*

Cryptographic functions—A set of procedures that provide basic cryptographic functionality. The functionality includes using various algorithms for key generation, random number generation, encryption, decryption, and message digesting.

Customer—The party, or his or her designee, responsible for the security of designated information. The customer works closely with an ISSE. Also referred to as the user.

Cut-and-paste attack—An attack conducted by replacing sections of ciphertext with other ciphertext, making the altered result appear to decrypt correctly, but in reality the message decrypts to plaintext that is used by the attacker for unauthorized purposes.

Cyberterrorist—An individual, or group of individuals, engaged in malicious activities against targeted computing infrastructure and/or resources, usually in the name of or on behalf of an entity the participants have considered to be greater than or serving a purpose greater than the specific individual(s) that are actually performing the malicious acts.

Data confidentiality—*See data privacy.*

Data diddling—An attack in which the attacker changes the data while en route from source to destination.

Data driven attack—An attack encoded in what appears to be ordinary data and is initiated by either a user or a process trigger. Such an attack may pass through the firewall in data form undetected and subsequently launch itself against system resources located behind the firewall.

Data Encryption Standard (DES)—The most common encryption algorithm with symmetric keys.

Data integrity—The reasonable assurance that data is not changed while en route from a sender to its intended recipient.

Data privacy—The reasonable assurance that data cannot be viewed by anyone other than its intended recipient.

Decision maker—A person who makes or approves policy. These are often the same people who are responsible for or own the resources to be protected.

Defense-in-depth—An approach for establishing an adequate IA posture whereby (1) IA solutions integrate people, technology, and operations; (2) IA solutions are layered within and among IT assets; and (3) IA solutions are selected based on their relative level of robustness. Implementation of this approach recognizes that the highly interactive nature of information systems and enclaves creates a shared risk environment; therefore, the adequate assurance of any single asset is dependent upon the adequate assurance of all interconnecting assets.

Delegation—The ability to empower a principal to act on behalf of another principal.

Denial of Service (DoS) attack—(1) An attack where an attacker floods the server with bogus requests, or tampers with legitimate requests. Though the attacker does not benefit, service is denied to legitimate users. This is one of the most difficult attacks to thwart. (2) The result of any action or series of actions that prevents any part of an information system from functioning normally.

Dictionary attack—(1) A crude form of attack in which an attacker uses a large set of likely combinations to guess a secret. For example, an attacker may choose one million commonly used passwords and try them all until the password is determined. (2) A brute-force technique of attacking by successively trying all the variations of words found in a (usually large) list.

Diffie-Hellman—A public key algorithm in which two parties, who need not have any prior knowledge of each other, can deduce a secret key that is only known to them and secret from everyone else. Diffie-Hellman is often used to protect the privacy of a communication between two anonymous parties.

Digital signature—A method for verifying that a message originated from a principal and that it has not changed en route. Digital signatures is typically performed by encrypting a digest of the message with the private key of the signing party.

Digital certificate—A structure for binding a principal's identity to its public key. A certification authority (CA) issues and digitally signs a digital certificate.

Digital electronic signature—A process that operates on a message to assure message source authenticity and integrity, and may be required for source non-repudiation.

Distributed tool—A tool deployed to multiple hosts that can be directed to anonymously perform an attack on a target host at some time in the future.

Digital Signature Algorithm (DSA)—This algorithm uses a private key to sign a message and a public key to verify the signature. It is a standard proposed by the U.S. government.

Distributed Computing Environment (DCE)—Open Group's integration of a set of technologies for application development and deployment in a distributed environment. Security features include a Kerberos-based authentication system, GSS API interface, ACL-based authorization environment, delegation, and audit.

Distributed Denial of Service (DDoS)—A denial-of-service technique that uses numerous hosts.

DNS spoofing—The action of assuming the DNS name of another system by either corrupting the name service cache of the victim or by compromising a domain name server for a valid domain.

Downgrade—The change of a classification label to a lower level without changing the contents of the data. Downgrading occurs only if the content of a file meets the requirements of the sensitivity level of the network for which the data is being delivered.

Dual-homed gateway—A firewall consisting of a bastion host with two network interfaces, one of which is connected to the protected network, the other of which is connected to the Internet. IP traffic forwarding is usually disabled, restricting all traffic between the two networks to whatever passes through some kind of application proxy.

Eavesdropping—An attack in which an attacker listens to a private communication. The best way to thwart this attack is by making it very difficult for the attacker to make any sense of the communication by encrypting all messages.

Effective key length—A measure of strength of a cryptographic algorithm, regardless of actual key length.

Egress filtering—The process of blocking outgoing packets that use obviously false IP addresses, such as source addresses from internal networks.

Elliptic Curve Cryptosystem (ECC)—A public key cryptosystem where the public and the private key are points on an elliptic curve. ECC is purported to provide faster and stronger encryption than traditional public key cryptosystems (e.g., RSA).

Encapsulating Security Payload—This message header is designed to provide a mix of security services that provides confidentiality, data origin authentication, connectionless integrity, an anti-replay service, and limited traffic flow confidentiality.

Entrapment—Deliberate placement of seemingly apparent holes or flaws in an information system in order to aid in detection of attempted penetrations.

Evaluation Assurance Level (EAL)—One of seven increasingly rigorous packages of assurance requirements from CC (Common Criteria (ISO 15408)) Part 3. Each numbered package represents a point on the CC's predefined assurance scale. An EAL can be considered a level of confidence in the security functions of an IT product or system.

Event—An occurrence that has yet to be assessed but may affect the performance of an information system.

False negative—A condition whereby an intrusion has actually occurred but the system allowed it to pass as if no intrusion ever occurred.

False positive—A condition whereby the system deems an action to be anomalous (indicating a possible intrusion) when it is actually an authorized, legitimate action.

File infector virus—A virus that attaches itself to a program file, such as a word processor, spreadsheet application, or game.

File integrity checker—Software that generates, stores, and compares message digests for files to detect changes to the files.

Fishbowl—Describes a scenario whereby specific actions are taken in order to contain, isolate, and monitor an unauthorized user found in a system so information about the user can be obtained.

Flooding—The unauthorized insertion of a large volume of data into an information system resulting in denial-of-service (DoS) condition.

Forensics—*See computer forensics.*

Frequency Division Multiple Access (FDMA)—FDMA is the division of the frequency band allocated for wireless cellular telephone communication into 30 channels, each of which can carry a voice conversation or, with digital service, carry digital data. FDMA is a basic technology in the analog Advanced Mobile Phone Service (AMPS), the most widely installed cellular phone system in North America. With FDMA, each channel can be assigned to only one user at a time. FDMA is also used in the Total Access Communication System (TACS).

Future Narrow Band Digital Terminal (FNBDT)—FNBDT is an end-to-end secure signaling protocol that will allow establishment of communications interoperability among communications devices that share the same communications capabilities, but are not configured to communicate with each other. FNBDT sets the common configuration. It is a network-independent/transport-independent message layer. FNBDT operates in the narrow-band portion of the STE spectrum (64 kbps and below).

Generic Security Services API (GSS API)—A programming interface that allows two applications to establish a security context independent of the underlying security mechanisms. GSS API is used to hide the details of the security mechanism. Typically both applications use the same mechanism at any given time. The security context is used to mutually authenticate the parties as well as protect the privacy and integrity of the communication. Some mechanisms also allow nonrepudiation and delegation. The GSS API is fully defined in Internet RFC's 1508 and 1509. Various RFCs and proposed RFCs define the implementation of the GSS API using a specific mechanism.

Global Command and Control System (GCCS)—A comprehensive, worldwide network of systems that provides the NCA, joint staff, combatant and functional unified commands, services, and defense agencies, Joint Task Forces and their service components, and others with information processing and dissemination capabilities necessary to conduct C2 of forces.

Global Information Grid (GIG)—It is a globally interconnected, end-to-end set of information capabilities, associated processes, and personnel for collecting, processing, storing, disseminating, and managing information on demand to war fighters, policy makers, and support personnel.

Global Network Information Environment (GNIE)—A composition of all information system technologies used to process, transmit, store, or display DoD information. GNIE has been superceded by Global Information Grid (GIG).

Guard(s)—A set of processes designed to limit the exchange of information between systems. A device used to defend the network boundary by being subjected to a high degree of assurance in its development; supports few services; services at application level only; may support application data filtering; may support sanitization of data and is often used to connect networks with differing levels of trust.

Hacker—An unauthorized user who attempts to or succeeds in gaining access to an information system.

Handler—A type of program used in DDoS attacks to control agents distributed throughout a network. Also refers to an incident handler, which refers to a person who performs incident response work.

Hijacking—*See IP splicing.*

Honey pot—(1) A system or a network resource designed to be attractive to potential crackers and intruders analogous to honey being attractive to bears. (2) A host that is designed to collect data on suspicious activity and has no authorized users other than its administrators.

Host-based security—The technique of securing an individual system from attack; host-based security is operating system and version dependent.

Host-based firewall—A firewall where the security is implemented in software running on a general-purpose computer of some sort. Security in host-based firewalls is generally at the application level, rather than at a network level.

Identification—The process of identifying a principal.

Identification & Authentication (I&A)—Identity of an entity with some level of assurance.

Impersonation—*See delegation.*

Inappropriate usage—A user violates acceptable computing use policies.

Incident—(1) A violation or imminent threat of violation of computer security policies, acceptable use policies, or standard computer security practices. (2) An occurrence that has been assessed and found to have adverse or potentially adverse effects on an information system.

Incident handling—The mitigation of violations of security policies and recommended practices.

Incident response—*See incident handling.*

Indication—A sign that an incident may have occurred or may be currently occurring.

Information infrastructure—An infrastructure comprised of communications networks, computers, databases, management, applications, and consumer electronics that can exist at the global, national, or local level.

Information protection policy—*See Security Policy.*

Information system—The collection of infrastructure, organization, personnel, and components used for transmission, handling, and disposal of information.

Information Systems Security Engineering (ISSE)—The art and science of discovering user information protection needs and then designing and making information systems, with economy and elegance, so they can safely resist the forces to which they may be subjected.

Information technology (IT)—The hardware, firmware, and software used as part of the information system to perform DoD information functions. This definition includes computers, telecommunications, automated information systems, and automatic data processing equipment as well as any assembly of computer hardware, software, and/or firmware configured to collect, create, communicate, compute, disseminate, process, store and/or control data or information.

Ingress filtering—The process of blocking incoming packets that use obviously false IP addresses, such as reserved source addresses.

Insider attack—An attack originating from inside a protected network, usually initiated by from inside the security perimeter by an authorized user attempting to gain access to system resources in an unauthorized manner.

International Data Encryption Algorithm (IDEA)—this is a symmetric encryption algorithm that is popular outside of the United States and Canada. However, DES is still the most popular symmetric algorithm anywhere.

Internet—a collection of myriad networks linked by a common set of protocols that make it possible for users in any one of the networks to gain access to or use resources located on any of the other networks.

Internet Control Message Protocol (ICMP)—A message control and error-reporting protocol between a host server and a gateway to the Internet. ICMP is used by a device, often a router, to report and acquire a wide range of communications-related information.

Intrusion—1) The act of bypassing the security mechanisms of a system without authorization in an attempt to obtain resources or to compromise the integrity, confidentiality, or availability of a resource. 2) An unauthorized act of circumventing security mechanisms enabled for protection of a system.

Intrusion detection—Detection of break-ins or break-in attempts either manually or via software expert systems that operate on logs or other information available on the network.

Intrusion Detection System (IDS)—(1) Software that looks for suspicious activity and alerts administrators. (2) A system that detects and identifies unauthorized or unusual activity on the hosts and networks; this is accomplished by the creation of audit records and checking the audit log against the intrusion thresholds.

IP splicing—A situation whereby a network session is intercepted and taken over by an unauthorized user. IP splicing often happens after a user has already authenticated. This allows the hijacker to assume the role of an already authorized user. Protection is effected by using strong encryption *(a.k.a. hijacking)*.

IPsec *(Internet Protocol Security)*—A security standard for protecting the privacy and integrity of IP packets.

Kerberos—A third-party trusted host authentication system devised at MIT within Project Athena. The Kerberos authentication server is a central system that knows about every principal and its passwords. It issues tickets to principals who successfully authenticate themselves. These tickets can be used to authenticate one principal (e.g., a user) to another (e.g., a server application). Moreover, Kerberos sets up a session key for the principals that can be used to protect the privacy and the integrity of the communication. For this reason, the Kerberos system is also called a Key Distribution Center (KDC).

Key Management Infrastructure (KMI)—Framework established to issue, maintain, and revoke keys accommodating a variety of security technologies, including the use of software.

Keystroke monitoring—A type of software used to record every key pressed by a user and every character that the system returns to the user.

Labeling—Process of assigning a representation of the sensitivity of a subject or object.

Layered solution—The judicious placement of security protections and attack countermeasures that can provide an effective set of safeguards that are tailored to the unique needs of a customer's situation.

Leapfrog attack—The use of illicitly obtained logon ID and password used on one host in order to compromise another host. Using Telnet to go through multiple hosts in order to avoid a trace.

Letterbomb—An e-mail containing data intended to do malicious acts to the recipient's system.

Local Area Network (LAN)—A limited-distance, high-speed data communication system that links computers into a shared system (two to thousands) and is entirely owned by the user. Cabling typically connects these networks.

Macro virus—A virus that attaches itself to documents and uses the macro programming capabilities of the document's application to execute and propagate.

Malicious code—Software or firmware designed to initiate an unauthorized process on an information system *(a.k.a. malware).*

Man-in-the-middle-attack—An attack in which an attacker insert itself between two parties and pretends to be one of the parties. The best way to thwart this attack is for both parties to prove to each other that they know a secret that is only known to them. This is usually done by digitally signing a message and sending it to the other party as well as asking the other party to send a digitally signed message.

Masquerading—An attack in which an attacker pretends to be someone else. The best way to thwart this attack is to authenticate a principal by challenging it to prove its identity.

MD5—A message digest algorithm that digests a message of arbitrary size to 128 bits. MD5 is a cryptographic checksum algorithm.

Message digest—The result of applying a one-way function to a message. Depending on the cryptographic strength of the message digest algorithm, each message will have a reasonably unique digest. Furthermore, the slightest change to original message will result in a different digest. Message digest functions are called "one-way" because knowing the message digest, one cannot reproduce the original message. Encrypted message digests give rise to integrity-protected messages.

Mimicking—*See spoofing.*

Mission Needs Statement (MNS)—Describes the mission need or deficiency; identifies threat and projected threat environment.

Mobile code—Software transferred across a network and executed on a local system without explicit installation or execution by the recipient. Such code usually has the intention of compromising performance or security, or it is used to grant unauthorized access in order to corrupt data, deny service, or steal data resources; examples of mobile code software are Java, JavaScript, VBScript, and ActiveX.

Motivation—The specific technical goal that a potential adversary wants to achieve by an attack (e.g., gain unauthorized access, modify, destroy, or prevent authorized access).

Multiple-component incident—A single incident that encompasses two or more incidents.

Multipurpose Internet Mail Extensions (MIME)—A specification for formatting non-ASCII messages so they can be sent over the Internet. MIME enables graphics, audio, and video files to be sent and received via the Internet mail system. In addition to e-mail applications, Web browsers also support various MIME types. This enables the browser to display or output files that are not in HTML format. The Internet Engineering Task Force (IETF) defined MIME in 1992. *See Secure Multipurpose Internet Mail Extensions, S/MIME.*

NAK attack—A penetration action leveraging a vulnerability in operating systems that cannot handle asynchronous interrupts properly in order to expose the system during such the occurrence of such interrupts *(a.k.a. negative acknowledgment).*

National Information Assurance Partnership (NIAP)—NIAP is a collaboration between the National Institute of Standards and Technology (NIST) and the National Security Agency (NSA) with a goal to help increase the level of trust consumers have in their information systems and networks through the use of cost-effective security testing, evaluation, and validation programs.

Network weaving—*See leapfrog attack.*

Nontechnical countermeasure—A security measure, that is not directly part of the network information security processing system, taken to help prevent system vulnerabilities. Nontechnical countermeasures encompass a broad range of personnel measures, procedures, and physical facilities that can deter an adversary from exploiting a system.

Nonrepudiation—(1) The reasonable assurance that a principal cannot deny being the originator of a message after sending it. Nonrepudiation is achieved by encrypting the message digest using a principal's private key. The public key of the principal must be certified by a trusted certification authority. (2) Assurance that the sender of data is provided a proof of delivery and the recipient is provided proof of the sender's identity so neither party can deny having electronically processed the data.

Open System Interconnection Model (OSI)—A reference model of how messages should be transmitted between any two endpoints of a telecommunication network. The process of communication is divided into seven layers, with each layer adding its own set of special, related functions. The seven layers are the application, presentation, session, transport, network, data, and physical layers. Most telecommunication products tend to describe themselves in relation to the OSI model. The OSI model is a single reference view of communication that provides a common ground for education and discussion.

Operations security—Process of denying information to others by identifying, controlling, and protecting seemingly generic activities or information that could be used by someone outside the organization to piece together usable, potentially damaging information about operations or intentions *(a.k.a. OPSEC)*.

Orange book—A Department of Defense publication, Series 5200.28-STD, "Trusted Computer System Evaluation Criteria," that is now superceded by the Common Criteria.

Packet—A grouped set of data sent over the network adhering to a specific protocol.

Packet filter—(1) A tool used to inspect each data packet transmitted in a network for user defined content, such as an IP address. (2) A type of firewall in which each IP packet is examined and either allowed to pass through or rejected. Normally, packet filtering is a first line of defense and is typically combined with application proxies for more security.

Packet filtering—The act of limiting the flow of data based on preset rules for processing the data, such as source, destination, or type of service being provided by the network. Packet filters allow administrators to limit protocol specific traffic to one network segment, isolate e-mail domains, and perform many other traffic control functions.

Packet sniffer—(1) Software that observes and records network traffic. (2) A device or program that monitors the data traveling between computers on a network.

Password cracking—The act of attempting penetration of a network, system, or resource with or without using tools to unlock a resource secured with a password.

Patch management—The process of acquiring, testing, and distributing patches to the appropriate administrators and users throughout the organization.

Perimeter-based security—The technique of securing a network by controlling accesses to all entry and exit points of the network.

Piggyback—The act of gaining unauthorized access to a system via another user's legitimate connection.

Port scanning—Using a program to remotely determine which ports on a system are open (e.g., whether systems allow connections through those ports).

Precursor—A sign that an attacker may be preparing to cause an incident.

Pretty Good Privacy (PGP)—A software package that uses public/private and secret keys for sending private mail messages as well as storing files securely. A de facto standard used for securing e-mail and file encryption on the Internet. Its public-key cryptography system allows for the secure transmission of messages and guarantees authenticity by adding digital signatures to messages.

Principal—Any entity that uses a security system. Users, systems, and client and server applications are all principals.

Private Communication Technology (PCT)—A standard created by Microsoft Corporation for establishing a secure communication link using a public key system.

Private key—A key that belongs to a principal and is never revealed to anyone. It is used by a principal to decrypt messages that are sent to it and are encrypted with the principal's public key. It is also used to encrypt a message digest sent by the principal to anyone else. This provides nonrepudiation, anyone can use the principal's public key to decrypt the digest and be sure that the message originated from that principal.

Probe—An attempt to gather information about an information system for the apparent purpose of circumventing its security controls. Access a target in order to determine its characteristics.

Profile—Patterns of a user's activity that can detect changes in normal routines. In computer security, a description of the characteristics of an entity to which access is controlled.

Profiling—Measuring the characteristics of expected activity so that changes to it can be more easily identified.

Protection Profile (PP)—A Common Criteria term for a set of implementation-independent security requirements for a category of Targets of Evaluation (TOEs) that meet specific consumer needs.

Protection Needs Elicitation (PNE)—A process of discovering a customer's prioritized requirements for the protection of information.

Proxy—Software agent that performs a function or operation on behalf of another application or system while hiding the details involved.

Public key—A key that belongs to a principal and is revealed to everyone. In order for everyone to trust that the public key really belongs to the principal, the public key is embedded in a digital certificate. The public key is used to encrypt messages that are sent to the principal as well as to verify the signature of a principal.

Public Key Cryptographic Standards (PKCS)—A set of standards proposed by RSA Data Security Inc. for a public-key-based system.

Public Key Infrastructure (PKI)—Public and private keys, digital certificates, certification authorities, certificate revocation lists, and the standards that govern the use and validity of these elements make up an infrastructure where principals can engage in private and nonrepudiable transactions. This combination is called the Public Key Infrastructure.

Quality of Protection (QOP)—Quality of protection refers to the set of security functions that are applied to what needs to be protected. The QOP can consist of any combination of authentication, privacy, integrity, and nonrepudiation.

Raike Public Key (RPK)—a public key cryptosystem invented by Bill Raike.

Replay attack—An attack in which an attacker captures a messages and at a later time communicates that message to a principal. Though the attacker cannot decrypt the message, it may benefit by receiving a service from the principal to whom it is replaying the message. The best way to thwart a replay attack is by challenging the freshness of the message. This is done by embedding a time stamp, a sequence number, or a random number in the message.

Replicator—Any program that acts to produce copies of itself. Examples include; a program, a worm, a fork bomb or virus. It is even claimed by some that UNIX and C are the symbiotic halves of an extremely successful replicator.

Retro-virus—A retro-virus is a virus that waits until all possible backup media are infected too, so that it is not possible to restore the system to an uninfected state.

Risk—The probability that one or more adverse events will occur.

Risk management— Process of identifying and applying countermeasures, commensurate with the value of the assets protected based on a risk assessment.

Risk plane—A graphic technique for depicting the likelihood of particular attacks occurring and the degree of consequence to an operational mission.

Rivest Cipher 2 (RC2)—a symmetric encryption algorithm developed by Ron Rivest (the R in RSA).

Rivest Cipher 4 (RC4)—a symmetric encryption algorithm developed by Ron Rivest (the R in RSA).

Robustness—A characterization of the strength of a security function, mechanism, service, or solution, and the assurance (or confidence) that it is implemented and functioning correctly.

Root CA—The Certification Authority that is trusted by everyone. The root CA issues digital certificates to other CAs.

Rootkit—A hacker security tool that captures passwords and message traffic to and from a computer. A collection of tools that allows a hacker to provide a backdoor into a system, collect information on other systems on the network, mask the fact that the system is compromised, and much more. Rootkit is a classic example of Trojan horse software. Rootkit is available for a wide range of operating systems.

Router-based firewall—A firewall where the security is implemented using screening routers as the primary means of protecting the network.

Routing control—The application of rules during the process of routing so as to choose or avoid specific networks, links, or relays.

RSA—Rivest, Shamir, Adleman; a public key cryptosystem invented by Ron Rivest, Adi Shamir, and Leonard Adleman.

Sandboxed environment—The enforcement of access control by a native programming language such that an applet can only access limited resources. Java applets run in a sandboxed environment where an applet cannot read or write local files, cannot start or interact with local processes, and cannot load or link with dynamic libraries. While a sandboxed environment provides excellent protection against accidental or malicious destruction or abuse of local resources, it does not address the security issues related to authentication, authorization, privacy, integrity, and nonrepudiation.

Sanitization—The changing of content information in order to meet the requirements of the sensitivity level of the network to which the information is being sent.

Scan—Software that performs an access check against a set of targets sequentially in order to identify which targets have specific characteristic is said to perform a scan.

Scanning—Sending packets or requests to another system to gain information to be used in a subsequent attack.

Screened subnet—A firewall architecture in which a "sandbox" or "demilitarized zone" network is set up between the protected network and the Internet, with traffic between the protected network and the Internet blocked. Conceptually, this is similar to a dual-homed gateway, except that an entire network, rather than a single host is reachable from the outside.

Screening router—A router that is used to implement part of the security of a firewall by configuring it to selectively permit or deny traffic at a network level.

Secret key—A key used by a symmetric algorithm to encrypt and decrypt data.

Secure Hyper Text Transfer Protocol (S-HTTP)—An extension to the HTTP protocol to protect the privacy and integrity of HTTP communications.

Secure Socket Layer (SSL)—A standard by for establishing a secure communication link using a public key system.

Secure Single Sign On (SSSO)—A sign-on methodology that satisfies three related sets of requirements: (1) From an end-user perspective, SSSO refers to the ability of using a single user ID and a single password to logon once and gain access to all resources that one is allowed to access. (2) From an administrative perspective, SSSO allows management of all security-related aspects of one's enterprise from a central location. This includes adding, modifying, and removing users as wells as granting and revoking access to resources. 3) From an enterprise perspective, SSSO provides the ability to protect the privacy and the integrity of transactions as well as to engage in auditable and non-repudiable transactions.

Secure hash—A hash value such that it is computationally infeasible to find a message which corresponds to a given message digest, or to find two different messages which produce the same digest.

Secure Hash Algorithm (SHA)—A message digest algorithm that digests a message of arbitrary size to 160 bits. SHA is a cryptographic checksum algorithm.

Secure Multipurpose Internet Mail Extensions (S/MIME)—A version of the MIME protocol that supports encrypted messages. S/MIME is based on RSA's public-key encryption technology. *See also Multipurpose Internet Mail Extensions, MIME.*

Security administrator—person responsible for the security of information and information technology. Sometimes, this function is combined with administrator.

Security Management Infrastructure (SMI)—A set of interrelated activities providing security services needed by other security features and mechanisms; SMI functions include registration, ordering, key generation, certificate generation, distribution, accounting, compromise recovery, re-key, destruction, data recovery, and administration.

Security mechanism—A piece of software that provides any combination of security functionalities including authentication, privacy, integrity, non-repudiation, delegation, audit, and authorization. A mechanism uses cryptographic functions and exports its services using an API.

Security policy—What security means to the user; a statement of what is meant when claims of security are made. More formally, it is the set of rules and conditions governing the access and use of information. Typically, a security policy will refer to the conventional security services, such as confidentiality, integrity, availability, etc., and perhaps their underlying mechanisms and functions.

Security Support Programming Interface (SSPI)—A standard programming interface developed by Microsoft Corporation where two applications can establish a security context independent of the underlying security mechanisms. SSPI is very similar to GSS API.

Security Target (ST)—A set of security requirements and specifications drawn from the Common Criteria for Information Technology Security Evaluation (CC) to be used as the basis for evaluation of an identified TOE.

Session key—A temporary symmetric key that is only valid for a short period. Session keys are typically random numbers that can be chosen by either party to a conversation, by both parties in cooperation with one another, or by a trusted third party. Also see Kerberos.

Signature—A recognizable, distinguishing pattern associated with an attack, such as a binary string in a virus or a particular set of keystrokes used to gain unauthorized access to a system.

Signed applet—An applet that is digitally signed by the source that provides it. Signed applets are integrity-protected and cannot be tampered with while en route from the server to the browser.

Simple Key Management for IP (SKIP)—A protocol for protecting the privacy and integrity of IP packets.

SmartCard—A tamper-resistant hardware device where sensitive information can be stored. Typically a SmartCard stores the private key(s) of a principal. SmartCards can also be used to encrypt of decrypt data on the card directly. This has the desirable effect of not exposing the private keys, even to the owner of the key. SmartCards are password protected; in order for an application to use the keys and functions of a smartcard the user must enter the correct password to open the card.

Smurfing—A denial-of-service attack where the attacker spoofs the source address of an echo-request using an ICMP (Internet Control Message Protocol, e.g., a ping) packet, altering it to a broadcast address for a network, causing the machines in the network to respond en masse to the victim thereby flooding its network with ICMP traffic.

Sniffer—A software tool used for auditing network traffic packets. Designed to capture data across a computer network, it is often used by hackers to capture user ID names and passwords.

Social engineering—(1) An attempt to trick someone into revealing information (e.g., a password) that can be used to attack systems or networks. (2) An attack based on deceiving users or administrators at the target site and is typically carried out by an adversary telephoning users or operators and pretending to be an authorized user, to attempt to gain illicit access to systems.

SOCKS—A networking proxy protocol that enables full access across the SOCKS server from one host to another without requiring direct IP accessibility. The SOCKS server authenticates and authorizes the requests, establishes a proxy connection, and transmits the data. SOCKS is commonly used as a network firewall that enables hosts behind a SOCKS server to gain full access to the Internet, while preventing unauthorized access from the Internet to the internal hosts.

Spam—The act of indiscriminately sending unsolicited, unwanted, pornographic or otherwise inappropriate messages enmass over a network, usually for advertising purposes.

Spoofing—Unauthorized use of legitimate logon data in order to mimic a subject and mask the existence of an attacker *(a.k.a. impersonating, masquerading, piggybacking, and mimicking).*

SSL—A session-layer protocol used to provide authentication security to applications. It uses a connection-oriented end-to-end encryption scheme to secure data traffic between a client and a server or for peer-to-peer applications security *(a.k.a. Secure Sockets Layer).*

Strength of encryption—The strength of encryption is measured by the amount of effort needed to break a cryptosystem. Typically this is measured by the length of the key used for encryption. The strength of encryption is algorithm-dependent. For example, the minimum acceptable key length for DES is 56 bits, while the minimum acceptable length for RSA is 512 bits.

Strength of Mechanism (SML)—A scale for measuring the relative strength of a security mechanism hierarchically ordered from SML 1 through SML 3.

Subversion—A scenario that occurs when an intruder subverts the operation of an intrusion detection system (IDS) to force false negatives to occur.

Symmetric algorithm—An algorithm where the same key can be used for encryption and decryption.

System Security Authorization Agreement (SSAA)—The SSAA is the formal agreement among the DAA(s), certifier, user representative, and program manager. It is used throughout the entire DoD DITSCAP to guide actions, document decisions, specify IA requirements, document certification tailoring and level-of-effort, identify potential solutions, and maintain operational systems security.

Tamper—Unauthorized modification that alters the proper functioning of cryptographic or automated information system security equipment in a manner that degrades the security or functionality it provides.

Target of Evaluation (TOE)—A Common Criteria term for an IT product or system and its associated administrator and user guidance documentation that is the subject of a security evaluation.

Technical countermeasure—A security feature implemented in hardware and/or software that is incorporated into the network information security processing system.

Technology gap—A technology that is needed to mitigate a threat at a sufficient level but is not available.

Third-party trusted host model—An authentication model in which a trusted third party authenticates principals to each other. The trusted third party shares a secret (password) with each principal. It uses a key derived from the password to issue tickets to these principals. *Also see Kerberos.*

Threat—An event with potential to adversely impact an information system via unauthorized access. The potential source of an adverse event.

Threat agent—Entities used to exploit vulnerabilities in an information system, operation, or organizational or governmental infrastructure.

Threat assessment—A process that formally defines and evaluates the degree of threat an information system may be exposed to in an attack scenario.

Ticket—A credential used in a third-party trusted host model. A ticket is encrypted with the password of the principal to whom the ticket is presented. A ticket contains a session key as well as the identity of the principal to whom the ticket is issued. Tickets have an expiration time.

Time Division Multiple Access (TDMA)—A technique to interweave multiple conversations into one transponder so as to appear to get simultaneous conversations.

Tinkerbell program—A program that operates in the background monitoring network traffic in order to generate alerts when calls are received from particular sites, or when logins are attempted using certain IDs.

Token—A token is an object that represents something else, such as another object (either physical or virtual). A security token is a physical device, such as a special SmartCard, that together with something that a user knows, such as a PIN, will enable authorized access to a computer system or network.

Trace packet—Used in packet-switching networks, a special type of packet that forces a report to be generated and sent to a Network Control Center (NOC) during each stage of its progression across the network.

Traceroute—An operation that uses trace packets and records the sequence of addressing obtained from UDP packets sent from the local host to a remote host. The output record normally displays time, address of the route taken, and a sequence number or "hop ID" used to reach its destination address.

Trojan horse—(1) A program that performs a desired task, but that also includes unexpected (and undesirable) functions. Consider as an example an editing program for a multi-user system. This program could be modified to randomly delete one of the users' files each time they perform a useful function (editing), but the deletions are unexpected and definitely undesired! (2) A software application containing hidden code that enables the unauthorized collection, alteration, or destruction of information. 3) A non-self-replicating program that seems to have a useful purpose, but in reality has a different, malicious purpose.

Trusted applet—*See signed applet.*

Trusted Computing Base (TCB)—The totality of protection mechanisms within a computer system—including hardware, firmware, and software—the combination of which is responsible for enforcing a security policy. A TCB consists of one or more components that together enforce a unified security policy over a product or system. The ability of a trusted computing base to correctly enforce a security policy depends solely on the mechanisms within the TCB and on the correct input by system administrative personnel of parameters (e.g., a user's clearance) related to the security policy. *[taken from Page 112 of the Orange Book]*

Trusted computer system—"A system that employs sufficient hardware and software integrity measures to allow its use for processing simultaneously a range of sensitive or classified information." *[taken from page 112 of the Orange Book]*

Trusted gateway—A firewall that uses a very secure, hardened operating system. These types of operating systems are typically rated B1 or better according to the Trusted Computing Base Evaluation Criteria (referred to as the Orange Book). The firewall system itself is divided into three software compartments: (1) that which interacts with the Internet, (2) that which interacts with the enterprise, and (3) a trusted gateway that mediates communications between the other two compartments. The operating system prevents applications that run in one compartment from accessing resources outside of that compartment. Any application that runs on the Internet compartment (e.g. a Web server) can only have access to resources in the Internet compartment (e.g., public HTML pages) or else it must use the trusted gateway to ask for information from the enterprise compartment.

Trusted operating system—A trusted operating system is part of a Trusted Computer Base (TCB) that has been evaluated at an assurance level necessary to protect the data that will be processed. *See Trusted Computing Base and Trusted Computer System.*

Tunneling—A term used to describe a connection process whereby both sender and receiver begin encapsulating a network protocol within packets carried by another network.

Tunneling router—A router or system capable of routing traffic by encrypting it and encapsulating it for transmission across an untrusted network, for eventual de-encapsulation and decryption.

Unauthorized access—A user gains access without permission to a network, system, application, data, or other resource.

Vaccine—A program that injects itself into an application in order to perform a signature check and provide warning if alterations are detected.

Victim—A machine that is attacked.

Virtual Network Perimeter—A network that appears to be a single protected network behind firewalls, which actually encompasses encrypted virtual links over untrusted networks.

Virtual Private Network (VPN)—A way of using a public network (typically the Internet) to link two sites of an organization. A VPN is typically set up by protecting the privacy and integrity of the communication line using a secret session key. The secret session key is usually negotiated using the public keys of the two principals.

Virus—Malicious code that self-replicates and attaches itself to an application or other executable and leaves no obvious signs of its presence. The new copy of the virus is executed when a user executes the new, copied host program. The virus may include an additional "payload" that triggers when specific conditions, such as time of day or specific date are met. For example, some viruses display a text string on a particular date. There are many types of viruses, such as variants, overwriting, resident, stealth, and polymorphic.

Virus hoax—An urgent warning message about a nonexistent virus.

Vulnerability—A weakness in a system, application, or network that is subject to exploitation or misuse. An exploitable flaw or weakness in an information infrastructure.

Vulnerability analysis—An evaluation of vulnerabilities in an information infrastructure.

Vulnerability assessment—A complete, orderly examination of an information system and/or infrastructure to determine the adequacy of security measures, identify any security vulnerabilities, gather data that will be used to predict the effectiveness of any proposed security measures, and confirm the adequacy of such measures post-implementation.

War dialer—A program that autodials a list of numbers and records those answer with handshake responses indicating possible entry points to networked systems.

War driving—The process of using a war dialer in a wireless or mobile environment where the hacker is often moving from location to location scanning for vulnerable computer systems and cataloging those numbers that return a handshake response so a crack can be attempted at a later time to try to infiltrate the system.

Wide Area Network (WAN)—A data communications network that spans any distance and is usually provided by a public carrier. Users gain access to the two ends of the circuit, and the carrier handles the transmission and other services in between.

Worm—(1) A self-replicating, self-propagating, self-contained program that uses networking mechanisms to spread itself. (2) An insidious, self-contained program that replicates from machine to machine across network connections often clogging networks as it spreads. (3) A self-replicating program, self-contained executable, able to propagate without need of a host program. The program creates a copy of itself and causes the copy to execute without user intervention. Worms commonly use network services to propagate to other host systems.

E.3 References

All.net. (2004). *A PBX Audit Checklist.* Retrieved August 9, 2004 from www.all.net/books/audit/pbx/general.html.

Ananthapadmanabha, T. V., & Fant, G. (1982). "Calculation of true glottal flow and its components." *Speech Communication*, 1(3-4):167–184.

Arango, M. et al. (1999). *RFC2705: Media Gateway Control Protocol (MGCP) Version 1.0.* Retrieved July 26, 2004 from http://rfc.sunsite.dk.

Archer, K. et al. (2001). *Voice and Data Security.* Indianapolis, IN: SAMS Publishing.

Bellovin, S., Ioannidis, J., Keromytis, A., & Stewart, R. (2003). *RFC 3554: On the Use of Stream Control Transmission Protocol (SCTP) with IPsec.* Retrieved July 18, 2004 from www.ietf.org/rfc/rfc3554.txt.

Biran, G. (2004). *Voice over Frame Relay, IP and ATM: The Case for Cooperative Networking.* Retrieved July 12, 2004 from www.protocols.com/papers/voe.htm.

Cavanagh, J. (2002). *Secure Business Telephony With VoIP: A Technical White Paper.* Retrieved August 3, 2004 from www.consultant-registry.com/delivery/TSWP1.pdf.

CERT Coordination Center. (2004). Carnegie Mellon Software Engineering Institute, CERT Coordination Center Web page. Retrieved August 9, 2004 from www.cert.org.

Cisco. (2002). *Configuring H.323 Gatekeepers and Proxies.* Retrieved August 5, 2004 from http://noc.caravan.ru/ciscocd/cc/td/doc/product/software/ios122/122cgcr/fvvfax_c/vvf323gk.htm.

Cloud, B. (2000). *PBX Audit Review and Questionnaire: Key Areas to Review During a PBX Audit.* Retrieved August 9, 2004 from www.auditnet.org/docs/pbxaudit.txt.

Coene, L. (2002). *RFC 3257: Stream Control Transmission Protocol Applicability Statement.* Retrieved July 18, 2004 from www.faqs.org/rfcs/rfc3257.html.

Dudley, H. (1950). "The speaking machine of Wolfgang von Kempelen." *Journal of the Acoustical Society of America*, 22(2):151–166.

Dudley, H. (1936). "Synthesizing speech." *Bell Laboratories Record*, 15:98–102.

Dudley, H., Riesz, R. R., & Watkins, S. S. A. (1939). "A synthetic speaker." *Journal of the Franklin Institute*, 2227(6):739–764.

Emmerson, B. (2004). *Convergence: the Business Case for IP Telephony.* Retrieved July 13, 2004 from www.acaimc.com/downloads/business-case.pdf

ENSC. (2004). *ENSC 835 Final Project Report.* Retrieved July 12, 2004 from www.ensc.sfu.ca/~ljilja/ENSC835/Projects/e.chan/Report.pdf.

Franks, J. et al. (1999). *RFC 2617: HTTP Authentication: Basic and Digest Access Authentication.* Retrieved July 26, 2004 from http://rfc.sunsite.dk.

Fuller, V. et al. (1993). *RFC 1519: Classless Inter-Domain Routing (CIDR): an Address Assignment and Aggregation Strategy.* Retrieved July 26, 2004 from http://rfc.sunsite.dk.

Gartner. (2003). *Business Planning for VoIP and IP-Telephony—train wreck or smooth ride?* Retrieved July 13, 2004 from www.gartner.com/teleconferences/asset_9148.jsp.

Gersho, A. & Gray, R. M. (1992). *Vector Quantization and Signal Compression.* Germany: Kluwer Academic Publishers.

Groves, C. et al. (2003). *RFC 3525: Gateway Control Protocol Version 1.* Retrieved July 18, 2004 from ftp://ftp.isi.edu/in-notes/rfc3525.txt.

Halpern, J. (2002). *IP Telephony Security in Depth.* White Paper, Cisco Systems. Retrieved August 13, 2004 from www.cisco.com/warp/public/cc/so/cuso/epso/sqfr/safip_wp.pdf..

Handley, M. et al. (1998). *RFC 2327: SDP: Session Description Protocol.* Retrieved July 26, 2004 from http://rfc.sunsite.dk.

Harkins, D. & Carrel, D. (1998). *RFC 2409– The Internet Key Exchange (IKE).* Retrieved July 18, 2004 from www.faqs.org/rfcs/rfc2409.html.

Haden, R. (2004). *Voice*. Retrieved August 5, 2004 from www.rhyshaden.com/voice.htm.

Hedrick, C. et al. (1988). *RFC 1058: Routing Information Protocol.* Retrieved July 26, 2004 from http://rfc.sunsite.dk.

ISACA. (2004). *Telecommunications.* Retrieved August 9, 2004 from www.isaca.org/gir/catDspl.cfm?catID=11&catName=Telecommunications#subcat97.

Jungmaier, A., Rescoria, E., & Tuexen, M. (2002). *RFC 3436: Transport Layer Security over Stream Control Transmission Protocol.* Retrieved July 18, 2004 from www.ietf.org/rfc/rfc3436.txt.

Kent, S. et al. (1998). *RFC 2402: IP Authentication Header.* Retrieved July 26, 2004 from http://rfc.sunsite.dk.

Kiser, C. (2003). *Regulatory Considerations for Cable-Provided IP Telephony.* Retrieved July 12, 2004 from www.mintz.com/images/dyn/publications/Kiser-IPTelephony.pdf.

Krawczyk, H. et al. (1997). *RFC 2104: HMAC: Keyed-Hashing for Message Authentication.* Retrieved July 26, 2004 from http://rfc.sunsite.dk.

Le, T. (2004). *Internet Firewalls: The Thin Red Line.* Retrieved August 9, 2004 from www-sal.cs.uiuc.edu/~steng/cs497_01/presentation.pdf.

Lemmetty, S. (1999). *Review of Speech Synthesis Technology.* Master's Thesis, Helsinki University of Technology, Finland.

Management Information Base. Retrieved July 12, 2004 from www.ietf.org/internet-drafts/draft-ietf-ccamp-gmpls-lsr-mib-05.txt.

McDermott, R. (1999). *Voice over IP.* Research Paper. Retrieved July 12, 2004 from http://people.bu.edu/rjm123/VoIP.htm.

Moorer, J. A. (1978). "The use of the phase vocoder in computer music applications." *Journal of the Audio Engineering Society,* 26(1):42–45.

National Cable and Telecommunications Association. (2004). *Balancing Responsibilities and Rights: A Regulatory Model for Facilities-Based VoIP Competition—An NCTA Policy Paper.* Retrieved July 12, 2004 from www.ncta.com/PDF_files/VoIPWhitePaper.pdf.

NexTone Communications, Inc. (2003). *Enterprise Voice Services*. Retrieved July 12, 2004 from www.nextone.com/pdfs/enterprise.pdf.

Munch, B. (2003). *VoIP Security: Part 3—Product Status*. Retrieved August 14, 2004 from http://techupdate.zdnet.com/techupdate/stories/main.

Nadeau, T. et al. (2004). Internet Draft: *Generalized Multiprotocol Label Switching (GMPLS) Label Switching Router (LSR)*.

National Institute of Standards and Technology. (2004). *NIST Special Publication 800-58: Security Considerations for Voice Over IP Systems Recommendations of the National Institute of Standards and Technology*. Retrieved August 3, 2004 from http://csrc.nist.gov/publications/drafts/NIST_SP800-58-040502.pdf.

National Security Agency. (2004). *NSA/SNAC Router Security Configuration Guide, Version 1.1*. Retrieved August 13, 2004, from http://nsa1.www.conxion.com/cisco/guides/cis-1.pdf.

NetIQ. (2001). *A Handbook for Successful VoIP Deployment: Network Testing, QoS, and More*. Retrieved July 13, 2004 from http://itpapers.zdnet.com/abstract.aspx?docid=29619&tag=tu.tk.6587.f1.

Netrake. (2004). Netrake Web site. Retrieved August 12, 2004 from www.netrake.com.

Networksorcery.com. (2004). *SIP, Session Initiation Protocol*. Retrieved August 4, 2004 from www.networksorcery.com/enp/protocol/sip.htm.

Ong, L. & Yoakum, J. (2002). *RFC 3286: An Introduction to the Stream Control Transmission Protocol (SCTP)*. Retrieved July 18, 2004 from www.faqs.org/rfcs/rfc3286.html.

Oppenheim, A. V. & Schafer, R. W. (1989). *Discrete-Time Signal Processing*. Englewood Cliffs, NJ: Prentice-Hall.

Pisello, T. (2003). *Ask the Expert: Questions and Answers—ROI and IT Investment*. Retrieved July 21, 2004 from http://searchcio.techtarget.com/ateQuestionNResponse.

Rekhter, Y. et al. (1996). *RFC 1918: Address Allocation for Private Internets*. Retrieved July 26, 2004 from http://rfc.sunsite.dk.

Roinetworks.com. (2004). *Business Case for VoIP, Remote Agents, and Converged Communications*. Retrieved July 13, 2004 from www.roinetworks.com/businessdiscussion.htm.

Rosenberg, J. et al. (2002). *RFC 3261: SIP: Session Initiation Protocol.* Retrieved July 26, 2004 from http://rfc.sunsite.dk.

Rosenberg, J. (2002). *SIP: Session Initiation Protocol.* Retrieved August 3, 2004 from www.jdrosen.net/papers/draft-ietf-sip-rfc2543bis-07.txt.

Samhassan.com. (2004). *Voice-Over-IP.* Retrieved July 12, 2004 from www.samhassan.com/Voice-Over-IP.htm#latency.

SANS Institute. (2004). SANS Institute Web page. Retrieved August 9, 2004 from www.sans.org.

Schulzrinne, H. et al. (1996). *RFC 1889: RTP: A Transport Protocol for Real-Time Applications*. Retrieved July 26, 2004 from http://rfc.sunsite.dk.

SecureLogix Corporation. (2004). *TeleWall: Telecommunications Firewall 4.1*. Retrieved August 3, 2004 from www.securelogix.com/applications/telewall.htm.

Shultz, T. (2000). *Voice over IP.* Retrieved August 5, 2004 from www.eicon.com/disv4bri/whtpap4.htm.

Spanias, A. (1994). "Speech coding: A tutorial review." *Proceedings of the IEEE*, 82:1539–1582.

Stewart, R. et al. (2004). *RFC 3758: Stream Control Transmission Protocol (SCTP) Partial Reliability Extension*. Retrieved July 18, 2004 from http://rfc.sunsite.dk/rfc/rfc3758.html.

Stone, J., Stewart, R., & Otis, D. (2002). *RFC 3309: Stream Control Transmission Protocol (SCTP) Checksum Change*. Retrieved July 18, 2004 from www.ietf.org/rfc/rfc3309.txt.

Techabulary. (2004). *Voice over IP (VoIP)*. Retrieved July 13, 2004 from www.techabulary.com/v/voip.html.

Thalhammer, J. (2002). *Security in VoIP—Telephony Systems*. Master's Thesis. Retrieved August 3, 2004 from www.iaik.tu-graz.ac.at/../teaching/11_diplomarbeiten/archive/thalhammer.pdf.

Villalona, S. & Lee, C. (2002). *Voice Over IP.* Retrieved July 12, 2004 from http://webcomposer.pace.edu/CL78352N/IPTelePP.ppt.

Vitel Software, Inc. (2003). *Voice Network Security: Strategies for Control.* Retrieved August 9, 2004 from www.ivize.com/pub/security_wp401.pdf.

Walker, J. & Hicks, J. (2004). *Taking Charge of Your VoIP Project.* Indianapolis, IN: Cisco Press.

Walker, J. & Hicks, J. (2002). *The Essential Guide to VoIP Implementation and Management.* Retrieved July 13, 2004 from www2.cs.uh.edu/~sujeetv/projects/Ad-Hoc/NetIQ_VoIP_Chapter1.pdf.

Wu, Y. et al. (2004). *SCIDIVE: A Stateful and Cross Protocol Intrusion Detection Architecture for Voice-over-IP Environments.* Retrieved August 14, 2004 from http://dynamo.ecn.purdue.edu/~sbagchi/Research/Papers/scidive_dsn04_submit.pdf.

ZVON. (2004). *RFC 3261: Security Considerations: Threat Model and Security Usage Recommendations.* Retrieved August 3, 2004 from www.zvon.org/tmRFC/RFC3261/Output/chapter26.html.

E.4 Wireless LANs and WLAN Security Policy

IM is considered one of the more vulnerable technologies used today. While it has great advantages in aiding in communications, it also poses great risks. When used on wireless devices, those vulnerabilities are increased many times because of the ease in which communications can be intercepted from wireless devices. As part of an IM network communications infrastructure, Wireless LANs (WLAN's) have unique network security requirements that must be adhered to in order to ensure network security. This Appendix will provide you with an overview of the basic WLAN security requirements and policy recommendations that we believe will help tighten security in an organization and prevent misuse of WLANs as part of a multi-level approach to information security as it relates to IM. These are just the minimum requirements for WLAN security as excerpted from our *Wireless Operational Security* [1] book with the permission of Digital Press, an imprint of Elsevier and we recommend it for an extensive coverage of this topic.

The security policy life cycle, as suggested by J. Craig Lowery [2] in a recent white paper, is a model incorporating nine phases of the security policy life cycle. These nine phases are shown below:

1. Draft—Representative committees write policies.
2. Adopt—Administration reviews and approves policies.
3. Implement—Administration defines procedures to implement the policies.
4. Educate—Users receive training about the new policies and procedures.
5. Deploy—Policies are put into effect; related technical solutions are deployed.
6. Monitor—Security team observes the computing environment for policy violations.
7. Enforce—Violators are punished as prescribed by policy.
8. Re-evaluate—Policies are reviewed for continued relevance and accuracy

9. Revise—Policies are revised as needed to keep them current, relevant, and accurate.

E.4.1 Purpose and Goals of WLAN IM Security Policies

A very good source to find samples of security policies is the SANS Security Policy Resource Webpage [3], which is maintained by the current Policy Project Director, Michele D. Guel [4]. SANS policy information is provided free of cost. The folks at SANS compiled those security policies originally to assist those attending SANS training programs, but because SANS feels security of the Internet depends on vigilance by all, they have made these resources available to the entire Internet community.

Another resource the reader can consult for security policy information is RFC 2196 [5]. This handbook is one of the early guides to developing computer security policies and procedures for sites that have systems on the Internet. Its purpose is to provide practical guidance to administrators trying to secure their organizational information and services. Topics covered include policy content and formation, a broad range of technical system and network security topics, and security incident response.

For all security policies developed in an organization, a standard template should be used to ensure consistency in presentation and format. We have provided a generic format we recommend for development of your security policies. The template may, of course, be modified to suit your organizational needs. The implementation of policies, as part of an overall organizational security plan, can greatly enhance the protective posture of any organization.

E.4.2 Basic Approach to WLAN IM Security Policy Development

One generally accepted approach to development of site security policy is that suggested by Fites [6] which recommends one take the following steps:

1. Identify what you are trying to protect.
2. Determine what you are trying to protect it from.
3. Determine how likely the threats are.

4. Implement measures to protect your assets in a cost-effective manner.
5. Review continuously, make improvements each time a weakness is found.

Most organizations will concentrate their efforts on item four above but, if an effective security plan is to be established at your site, the other steps cannot be avoided. An axiom to remember is that the cost of protecting yourself against a threat should be less than the cost of recovering if the threat were to strike you. Cost in this context should factor in losses expressed in dollars, reputation, trustworthiness, and other less obvious measures. Without reasonable knowledge of what you are protecting and what the likely threats are, following this rule could be difficult. We will briefly review each of the five items in the box above.

E.4.3 Identify What Needs Protection and Why

These two steps are initially accomplished in the Risk Analysis phase (which is described later in this chapter). A list of asset categories (disposable office supplies, non-disposable office supplies, computer equipment, computer peripherals, etc.) should be developed. For every organization, the inventoried assets will be different, but most will fall into one of the above categories. Conduct your asset inventory, listing every item, grouped by category. This may help you to determine potential threats for an entire group of assets versus an item by item approach. For example, mandating all disposable supplies should be locked in a cabinet may be more cost effective and equally effective as having separate procedures for ribbons, paper, etc. Once the assets requiring protection have been identified, an organization should take steps to identify corresponding potential threats for those assets. These threats can subsequently be evaluated to determine if any potential for loss may exist.

E.4.4 Determine Likelihood of Threats

A computer security policy is generally created to ensure that efforts spent on security yield cost effective benefits. Most surveys of computer security show that, for most organizations, the actual loss from "insiders" is a much greater risk than attack by an outsider. We have discussed a process that involves determining what a site needs to protect, what they need to protect it from, and how to actually protect it. The process of examining all of the risks associated with each of these three items, to include ranking those risks by level of severity is what we mean by determining the likelihood of a threat. This process involves making cost-effective decisions on what you want to protect. After all, it does not make good business sense to spend more to protect something than it is actually worth.

E.4.5 Implement Protective Measures

The security-related decisions you make, or fail to make, largely determine how secure your network is. However, you cannot make good decisions about security without first determining what security goals need to be set for your organization. Until you determine what your security goals are, you cannot make effective use of any collection of security tools because you simply won't know what to check for and what restrictions to impose. Your goals will be largely determined by the following key tradeoffs:

1. **Services offered versus security provided**—Each service offered to users carries its own security risks. For some services, the risk outweighs the benefit of the service and the administrator may choose to eliminate the service rather than try to secure it.
2. **Ease of use versus security**—The easiest system to use would allow open access to any user and require no passwords. Of course, there would be no security. Requiring passwords makes the system a little less convenient, but more secure. Requiring device-generated one-time passwords makes the system even more difficult to use, but much more secure.
3. **Cost of security versus risk of loss**—There are many different costs to security: monetary, performance, and ease of use, to name a few. There are also many levels of risk: loss of privacy, loss of data, and the loss of service. Each type of cost must be weighed against each type of loss.

Goals should be communicated to all users, operations staff, and managers through a set of security rules, called a "security policy."

E.4.6 Definition of a Security Policy

A security policy is a formal body of the rules by which people who are given access to an organization's technology and information assets must abide. It is part of an overall organizational site security plan. It's purpose is to inform members of the organization of their responsibilities under certain circumstances which could pose potential risk to the company.

E.4.7 Purposes of a Security Policy

The main purpose of a security policy is to inform users, staff and managers of their obligatory requirements for protecting technology and information assets. The policy should specify the mechanisms put in place to meet these requirements. Another purpose is to provide a baseline from which to acquire, configure and audit computer systems and networks for compliance with the policy. An Acceptable Use Policy (AUP) should be part of any security policy. The AUP should spell out what users shall and shall not do on the various components of the system, including the types of traffic allowed on the networks. The AUP should be as explicit as possible to avoid any ambiguity or misunderstanding.

Generic Policy Template

<Policy Title>

June 21, 2005

1.0 Purpose

The purpose of this policy is to provide guidance …

2.0 Scope

This policy applies to all <Company Name> employees and affiliates.

3.0 Policy

…

4.0 Enforcement

Any employee found to have violated this policy may be subject to disciplinary action, up to and including termination of employment.

5.0 Definitions

Term	Definition

6.0 Revision History

Date of last change	Summary of change	Change made by

7.0. Signature(s)

______________________________ Date __________

Chief Security Officer (or equivalent)

______________________________ Date __________

Chief Executive Officer

Note: *It is often the practice in many organizations for the CIO, legal, and HR to sign off on policy documents as well as the CSO and CEO. It is a good idea to check with your organization to be sure which signature blocks are required before publishing policies.*

E.4.8 WLAN Risk Management

In this section, we will take a look at what risks are faced by security managers when implementing WLANs, especially when connecting WLANs to LANs. The best weapon to combat these weaknesses is knowledge – administrators that are aware of the risk can defend against it more effectively. Administrators that procrastinate or choose not to continually review their security profiles only increase the risk that a breach in the defenses will occur. Now, lets take a look at what it takes to secure the WLAN.

Necessary Steps to Securing the WLAN Configuration

According to NIST SP800-48 [7] (draft), network administrators need to configure APs in accordance with established security policies and requirements. Properly configuring administrative passwords, encryption settings, reset function, automatic network connection function, Ethernet Medium Access Control (MAC) Access Control Lists (ACL), shared keys, and Simple Network Management Protocol (SNMP) agents will help eliminate many of the vulnerabilities inherent in a vendor's software default configuration. What follows are some other NIST recommended steps for administrators should take to ensure WLAN IM Security:

Updating Default Passwords. Each WLAN device comes with its own default settings, some of which inherently contain security vulnerabilities. The administrator password is a prime example. On some APs, the factory default configuration does not require a password (i.e., the password field is blank). Unauthorized users can easily gain access to the device if there is no password protection. Administrators should change default settings to reflect the organization's security policy, which should include the requirement for strong (i.e., an alphanumeric and special character string at least eight characters in length) administrative passwords. If the security requirement is sufficiently high, an organization should consider using an automated password generator. An alternative to password authentication is two-factor authentication. One form of two-factor authentication uses a symmetric key algorithm to generate a new code every minute. This code is a one-time use code that is paired with the user's personal identification number (PIN) for authentication. Another example of two-factor authentication is pairing the user's smart card with the user's PIN. This type of authentication requires a hardware device reader for the smart card or an authentication server for the PIN. Several commercial products provide this capability. However, use of an automated password generator or two-factor authentication mechanism may not be worth the investment, depending on the organization's security requirements, number of users, and budget constraints.

Establishing Proper Encryption Settings. Encryption settings should be set for the strongest encryption available in the product, depending on the security requirements of the organization. Typically, APs have only a few encryption settings available: none, 40-bit shared key, and 128-bit shared key (128-bit being the strongest). Encryption such as that used in WEP, simple stream cipher generation, and exclusive-OR processing does not pose an additional burden on the computer processors performing the function. Consequently, organizations do not need to worry about computer processor power when planning to use encryption with the longer keys. However, it should be noted that some attacks against WEP yield poor results regardless of the key size.

Controlling the Reset Function. The reset function poses a particular problem because it allows an individual to negate any security settings administrators have configured in the AP. It does this by returning the AP to its default factory settings. The default settings generally do not require an administrative password, and may disable encryption. An individual can reset the configuration to the default settings simply by inserting a pointed object such as a pen into the reset hole and pressing. If a malicious user gains physical access to the device, that individual can exploit the reset feature and cancel out any security settings on the device. The reset function, if configured to erase basic operational information such as an IP address or keys, can further result in a network DoS, because APs may not operate without these settings. Having physical access controls in place to prevent unauthorized users from resetting APs can mitigate the threats. Organizations can detect threats by performing regular security audits.

Using MAC ACL Functionality. A MAC address is a hardware address that uniquely identifies each computer (or attached device) on a network. Networks use the MAC address to help regulate communications between different computer NICs on the same network subnet. Many 802.11 product vendors provide capabilities for restricting access to the WLAN based on MAC ACLs that are stored and distributed across many APs. The MAC ACL grants or denies access to a computer using a list of permissions designated by MAC address. However, the Ethernet MAC ACL does not represent a strong defense mechanism by itself. Because MAC addresses are transmitted in the clear from a wireless NIC to an AP, the MAC can be easily captured. Malicious users can spoof a MAC address by changing the actual MAC address on their computer to a MAC address that has access to the wireless network. This countermeasure may provide some level of security; however, users should use this with caution. This may be effective against casual eavesdropping but will not be effective against determined adversaries. Users may want to consider this as part of an overall defense-in-depth strategy—adding levels of security to reduce the likelihood of problems. However, users should weigh the administrative burden of enabling the MAC ACL (assuming they are using MAC ACLs) against the true security provided. In a medium to large network, the burden of establishing and maintaining MAC ACLs may exceed the value of the security countermeasure.

Changing the SSID. The SSID of the AP should be changed from the factory default. Although an equipped adversary can capture this identity parameter over the wireless interface, it should be changed to prevent unsophisticated adversary attempts to connect to the wireless network.

Changing Default Cryptographic Keys. The manufacturer may provide one or more keys to enable shared key authentication between the device trying to gain access to the network and the AP. Using a default shared key setting is a security vulnerability because many vendors use identical shared keys in their factory settings. A malicious user may know the default shared key and use it to gain access to the network. Changing the default shared key setting to another key will mitigate the risk. For example, the shared key could be changed to "954617" instead of using a factory default shared key of "111111." No matter what their security level, organizations should change the shared key from the default setting because it is easily exploited. In general, organizations should opt for strong encryption (e.g.,128-bit), regardless of their security levels, whenever it is available. If it is not available or feasible, organizations should, assuming they have already performed a risk analysis, use 40-bit encryption. Finally, a generally accepted principle for proper key management is to change cryptographic keys often.

Changing Default SNMP Parameter. Some wireless APs use SNMP agents, which allow network management software tools to monitor the status of wireless APs and clients. The default SNMP community string that SNMP agents commonly use is the word "public" with assigned "read" or "read and write" privileges. Using this well-known default string leaves devices vulnerable to attack. If an unauthorized user were to gain access and had read/write privileges, that user could write data to the AP, resulting in a data integrity breach. Organizations that require SNMP should change the default community string, as often as needed, to a strong community string. Privileges should be set to "read only" if that is the only access a user requires. If SNMP is not required on the network, the organization should disable SNMP altogether.

Changing Default Channel. One other consideration that is not directly exploitable is the default channel. Vendors commonly use default channels in their APs. If two or more APs are located near each other but are on different networks, a DoS can result from radio interference between the two APs. Organizations that incur radio interference need to determine if a nearby AP(s) is using the same channel or a channel within five channels of their own, and then choose a channel that is in a different range.

Using DHCP. Automatic network connections involve the use of a Dynamic Host Control Protocol (DHCP) server. The DHCP server automatically assigns IP addresses to devices that associate with an AP when traversing a subnet. For example, a DHCP server is used to manage a range of TCP/IP addresses for client laptops or workstations. After the range of IP addresses is established, the DHCP server dynamically assigns addresses to workstations as needed. The server assigns the device a dynamic IP address as long as the encryption settings are compatible with the WLAN. The threat with DHCP is that a malicious user could easily gain unauthorized access on the network through the use of a laptop with a wireless NIC. Since a DHCP server will not necessarily know which wireless devices have access, the server will automatically assign the laptop a valid IP address. Risk mitigation involves disabling DHCP and using static IP addresses on the wireless network, if feasible. This alternative, like the MAC ACL countermeasure, may only be practical for relatively small networks, given the administrative overhead involved with assigning static IP addresses and the possible shortage of addresses. Statically assigning IP addresses would also negate some of the key advantages of wireless networks, such as roaming or establishing ad hoc networks. Another possible solution is to implement a DHCP server inside of the wired network's firewall that grants access to a wireless network located outside of the wired network's firewall. Still another solution is to use APs with integrated firewalls. This last solution will add an additional layer of protection to the entire network. All users should evaluate the need for DHCP taking into consideration the size of their network.

E.4.9 Risks to Wired Networks from Wireless Networks

With the prevalence of wireless devices, more users are seeking ways to connect remotely to their own organizations' networks. One such method is the use of untrusted, third party networks. Conference centers, for example, commonly provide wireless networks for users to connect to the Internet and subsequently to their own organizations while at the conference. Airports and even some coffee franchises are beginning to do the same. These untrusted public networks introduce three primary risks:

1. Because they are public, they are accessible by anyone, even malicious users.
2. They serve as a bridge to a user's own network, thus potentially allowing anyone on the public network to attack or gain access to the bridged network.
3. They use high RF transmission power levels for a strong signal strength, thus allowing malicious users to eavesdrop more readily on their signals.

In connecting to their own networks via an untrusted network, users may create vulnerabilities for their company networks and systems unless their organizations take steps to protect their users and themselves. Users typically need to access resources that their organizations deem as either public or private. Organizations should protect their public resources using an application layer security protocol such as Transport Layer Security (TLS), the Internet Engineering Task Force standardized version of Secure Sockets Layer (SSL). Organizations should use a VPN solution to secure their connections, since this will help prevent eavesdropping and unauthorized access to private resources. Lastly, as with any network, social engineering and dumpster diving are also concerns. An enterprise should consider all aspects of network security when planning to deploy a wireless network.

E.4.10 Security Issues for Wireless Public-access Network Use

WLANs that are installed at airports, hotels, and other establishments present high security risks. Typically you would disable any wireless encryption or access control on your laptop before connecting to a public LAN. Thus, any information you exchange is sent unencrypted, and furthermore your laptop may be subject to probes and scanning from other clients connected to the LAN. Therefore, the following recommendations should be followed:

- Do not use a public LAN with your work-related laptop unless it is absolutely necessary.
- Use a VPN, as otherwise all messages can be intercepted.
- Use a personal firewall and ensure its settings are set at maximum protection.
- Upon leaving the LAN, immediately restore all security settings.
- Scan the laptop for viruses and spyware.

E.4.11 Sample WLAN IM Security Checklist

The following checklist provides a good start on creating a security checklist for your organization. This checklist was taken from draft version of NIST SP-800-48 [8]. It is recreated below for your review.

Table E.1 *WLAN IM Security Checklist.*

Recommendation	Best Practice	May Consider	Done
Develop an organizational security policy that addresses the use of wireless technology, including 802.11.	√		
Ensure users on the network are fully trained in computer security awareness and the risks associated with wireless technology.	√		
Perform a risk assessment to understand the value of the assets in the organization that need protection.	√		
Ensure that the client NIC and AP support firmware upgrade so that security patches may be deployed as they come available (prior to purchase).	√		
Perform comprehensive security assessments at regular intervals (including validating that rogue APs do not exist in the 802.11 WLAN) to fully understand the wireless network security posture.	√		
Ensure external boundary protection is in place around the perimeter of the building or buildings of the organization.	√		
Deploy physical access controls to the building and other secure areas (e.g., photo ID, card badge readers).	√		
Complete a site survey to measure and establish the AP coverage for the organization.	√		
Take a complete inventory of all APs and 802.11 wireless devices.	√		

Table E.1 *WLAN IM Security Checklist.*

Recommendation	Best Practice	May Consider	Done
Empirically test AP range boundaries to determine the precise extent of the wireless coverage.	√		
Ensure AP channels are at least five channels different from any other nearby wireless networks to prevent interference.	√		
Locate APs on the interior of buildings versus near exterior walls and windows.	√		
Make sure that APs are turned off during all hours during they are not used.	√		
Make sure the reset function on APs is being used only when needed and is only invoked by an authorized group of people.	√		
Restore the APs to the latest security settings when the reset functions are used.	√		
Change the default SSID in the APs.	√		
Disable the "broadcast SSID" feature so that the client SSID must match that of the AP.	√		
Validate that the SSID character string does not reflect the organization's name (division, department, street, etc.) or products.	√		
Understand and make sure all default parameters are changed.	√		
Disable the broadcast beacon of the APs.		√	
Disable all insecure and nonessential management protocols on the APs.	√		
Enable all security features of the WLAN product, including the cryptographic authentication and WEP privacy feature.	√		

Table E.1 *WLAN IM Security Checklist.*

Recommendation	Best Practice	May Consider	Done
Ensure that encryption key sizes are at least 128-bits or as large as possible.	√		
Make sure that default shared keys are periodically replaced by more secure unique keys.	√		
Install a properly configured firewall between the wired infrastructure and the wireless network (AP or hub to APs).	√		
Install antivirus software on all wireless clients		√	
Install personal firewall software on all wireless clients.		√	
Deploy MAC access control lists.		√	
Consider installation of Layer 2 switches in lieu of hubs for AP connectivity		√	
Deploy IPsec-based Virtual Private Network (VPN) technology for wireless communications.		√	
Ensure encryption being used is as strong as possible given the sensitivity of the data on the network and the processor speeds of the computers.		√	
Fully test and deploy software patches and upgrades on a regular basis.	√		
Ensure all APs have strong administrative passwords	√		
Ensure all passwords are being changed regularly.	√		
Deploy user authentication such as biometrics, smart cards, two-factor authentication, or PKI		√	

Table E.1 *WLAN IM Security Checklist.*

Recommendation	Best Practice	May Consider	Done
Ensure that the "ad hoc mode" for 802.11 has been disabled unless the environment is such that the risk is tolerable.	√		
Use static IP addressing on the network.		√	
Disable DHCP.		√	
Enable user authentication mechanisms for the management interfaces of the AP.	√		
Ensure management traffic destined for APs is on a dedicated wired subnet.		√	
Make sure adequately robust community strings are used for SNMP management traffic on the APs	√		
Configure SNMP settings on APs for least privilege (i.e., *read only*). Disable SNMP if it is not used.	√		
Enhance AP management traffic security by using SNMPv3 or equivalent cryptographically protected protocol		√	
Use a local serial port interface for AP configuration to minimize the exposure of sensitive management information		√	
Consider other forms of authentication for the wireless network such as RADIUS and Kerberos		√	
Deploy intrusion detection sensors on the wireless part of the network to detect suspicious behavior or unauthorized access and activity.		√	
Deploy an 802.11 security product that offers other security features such as enhanced cryptographic protection or user authorization features		√	

Table E.1 *WLAN IM Security Checklist.*

Recommendation	Best Practice	May Consider	Done
Fully understand the impacts of deploying any security feature or product prior to deployment	√		
Designate an individual to track the progress of 802.11 security products and standards (IETF, IEEE, etc.) and the threats and vulnerabilities with the technology.		√	
Wait until future releases of 802.11 WLAN technology that incorporates fixes to the security features or enhanced security features		√	

E.4.12 Creating WLANs in Public Space

In order to deploy a WLAN in a public space, such as an airport or shopping mall, you need to design the WLAN to meet some additional requirements unneeded in a wired only environment. It is advised that you plan for a single wireless network infrastructure that can be shared across multiple vendors and accessed by multiple groups (segments) of users. The use of a single wireless network infrastructure will help to eliminate any radio frequency interference that may be encountered in the public space. Due to the limited number of non-overlapping channels that are made available in 802.11b devices, having multiple wireless network infrastructures (zones) in the same location can cause interference among wireless APs with overlapping channel frequencies.

E.4.13 Virtual Local Area Networks (VLANs)

For the best level of security, we recommend that you make sure your APs support Virtual Local Area Networks (VLANs). VLANs can provide you with the capability for beaconing multiple SSIDs. They also have the capability for binding each SSID to a separate VLAN. VLAN support enables the AP to route the wireless client to the correct network path. The capability for beaconing multiple SSIDs enables multiple service providers to share the same wireless network infrastructure. After the wireless client associates with the correct SSID, the AP must bind that SSID to the correct VLAN in order to route the network traffic to the correct destination. The AP maintains a network address table that maps each SSID to its respective VLAN number. The public space WLAN often must provide for and allow non-802.1X wireless clients access to the Internet. To support this capability, the administrator must assign a VLAN number for all non-802.1X wireless clients. The VLAN number routes the non-802.1X clients to a VLAN that is configured to provide non-802.1X clients with 802.1X credentials. As you can see, it is necessary to use Enhanced APs for WLAN deployment in a public space.

To provide security for the WLAN environment, an IEEE 802.1X and RADIUS-capable wireless AP is needed. An EAP-capable RADIUS server such as Windows Server 2003 IAS is recommended. In the public space WLAN environment, it may be necessary to provide billing and accounting services when customers connecting through the public space WLAN are charged for such access. A public space WLAN usually charges for services that it provides. These services are typically provided by an ISP to public space customers connecting through the public space WLAN. An ISP can charge the customer for this service in several ways. It can bill for the total time connected, the quantity of data transferred, or a combination of the two methods.

It is possible to configure the IAS server used for the authorization of wireless users to capture connection data and save it to an accounting log file. The log file contains the connection time, the amount of data transferred during a session, and other data that can be used to produce billing records for ISP customers. Tools that import the log file into a database are frequently used. These utilities convert the log files into a format that can be read and interpreted from the database using a reports generator or reporting module to provide detailed billing records. Very often, in Windows environments, the IAS for Windows Server 2003 is configured to send such accounting information directly to a SQL server database.

E.4.14 Designs for Scalable and Secure WLAN Solutions

When designing WLANs, for public or secured spaces, it is very important to provide sufficient bandwidth to support the expected volume of users likely to use the WLAN. When designing your WLAN, it is a good practice to first consider how many users will need to connect simultaneously through each deployed AP. For example, if you design for an average bandwidth of 28 kilobits per second (Kbps), more users will be able to associate with the network than if you design the average bandwidth to be 56 Kbps. The tradeoff between slower connect speed and more users versus higher connect speed but fewer user connections is a business decision that should not be made hastily. Keeping users on the correct segments of the network can be tricky business. Using VLANs and DMZs are essential to good security practice.

E.4.15 VLANs and Wireless DMZ Configuration

A DMZ is defined as a small network that is inserted as a "neutral buffer zone" between a company's private network and the outside public network. This neutral buffer zone, or **D**e-**M**ilitarized **Z**one (the DMZ term is derived from the geographic buffer zone set up between North and South Korea following the United Nations directive issued in the early 1950s), is designed to prevent outsiders from obtaining direct access to any servers that contain proprietary data.

DMZs are not mandatory in a network architecture but good network practice dictates that administrators build DMZs to provide a more secure approach to the firewall. The DMZ and effectively acts as a proxy server. Conventional DMZs mandate strong encryption (IPSEC) and authentication. This strong encryption and authentication avoids many of the problems swirling around Layer 2 wireless security schemes such as WEP that can be broken or easily compromised. Today, most corporations place WLANs users outside the Intranet within a DMZ. This seems like a logical approach given that remote access over the Internet using VPNs is a well-understood security and "best-practice template." As long as IT can treat all wireless users as insecure until they prove otherwise, security problems can effectively be eliminated.

However, putting wireless users in a DMZ essentially causes the corporation to forego any options of secured scalability down the road. DMZs were originally intended to support large numbers of remote users connecting through dial-up methods or by using asynchronous or DSL connections to gain access to the corporate network. These methods used relatively low-speed connections. Today's modern WLAN users generally connect at 11 mbps or higher and as a result put more usage onto the network. For this reason, it is frequently the case where WLAN users are quarantined from corporate network resources that lie behind VPNs and/or firewalls which are designed to aggregate traffic for all low-speed users coming into the DMZ. It is now common practice for administrators to partition their wireless users from wired users using VLAN technology.

Many corporations attempt to solve the problem by designing a single, large broadcast WLAN domain that spans the enterprise. As the broadcast domains grow, performance and reliability shrink due to broadcast storms, congestion and all the well-known problems solved by using intelligent switches for the wired world. Even in this so-called "*secure environment*" rogue APs can be plugged into wired data ports. This action has the adverse effect of compromising the entire corporate network. Point solutions for security (solutions which address a single security issue) don't offer the kind of comprehensive protection needed to allow ubiquitous connection to the wired infrastructure. Security solutions that are effective require a more holistic approach. Because network services and security break down when mobility is introduced, the wireless network should be considered carefully before allowing it to become an extension of the wired network.

E.5 Endnotes

1. Rittinghouse, John W. and Ransome, James F., Wireless Operational Security, 1st Edition, March, 2004. Digital Press, New York, NY.
2. J. Craig Lowery, Ph.D., "Developing Effective Security Policies," Dell Power Solutions, November, 2002, Dell Computer.
3. URL Reference is: http://www.sans.org.
4. Michele Guel, "Proven Practices for Managing the Security Function." from the SANS certification program for Certified Information Security Officers.
5. RFC 2196, "Site Security Handbook", Sep 1997, ed. B. Fraser, IETF NWG, URL Reference is: http://www.ietf.org.
6. M. Fites, P. Kratz, and A. Brebner, "Control and Security of Computer Information Systems", Computer Science Press,1989.
7. NIST Special Publication 800-48 (Draft), "Wireless Network Security 802.11, Bluetooth™ and Handheld Devices," ed., Tom Karygiannis and Les Owens, July 2003, U.S. Department of Commerce.
8. NIST Special Publication 800-48 (Draft), "Wireless Network Security 802.11, Bluetooth™ and Handheld Devices," ed., Tom Karygiannis and Les Owens, July 2003, U.S. Department of Commerce.

Index